WOMEN/MEN/MANAGEMENT

Ann Harriman

PRAEGER SPECIAL STUDIES • PRAEGER SCIENTIFIC

New York • Philadelphia • Eastbourne, UK
Toronto • Hong Kong • Tokyo • Sydney

Library of Congress Cataloging-in-Publication Data

Harriman, Ann.
    Women/men/management.

    Bibliography: p.
    Includes index.
    1.   Sex discrimination in employment—
United States.   2.   Women—Employment—
United States.   3.   Sexism—U.S.
4.   Organizational behavior.   I.   Title.
HD6060.5.U5H37   1985   658.3'042   85-12034
ISBN 0-03-063362-1
ISBN 0-03-063363-X (pbk.)

Published in 1985 by Praeger Publishers
CBS Educational and Professional Publishing, a Division of CBS Inc.
521 Fifth Avenue, New York, NY 10175 USA

56789 052 987654321

Printed in the United States of America on acid-free paper

INTERNATIONAL OFFICES

Orders from outside the United States should be sent to the appropriate address listed below. Orders from areas not listed below should be placed through CBS International Publishing, 383 Madison Ave., New York, NY 10175 USA

Australia, New Zealand

Holt Saunders, Pty, Ltd., 9 Waltham St., Artarmon, N.S.W. 2064, Sydney, Australia

Canada

Holt, Rinehart & Winston of Canada, 55 Horner Ave., Toronto, Ontario, Canada M8Z 4X6

Europe, the Middle East, & Africa

Holt Saunders, Ltd., 1 St. Anne's Road, Eastbourne, East Sussex, England BN21 3UN

Japan

Holt Saunders, Ltd., Ichibancho Central Building, 22-1 Ichibancho, 3rd Floor, Chiyodaku, Tokyo, Japan

Hong Kong, Southeast Asia

Holt-Saunders Asia, Ltd., 10 Fl, Intercontinental Plaza, 94 Granville Road, Tsim Sha Tsui East, Kowloon, Hong Kong

Manuscript submissions should be sent to the Editorial Director, Praeger Publishers, 521 Fifth Avenue, New York, NY 10175 USA

To Mac:

Without him it would have been finished sooner
and it never would have been finished at all.

Acknowledgments

Acknowledging one's scholarly debts is a little like accepting an Academy Award for best third assistant sound effects director, but not much. When one stands up to receive an Oscar, the accepted practice is to thank everyone who had anything at all to do with the production and to minimize one's own effort or contribution. And so it is with authorship. My list of debts is long, too long to be presented in its entirety.

Several graduate assistants have made invaluable contributions; two stand out. Douglas Higgins spent endless hours in the library, scouting elusive sources, locating missing articles and books, trailing items from partial or illegible or faulty references, coping with the vagaries of other students and the complexities created by too few copy machines in too poor repair. Loretta Lentzner read and reviewed and rewrote and reread. Each of them worked tirelessly. Their work was absolutely invaluable; so was their support and encouragement.

Hundreds of students have passed through my course on Women/Men/Management over the years. I owe a great debt to each of them. It is a truism that the teacher always learns more than the students. From mine I have greatly expanded my own perception of the topic of men and women in organizations. I've become increasingly aware of the different social worlds of students from ethnic and religious backgrounds different from my own. I've become more sensitive to the perceptions of those from poor and disadvantaged backgrounds. I understand better the isolation felt by lesbians and gays in a straight world and the fear and frustration of women and men making major life changes at mid life. And I've become convinced that we who study and teach about organizational behavior must recognize not only that this pluralistic world exists but that it has important implications for management. We need to understand where we have been, where we are, and where we are going if we are to manage either our present or our future.

My "boys"—Paul, Dan, Tom, and Steve Harriman and Scott White—are all grown men now; they've provided a wonderful training laboratory for learning about masculinity. It's not easy raising parents these days, but they've been very patient with me, and I've learned a great deal from each of them. I'm very proud of them. My daughter-in-law, Eva, and my grandchildren, Christopher and Sarah, serve to remind me that each new generation offers both tradition and change. For all the efforts to raise androgynous children, Sarah at two-and-a-half smiles ever so sweetly and says coyly: "Girls can't do that."

The list goes on. Students, faculty colleagues, friends, and family—too many to mention but not to forget. The difference between this and an

Academy Award, however, is that an Oscar is awarded after the work has been received and judged, not before. For whatever good there is in the book, I freely and willingly acknowledge the contributions of others. Whatever faults it may have, and it has many, they are no one's but my own.

Contents

WOMEN/MEN/MANAGEMENT

1
Point of Departure

"What is the very first thing that you notice when you meet someone for the first time?" That question, a favorite of roving reporters or cocktail party guests, usually evokes answers such as "his smile," "her eyes," or "his hair." But the only true answer, of course, is "sex." Some people argue that race is more fundamental than sex to identity, and therefore the primary identifying characteristic, and that may be so. Nevertheless, most people find it essential to determine immediately the sex of another person with whom they interact. On the rare occasion when sexual identity is ambiguous, or, even worse, in a case of mistaken identity, we are uncomfortable and embarrassed (Nielsen 1978).

A friend calls and says "Susie had her baby." Your first question inevitably is "What did she have?" Your friend understands, of course, that your question is "Is it a boy or a girl?" For almost everything that happens to that baby from that point on will be affected by the answer to that question—the name it is given; the kinds of toys it will play with; the way it is handled, dressed, played with, and talked to; the nature of its relationships with other people; the way it will speak and be spoken to; the way it will be educated, evaluated, and entertained—all these and more will depend on whether it is male or female. And these differences will begin at the moment of birth.

While the child is still very small, adults will begin to ask it "What are you going to be when you grow up?" And here the differences between boy children and girl children become critical. A boy child will very soon come to understand that what he will *be* will be determined by what he *does,* that is, by his occupation or his profession. He will answer "I want to be an astronaut" or a fireman, or a doctor. A girl child, on the other hand, will soon come to understand that what she will *be* is a function of

1

who she *is*. She will soon learn to answer "I'm want to get married" or "I want to be a mommy" (Ireson 1978). She will take her identity and her status not from her own achievements but from those of her husband and children. She probably *will* get married and have children; so will the boy child. The difference is that each of them will already have learned an essential element of sexual identity. Men in our society are perceived first as jobholders, second as husbands and fathers; women, no matter what their status as jobholder, will be perceived first as homemakers, second as workers.

Many books and articles have been written, are being written, and will no doubt continue to be written about the problems faced by women entering traditionally and historically male-dominated work organizations. Many others, although perhaps fewer, concern themselves with the problems that managers, presumably males, face in managing the army of new women workers entering the labor market. Why, then, do we need another book on the topic of women and men in management? In what way will this book differ from all the others?

Furthermore, endless numbers of books and articles have been written, are being written, and no doubt will continue to be written on the general subject of management and organizational behavior. In the absence of new theoretical breakthroughs, what more could possibly be said. Why, then, do we need another book on the subject? In what way will this book differ from all the others?

There are three considerations that make this book different from the others:

1. The current literature, including much that is written expressly for women, tends to assume a "male model" of work. This model, on the one hand, is based on implicit assumptions about masculinity and femininity and about the relationship of work roles and family roles. On the other hand, it manages to ignore the whole issue of human sexuality in complex organizations. While assuming that "male is normal," it fails to consider if, why, or in what ways masculinity affects the organization's structure or processes. To the extent that sex roles are studied at all, it is the feminine role that receives attention.

2. The current literature assumes a "breadwinner model." This model assumes that the typical worker is a male head of household with a homemaker wife and dependent children. It fails to take adequate note of such social changes as the increased labor force participation of women, particularly married women, the decreased labor force participation of men, plural family forms, a rapidly aging work force, decreased fertility, increased education, and other social and economic changes. While obviously these changes and trends have not gone unreported, the majority of the literature on organizations fails to adequately address the implica-

tions that they will have on work organizations themselves and the adaptive responses that will be required.

3. The current literature is rooted in the Industrial Revolution and is therefore based on an "industrial model." It fails to address adequately the implications of electronic technology and the postindustrial society for the organization of work, the distribution of income, and the relationship of work and family for contemporary workers.

None of this literature examines in sufficient depth the issues of sex and gender as organizational variables. Some recent studies have focused on specific characteristics or problems of female workers. Others have attempted to address the organizational problems that have arisen from the efforts of women to move into traditionally male-dominated occupations or organizations. Still others have noted the growing phenomenon of the two-paycheck or two-career family and have addressed coping mechanisms for the couple. None of it examines the impact or implications of masculinity on organizations; little of it examines the implications of changing roles of both women and men. Some efforts have been made to study the problems of sexual attraction and sexual harassment in the organization, but almost no attempt has been made to address the whole issue of human sexuality and its role in organizational dynamics.

None of this literature examines in sufficient depth the interactive implications of changing sex roles and changing technology. Just as the Industrial Revolution brought about major changes in the social world that affected every sector of life, so too does the "electronic revolution" portend vast social change. Since jobs are a major factor in our existence, determining to a great extent our self- and public identities, major changes in the nature of jobs must result in major changes in our society and its institutions. Since contemporary organizational structures and processes are designed for efficiency, and their design rests upon an assumption of the traditional nuclear family, major changes in both technology and family life must ultimately be reflected in organizational design.

Much of the literature, as it applies to sex differences, is based on the shakiest methodological grounds. Some of the most popular and oft-quoted works are based on purely anecdotal evidence. Others are pure speculation. Still others, while attempting to meet more rigorous standards of validity and reliability, incorporate without examination assumptions about the stereotypical roles of men and women.

SEX AND THE CENTRALITY OF WORK

The "male model" of work perceives organizational behavior as consistent with a sex-differentiated view of life. Holding a paid job is universally assumed to be central to the lives of male workers and secondary to the lives of women workers. Further, men are assumed to be the primary members of the work force; women are perceived as only secondary, a kind of "reserve army" of workers. The study of work often either excludes women altogether or treats them as a footnote. Research on male workers is often generalized to women workers, completely ignoring the possibility of sex differences; when women are included they are often treated differently from men (Acker and Van Houten 1974; Acker 1978). In some cases the analysis is shaped by sex-biased interpretations: for example, that men, but not women, are concerned about success on the job. In other cases the entire analysis of work is distorted because certain factors are defined as appropriate to either women's work or to men's work but not to both. Stress and fatigue, for instance, may be attributed to the job itself for men's jobs, but may be attributed to family responsibilities or the demands of dual roles for women's jobs.

This segregation of male and female roles has led to separate models for studying work, a "job model" for studying males and a "gender model" for studying females (Feldberg and Glenn 1979). The job model assumes that the job is central to the lives of male workers; it treats the job itself as the primary independent variable. Items like complexity, routineness, autonomy, and working conditions are used to explain performance on the job and job satisfaction, as well as off-the-job behavior, activities, and mental health for male workers.

The gender model assumes that the family is central to the lives of women workers; it virtually ignores the job itself or the working conditions and relies on personal characteristics or family situations to explain the job attitudes and behaviors of married women. Rather than looking at the tasks that women workers perform, it looks at such variables as their marital status, number and age of children, education, or husband's income, even sometimes at the husband's attitude toward his wife working, to explain behavior and attitudes toward work. Rather than looking at differences in the organizational experiences of women and men, it looks at factors external to the organization to explain women's organization behavior (Acker and Van Houten 1974).

This bifurcated view of the work world has its historical roots in the industrial era. The Industrial Revolution brought about a separation of women's and men's roles that was virtually complete; men worked for wages while women worked in the home. It was in this milieu that the study of organizations and organizational behavior had its foundations. Frederick W. Taylor's (1947) seminal work on *Scientific Management*, first published in 1911, is based upon his experience working with men doing hard, heavy, physical work in the mills and foundries. By the 1920s, when the famous Hawthorn Studies were undertaken, women were already experiencing differential status and treatment, but these differences were simply ignored (Acker and Van Houten 1974). Subsequent studies simply continued to ignore or misinterpret sex differences.

Enormous changes have taken place in recent years in both technology and women's labor force participation. An ever-increasing body of research has applied the job model to study women workers. However, relatively little research has employed a gender model to study men workers. What evidence there is has shown repeatedly that the degree to which work is a "central life interest" varies by occupation and not by marital status for both women and men (Dubin and Goldman 1972). Despite these well-publicized findings, the assumption persists that differences are based on sex, not on occupation (Feldberg and Glenn 1979).

PREVIEW OF THE BOOK

In the succeeding chapters we will be looking at the very broad range of personal, social, and organizational influences that shape sexual identity and behavior and at the way in which sexual behavior, in turn, affects organizational behavior.

We start with a history lesson. Chapter 2 traces the evolutionary process by which social and technological changes in the Industrial Revolution contributed to the division of labor within the household and the segregation of women's and men's occupations in the workplace. It also looks at contemporary changes in technology and social life and considers what effects they are having or may have in the future. Chapters 3 and 4 look specifically at the economic and political implications of occupational segregation, low pay, and sex discrimination in employment. Chapter 3 traces changes in the composition of the work force and outlines major economic theories that attempt to explain sex differences. It concludes that at least some of the differences can be explained only by sex discrimination. Chapter 4 describes the major federal legislation aimed at removing sex discrimination in employment and the ways in which that legislation has been applied by government agencies and by the courts.

Chapter 5 turns to social psychology, specifically to the pervasive sex roles and sex role stereotypes that sustain and perpetuate differences in behavior, in expectations, and in outcomes. It concludes with a discussion of psychological androgyny and its implications for freeing both women and men from the dysfunctional aspects of sex stereotypes. Chapter 6 focuses specifically on relationships among and between the sexes in the workplace, including male/female, male/male, and female/female relationships. Chapter 5 and 6 together challenge the assumption of most of the literature that sex and sex role are not significant organizational variables.

Chapters 7, 8, 9, and 10 deal with the fundamentals of organizational behavior through the lens of sex and sex roles. Chapter 7 studies communication, both verbal and nonverbal, concentrating especially on the ways in which sex differences in communication affect power and status within the organization. Chapter 8 reviews the literature on motivation. It challenges the conventional wisdom of the "gender model" that women are less motivated than men and concludes that what differences exist are more a function of situational variables than of sex. Chapter 9 addresses major theories of leadership and power. It finds that there is little conclusive evidence of sex differences in leadership style but considerable difference in the ability to get and use power. Chapter 10 covers the multiple topics of performance, perceptions of performance, and outcomes of performance. It leads to the ineluctible conclusion that while there are no sex differences in performance, women and men tend to be evaluated quite differently for the same work and women's work tends to be systematically devalued. As a result, women suffer from both "access discrimination" and "treatment discrimination."

Chapter 11 compares the career aspirations of women and men and questions the extent to which women and men have equal access to training and development opportunities. It reveals that most organizational training and development programs lack systematic objectives or adequate evaluation. Although women are less likely than men to have access to mentors, an important form of career development, the majority of men are also excluded from this elite system. It offers some alternatives for both organizations and individuals.

Chapter 12 looks at the future. It is a utopian view of the world, one in which division of labor is allocated on grounds of ability or fairness, not sex, opportunities for both achievement and leisure are equally distributed between the sexes, and wealth is distributed equitably through the society. It sees electronic technology as liberating individuals from the necessity to do onerous work and creating opportunities for them to lead fulfilling and rewarding lives. It may be a fantasy, but it is at least as likely a scenario as gloomy forecasts of idleness, poverty, and despair. The social world was changed immeasurably by the Industrial Revolution, mostly for the good. The social world will be changed again by the electronic revolution. We have enormous power to make that change a positive one, if we will.

Let us begin!

2
The Social-Technological Environment

In the chapters that follow we will examine the twin problems of the occupational segregation of women and men and discrimination against women in the work force. We will then review the major political approaches to reducing sex discrimination. Before we take up these topics, however, we will look at the broader issue of division of labor between women and men in the family. To a very great extent that division of labor is a function of the organization of work, which in turn is strongly related to technology.

The word "technology" has a great many definitions. To some it means mechanization or automation, to others it has come to be limited specifically to electronic inventions. However, here we will be using it in its more generic sense, to mean "technique," or the whole complex of standardized means—scientific, mechanical, and organizational—for achieving some predetermined result (Ellul 1964). While the history of technology, using this definition, is as old as mankind, we are particularly interested in the period from the start of the Industrial Revolution to the present postindustrial period.

This chapter will look at the effect of technology on women's and men's work roles and family roles. It will also analyze the relationship between postindustrial technology and changing family roles.

THE INDUSTRIAL SOCIETY

The period of the Industrial Revolution is usually dated from about 1750 to the beginning of the twentieth century, and the industrial *era* continued until at least the mid twentieth century. The Industrial Revolution brought about not only the change from an agricultural to a manufacturing society but enormous social change as well. Chief among these changes was the transformation of the family from a producing unit to a consuming unit, a change that increased the segregation of roles within the family and decreased the value of the woman's work both at home and in the labor force.

The Family

The family has been considered the basic economic unit of society since the days of the preindustrial, agricultural era, both in this country and in the United Kingdom. In rural societies, the family was a productive unit, characterized by a high degree of interdependency; all members of the family who were able, old and young, worked to contribute to the family enterprise. The family typically was a large, extended one, and while division of labor tended to be separated along sex lines, the contribution of all family members was essential to the family's well-being. Whether the family enterprise was farming or craft production, all able-bodied members worked. Based on biblical teachings, the father served as the authority figure, the head of the household (Young and Willmott 1973). However, a very significant priority for the family was the getting and preparing of food, a task that almost always fell to the woman and occupied a major portion of her time. It also made her largely responsible for handling whatever money the family acquired and, since the majority of cash was spent on food, gave her a certain amount of power in the family (Tilly and Scott 1978).

Since each member of the family was involved in the production of necessities of life, both the allocation of time between work and nonwork and the scheduling of time were left to the individual, or at least to the family. A great many factors—weather, size of the family, availability of resources, demand for surplus production, family and religious customs—contributed to the allocation and scheduling of time. There was no standard work day, no overtime, no paid vacation.

With the coming of industrialization the family as a production unit tended to be replaced by a "family wage economy" in which each family member exchanged labor for money, which was then pooled and used for the maintenance of the family's welfare. In some cases families hired themselves out as a unit, with the father bargaining for a wage rate that included himself and each of his children. Transportation was limited and cities grew as workers moved closer to the factories. Large extended families became less common than nuclear families; living quarters were cramped, large families were less mobile, hence less able to move to find work, and the wage system made it nearly impossible to support aged or infirm family members unable to work. Many services that had been performed by members of the extended family came to be turned over to other institutions: schools for the young, old age homes for the elderly (Toffler 1980). Among families that remained in rural areas, both boys and girls often migrated to the cities to find work; their wages, in whole or in part, were sent home to the family, sometimes directly by the employer (Tilly and Scott 1978).

The transition from an agricultural to a manufacturing society was gradual, and labor for the mills was in short supply. Women and children helped to fill the demand, and the religious values of the time, a puritan ethic that abhorred idleness, looked with favor on their industry. In many cases, work that had previously been done at home, such as spinning and weaving, was moved to the plants (Blau 1978). Single women sometimes continued to live at home or to work in "service"; many went to live in dormitories provided by the mills until they married. In England, some unmarried women lived and worked at home their whole lives, spinning yarn for the weavers. Because their families relied on their earnings for survival, they were never allowed to leave home to marry. They came to be known as "spinsters" (Tilly and Scott 1978).

The move from work in the home to work in the factory did not mean a significant social change, however. The work of the factory girls continued to be viewed in very traditional terms, both by their employers and to some extent by the women themselves. The daughters of farmers or artisans, they had always worked; the only change was in the setting. Wage work was considered a secondary occupation for them; women's real work was raising children and running a household. Employers preferred to hire young, unmarried women; most machine operators were between 16 and 25 years old. Their wages were low and turnover was high. The women accepted the low wages because they didn't expect to stay long (and typically didn't). The mill owners accepted the high turnover because the tasks were easy to learn and labor was cheap (Scott 1982).

Married women in urban working-class households were less likely than men or single women to work for wages outside the home. Food continued to be a major concern for the family, and while the urban wife no longer raised vegetables and chickens and milked the cows or goats, a great deal of her time was spent in both buying and preparing food. Both fertility rates and infant mortality rates continued to be very high, and children typically remained at home until they married, so there was a great deal of work to be done. These home duties made it nearly impossible for women to work the 12-hour shifts demanded by the mills and factories, and they went out to work only if their husbands were unemployed or ill and if there were no children to send out to work. When they did work, it was often only sporadically; women formed a fairly large class of temporary and seasonal workers. Nevertheless, in the family wage system, women needed to continue to earn, and they did so by taking in boarders, by doing piecework at home, or by selling the surplus food or clothing that they produced for their own family's use (Tilly and Scott 1978).

This change from a rural, producing economy to the family wage economy brought with it a greater degree of sex role segregation. Although the wife's work continued to be vital to the welfare of the family, it was the husband's wages (and to a lesser extent the children's wages) that provided the essential goods and services for the family. While the wife continued to manage the family's money, since most of it went for food, the loss of her spouse usually meant that she was reduced to a life of poverty. The interdependency of the farm family was replaced by a different and less equal interdependency in the city.

As the industrial era continued, the occupational mix of the work force gradually changed. The number of factory and mill jobs available to women, as well as the number of jobs in domestic service, began to decline, but jobs in the "tertiary sector" of the economy, the services sector, began to increase. Office work had always been a male-dominated occupation: Young men did clerical work as part of a general apprenticeship in business, often in preparation for a partnership or an inheritance (Scott 1982). In the mid-1800s, the main technology of the office was pen and paper, a time-consuming and monotonous method (Giuliano 1982). Gradually, as the volume of paperwork increased, clerical work was separated from administrative work and from the opportunity for advancement. Copy work was given out to women, usually married women or widows supplementing the household income, to be done at home. They were paid by the word, and of course the pay was low (Scott 1982).

Technology, specifically the telephone, the telegraph, and the typewriter, had a significant impact on the performance of office work and on women's employment. Typewriters, called "writing machines," started to be available by about 1850, and by 1900 they were widely available at affordable prices (Giuliano 1982). Typing, filing, and stenography, that is, the management of information, became components of full-time occupations. Secretaries were frequently called "female typewriters." Ambitious young men moved into sales, advertising, or administrative positions; women moved into and soon dominated almost completely the new clerical occupations (Scott 1982).

Office work differed from factory work in that it was cleaner and safer. Like nursing and teaching, which also came to be female-dominated fields, it was considered respectable for middle-class women. But, like factory work, office work kept women in a labor market separate from that of men and perpetuated cultural stereotypes of women's capabilities. The jobs of secretary and telephone operator quickly replaced factory work as the typical female occupation. Like factory work these jobs were designated as employment for single women, and many employers enforced age limits of between 18 and 25. Women were often required to leave their jobs when they married, whether they wanted to or not (Scott 1982). The separation of home and work for women was increased, and women's need for education also increased slightly, but in no way were either women's wages or women's integration into the male labor force enhanced. Wherever women worked they earned less than men; whatever occupations women entered, men left (Tilly and Scott 1978).

By the turn of the century the family had begun to shift from a producing unit to a consuming unit. Men's wages had risen sufficiently that the family no longer needed to concern itself with survival alone. An increased quantity of consumer goods was available and families had increased income to purchase them. The target income for families tended to rise, and while family life didn't change dramatically, the separation of male and female roles became even more distinct. Infant mortality rates fell, and so did fertility rates; child labor laws and compulsory education laws kept children out of the work force for a longer period. Adult children continued to live at home until they married, continuing to contribute their wages to the family income but usually reserving some money for their own use (Tilly and Scott 1978).

Contrary to popular belief, increased prosperity and the development of labor-saving technologies did not lighten the domestic work load of women (Goode 1971). To be sure, they made housework less onerous. Technological changes were slower in coming to the household than to the factory, but some improvements were available as early as the nineteenth century. Items like soap, candles, textiles, and clothing, once made in the home, could now be purchased. Stoves replaced the open hearth for cooking and heating. Later, gas and electricity became available for heating, cooking, and lighting; indoor plumbing and the washing machine certainly reduced the back-breaking burden of the housewife. Still later, vacuum cleaners, refrigerators, dishwashers, freezers, and convenience foods saved time and made the work easier (Rothschild 1983).

This array of appliances and conveniences dramatically changed the housewife's job without necessarily easing it. New tasks took on significance as old ones were replaced; shopping, servicing household equipment, and travel to do household errands all took time. Urban children required more supervision than farm children; city smoke and grime required more laundry and housecleaning (Vanek 1978).

Further, attitudes about the housewife's job were changing. Along with the availability of household appliances came a rise in the standards of household cleanliness. Around the turn of the century, advocates of the "domestic science movement" were interested in raising housework to the status of a profession and in educating women to do it well (Vanek 1978). Lillian Gilbreath, a pioneer in industrial engineering and the Scientific Management movement, conducted research into the improvement of housework (Trescot 1983) and the application of the principles of Scientific Management to the home. The American Home Economics Association successfully lobbied the government for money to educate women in principles of health, sanitation, and nutrition. Women's magazines gave advice on how to keep husbands happy, children polite, and the house clean (Vanek 1978). Women were urged to keep their homes not only clean but attractively decorated; meals were expected to be not only nutritious but creative and artistic as well. A new emphasis on childrearing required mothers to be experts in the psychological, physical, and educational development of their children (Scott 1982).

Household technology to some extent reversed the trend away from the production of goods and services. For one thing, at the same time that labor-saving devices were becoming more available, household help was becoming less available. Women who had relied on domestic servants now found themselves pushing the vacuum cleaner or cooking the meals (Vanek 1978). For another, appliances like the washing machine, the iron, and the home freezer reduced the urban housewife's reliance on services provided outside the home. When women produced these goods and services within the home, the work was removed from the family wage economy. Women did not receive wages for their productive activity; therefore, as far as the society was concerned they did not work.

The home sewing machine also made it possible for women to produce goods in the home. As in preindustrial times, women could again make clothing at home instead of purchasing it ready-made. But the sewing machine soon became an instrument for exploiting women as well. Factories had, of course, used sewing machines for many years (sometimes owned by the women workers, who were forced to buy them from their employers with weekly deductions from their wages). When lightweight machines suitable for home sewing became available, many machines were sold along with a contract with a clothing manufacturer. The woman could pay for her machine and earn additional money by doing piecework for pay in her home. For middle-class women, such employment was a supplement to the family income and provided a few hours a day of profitable employment during times that were convenient to her. But for many poor women, seeking to earn a living, the low rates made long hours a necessity and turned many urban homes into mini-sweatshops (Scott 1982).

Industrial technology, then, took some tasks that had been performed in the home and moved them to the factories; it created factory jobs for young women until they married. Technology also split clerical work from administrative work and created office jobs for young, unmarried women. Technology made the work of married women in the home less unpleasant and physically demanding but no less time-consuming. In so doing it increased the occupational segregation and the division of labor between the sexes. It did nothing to increase the earnings of female-dominated occupations or the job opportunities for married women.

By the early twentieth century the split between production and consumption was nearly complete. Single women worked for wages until they married or perhaps until their first child was born; married women toiled in the home, preparing food, bearing and raising children, and managing the home. If they did paid work, it was likely to be only temporarily, it was likely to be in a sex-segregated occupation, it often entailed piecework done at home, and it was very likely to be low paid. White women rarely worked for wages outside the home unless there was some serious family problem, and a strong sentiment against women intruding into the labor force discouraged them from doing so. Black women, mostly in the South, and immigrant women in the Northeast, however, were much more likely to be in the paid labor force (Blau 1978). Woman's role became increasingly one of caretaker and her work unpaid and devalued (Baxandall, Ewen, and Gordon 1976; Baxandall, Gordon, and Reverby 1976). Women's roles came to be associated with consumption and men's with production. Their role segregation was nearly complete, and while there continued to be a great deal of interdependency, there was less and less equality.

The Work Organization

The invention of the steam engine, perhaps more than any other single breakthrough, changed the way in which work was performed the world over. Machines in all productive processes—mines, mills, steelworks, or woodworking—could and did work harder, faster, and more reliably than men. Factories grew up around the engine. For the first time it was possible to have many hundreds of people working in one place purely because it was more productive to do so (Jenkins and Sherman 1979).

Factories, however, demanded huge amounts of both labor and capital. The need for labor was urgent. Each machine needed tending and maintenance; each factory needed many indirect production workers, such as carriers, sweepers, folders and stackers. Employers would hire anyone who could produce the work, but women and children were preferred because they were paid even less than the men. Most of the work required no education and little skill; such crafts as were necessary were taught by example. Management was done by owners; clerical work was rudimentary and administrative work almost nonexistent. Working conditions were arduous, dangerous, and uncomfortable. Families lived in squalid, overcrowded housing. Attendance at church was the primary diversion, aside from drinking in the pubs. The church, rather than protesting the appalling conditions, preached the "puritan work ethic," which espoused the dignity of work and exhorted workers to accept their lot (Jenkins and Sherman 1979).

The urgent need for capital and for economies of scale demanded that small owner-managed businesses give way to ever larger and more complex entities, and the modern corporation was born. Industrialization and the growth of large corporations, in turn, introduced several "rules or principles" of organization: standardization—of both work and workers; specialization—division of labor and professionalism; synchronization—concern with the use of time and with punctuality; concentration—of capital, of resources, and of workers; maximization—of profits, of growth, and of size; and centralization—of political and economic power (Toffler 1980).

Standardization of work schedules was a necessity. In order to maximize profit returns from the capital investment, plans had to operate 24 hours a day, and shift work was the result. Because workers were highly interdependent on each other, synchronized schedules were a necessity. Unlike the preindustrial era, workers were no longer able to decide for themselves the allocation of time to work or leisure, nor were they able to decide their own working schedules. Workers were now required to work long shifts, night or day, at times prescribed by their employers. Even leisure time was standardized and synchronized; vacations and holidays, paid or not, were taken when and in the amount determined by the employer or by the union contract. Toffler (1980) argues that mass education had a "covert curriculum" consisting of three courses—one in punctuality, one in obedience, and one in doing rote, repetitive work—the three subjects most needed by workers on the modern assembly line.

These changes were not without their protestors. Two major opponents in England were the Luddites and the Chartists. The Luddites were named after Ned Lud, who had led his fellow workers in destroying "frames," the knitting machines employers had begun to install in the workshops of the textile industry (Leontief 1982). Lud and his followers believed that the machines created widespread unemployment. But they were mainly concerned that traditional skills would not be needed and that, while jobs might be available, they would be less attractive and require less expertise. The Chartists, a more radical group, focused more on working conditions. Luddism was a short-lived but bitter movement; Chartism lasted somewhat longer, but it too lost momentum and died in the mid-1800s (Jenkins and Sherman 1979).

The protest movements were futile: Workers had no choice but to conform to management's terms. They were no longer able to produce for themselves the requirements for their existence and were dependent on the corporation for their livelihood. Finding or keeping work often required the family to be geographically mobile. Workers were able to conform to these schedules because of the division of labor in the family.

These schedules were possible because the worker had a homemaker wife who prepared his food, raised his children, and managed his household, and if necessary supervised a move.

Over time, partly as a result of the advancing mechanical technology, conditions improved. The development of the internal combustion engine and the motor car transformed the transportation industry, and as mass production brought price reductions, both mass transit and private motor cars became available. Mass production methods made work even more intense and repetitious and the environment more hostile, but mass transit made it possible for people to live further distances from the factory and eased the crowded housing conditions. The electric motor, far smaller and more efficient than the steam engine and capable of enormous adaptation, made possible a plethora of manufacturing technologies and no doubt was responsible for creating an enormous number of jobs. It also became the basis for most of the "labor saving" household appliances. The deskilling of jobs and the decline of crafts continued, however (Jenkins and Sherman 1979).

As the work became more and more routinized, standardization came to be extended to wages as well as to hours and performance. With impetus from the labor movement, standardized hourly wages became the accepted practice. In preindustrial times, labor was rewarded on the basis of its output, that is, farm produce or craft products were used or exchanged according to their relative value. In the industrial system, labor was rewarded for its input—that is, the worker was separated from the results of his labor; he was paid for the time that he spent on the job. Since the family continued to be the basic economic unit of the society, hourly wages were set at a rate that was consistent with the wage earner's family responsibilities.

In the early twentieth century, the labor movement began to bargain for "in kind" services as well as wages, later to be dubbed "fringe" benefits. The amount and kind of these benefits were based not only upon the needs of the worker, the breadwinner, but also upon the needs of his dependent family as well. Clearly, health insurance was a great advantage to the worker, particularly in the days that preceded workmen's compensation, disability insurance, social security, vested pension plans, or unemployment insurance. But health insurance for the worker alone did not protect him from financial ruin if a member of his family suffered catastrophic illness; high wages alone did not protect the worker's family in the event of his death or disability. Since wives typically did not work for wages, and in fact were encouraged to remain out of the paid labor force, social protections for workers and their families came to be the responsibility of the employer.

Thus a "breadwinner model" evolved. In the social and economic times that accompanied the growth of large work organizations, this kind of symbiotic relationship between job and family served both satisfactorily, if not well. The family was utterly dependent on the breadwinner for his earnings; he, in turn, was equally dependent on his employer. On the other hand, the corporation was dependent on the worker for his labor, and he, in turn, was dependent on his wife to maintain the home and raise the children while he worked. The system required both in order to function (Goode 1971).

The important question, however, is to what extent this breadwinner model is functional today, given the changes that have occurred in family life, in women's participation in the paid work force, and in technology. Are contemporary organizational processes built on this breadwinner model the most rational for the organization? To what extent do they create institutional barriers that inhibit the performance of women workers? Of men workers?

THE POSTINDUSTRIAL SOCIETY

The beginning of the end of the industrial era came in the middle of the 1950s when two events occurred. The balance of the American work force shifted from manufacturing goods to delivering services, and the first commercial computer became available. The first event made this country the first "postindustrial" nation; the second allowed the computer (the twentieth-century steam engine) to become more than just an instrument of science, but a tool of the booming service industry (Hallblade and Mathews 1980).

The shift from a manufacturing to a service society has the potential for social change as great as those associated with the coming of mechanization. What these impacts will be, either for workers or for work organizations, we can only begin to perceive. In the four decades since the end of World War II, enormous change, both technological and social, has already taken place.

Changes in the Family

By the end of the nineteenth century American newspapers and magazines were full of speculation about the crisis of marriage and the family. From the 1900s down to the 1930s, discussion of the decline of the family became increasingly intense. Four developments gave rise to a steadily growing alarm: the rising divorce rate, the falling birth rate among "the better sort of people," the changing position of women, and the so-called revolution in morals (Lasch 1980).

The French have an axiom that translates roughly as "The more things change, the more they stay the same." Certainly the four developments just mentioned could be said to be the cause of as much alarm at the end of the twentieth century as they were at the end of the nineteenth. Divorce rates are at an all-time high; birth rates are falling among middle-class couples and rising among poor teenagers (and especially poor black teenagers); feminism and the entry of married women into the labor force are dramatically affecting the lives of American women; and the sexual revolution has certainly affected the whole fabric of society.

Yet despite these obvious changes, it is as true today as it was a century ago that the American family is alive and well; it is still the basic economic unit of our society. The most significant difference between then and now is that, rather than one modal class breadwinner family, there now exists a plurality of family and household forms. Some sociologists, in fact, argue that the contemporary family is, in some ways, returning to a form more like that which existed in preindustrial times, a form characterized by less segregation of roles and greater equality (Young and Willmott 1973).

Divorce Rates

Divorce rates have risen dramatically over the past several decades. However, to paraphrase Mark Twain, accounts of the death of the American family have been greatly exaggerated. Although families are smaller than ever before, nine out of ten people continue to live in households as family members (*Newsweek* 1983).

Prior to World War II, the divorce rate was 2 per 1,000 population (2 divorces per year for every 1,000 people). The war brought a sharp increase in the number of marriages, which in turn brought an increase in the number of divorces—a pattern that was repeated in the era of the Vietnam war. In 1946 the divorce rate reached 4.3, then dropped during the 1950s. It began to climb during the decade of the 1960s and by 1979 had reached 5.2 (Levitan and Belous 1981).

After 1975, however, the rate of increase in divorce dropped substantially. Between 1968 and 1975, the average annual increase in the divorce rate was 8 percent; in the four succeeding years the rate of increase dropped to only 2 percent (Levitan and Belous 1981). In 1979 one divorce occurred for every two marriages, but this often-quoted figure is meaningless, since the people getting married are not the same ones getting divorced. A lower and more accurate rate, called the "refined rate," is determined by comparing divorce rates among married women with marriage rates among single women. The average refined rate for the years 1975-77 was 37 divorces per 1,000 married women. Using that figure, we see that under 4 percent of married couples ended their marriages in those years (Scanzoni and Scanzoni 1981).

Further, high or rising divorce rates do not necessarily signal the end of the American family. About two out of every three (66 percent) of all first marriages survive. The high divorce rate reflects the fact that most divorced individuals remarry, and 44 percent of second marriages end in divorce. Thus 40 percent of all marriages, including second and succeeding marriages, may end in divorce.

These data can be interpreted in several ways. One can say: "Isn't it awful that so many second marriages fail?" or "Isn't it terrific that so many first marriages last?" Or even, "Isn't it grand that so many divorced people are willing and able to form new families?" Another positive way of looking at the situation is to observe that in earlier periods marriages were frequently disrupted by the death of a spouse, usually the husband. As life expectancy has increased, fewer and fewer marriages end with the death of a spouse. Until very recently, the increase in the divorce rate tended to be offset by the decrease in the death rate. Until 1970, the percentage of "ever married" women living with their first husbands had changed very little throughout the twentieth century (Bane 1976).

Families are, however, getting smaller and more diverse in form. The average family size for white families is now 3.2 persons; for blacks it is 3.7 and for Hispanics it is 3.9 (*Newsweek* 1983). The last several decades have seen not only an increase in the divorce rate but also a considerable growth in the number of nontraditional family forms, including cohabitation, voluntary childlessness, joint custody and coparenting, stepparenting, the so-called blended or reconstituted family, "open marriage," homosexual relationships, and multiadult relationships (Macklin 1980). The greatest increases have come in the number of married couples with no children present, the number of female-headed families, and the number of men and women living alone (Bane and Masnick 1980).

Out of 20 adults, 19 marry at least once in their lifetime, and the great majority of people, young and old, expect to marry and to live in a family setting (Levitan and Belous 1981). Even if they fail at a first marriage, the majority of people are willing to enter into a second one. What is significant for our purposes, and for American managers, is not that divorce is shattering the American family, but that myriad family forms now exist. The typical family of the industrial era, the breadwinner husband with the homemaker wife and several children, is now in the minority.

Birth Rates

Another phenomenon apparently troubling society at the end of the nineteenth century was the declining birth rate, particularly among middle-class and upper-middle-class couples. In 1897, Theodore Roosevelt worried about "the diminution of the birth rate among the highest classes;" fears abounded that the "highest races" would soon be outnumbered by their inferiors, who were thought to reproduce with total disregard for their ability to provide for the rising generation (Lasch 1980).

Today, the birth rate is still low, and dropping, among middle- and upper-middle-class families. Few women, less than 5 percent, voluntarily choose not to become mothers at all (Veevers 1973; Macklin 1980). But more and more couples are choosing to have only one, or at most two, children. Paradoxically, and at the same time, the birth rate is very high among teenagers, particularly among poor black girls (*Public Administration Times* 1983).

The American birth rate has dropped steadily since the 1800s, with black birth rates always higher than the white rate, but dropping at about the same rate. The steady downward trend was interrupted by the "baby boom" following World War II, but by the 1960s it had resumed. During the period between 1957 and 1978, the fertility rate dropped by nearly half (Levitan and Belous 1981). However, in 1977 the birthrate increased for the first time in seven years. The biggest rates of increase were among women in their late 20s to middle and late 30s, many of whom were having their first baby. Rather than signaling a new baby boom, this increase more likely reflects the decision of many women who had postponed childbirth while pursuing educational or career objectives (Scanzoni and Scanzoni 1981).

The reasons for the declining birth rate are numerous. Rates dropped rather precipitously during the early 1960s, a time associated with the increased availability, efficacy, and safety of birth control methods, especially the birth control pill. The Supreme Court decision to permit legal abortion, handed down in 1973, may also have had an effect, but its impact is less obvious or observable (Scanzoni and Scanzoni 1981). Other explanations include the changing roles of women, including the increased participation of married women in the paid labor force, the increased cost of childrearing, changing values, longer years spent in education for both women and men, and the somewhat later age at which young people are entering first marriage.

Families with high socioeconomic status, based on occupation, education, and income, have fewer children and they have them at an older age than families of low socioeconomic status. These high-status families are able to give their children a great many privileges, both in the amount of time spent in family activity and in the quality of education and other resources available. Their children are highly privileged (Levitan and Belous 1981).

About one-third of black families and one-tenth of white families fall below the poverty line. In the 1970 U.S. Census, lower status white families averaged one more child per family than did the upper status group; lower status black families averaged three more children per family than did higher status blacks. A very large proportion of poor families are headed by single women; 71 percent of the black families living below the poverty line in the 1970 census were headed by women (Scanzoni and

Scanzoni 1981). Between 1970 and 1982 the number of unwed mothers rose by 367 percent, and the number among teenagers doubled. Among white teenagers, 33 percent of all births were illegitimate; among blacks 86 percent were out of wedlock (*Newsweek* 1983).

The point at issue here is the contrast between the highly privileged children in small middle- and upper-middle-class families, and the diminished opportunities available to children in large lower-class families, regardless of race. The dual problems of illegitimacy and teenage pregnancy among poor blacks have reached such major proportions that the Urban League and a number of other civil-rights groups have made it a priority issue. The problem is one of social class, not of race. Poor white families, often headed by women, suffer the same lack of opportunity and access to educational resources, and they face the same downward spiral. If, as many predict, the postindustrial society has fewer jobs and will require workers with higher levels of technical and scientific knowledge, they are more likely to come from the privileged few than from the underprivileged many.

Changing Roles

The changing roles of women and men will be a major topic of this book. For the purposes of understanding the postindustrial society it is only important to understand how significant womens' roles were to the development of the industrial society to understand how changing those roles will change the fabric of society and the composition of work organizations.

At the turn of the century only about 5 percent of middle-class wives were members of the paid work force. Those who did work were usually forced to do so by adversity. They had little formal education, their attachment to the work force was episodic, and they were concentrated in a few low-paid, low-skilled occupations in the services sector. Single women worked until they married; some married women continued to work until the birth of their first child. After that it was considered a poor reflection of the husband's role as breadwinner if his wife went out to work. Instead she managed his household, and he gave full attention to his role as provider. Women typically married by the age of 22, had their first child by age 23, bore four or more children, had their last child at age 38, and lived to the age of 55. A significant portion of their lives was spent in bearing and raising children. They were completely dependent on their husbands for financial support; husband and wife roles were highly differentiated and the husband tended to have a great deal more power in the relationship.

Today women are marrying later, bearing their children later, bearing fewer children, and living longer. They are better educated than their grandmothers, in fact as well educated as their male counterparts. They, like their grandmothers, tend to start work when they are single, but few can afford the luxury of choosing to stop work when they marry or when their first child is born. Even those without a financial need often choose to combine marriage, childrearing, and paid work. They typically marry by age 24, bear their first child by age 26, their last by age 30; they typically have only one, or at most two children, and live to be 76 years old. Consequently, unlike their grandmothers, a relatively small portion of their lives is devoted to bearing and raising children and a very significant share is spent in the labor market.

Like their grandmothers, however, they still find their job opportunities limited largely to the services sector (although this sector has grown enormously while the industrial sector has declined) and they still find themselves receiving significantly lower pay than male workers. Husband and wife roles are less differentiated, with both sharing breadwinner and caretaker responsibilities. Although the true egalitarian marriage is rarely a reality, contemporary working wives who earn a major and essential portion of the family's income enjoy more equality in their relationships than did their Victorian grandmothers.

These changes have important implications for modern managers, as yet only faintly realized. Women workers are better educated and more highly skilled than in the past; they are more independent both sexually and financially; they are permanently attached to the labor force; they have smaller families and are involved in childrearing for a shorter period of their lives; they rely on their own earnings for a substantial portion of their livelihood, sharing with their husbands both breadwinner roles and the responsibility for household duties. They regard their organizational role as a significant one.

An equally important and more frequently overlooked aspect of these changes, however, lies in their impact on men's lives and on their roles as breadwinners. The contemporary male, unlike his grandfather, does not have a full-time homemaker wife to bear and raise his children and manage his household. The working male with an employed wife may have neither the freedom nor the responsibility to devote his main energies to his roles of breadwinner and job holder. He no longer bears sole responsibility for his family's income and welfare; that burden is shared not only by his wife, if she holds a job, but also by a variety of government-mandated and -managed social programs. He no longer suffers shame if his wife works; he may, in fact, enjoy the benefits of the high combined incomes that they share. His family role is a significant one. He no longer must rely on the employer as his protection against catastrophy. His employer can no longer assume his unconditional dependency, loyalty, or obedience. The modern corporation, built upon the breadwinner model, has lost its breadwinner.

The Revolution of Morals

The "sexual revolution," cause of much consternation in the 1960s and 1970s, is of course not really a revolution at all but instead a rather abrupt change in sexual attitudes and behavior. The current period of change is, in many ways, a repeat of the period of change occurring at the turn of the century. What one means by the term, of course, is open to debate. For many people, apparently, a sexual revolution connotes an increase in female (but not male) nonmarital sex (Scanzoni and Scanzoni 1981). For others, it means an increased acceptance of a wide repertory of sexual behaviors. Many blue-collar couples have experienced pressure and conflict in their marital sexual relationships simply as a result of increased openness and frankness in public discussions of sex (Rubin 1976). For still others it means increased acceptance of and openness toward a variety of sexual lifestyles.

Unquestionably changes have occurred in sexual mores in recent years, no matter what definition you use. During two time periods, one beginning around 1915 the other around 1965, rather sharp increases occurred in female sexual behavior. Prior to that time, Protestant values and Victorian prudery had assigned to women the necessity of remaining virginal until marriage and faithful to their mates after marriage. Although these moral expectations also applied to men, they were mainly honored in the breach. Somewhere in the early part of this century, probably starting about 1915, the number of women who had experienced premarital sex doubled in one decade. From that point until the mid-1960s, change could be described more as evolution than revolution. Then, once again, there was a sharp increase in the number of women who had had sex prior to marriage, an increase in the number of women pregnant at the time of marriage, a lowering of the age of first coitus, an increase in the extent of noncoital sexual activity among adolescents, and an increase in the number of women reporting extramarital affairs (Scanzoni and Scanzoni 1981).

Although these two periods of change occurred 50 years apart, they occurred under very similar social contexts. Both the first and second sexual revolutions coincided with unpopular wars; World War I in the earlier period; Vietnam in the second. Each was concurrent with an active women's movement. The first period marked the culmination of nearly 70 years of effort to win the vote, an effort that was resisted vigorously on the grounds that it would have a negative effect on women's virtue and purity. The second period coincides with the rebirth of the women's movement, after nearly 40 years of hiatus, and the effort to enact the Equal Rights Amendment. The first feminist movement involved itself in other issues as well as suffrage, notably the right to disseminate and use birth control. The second movement's rebirth was coincident with the availability of the birth control pill and the IUD (intrauterine device). Each period was marked by a high level of hedonism: the roaring twenties and the rebellious sixties (Tannahill 1981).

The significance of a sexual revolution is not a breakdown of moral values or a rise in permissiveness but its association with larger social issues. When women demand increased autonomy, increased equality, and decreased paternalism, they also demand and exercise the right to greater sexual freedom. These changes do not spell a threat to the family. They do, however, underline for management the fact that women are seeking and demanding autonomy and equality in both their family and work environments.

As we approach the end of the twentieth century, the social issues concerning us are the same ones confronting our forefathers a century ago: the breakdown of the family, a declining birth rate, a revolution in morals, and the changing roles of women. Yet enormous change has taken place in the last century. From the standpoint of the organization, these changes add up to a very different social world from the one that existed at the turn of the century. Fears of the breakdown of the family have been greatly exaggerated, yet the nuclear family of the nineteenth century has been replaced by an enormous variety of family forms. Because of the steady decline in the birth rate, and despite a significant increase in the number of births to unwed teenage mothers, we are faced with an ever-decreasing work force. As the baby boom cohort moves through the life cycle, the succeeding cohorts are becoming increasingly smaller. By the time the baby boomers reach retirement age, there will be only two workers in the labor force for every retired worker. Changes in sexual mores and in women's roles have led to very different expectations of women's participation in and rewards from paid employment.

A number of questions are raised by these social phenomena. What effects will social change have on work organizations? How will technology affect the work organizations? How will it affect the family?

Changes in the Work Organization

There are two possible scenarios for the future. One is that economic growth and the declining birth rate will create labor shortages. The demand for skilled workers will increase to such an extent that government and industry will be forced to create educational and training programs. These programs will qualify the less-privileged workers for high-paid jobs, which in turn will help to raise them to middle-class status. Older workers will be offered inducements such as shorter hours to persuade them to remain in the work force; couples with children will be offered extended parental leaves, employer-sponsored day care, educational tuition, and other inducements to produce children while continuing employment.

The other scenario is that technology will eliminate many jobs and deskill many more. Only those with the highest technical knowledge and skills will be able to find satisfactory employment. Others will work at increasingly low-paid, low-skilled jobs, and many will be unable to find any paid work at all. Wealth will tend to be increasingly concentrated in the hands of the elites who own the means of production. Lower-class families, rather than using jobs to raise their socioeconomic status, will find themselves slipping ever deeper into poverty and will increasingly rely on transfer payments for survival. Women will continue to work in sex-segregated jobs that are low-paid and low-skilled, and they will continue to bear an unequal share of the household labor.

Unfortunately, the latter scenario is the one that appears to be increasingly likely. The computer and, more particularly, the transistor and the microchip have dramatically changed the way we work and the kind of work that we do. The immeasurable speed, miniature size, and daunting capacity of the microchip are almost inconceivable to most of us. The number of uses to which they can be, and have already been, put seems to be infinite, and we're constantly reminded that electronic technology is still in its infancy. Given the awesome possibilities, the impacts of developing technology on our society can be no less than revolutionary.

Let's look at some examples.

Computers may be bringing about the demise of the printed word. The invention of writing was the most revolutionary of all human inventions; it freed human communication from its temporal and regional restrictions. Thoughts could be written down at one time and place and read and reread in others. But written words must be stored and transported. Man has moved from stone tablets, to paper, to microfilm, but all of these require storage and they require the reader and the written material to be at the same place at the same time. The computer can store enormous amounts of information in an extremely small space, and it can do it for a tiny proportion of the cost of pen and ink. Further, it can sift and interpret the information in almost any way that the reader chooses. Bookstores, libraries, even references materials such as encyclopedias and dictionaries, seem old-fashioned and inefficient by comparison (Evans 1979).

Professions, like books, have long been repositories of knowledge, and access to that knowledge has been closely guarded—for example, by severely limiting admission to medical or law school. Will computers make the professions irrelevant? Probably not, but they can certainly decrease their power. Already, computers can take a patient's medical history on a large variety of common complaints, make simple recommendations for follow-up studies, and offer tentative diagnoses. In law, computers can store the enormous amount of case law whose precedents are so important; further, they can sift and sort through the stored data to find the relevant information in a fraction of the time it would take a law clerk. In teaching, early attempts at computerized instruction have turned out to be expensive, cumbersome, and ineffective. But portable, pocket-sized personal teaching computers can now be used as dictionaries, as drill and practice aids in math and languages, and as game partners. These "smart," interactive computers can adjust their responses in a number of ways that closely resemble that of the human teacher (Evans 1979).

Money as we know it today may cease to exist. The first step toward the replacement of physical money was the credit card. At first these were simply plastic promissory notes, useful for testifying to the holder's creditworthiness and for recording financial transactions (Evans 1979). Credit cards are issued that can be used almost any place in the country and even overseas. Now the cards can be fed into a computer to ensure that they have not been stolen nor the credit privilege abused. Debit cards make it possible to make "cash" payments with a card that automatically transfers money from the buyer's bank account to the seller's. Almost all checks are sorted by means of a nationwide system of machine-readable code numbers. Computer-based equipment for tellers has been available for many years; automatic teller machines now transfer much of the teller's work to the client (Ernst 1982).

Robots are becoming increasingly available to perform tasks in the manufacturing area that are too dangerous or too monotonous for humans to perform. Much emphasis has been placed on the capacity of industrial robots to replace production workers. In reality, however, the greatest impact of electronic technology has been on information processing and on the design of products and processes. "Computer integrated manufacturing" is achieved by linking design, the storage and retrieval of information about the parts being manufactured, the management and control of resources, the handling of materials, the control of machine tools and other single purpose machinery, and the control of robots (Gunn 1982).

Some of the most miraculous innovations, however, have come in telecommunications. The typewriter, the telephone, and the telegraph revolutionized office work in the Industrial Revolution and created an enormous number of jobs, especially for women. Since then the technology has gradually replaced a great deal of that labor, through the introduction of the dial system, solid-state switching, fiber optics, modularization, and more (Ernst 1982). Workers in a wide variety of occupations and locations now communicate through "electronic mail" networks. Telecommunications link people from office to office, but also from their homes, from the factory floor, or from anywhere in the world where they have a personal computer and a telephone. More and more workers, managers, economists, librarians, and airline personnel now rely on personal "work stations," computerized facilities that often include a personal computer and are ultimately linked to one or more central computers, data bases, communications systems, and any of thousands of support systems. These stations become increasingly sophisticated and complex; as with most electronic technology, change is occurring at a dizzying rate (Giuliano 1982).

All of these innovations have had the effect of increasing productivity enormously; without them our whole system of commerce would be impossible. It's hard to imagine what business would be like without automatic dialing, computerized check sorting or credit checks, and electronic record keeping.

Technology in the postindustrial era, as in the industrial era, has the potential for making enormous social change. For many types of work, there is no longer any need to assemble all workers at the same time and place. Portable terminals and computers, equipped with appropriate software and communications facilities, including telephones, create an office anywhere the worker happens to be. The remote work station can communicate with the central office and extends the range of places where written and numerical material can be generated, stored, retrieved, manipulated, or communicated. The telephone made it unnecessary to go to a particular place to communicate orally; the small computer makes it unnecessary to go there to communicate in writing. The job is no longer tied to the flow of paper across a designated desk; it is tied to the worker himself (Giuliano 1982).

Today's problems are often yesterday's solutions. Enormous increases in productivity have also brought about their share of problems. The major concern, for our purposes, is the same one that was raised by critics of the Industrial Revolution: the displacement of labor. Two questions are raised: does technology eliminate jobs? and does it deskill jobs? The conventional wisdom has always argued that automation creates more jobs than it eliminates, and to a great extent that was true of the industrial era. Successive waves of technological innovation brought with them "a spectacular growth of both employment and real wages" (Leontief 1982). The conventional wisdom has also argued that the new jobs are more highly skilled than the old ones, but in this case the Luddites were right. Industrialization did, in fact, lead to the deskilling of many jobs and the decline of crafts (Jenkins and Sherman 1979).

Machines in the industrial era displaced human muscle, but machines in the postindustrial era increasingly replace the human nervous system in both production and service industries. The relationship between man and machine is being transformed. Human labor has always been a principal factor in production, but electronic technology has so increased productivity as to make traditional definitions meaningless. Some types of labor are being replaced faster than others. Agriculture has been so transformed that it is now more highly mechanized than manufacturing. Mining, manufacturing, and construction industries, despite resistance from labor unions, have become highly mechanized and employment is down dramatically. On the other hand, the number of white-collar workers has increased dramatically (Ginzberg 1982). But technology appears to have checked the growth in this sector as well (Wheale 1984). Usually less-skilled workers are replaced first and more-skilled ones later, but there are exceptions to this rule (Leontief 1982).

Despite many efforts to reverse the trend, through training and retraining programs, investment credits, or reduced working hours, unemployment levels have risen steadily in the last four decades. In 1945 the irreducible level of unemployment was considered to be 2 percent; by the 1960s that figure had risen to 4 percent. In the 1980s it is closer to 9 percent. While not all of this increase can be attributed to technological unemployment, neither can its existence be ignored (Leontief 1982). Considerable evidence supports the view that, as computers become more and more sophisticated, the trend to technological unemployment will increase.

Contrary to most expectations, this displacement appears to have a disproportionate effect on women workers. Longitudinal analysis of changes in the occupational structure at American Telephone and Telegraph (AT&T) prior to its divestiture of local operating companies, for example, showed that technological displacement affected both management and nonmanagement women (S. Hacker 1979).

In 1971 an investigation by the Equal Employment Opportunity Commission had found that women and minorities at AT&T were clustered at the lowest levels of both management and nonmanagement categories. The two largest categories in the operating companies were heavily sex-segregated: traffic (operators and their supervisors) was 96 percent female, and plant (craft and some clericals) was 84 percent male.

The government required the company to produce affirmative action plans with a three-year timetable of goals for the employment of women and minorities at each organizational level. The outcome, however, showed an overall decline in the proportion of women working anywhere in the system. While some women were moved up, more moved out. Despite AT&T's apparent good-faith effort to achieve its goals, at the end of the three years gains made through affirmative action were offset by losses through technological displacement.

The period covered by the plans coincided with a period of rapid technological change. In the female-intensive traffic departments, 36,000 jobs for operators and clericals and 1,500 of their supervisors were eliminated as automatic equipment was installed to handle calls and billing.

Because of affirmative action efforts, both men and women were moved into nontraditional positions. Over 16,000 men moved into traditionally female jobs; many men became operators and moved into supervisory jobs. Only 9,000 women moved into traditionally male jobs. During the period men as a group gained over 14,000 positions, women as a group lost over 22,000.

Further, by the mid-1970s, just as women were being encouraged to move into traditional male jobs (crafts and semiskilled labor), significant technological changes got under way that would reduce jobs in these categories, in some cases by up to 80 percent. Many traditionally male jobs, especially semiskilled and crafts jobs, were reduced or eliminated, along with many management positions. To avoid the layoffs that were sure to occur, the company increased the work load of present workers, reduced flexibility on the job, and hired temporary workers. At AT&T, technological displacement affected both male and female workers, but both technological change and affirmative action benefited men more than women (S. Hacker 1979).

A parallel concern about technology is that it will not only eliminate many jobs but will make the remaining ones increasingly repetitious. Some experts have predicted that computer technology will result in greater decentralization, structural complexity, and autonomy for administrators and higher levels of skill and responsibility for workers (P. Blau et al. 1976). But the preponderance of the evidence suggests that both administrative and operating jobs will become more routine and repetitive. Also, women again seem to be disproportionately affected by this deskilling of jobs.

Studies of office automation in the insurance industry, a fairly typical service industry, between 1961 and 1980 found that:

- The introduction of new technology was labor-saving, and some occupations were eliminated altogether.
- The continued expansion of clerical activity more than offset savings in labor, so that the clerical force grew slightly overall; however, there was a sizable reduction in the number of traditional clerical jobs.
- The new technology has been used not only to reduce the number of jobs but to reorganize the work. Occupations are narrower, more specialized, and more standardized.
- The expansion of computer-related occupations has increased the total number of jobs and created some new, higher paid occupations. But the workers displaced by automation do not appear to benefit; the new jobs are at the technical level and largely held by males. Women from traditional clerical jobs are unlikely to be moving up into these jobs. Rather, a new layer of largely male workers,

recruited from a different labor pool, has been inserted into the office. The women in the traditionally female clerical categories are likely to find not only higher unemployment but also the deskilling of their jobs and reduced opportunities for advancement (Feldberg and Glenn 1983).

Further, the reorganization of work brought about by automation may also involve changes in worker autonomy. For instance, with computerization, a great deal of information can be centralized in one place, be available simultaneously to many employees, and be constantly updated or revised. This centralization allows low-level clerical jobs to be redesigned to cover a broader scope of information. But it also allows closer supervision. Monitoring systems can keep track of the work done by each clerk, and automatic call distributors can allocate incoming phone calls and record the number of calls answered or lost. A tally can be kept of each clerk's errors. Jobs can be designed so that each task must be handled according to specified procedures and within a specific time frame. Although the clerk has access to more information, and appears to be performing a wider range of duties, in fact she is required to have less knowledge of procedures and she has less opportunity to use her judgment about modifying those procedures (Feldberg and Glenn 1983).

Technological advances since the mid-1950s, the beginning of the postindustrial era, have already dramatically reshaped the social world we live in. We have come to accept as commonplace many achievements and innovations that were outlandish fantasies only a short time ago. We have come to accept change at an unprecedented rate. In spite of the wonders of technology, however, in medicine, in telecommunications, in business, and in our homes, we need to be aware of some of its broader impacts. Technology has caused displacement. Many occupations have been eliminated altogether, and in others growth has slowed. Those eliminated are often, but not always, the least skilled. Further, technology has resulted in many jobs becoming more routine and repetitious, which in turn makes them susceptible to further automation. Other jobs that appear to have been enriched have, in fact, become less autonomous. New, more technical jobs are often created, but they rarely go to the displaced worker.

These changes have affected different sectors of the labor market differently. Contrary to popular belief, the greatest changes have not occurred among blue-collar male workers in manufacturing industries but among white-collar women workers. These workers are confronted with a dwindling job supply and increasing competition from male workers for such improved jobs as become available. Those women who have moved into the skilled and semiskilled trades, on the other hand, may also find themselves competing with males for jobs in declining occupations.

SUMMARY

The Industrial Revolution brought about enormous social change. The development of the factory system enhanced the division of labor within the family and the occupational segregation of women and men in the work force. Because of the rigorous demands on male workers, families relied on the services of a full-time homemaker wife. Because of the economic conditions, the size of the family, and life expectancy, most women spent all of their adult lives in childbearing and childrearing. Even when labor-saving devices that made women's work less onerous became available, the amount of time women spent in housework and child care did not decrease. Instead standards and expectations increased. The household division of labor was thoroughly established. Man was the breadwinner; woman was the wife.

From the beginning of the factory system young women typically worked until the time they married. After marriage they seldom worked for wages outside the home except in cases of emergency, but they often earned extra money by taking in boarders or by doing piecework—sewing or copying—at home. In fact, some homes became minisweatshops.

Men, the breadwinners, became the mainstay of the industrial system. As wages and benefits were improved over time, partly through the efforts of the labor movement, they were expanded to provide not only for the worker himself but for his wife and children as well. Women were episodic members of the work force. They worked in only a small number of occupations; their pay was low and their benefits minimal.

In the postindustrial era, much has changed and much has stayed the same. The family is still the basic economic unit of society, and most people live in families, but the definition of family has changed greatly. Families are smaller, divorce and remarriage are more frequent, and widowhood is less frequent. The birth rate is very low, except among teenagers and especially among black teenagers. Women are more independent, both financially and sexually, than ever before. The majority of women work more or less continuously throughout their lives, and women have come to expect equal opportunity and equal treatment in the workplace. As women share the breadwinner role with their husbands, increasingly they look to their husbands to share their homemaker roles.

Postindustrial technology has brought about, and is sure to bring in the future, social changes as great or greater than those brought about by industrialization. These changes, especially those that affect the workplace, fall differentially on women and men. Telecommunications free workers from the necessity to work in a particular place at a particular time, surely a great advantage to the two-career family. But they also create the possibility of a modern sweatshop where women are paid piecework wages, without benefits, for the privilege of working at home while they have a break from child care or household work. Technology eliminates some jobs and deskills others. At the same time it creates new, more technical jobs. Unfortunately, the available evidence seems to indicate that these changes adversely affect women workers. Traditional female jobs are the ones most likely to be eliminated, and these displaced workers are not generally the ones who move into the new and better ones.

The implications are positive or negative, depending on your point of view. For women at the low end of the scale, for those lacking education or job training, the prospects for finding employment are dim indeed. The clerical jobs that have historically been available to them, while admittedly low paid and lacking in advancement opportunities, are no longer available at all. Middle-class workers, on the other hand (those who are able to find employment), might expect some positive outcomes, such as shorter working hours, higher pay, flexible pay, fringe benefit programs, and employer-sponsored child care.

These futuristic opportunities will be discussed in Chapter 12. In the intervening chapters we will be looking at the contemporary world of women and men in organizations.

3

The Economic Environment

The "woman problem" in organizations is one that is always susceptible to argument, some of it vehement. In recent years conflict and confusion created by Affirmative Action and Equal Employment Opportunity
programs have exacerbated the perception of the woman problem. Inevitably, a book such as this one will cause someone—usually but not always
a white male—to protest that problems no longer exist *for* women, only
problems *about* women. Women, they will argue, now are at least the organizational equals of men, and in fact the men are the victims of something ambiguously referred to as "reverse discrimination."

Before we begin our discussion of sex roles and organizational roles
we need to consider these charges. We will do so by examining some data
on the actual experience of women and men in the labor force and the
trends in that experience over the last two or three decades. These data
show that despite the enormous changes that have occurred, women and
men still tend to work in different occupations and women still earn less.

Next we will turn to economic theories that attempt to explain these
differences. Neoclassical theories, especially the Human Capital theory,
argue that the differences occur because women choose to allocate their
time to family responsibilities and elect not to invest in their earnings ability. Segmented Labor Market theories argue that women are relegated by
employers to secondary jobs with low pay and little opportunity to acquire firm-specific skills, that is, that the differences are a result of discrimination.

Finally, we will look at evidence from organizational studies of the
"comparable worth" of jobs. These studies attempt to assess the degree to
which differences in pay between female- and male-dominated occupations are a function of productivity or of sex discrimination.

32

LABOR FORCE PARTICIPATION

The myths about women workers assume that all or nearly all women are married and are supported by their husbands; if they work at all it is assumed to be either for a specific purpose—for the down payment on a house or to send the children to college—or as a supplement to the breadwinner's earnings. Thus men are perceived to be the "primary" workers, the mainstay of the labor market; women are perceived to be "secondary" workers, only episodically members of the labor force.

It would be hard to imagine that anyone could be unaware of the increased role of women in the work force in recent years. On the other hand, few are aware of the extent to which men's labor force participation has declined. In 1960, 37.3 percent of adult women were in the workplace; by 1981 that number had risen to 52.1 percent. In 1960, 83.3 percent of adult males were in the work force; by 1981 that number had shrunk to 77 percent (Sorrentino 1983) as seen in Figure 3.1. The increase in women's participation has come in the middle years of life—between ages 24 and 54—a period when women in the past tended to leave the work force to raise their families. For men, the decrease has occurred at the beginning and end of their work lives. Men tend to stay in school longer, thus entering the labor market later (although the majority combine work and school), and many are leaving it earlier, mostly because of poor health.

By 1980, 45 percent of the labor force consisted of women (Waldman 1983). As a result of these changing patterns of labor force participation, the average 16-year-old male today can expect to spend 38.5 years in the labor force and a typical female of that age can expect 27.7 years of labor force involvement (S. Smith 1982).

The Increase in Women's Labor Force Participation

Since 1959, women workers have accounted for 57 percent of the increase in the size of the labor force. Factors that contribute to women's increased labor force activity include:

- Expansion of the service sector. The service sector has been the fastest growing sector of the economy, and four-fifths of all working women are in that sector.
- Declines in fertility rates. The fertility rate is measured by the number of live births per 100 women between ages 15 and 44. In 1960 the rate was 11.9; in 1980 it was 7.0. Labor force participation is inversely related to fertility: the fewer children a woman has, the more likely it is that she will be in the labor force.
- The increased availability of part-time work. In 1980, 19 percent of all employed women were working part time. But at the same time

14 percent of women in the work force were working *more* than 40 hours a week, often because they were working at two part-time jobs (Taylor and Sekscenski 1982).

- Increased higher education. For both women and men, the higher the level of education, the higher the probability that they will be in the labor force. Of workers with four or more years of college, 95 percent of the men and 74 percent of the women were in the labor force in 1981. In 1981, men were more likely than women to have at least some college education, but women were more likely than men to have finished high school (Young 1982).

FIGURE 3.1
Trends in Labor Force Participation Rates For All
Persons and by Sex, 1960-81

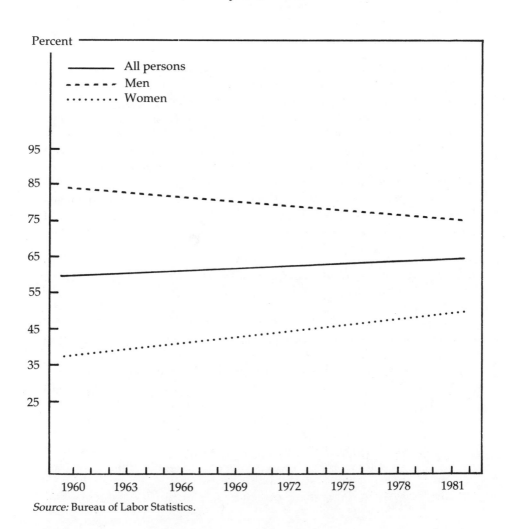

Source: Bureau of Labor Statistics.

- Abating job discrimination among women.
- Changing attitudes toward women's role in society (Sorrentino 1983).

The Decrease in Men's Labor Force Participation

Since 1960, and especially since 1974, labor force participation of males aged 60 to 64 has declined sharply; participation among men aged 45 to 59 has also declined, but more gradually (Rosenfeld and Brown 1979). Some withdrawals (about 30 percent) are voluntary, but the majority are not.

The reasons for involuntary withdrawal include:

- Poor health. Between 1966 and 1972, 43 percent of white retirees and 52 percent of black retirees between the ages of 55 and 69 left the labor force because of poor health. These men who retire because of poor health are likely to have been in a low-level occupation and to receive lower retirement income.
- Unemployment. Retirement is a more honorable estate than unemployment, and some workers retire as a way of dealing with long-term chronic unemployment. Older workers with low educational attainment or low skill levels who are laid off often find it especially difficult to find new employment.
- Mandatory retirement. About 5 percent of workers between 59 and 73 who retired in 1980 were forced into retirement by mandatory programs (Sproat 1983).
- Education level. Among men 45-54, the largest decrease in participation was among the least educated. It may be that these men, if they become unemployed, are unable to find another job. Also, employers may increase the educational requirements of jobs if a supply of unemployed men is available to meet those requirements. Finally, the number of jobs in which the average years of schooling tends to be lowest has decreased (Rosenfeld and Brown 1979).

The primary reason for increased voluntary retirement is financial. Increasingly, improved private pension plans make it possible for men to retire before they reach 65. The decision to retire voluntarily is often also influenced by such factors as the absence of dependents, the desire for leisure, increases in social security benefits, and the conditions on the job, for example, boring or monotonous tasks (Rosenfeld and Brown 1979).

Family Membership and Labor Force Participation

Married men are no longer the mainstay of the labor market. In 1955 husbands constituted 52 percent of the labor force. By 1977 that figure had shrunk to 41 percent, and by 1982 it was down to only 35 percent. At the same time the percentage of the labor force made up of wives was on the increase: by 1982 they made up almost 25 percent. In 1982 more than 70 percent of the labor force lived in married-couple families (Klein 1983) and half of all married couples were in multiearner families (Waldman 1983). Another 10 percent of the work force lived in families maintained by women on their own, most of which were single-earner families (Klein 1983).

Married men are no longer the mainstay of the family, either. In 1983, 52 percent of all wives and 79 percent of all husbands were in the labor force, and these rates varied very little even for families with children. Some 45 percent of mothers of infants (0 to 2 years old) were in the labor force; for mothers of 2-5 year olds the rate was between 50 and 57 percent; and for mothers of school-age children the rate ranged as high as 67 percent. Sixteen percent of all families were maintained by women, over half of whom had children under 18 and were in the work force (Johnson and Waldman 1983). Unemployment rates tend to run high, especially for mothers with children under age 3, but when mothers are employed, 60 percent of them work at full-time jobs (Waldman 1983).

Men are more likely than women to put in overlong work weeks, and the patterns differ according to marital status. Married men are more likely than single men to work long schedules; but single women are more likely than married women to exceed the standard. Over the last decade the number of married women holding more than one job has increased, while the number of married men holding more than one job has decreased (Taylor and Sekscenski 1982).

When a worker retires involuntarily for health reasons, the family's situation is often poor. These workers often come from the lowest economic strata, and their economic hardships are intensified by rising medical costs and declining income. Wives typically do not enter the labor market during the husband's illness. If they do find work after his death, the wages are typically very low. Just under 30 percent (almost one in three) of white widows live below the poverty line. However, when older workers retire voluntarily, the situation is less dire. Family income drops, usually by about one-third, but retirement income is often supplemented by the wife's earnings, which may be as much as the retiree's own income (Sproat 1983).

Unemployment

From 1947 until very recently, women have had higher rates than men for both secular and cyclical unemployment. That is, unemployment rates have been chronically higher for women than for men, and women workers have been harder hit by recession than men workers. However,

after the most recent (1980-82) recession, for the first time the rate of unemployment was higher for men than for women. Several factors contributed to the reversal. A great many jobs were lost in manufacturing, but
during the same period the number of jobs in the service sector increased.
Also, within specific industries, women's unemployment rates were
lower than they had been in the previous recession of 1972-74, suggesting
that perhaps more women had accumulated enough seniority to make
them less vulnerable (Nilsen 1984).

The impact of the 1980-82 recession was much less severe for married
women than for married men, but unemployment tends to run in
families. Persons with highly marketable education and training tend to
marry each other, as do persons with more limited labor market skills. But
an even more important factor is that when high unemployment hits a
specific geographical area it can affect more than one member of the family. The unemployment rate for people with unemployed spouses tends
to run about three times as high as the rate for people with employed
spouses. For example, in 1982 the unemployment rate for wives with unemployed spouses was 20.7 percent and for wives with employed
spouses it was 6.3 percent (Klein 1983). However, the presence of children also affects unemployment; for mothers with children under age 3
the rate was 23 percent (Waldman 1983).

Unemployment falls especially hard on women who maintain their
own families, higher than for either husbands or wives. Since the early
1970s their rate has increased over that of married women and has shown
little response to economic expansion. These women tend to be young, to
have young children, to have fewer years of education, and to be concentrated in lower skilled, lower paying jobs having considerable turnover.
Because their children tend to be too young to hold jobs, they usually lack
the economic cushion of a second wage earner in the family (Klein 1983).

Thus we can see that over the last two decades the nature of the work
force and of the family has changed dramatically. While the majority of
workers continue to live in married-couple families, men's labor force
participation has fallen, the percentage of the labor force made up of husbands has fallen, the number of married men working at multiple jobs has
fallen, and the number and percentage of single-earner families has fallen. During the same time the proportion of the labor force made up of
women has risen, the number of wives and mothers in the labor force has
risen, the number of married women working at two jobs has risen, and
the number of women working full time and maintaining their own
families has risen. Unemployment rates for men have risen higher and
faster than rates for women, but the rates continue to be very high for
married women with young children and especially for single women
maintaining their own families. Clearly we can no longer divide the labor

market into "primary" and "secondary" workers on the basis of sex or family responsibility.

Clearly, however, the labor market is segregated into women's jobs and men's jobs and the latter are a good deal more rewarding than the former.

OCCUPATIONAL SEGREGATION

The sexual division of labor is characteristic of every society and every historical period, although the sexual assignment of specific tasks varies from culture to culture. In our society, the majority of occupations have typically been assigned to one sex or the other, although those assignments have tended to shift over time. For example, the job of bank teller, once an almost exclusively male job, has become a predominantly female one. In 1982, women accounted for about 6 percent of all craftsworkers and 78 percent of all clerical workers. Women were *more* likely than men to work in professional and technical occupations, but they held different jobs (and lower paying jobs) within that category. They account for only 5 percent of the engineers, 23 percent of the lawyers, and 22 percent of the physicians employed as wage and salary workers. On the other hand they made up very large shares of the lower paying professional and technical jobs: 94 percent of the registered nurses, 67 percent of teachers below the college level, 70 percent of the health technologists and technicians, and 65 percent of the social and recreational workers. Among sales workers, about half the women were sales clerks in retail trade, one of the lowest paying sales occupations. Only one-sixth of the male sales workers were in retail trade. Men were more likely to be sales representatives in wholesale trade or manufacturing, sales workers other than sales clerks in the retail trade, and stock and bond sales agents—all relatively high-paying sales jobs (Mellor 1984).

Because female-intensive occupations tend to be the lowest paid ones, substantial efforts have been made in the last two decades to reduce occupational segregation. However, even though the percentage of adult women in the work force has increased dramatically in those years and the proportion of the labor force who are women has increased substantially, the degree of occupational segregation has declined only slightly. Women workers continue to be found clustered in a fairly small number of occupational categories. What changes have taken place appear to be more a function of the decline in employment in male-intensive jobs than an indication of the breakdown of segregation.

Looking only at major occupational groups, one could find cause for optimism. Clearly, some groups are either male- or female-intensive and have remained so at least for the last decade. For example, laborer, transportation worker, and craft worker categories (all male-intensive) have changed very little in their proportion of male and female workers. Administrative support, clerical, and household worker categories (all female-intensive) show equally little change. However, some categories appear to be sex-neutral. Professional specialties, technicians, and salesworkers, for instance, show greater than average increases in female percentages. But these figures are misleading. Within these broad groups a great deal of sex segregation exists. For example, nearly half of all the female professionals are either nurses or teachers, heavily female-dominated occupations (Rytina and Bianchi 1984). To be sure, the number of males in these professions has increased slightly, but the males are much more likely, proportionately, to be found in the administrative positions of these professions. In fact, males tend to be attracted to female-dominated professional fields during periods when the number of administrative positions is expanding (Grimm and Stern 1974).

Actually, the degree of sex segregation has decreased in the last decade or two, but not so much because women have penetrated male-dominated occupations as because of shifts in the types of jobs available. In 1970, 75 percent of women workers were in female-intensive occupations, 16 percent were in neutral occupations, and only 9 percent were in male-dominated occupations. In 1980, these percentages were about the same. However, the degree of sex segregation had decreased because of a change in "occupational mix," that is, a change in the proportion of jobs in various occupational categories (Rytina and Bianchi 1984). Since 1950 three trends have occurred: a decline in the relative importance of agricultural work, resulting in a drop in the proportion of workers who are farmers or farm workers; a decline in the importance of unskilled work, resulting in a decrease in the proportion of workers who are nonfarm laborers; and a shift away from self-employment. All of these are male-intensive occupations. During the same period jobs have expanded in the clerical and services sectors, which include many women workers, and in the predominantly female professions (Blau and Hendricks 1979).

Nevertheless, occupational segregation persists. If we were to examine the 25 largest occupational categories for women and men, we would see that there are only seven occupations that appear on both lists. The men are dispersed over a large number of occupations. In 1980, 42 percent of the male labor force (approximately 4 out of 10 workers) worked in the 25 largest occupational categories for men; only 15 of these categories were male-intensive (see Figure 3.2). Between 1970 and 1980, the category with the greatest proportional rise in female participation was accountants and auditors (from 25 percent in 1970 to 38 percent in 1980). On the other hand, women are concentrated in a small number of occupations. As Figure 3.2 shows, 57 percent of women workers, almost 6 out of 10, were concentrated in the 25 largest occupational categories for women, and 18 of the 25 were female-intensive (Rytina and Bianchi 1984).

FIGURE 3.2
Occupational Segregation by Sex

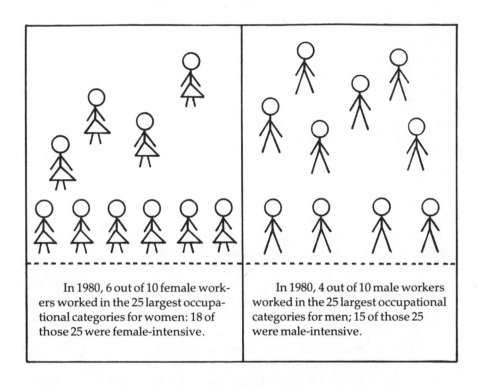

| In 1980, 6 out of 10 female workers worked in the 25 largest occupational categories for women: 18 of those 25 were female-intensive. | In 1980, 4 out of 10 male workers worked in the 25 largest occupational categories for men; 15 of those 25 were male-intensive. |

Source: Current Population Survey, Bureau of Labor Statistics.

The largest occupational category for men workers was "executive, administrative, and managerial." This category ranked only sixth for women workers, even though it was the one in which they showed the greatest gain during the 1970s (from 18 to 31 percent). Women are still underrepresented among managers, and that underrepresentation is greater than the data reveal because women and men managers tend to be employed in different settings with different levels of responsibility and power (Rytina and Bianchi 1984). No matter how we examine the data, we cannot avoid the certainty that workers tend to be concentrated in sex-segregated occupations, and that those occupations designated as "women's work" are paid less.

DIFFERENCES IN EARNINGS

On average women earn two-thirds as much as men. Depending on what figures are used to calculate median earnings, estimates range from 60 percent to 65 percent, a differential that has persisted over several decades (Shack-Marquez 1984). Average weekly earnings in 1982 were $309; the median for women was $241 or 65 percent as much as men at $371. However, median earnings figures mask the extent of the problem because they don't reveal the range of earnings on which the medians are calculated. For example, salaried lawyers had median weekly earnings of $626, but nearly 10 percent had earnings under $300 and nearly 20 percent

FIGURE 3.3
Earnings Differences by Sex

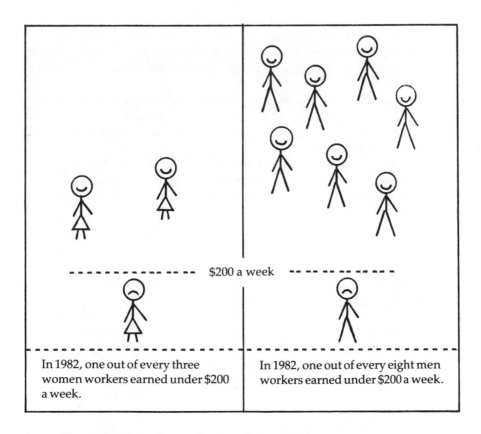

$200 a week

In 1982, one out of every three women workers earned under $200 a week.

In 1982, one out of every eight men workers earned under $200 a week.

Source: Current Population Survey, Bureau of Labor Statistics.

had earnings of $900 or more. And the differences by sex are greater than a comparison of medians reveals. Figure 3.3 illustrates the point; one of three full-time women workers earned under $200 a week, compared to only one in eight men. For most occupational groups, women were two to five times as likely as men to earn under $200 a week. Almost half (48 percent) of male managers, but only 16 percent of female managers, earned over $500 a week. Among retail clerks, 35 percent of the men and 71 percent of the women earned under $200 a week (Mellor 1984).

Another way to compare male and female earnings is to find the top decile of women's earnings and ascertain how much a woman must earn to be among the top 10 percent of women in an occupation, and then estimate the proportion of men who are earning at that level. For most major occupations, about 40 percent of the men earn at least as much as the highest 10 percent of women workers. For example:

- Among managers and administrators, a woman must earn $568 a week to be among the top 10 percent of women, and 40 percent of all male managers earn at least that much. To be among the top 10 percent of male managers a man would have to earn over $900 a week.
- Among clerical workers, a woman must earn $386 to be in the top decile, an amount earned by 42 percent of all male clerical workers. To be among the top decile of male clerical workers, a man would have to earn $571.
- Among accountants, the lower boundary for the top decile for women was $532, an amount earned by 39 percent of all male accountants; the lower boundary for the top decile among men was $776 (Mellor 1984).

Even when women and men do equal work, at least within narrowly defined white-collar occupational skill levels, men still earn higher wages, although the differences are smaller. A 1981 study by the Bureau of Labor Statistics of women and men in professional, administrative, technical, and clerical positions found that the female-male pay ratio ranged from 78 to 92 percent. However, the gap narrowed to around 90 percent when the comparisons were limited to work levels within occupations. These results might be more reassuring, however, if pay disparity didn't *increase* as experience level rose. For example, at the entry level of Director of Personnel I, women actually earned more—101 percent of the male rates. However, by level II the men had moved ahead and the ratio of women's earnings to men's was 94 percent. By level III the gap had widened to 90 percent. The only occupation in the survey in which the gap failed to widen with experience was Job Analyst. At the entry level women earned 87 percent of men's earnings. By level IV the difference had narrowed to 94 percent (Sieling 1984).

The overall ratio of female to male earnings did change significantly between 1979 and 1982. For workers over age 25, the sex-earnings ratio rose from 61 to 64 percent, but there is no evidence to suggest that this change was due to a change in the mix of occupations. A more likely explanation is that it resulted from the higher unemployment rate for men during the recession (Mellor 1984).

Despite the gains women have made in labor market penetration, they still tend to be concentrated in female-intensive occupations, and these occupations are low paid relative to male-dominated occupations. Even when they move into male-intensive occupations, they tend to occupy different positions from men and to earn substantially less. Even when they occupy the same positions, they still earn less than men. Although the difference is smaller, it tends to widen as experience increases. These wage differences can be partially explained by factors such as age, skill level, job tenure, industry, and hours worked, but these factors are insufficient either individually or in combination to explain either occupational segregation or the lower earnings of women.

ECONOMIC THEORIES OF OCCUPATIONAL SEGREGATION

Economists have long struggled with the constant and unrelenting reality of sexual inequality in the labor market. Some economic theories try to explain this inequality, and they can be divided into four categories: neoclassical, institutional, Marxist, and radical. We will examine the first two in some detail.

Neoclassical Theory

In neoclassical theory the primary analytical category is the individual, who is assumed to exercise freedom of choice and to behave rationally to maximize his or her utility. But maximization of welfare is subject to constraints, mainly income and prices, which also are the main determinants of individual behavior. The neoclassicists assume individuals to be identical, "timeless, classless, raceless, and cultureless" creatures (Amsden 1980). Individual preferences and social, cultural, or ideological influences are referred to as "tastes"; they are beyond the interest or concern of the neoclassicist, who assumes them to be trivial and idiosyncratic.

Among neoclassicists, two major theoretical propositions are used to explain sexual inequality in the workplace: one is the Human Capital approach, the other is the Overcrowding Theory.

The *Human Capital* approach is concerned with the allocation of time and also with the division of labor within the family. An individual "invests" in his or her human capital through time spent in education or on-the-job training; employers invest in their employees' human capital by providing on-the-job training. A worker's productivity is a function of his or her human capital, and earnings are a function of productivity. But women and men choose to allocate their time differently, men in paid work and women in family duties and responsibilities. Women's lower earnings, then, are not ascribed to injustice but to their lower acquisition of human capital. Women earn less because their labor market participation is discontinuous, that is, they leave the labor market during periods of childbearing and childrearing, because they spend fewer years in the market, and because during periods of discontinuity their skills tend to depreciate. Further, women anticipate these discontinuities in employment and avoid jobs that contain skill training or learning components, since they perceive little return for such investment. Women's lower earnings, in this model, are a result of their choice not to invest in their human capital (Mincer and Polachek 1974).

Women's occupational segregation is also explained by human capital theorists as a matter of choice. The argument goes as follows. Wages on the job rise continuously over the life cycle as experience mounts. Dropping out of the labor force through intermittent participation has adverse effects on earnings potential. Aside from the period of no earnings, reentry earnings levels are lower than what they would have been if the individual had worked continuously. This loss of earnings that can be attributed to periods of work intermittency is referred to as "atrophy." But atrophy occurs in different occupations at different rates and hence influences occupational choice. In other words, the woman who anticipates that her labor force participation will be interrupted by childbearing and childrearing will choose those occupations where the least atrophy occurs. Specifically, time out of the labor force increases the probability of being in all occupations except managerial; women with the greatest "home time" are least likely to enter managerial and professional occupations. Polachek's (1981) analysis of data led him to conclude that

> if women were to have a full commitment to the labor force, the number of women professionals would increase by 35 percent, the number of women in managerial professions would more than double, and women in menial occupations would decrease by more than 25 percent.

The *Overcrowding Theory* is also based on supply and demand analysis. It argues that women (and blacks) are restricted to a limited number of menial occupations because of "demand factors," that is, demand exists for them in menial occupations and not in prestige ones. Employers will hire women and blacks in prestige occupations only on condition that they will work for less money than the employer would have to pay white males. The result is that those in restricted occupations receive lower wages and those in nonrestricted occupations receive higher ones (Bergmann 1974).

That neoclassical theories come in for substantial criticism should come as no surprise. Proponents of the Human Capital theory present empirical data that show that as much as half of the differences in wages between women and men can be explained by differences in their work-experience histories (Miner and Polachek 1974), but critics put the figure at closer to one-fourth (Sandell and Shapiro 1978). In either case, a good deal of the difference is left unexplained (Rosenfeld 1979).

But regardless of these discrepancies, the theory does not resolve the chicken and egg question; it does not reveal the extent to which low levels of human capital are the cause or the effect of labor force instability. Low wages due to discrimination may discourage women from investing in human capital, and low investments in human capital perpetuate women's lower earnings (Amsden 1980).

Another criticism of the Human Capital theory is that it relies heavily on tastes. For example, it argues that as a result of the division of labor within the family women choose those occupations that are lowest paid. But it ignores the fact that both male and female occupations require varying amounts and types of skills. Some female and some male occupations require lengthy general training; some require lengthy firm-specific training. Some male and some female occupations require few skills and do not provide a potential for productivity increases through experience. Some male and some female occupations experience atrophy of skills during periods of absence from the labor market. Reliance on women's role in the family might explain a greater tendency to find women in low-skilled jobs but not in the other types of jobs. Finally, the model assumes that women choose female-dominated occupations, knowing that they pay less, as a matter of personal preference. It does not explain why only women have "tastes" for these lower paying jobs or why such a large proportion of women should exhibit such tastes (Blau and Jusenius 1976).

The Human Capital theory also assumes that individuals choose an occupation fairly early in life and stick to it. But those choices may be significant for only a small number of occupations in which individuals acquire occupation-specific preemployment training. In many cases, employees apply for work within a broad framework of vaguely defined job categories; the employer decides who will be hired and for which entry-level job. This initial decision will determine what promotional opportunities will be open to employees if they remain with the firm. So the concept of occupational assignment may be more relevant than that of occupational choice (Blau and Jusenius 1976).

The Overcrowding hypothesis has come in for criticism on the grounds that it is insufficient and may be a better explanation of the consequences of segregation than of its causes. It, too, relies on tastes. It argues that workers are perfectly substitutable for each other and that employer tastes prevent integration—that is, that employers have a taste for discrimination against women and will hire them only when the wage difference between female and male labor is large enough to compensate for the disutility they incur by hiring women. But it doesn't explain why so many employers would have these tastes or why they should be so strong (Blau and Jusenius 1976).

Because of these shortcomings, critics of neoclassical theory turn to institutional approaches to try to explain the dual phenomena of occupational segregation and differential earnings.

Institutional Approaches

This body of literature is sometimes referred to as the Segmented Labor Market (SLM) theory. It argues that the problem of wage inequality is due to occupational differences between women and men of equal qualifications. Discriminatory hiring practices, not tastes, crowd women into sex-typed jobs, which in turn exert downward pressure on their pay. The problem, then, is really one of job discrimination, not wage discrimination (Amsden 1980).

The explanation for this job discrimination lies in a concept of dual labor markets: a primary market and a secondary market. Jobs in the primary market possess such characteristics as high wages, good working conditions, employment stability, chances of advancement, equity, and due process in the administration of work rules. Jobs in the secondary market tend to have low wages and fringe benefits, poor working conditions, high turnover, little chance of advancement, and often arbitrary and capricious supervision (Rosenfeld 1979). Since jobs in the primary market require the development of job-specific skills, employers want to screen out those who are likely to be unreliable or intermittent workers (Doeringer 1967). If employers believe that women (or blacks) are on the average less qualified, less reliable, or less stable than men and whites, and if the cost of obtaining information about individual applicants is excessive, they will discriminate against blacks and women by assigning them only to the secondary market. Sex or skin color becomes a proxy for relevant data not sampled and the employer engages in "statistical discrimination" (Phelps 1980).

Another SLM theory defines typologies of sectors of the economy based upon the development of the capitalist system. In this analysis, one sector is defined by large *centralized* (monopoly) *capital,* that is, a small number of large firms that wield virtual monopoly power in their environment. The second sector is defined by *decentralized capital,* that is, many small firms in a highly competitive economy. The nature of these capital sectors is such that jobs in the monopoly sector tend to have characteristics similar to those in the primary labor market, while those in the competitive or periphery sector tend to be like those in the secondary market (Rosenfeld 1979). These are sometimes referred to as "structured" and "unstructured" labor markets (Rubery 1980).

A refinement of the dual labor market theory posits an "internal labor market" theory (Blau and Jusenius 1976). In this model the job structure of a firm can be divided into two categories of occupations on the basis of how they are filled. First are those job categories that are filled from sources external to the firm through the recruitment of new workers. Such jobs are generally restricted to lower-level positions. Second are those categories that are filled from internal sources through the promotion and upgrading of presently employed workers. Access to this second type usually occurs through advancement up well-defined promotion ladders. The process by which workers move up these career ladders is through the acquisition, either formally or informally, of added knowledge or skills that are mostly specific or unique to the firm.

Competitive market forces, according to this model, operate principally at the entry level. Those jobs that are filled from within typically require firm-specific skills. These skills are acquired through the performance of some jobs and not others, hence some jobs are preparation for promotion up the organizational ladder and some are not, which tends to work against the development of a purely competitive market. Instead, an *internal labor market* develops—an administrative system that both allocates labor and determines wage rates within the firm.

Labor is allocated through the administrative system that determines the job categories within which both horizontal and vertical mobility will take place. As a result, advancement opportunities open to workers are generally determined by the entry-level job to which they were originally assigned. Clearly not all workers in a given entry-level job will be promoted to higher level ones, but promotional opportunities are limited to workers in those specific occupations.

Wages are determined by job evaluation plans or other administrative arrangements that establish base pay rates for each occupational category and that specify wage relationships among occupations. Custom and administrative arrangements typically work to maintain relationships among occupations; merit and seniority typically determine pay differentials within occupations. The internal labor market, then, specifies a relatively rigid set of wage relationships and promotional possibilities, both of which are primarily defined by job categories.

Two elements of this internal labor market model are relevant in explaining both occupational segregation and the male/female wage differential. First, because of its reliance on merit and seniority, the internal market tends to treat workers as groups, rather than individuals, hence the greater the homogeneity of the group the greater the efficiency of the process. And sex is an obvious basis for differentiation. Second, there is a vital link between job segregation and wage differentiation. The organization has the greatest latitude to differentiate among individuals or groups at the entry level. It has narrower but still broad discretion in allocating workers among job categories filled from internal sources, where it must select individuals only from appropriate promotion ladders. It has the least discretion in wage differentiation among individuals within the same job category. By assigning women to those entry-level jobs that have the least promotional potential, and by paying these jobs at the lowest rate, the organization is able to differentiate between female and male employees and to maintain its internal relationships. Hence, "wage rates might almost be considered the monetary (or value) dimension of the job structure" (Blau and Jusenius 1976).

The internal labor market model relates to Segmented Labor Market theory in that the jobs in the internal labor market share characteristics with jobs in the primary market. Entry is restricted to relatively few lower level jobs; promotion ladders are long; and worker stability is encouraged by high wages, opportunities for advancement, good working conditions, and provisions for job security. At the other extreme, the secondary market is more like a set of "unstructured markets." It offers numerous ports of entry and short or nonexistent promotion ladders, while discouraging worker stability by low wages, little opportunity for advancement, poor working conditions, and little job security. Since long-term attachment between worker and firm is important to jobs in the primary sector, employers tend to select new workers whom they perceive as having the potential for job stability. Thus both pure discrimination and statistical discrimination tend to keep women from primary-sector jobs, even if they possess the relevant qualifications.

Like neoclassical theory, institutional theories have also come in for their share of criticism. Some truth attaches to the assumption of the labor market that women are less stable workers than men. The question is whether this is a cause or an effect of occupational segregation. Neoclassical theory argues that it is a cause, that because of individual women's family obligations, they choose or are chosen for those occupations where the negative effects of intermittent labor force participation are least. Their low pay is the price they pay for childbearing and childrearing. Institutional theory, particularly internal labor market theory, argues that it is both a cause and an effect. Women are treated as a class, not as individuals, and the class is perceived as being unstable in its labor market participation. As a result of this statistical discrimination, women are segregated into jobs in the secondary sector. And because jobs in this sector offer little or no reward for stability, its occupants tend to be unstable workers. Critics argue that the theory, while useful, doesn't go far enough, that in fact we must go outside of economics for an explanation of discrimination (Arrow 1976).

One such approach is to analyze the process by which firms evaluate jobs and set wages. Increasingly, results of such analysis show that seemingly benign, sex-neutral job evaluation methods are in reality often biased in favor of male-intensive job categories.

Job Evaluation

Proponents of discrimination theory believe traditionally female jobs are undervalued and underpaid for no other reason than because they are held by women. To test this notion, in 1975 researchers at the University of Wisconsin analyzed the Department of Labor's *Dictionary of Occupational Titles (DOT)*, which rates the complexity of 30,000 job titles and is the world's most comprehensive and widely used compensation reference. The *DOT*, they found, rates health and child care professionals, including nurses, on the same level of complexity as dog pound attendant. The work that women do caring for children and adults, sick or well, is considered no more complex nor valuable than the work men do caring for dogs.

Employers typically determine the worth of jobs within the firm by job evaluation studies, a concept developed nearly 100 years ago by Taylor, whose concept of Scientific Management was concerned with industrial organizations. He argued that jobs should be designed for the utmost efficiency, workers should be trained to do a job exactly as it had been designed, and evaluation and compensation should be based upon the relative difficulty of the job, entirely separate from the personal characteristics or abilities of the jobholder. Most job evaluation methods in use today were developed in the 1930s and 1940s, a time when both jobs and jobholders were very different from what they are today.

Job evaluation determines the relative complexity of jobs within an occupational group. To determine pay, a wage survey determines the amount paid for a limited sample of equivalent jobs within the labor market. Each occupational category is treated separately. Clerical jobs, for instance, are evaluated as a class. Once the relative complexity of the jobs has been established, pay is determined by surveying the market to find what similar clerical jobs are being paid. If women's jobs are underpaid because they are filled by women—that is, if the market is inherently biased against female-dominated occupations—then using the labor market data simply perpetuates long-standing, institutionalized discrimination (Doherty and Harriman 1981). One way to demonstrate whether discrimination exists is to make comparisons within the firm across occupational boundaries, to compare such female-dominated occupations as clerical workers with male-dominated ones such as craft workers or laborers.

The most difficult aspect of job evaluation is and always has been achieving objectivity. No system is or can be completely objective. The critical question is what compensable factors are included, and that is always a subjective decision.

The four methods of job evaluation, in order of objectivity, are: ranking, classification, point plans, and factor comparison plans:

- The *ranking* system is the simplest and also the most subjective.
- The *classification* system, used by many public employers, uses only one compensable factor, skill. Since many variations of skill are possible, that too is highly subjective.
- The *point* plan, originally developed by a private consulting firm, Hay and Associates, is the one most frequently used. It identifies several compensable factors that are of value to the organization, then assigns a complex system of weights and points. The compensable factors that the Hay system uses are Know-how, Problem Solving, and Accountability; working conditions are also factored in where they are relevant. The Equal Pay Act of 1963 considers skill, effort, and responsibility. This system has gained a good deal of popularity because it has a semblance of objectivity but permits a great deal of subjectivity in its administration.
- The *factor comparison* method, the most objective and least used, is complex and expensive. It involves the comparison of jobs with other jobs to determine which jobs contain greater amounts of identifiable compensable factors. But even this system is subject to question. It depends on correctly identifying "key jobs" within the organization; it requires the evaluator to estimate what portion of the current wage is allocable to each of the compensable factors, and it assumes that the current wage for the key jobs is the correct one (Berg 1976).

It's essential to emphasize that these job evaluation methods were not designed to measure the comparable worth of male- and female-dominated jobs; they were designed to determine the comparable worth of jobs within occupational families. They are highly subjective and highly dependent on the choice of factors and the weighting of factors.

Many employers have used several different job evaluation plans for different job categories, making comparisons impossible. Beginning in the mid-1970s, women employees in many organizations, often supported by their unions, began to seek and get job evaluation studies that do cut across occupational boundaries to compare sex-segregated jobs. They have used a variety of increasingly sophisticated methods and complex compensable factors. In addition, state and local governments have sponsored hearings or research projects, and a growing number are mandating and implementing pay equity for their employees (Hartmann and Treiman 1983).

In 1978, the Equal Employment Opportunity Commission (EEOC) invited the National Academy of Sciences to study the issues involved in measuring the comparability of disparate jobs. The result was an extremely comprehensive review of the overall situation of women in the labor market.

The committee conducting the research reviewed 25 years of studies based on the Human Capital model. It found that studies that focus only on the characteristics of workers generally explain only about one-fourth of the earnings gap and never more than half. The remaining gap is often attributed to discrimination. Other studies that attempt to incorporate characteristics of jobs in addition to characteristics of people generally explain more of the gap, leaving a smaller residue to be considered the result of discrimination. However, it found little evidence that particular characteristics of occupations (for example, measures of skill, effort, or responsibility, working conditions) actually contribute to the explanation of earnings differentials. Occupational classification offers a better explanation. The study concluded that "discrimination is likely operating in the labor market with significant effects on women's earnings and the pay rates of women's jobs in particular" (Hartmann and Treiman 1983).

The committee also reviewed the operation of labor markets, focusing on the institutional model, a useful approach since issues of pay equity tend to emerge most clearly in situations in which a single firm employs a large work force across many different jobs. They concluded that most firms exhibit job segregation by sex and that much of that segregation is the result of the placement of newly hired individuals. To some extent placement is determined by supply, but even so, several studies showed that much of the earnings differential between women and men was the result of differential placements when individuals first enter. Men and women with equal qualifications are assigned to different entry-level jobs with differing implications for their futures (Hartmann and Treiman 1983).

The commitee also reviewed several studies specifically aimed at assessing whether jobs of equal worth are equally paid. Many studies are available, and they tend to show that they are not. In Minnesota, equal points were awarded to Registered Nurses and Vocational Education Teachers, but the Nurses' monthly salary was $1,723 and the Voc. Ed. Teachers' was $2,260. In San Jose, California, similar points were awarded to Senior Librarian and Senior Chemist, but the Librarians' biweekly salary was $898 and the Chemists' $1,119. In Washington State, Secretaries earned $1,122, while the Maintenance Carpenter's job, judged comparable, paid $1,707 (Grune and Reder 1983).

The committee concluded that substantial discrimination exists in the labor market and that "the wage rates of jobs held traditionally by women are depressed relative to what they would be if women had equal opportunity in the labor market."

Needless to say, these conclusions have not gone unchallenged. Critics of the report include those who say it goes too far in finding discrimination and those who say it doesn't go far enough in recommending solutions. The committee looked at the concept of comparable worth as an approach to adjusting pay rates within individual firms. But it took note of the many different job evaluation plans, economic circumstances of employers and industries, and values regarding the hierarchy of job worth, and refused to recommend any universal system of job evaluation that would apply across the economy. Employers are told that long-standing business practices are probably discriminatory and they are urged to adopt a single, nondiscriminatory job evaluation method for all employees, but no preferred methodology is proposed. Employees and their unions are told that in fact they are victims of systematic, societal, sex-based discrimination but are urged to address it at the organizational level. On balance, however, the report has been a useful tool for advocates of pay equity.

SUMMARY

The labor market has undergone enormous change in the last two decades. The number of women in the labor market has increased dramatically, with the greatest change among women in the middle years. The majority of married women, even married women with children, are in the work force. During the same period the percentage of men in the work force has declined, and the changes for men occur at the beginning and ending of their careers. Men often stay in school, hence out of the labor market, longer, but most of the decline has come from older men who leave the labor market either voluntarily, through early retirement, or involuntarily, because of poor health.

The composition of the labor force has also changed; the proportion of jobs in male-intensive industries, such as agricultural workers and laborers, has declined, and the proportion in the clerical and service sectors has increased. Nevertheless, a high degree of occupational segregation still persists, especially among women, and women still earn on the average only about 60 percent of what men earn.

Economic theories that attempt to explain occupational segregation and the lower wages of women fall into two categories. The neoclassical theories, and specifically the Human Capital theories, explain the differences on the basis of choice—that is, women put greater value on their family roles than on their work roles and therefore choose occupations that require a lower investment in human capital. Segmented Labor Market theories, on the other hand, assume that occupational segregation and pay disparity occur as a result of discrimination against women.

Job evaluation models extend the segmented or internal labor market theories and focus on the evaluation of disparate jobs within the individual firm. They agree that differential job placement perpetuates job segregation, and they argue that those jobs to which women are relegated are underpaid because of long-standing bias in the market. They assume that the comparable worth of jobs should be determined in relationship to dissimilar occupational classifications within the firm, rather than to similar occupations in the labor market.

In Chapter 4, we turn to political and legal remedies for job segregation and pay inequity.

4
The Political Environment

From the onset of the Industrial Revolution, workers struggled with business owners for better working conditions. They were joined in their struggle by labor leaders and various reform movements. The struggle was waged on two fronts: through collective bargaining and through legislation. Legislation, in turn, depended for its effectiveness on both the agencies that administer it and the courts that interpret it.

In the nineteenth and early twentieth centuries, these two basic approaches came to be divided, at least to some extent, by sex. In a very general sense, men came to achieve their employment gains through participation in the labor movement, women through legislation. Early legislation aimed at protecting women and children from exploitative employers had the effect, if not the intent, of increasing the discrimination against women. More recent legislation has been aimed at protecting women (and minorities) from discrimination.

It would be impossible to understand the contemporary political/legal environment without some knowledge of these historical origins. We will start with a review of state "protective legislation," then turn to an overview of the major pieces of federal civil rights legislation. We will review the role of the government and of the courts in interpreting and applying the legislation to the elimination of sex discrimination. Finally, we will conclude with a brief overview of the contemporary political environment.

PROTECTIVE LEGISLATION

The industrial movement that began in the early nineteenth century gradually took over many of the tasks that women had traditionally performed in the home. As this occurred, more and more women left the home to work as weavers, spinners, seamstresses, laundresses, and waitresses. While working conditions for all workers during this period were deplorable, they were much worse for women than for men. Women worked longer hours, their work rules were stricter, and their workplaces were more unsafe and unhealthy than those of men. Aside from the long hours, factory women were subjected to incredible noise, heat, and air pollution. Tuberculosis was common and incurable.

Further, as the nineteenth century progressed, the disparity increased. The labor movement began as early as 1825 to agitate for a ten-hour day for male workers, and eventually a ten-hour, six-day week became commonplace in most occupations. The major exception was factory work, which still had the most women workers. Women often worked 11 to 13 hours, sometimes seven days a week, while men in some occupations worked only 50 hours or less (Baer 1978).

Public attention was focused on these appalling conditions in 1911 when a fire at the Triangle Shirtwaist Company in New York City burned at least 143 women workers to death. Triangle was an exceptionally anti-union company that had been the target of a prolonged strike just two years earlier. It was notorious for its terrible working conditions. When fire broke out in the loft of the factory, the women workers were unable to escape because the company had locked the doors to the stairs from the outside to keep employees from stealing or escaping. There were no fire extinguishers; the only fire escape would have taken three hours to clear the building. Most of the women died within 20 minutes. Most of their bodies were never identified; they were buried in numbered coffins (Baxandall, Gordon, and Reverdy 1976).

The reasons why differences arose between female workers and male workers in hours and working conditions, and why they persisted, are too complex to examine in detail here. However, two questions are significant. One is why relief was sought through legislation rather than collective bargaining; the other is why legislation was sought, and enacted, to protect women and children and not adult males.

Legislation or Negotiation

Many of the gains that were made in the working conditions of men came about through unionization and collective bargaining. The unions began in the early nineteenth century to pressure for reductions in hours and for improved working conditions. Strong unions in heavily organized industries were successful in achieving these goals. Where they lacked the strength to accomplish their goals collectively, they often turned to legislation to accomplish reform. For example, as early as 1842, employees in Massachusetts petitioned the state legislature for a law imposing explicit, enforceable limits on their work week. After nearly two decades of effort, the workers finally settled in 1867 for a bill that set maximum working hours only for women and children. The legislature was willing to adopt this measure to protect women's (but not men's) health; the male workers were willing to accept it because they believed that the restrictions would be applied to all workers. Hence the workers were accused of having decided to "fight the battle from behind the women's petticoats" (Ratner 1980).

With few exceptions, the unions rarely sought universal hours legislation thereafter. Many states enacted laws limiting the number of hours that women could work, prohibiting their work during certain hours (typically at night), restricting them from certain occupations that were considered hazardous, barring them from places where liquor was served, prohibiting or limiting work during pregnancy, and requiring pay equal to that of men.

Legislators were unwilling to enact protective legislation for men, but they would adopt it for women because of what was perceived as the state's legitimate interest in women's role in childbearing and childrearing. Proponents argued that because women on the whole were weaker than men, and because only women were capable of bearing children, working conditions that were tolerable for men were dangerous for women and should therefore be prohibited. Further, since a woman's primary duties were assumed to be in the home, the state took an interest in "easing the burden of motherhood," not by reducing her share of the home duties but by ensuring that she was not overtaxed in the workplace. In 1908 the Supreme Court turned back a challenge to Oregon's protective legislation by agreeing that the state had a legitimate interest in women's reproductive health, and that precedent was not overturned until after the passage of the Civil Rights Act of 1964 (Baer 1978).

Women and Men in the Labor Movement

From the beginning of the labor movement, women were far less active than men, for several reasons. The industries they worked in had the worst conditions and were also the least amenable to change. Women were not perceived by labor leaders to be permanent members of the labor force, and indeed women workers tended to perceive themselves as temporary workers. Since they expected the leave the labor force when they married, they had less incentive to work for change. Further, since participation in a union was illegal and highly risky, as well as time consuming, workers with the most to gain also had the most to lose. Thus women workers, who needed the most from labor organizations, were the least organized.

Pressure for legislation to protect women and children workers came not only from male union leaders but also from the growing army of social reformers and the few women who were labor leaders and organizers. The reformers supported sex-specific legislation because they were genuinely concerned about the plight of women workers, and unions accepted it in hopes that its protections would be extended to male workers.

But the male-led unions have been accused of having another reason for pursuing protective legislation for women, a less benevolent and purely economic one. Male workers viewed women as a threat to their jobs, and since women were paid lower wages, the threat was exacerbated. Their response was to exclude women, rather than to organize them, because excluding them would also assure that they would continue to be available to perform the appropriate tasks at home (Hartmann 1976). The union movement, its critics charge, deliberately sought protective legislation as a means of excluding women from some occupations and reducing their participation in others. Statutes that restricted the number of hours that women could work, or that proscribed their participation in specified occupations, made women on the whole less desirable employees than men. Statutes that required equal pay for equal work greatly reduced an employer's incentive to hire women if men were available. The net result was to reduce the competition from women for the best paid, most-sought-after jobs (Berch 1982). While there is some evidence that the unions were more concerned with men workers than with women, there is little support for the contention that these motives were either widespread or effective (Ratner 1980).

So to answer, in a greatly oversimplified way, the questions raised above, we can say that legislation was pursued over negotiation because it was more effective in areas and in industries that were not heavily unionized. The legislation that was enacted was sex-specific because lawmakers could be persuaded that the state had a legitimate interest in protecting women's childbearing ability but not in protecting men's overall health, and the labor movement accepted the compromise. The charge has been made, but not satisfactorily proven, that the unions were more interested in keeping women out of the labor force than in protecting their rights in it.

From 1867 until 1964, states continued to enact sex-specific legislation limiting the hours and working conditions of women workers. These laws were repeatedly challenged in the courts and just as repeatedly upheld as legal and constitutional (Baer 1978). During the 1930s the U.S. Congress adopted the Fair Labor Standards Act of 1938, which extended uniform hours protection to all workers. Most of the protective laws were suspended during World War II because of a national "manpower" shortage. At the same time, the War Manpower Commission issued guidelines providing for equal pay and prohibiting sex discrimination. But when the war ended the legislation was reimposed. For the next 25 years, sex-specific legislation that restricted women from certain occupations remained on the books in many states, despite all court challenges to its constitutionality and political efforts to amend or appeal it.

FEDERAL LEGISLATION

Congress took up the issue of discrimination against women in the early 1960s, first with the Equal Pay Act of 1963 and later with the Civil Rights Act of 1964.

The Equal Pay Act of 1963

The Equal Pay Act of 1963 can hardly be said to be a major departure from the paternalistic posture of protective legislation. An amendment to the Fair Labor Standards Act of 1938, it was carefully drawn as a limited, narrow assurance of pay equity. Although the Kennedy administration had proposed a broader bill, the Congress was willing to adopt only the narrowest of statutes. The act forbids:

> paying wages to employees . . . at a rate less than the rate at which [the employer] pays wages to employees of the opposite sex . . . for equal work on jobs the performance of which requires equal skill, effort, and responsibility, and which are performed under similar working conditions . . . (29 U.S.C. @206 [d][1]).

The legislative history of the bill shows clearly that the Congress understood that women and men seldom work at jobs that meet this equal work standard, that is, that are the same or substantially the same and are performed under similar working conditions. It's quite clear also that they did not intend in this bill to assure equal pay between jobs that were comparable but markedly dissimilar. Lest there be any doubts, the lawmakers provided employers with four affirmative defenses against charges of sex discrimination in pay. Differences in pay are not in violation of the act if they are based on (1) a seniority system, (2) a merit system, (3) a system that measures earnings by quantity or quality of production, or (4) a differential based on any factor other than sex. Responsibility for enforcement of the act was placed with the Wage and Hours Division of the U.S. Department of Labor, which was permitted to issue "interpretive bulletins" but not binding regulations. The Department of Labor could bring suit for back wages and injunctions, but only the Department of Justice could file criminal actions in the case of willful violation (Bureau of National Affairs 1963).

In 1979, enforcement of the Equal Pay Act was transferred to the Equal Employment Opportunity Commission, which issued new and more restrictive guidelines to employers (Greenlaw and Kohl 1982). A number of court cases have established that jobs need not be identical, only substantially equal, in order to be compared. Job descriptions or classifications are irrelevant in showing that work is unequal unless they accurately reflect the actual content of the job. Thus, despite its narrow scope, the Equal Pay Act has been successful in reducing pay disparities based on sex alone or on artificial or superficial job differences that serve as thinly veiled justifications for sex discrimination (Doherty and Harriman 1981).

The Civil Rights Act of 1964

The Civil Rights Act of 1964, while a much broader based bill, was designed primarily to address the problem of race discrimination. An extremely controversial bill, it was passed in the wake of the assassination of President John Kennedy, but not without the strongest possible protests of representatives from the Southern states. Title VII of the bill covers employment discrimination; in its original form it covered discrimination on the basis of race, color, religion, and national origin.

When the bill reached the floor of the Congress, after having proceeded painstakingly through the committee process, a number of amendments were proposed by its opponents, in the hope that by confusing and weakening it they could ultimately defeat it. Among the amendments was one proposed by Congressman Howard Smith of Virginia to add the word "sex" as a protected category, setting off what came to be known as "ladies day" in the Congress (EEOC 1964).

Mr. Smith assured the Congress that he was

> very serious about this amendment . . . I do not think it can do any harm to this legislation; maybe it can do some good. I think it will do some good for the minority sex . . . I think we all recognize and it is an indisputable fact that all throughout industry women are discriminated against in that just generally speaking they do not get as high compensation for their work as the majority sex. . . . That is about all I have to say about it except, to get off of this subject for just a moment to show you how some of the ladies feel about discrimination against them, I want to read you an extract from a letter I received the other day. . . . This lady has a real grievance on behalf of the minority sex.

He then went on, apparently amid great laughter, to read a letter from a woman in New York asking for an amendment to correct the present imbalance that exists between the number of males and females in the country, "a grave injustice to womankind" that "shuts off the right of every female to have a husband of her own."

> I read that letter just to illustrate that women have some real grievances and some real rights to be protected. I am serious about this thing. I just hope that the committee will accept it. Now, what harm can you do this bill that was so perfect yesterday and is so imperfect today—what harm will this do to the condition of the bill?

Congressman Emanuel Celler from New York, chair of the House Judiciary committee, arose to read a letter from the Women's Bureau of the Department of Labor (signed by a man), asking that the amendment be withdrawn so that it could submit a separate bill. But first he felt compelled to argue that women were not in the minority in his home. "The reason we have been living in such harmony for almost half a decade is that I usually have the last two words, and those words are 'yes dear.'" However, he went on to argue quite seriously (presumably) that the bill would cause social upheaval by requiring total equality.

> Would male citizens be justified in insisting that women share with them the burdens of compulsory military service? What would become of traditional family relationships? What about alimony? Who would have the obligation of supporting whom? Would fathers rank equally with mothers in the right to custody of children? What would become of the crimes of rape and statutory rape? Would the Mann Act be invalidated? Would the many State and local provisions regulating working conditions and hours of employment for women be struck down? You know the biological differences between the sexes. In many states we have laws favorable to women. Are you going to strike those laws down?

But the frivolous nature of the debate continued. The men repeatedly pointed out that they, not the women, were the minority sex, and several congressmen referred to themselves as "second-class citizens." Mr. Cellar offered such wisdom as:

> Lives there a man with hide so tough
> Who says "Two sexes are not enough?"

Congresswoman Martha Griffiths of Michigan led the serious debate in favor of the amendment. Arguing that "if there had been any necessity to have pointed out that women were a second-class sex, the laughter would have proved it," she went on to present a cogent example to demonstrate that if the bill passed without including sex in its coverage that it would provide less coverage for black women than for black men and that "white women will be last at the hiring gate."

Mrs. Griffiths was joined by several other congresswomen in serious support of the bill. Facetious support came from many Southern congressmen, some of whom had been among the most vigorous opponents of the Equal Pay Act the previous year. Some sincere opposition was raised by proponents of the act who feared that the amendment would "clutter up the bill" and be used later to destroy it; they too were joined by the act's opponents. Despite the antics of its opponents, the amendment was adopted on the floor by a vote of 168 to 133. Title VII of the Civil Rights Act of 1964 was passed into law providing protection for women as well as minorities against discrimination in employment.

Unlike the bill itself, the issue of sex discrimination never received serious consideration or debate in any committee of the Congress. So hastily and so poorly drawn was the amendment that two days later the House again took up the matter, to add the word "sex" in several places where it had been accidently omitted (to make the bill consistent throughout) and "to make the requirement for no discrimination on the basis of sex subject to a bona fide occupational qualification exception" (EEOC 1964). This lack of careful consideration has raised doubts in the enforcement agencies and in the courts as to the serious intent of Congress to prohibit sex discrimination and has made it more difficult, but not impossible, for women to find remedies to sex discrimination under Title VII.

Title VII, with the 1972 amendments added to extend coverage and strengthen enforcement, makes it unlawful for employers, labor unions, joint apprenticeship committees, or employment agencies covered by the act to discriminate in the areas of hiring, firing, or terms of employment. Subsequent amendments have added older workers, the disabled, and Vietnam-era veterans to the list of protected classes (Belohlav and Ayton 1982). It prohibits employers from limiting, segregating, or classifying employees or applicants in protected groups in any way that would deprive an individual of employment opportunities. It prohibits discrimination as it relates to wages, fringe benefits, assignments or promotions, use of facilities, or training. For the first time, Title VII gave women a legal basis for insisting that they be allowed to compete with men for jobs and promotions, as well as that they be paid the same as men once such jobs and promotions are secured (Doherty and Harriman 1981).

The Executive Orders

A third body of federal regulation on discrimination in employment is found in a series of Executive Orders (orders issued by the president of the United States). Executive Order No.11246, issued in 1964 and subsequently amended several times, prohibits employment discrimination on the basis of race, color, religion, national origin, age, or sex, by em-

ployers with federal contracts and by contractors working on federally as-
sisted construction projects. In other words, "any person" who contracts
with a federal agency to furnish supplies or services or for the use of real
or personal property. It may also apply to labor unions and employment
agencies. Responsibility for the administration of the order lies with the
Office of Federal Contract Compliance (OFCC) within the Department of
Labor (Pemberton 1975).

A paradox created by the major difference between Title VII and the
Executive Orders lies in the issue of "affirmative action." Title VII requires
employers to be color- and sex-blind; it states specifically that no employer is required "to grant preferential treatment to any individual or group
on account of any imbalance which may exist." The Executive Orders, on
the other hand, have required the use of affirmative action, a term that
has been interpreted by the compliance agencies and the courts to mean
active, affirmative plans to overcome the effects of past discrimination,
often by pursuing numerical "goals and timetables" (Block and Walker
1982). Affirmative actions include not only widespread and extensive recruitment efforts to reach qualified minorities and women, but also special training programs, identification of career ladders, creation of sub-
professional job classifications as "bridging classes," and the reevaluation
of minimum job qualifications to recognize alternative education and experience categories. Opportunities must be expanded, not only for qualified but also for "qualifiable" candidates. In other words, Title VII requires that employers not grant preferential treatment; the Executive Orders require that they do.

Not surprisingly, these affirmative action programs have caused an
enormous amount of controversy. Charges of "reverse" discrimination
(as opposed to "forward" discrimination?) have been brought by white
males barred from educational or training programs. Allan Bakke, a white
male twice denied admission to the medical school at the University of
California at Davis, sued the Regents of the University on the grounds
that students admitted under a special admissions program for disadvantaged students had lower grades and test scores than he. While the U.S.
Supreme Court ordered his admission to the school, it also upheld the
right of schools to devise special admissions programs so long as they
didn't constitute numerical quotas. A year later the court upheld the right
of Kaiser Aluminum and Chemical Company to use a voluntary quota
system to reserve 50 percent of the positions in its training program for
blacks, who made up only 2 percent of their employees and 39 percent of
the local labor force (Block and Walker 1982).

Critics and supporters of affirmative action programs do agree on
one thing: that they have had only minor effect on achieving equity in the
workplace. Both agree that some progress has been made in reducing the
disparity between white and minority earnings, and both agree that the

progress is more likely attributable to economic growth, to civil rights protests (Feagin and Feagin 1978), or to geographic mobility (Sowell 1982)
than to affirmative action programs. Supporters argue that programs
have been less than successful because too little in the way of government
resources have been devoted to the effort; critics believe that the very concept of compensation for past discrimination is ill-conceived and unwork-
able (Glazer 1975; B. Gross 1978). Opponents include many members of
the protected groups themselves, who often find that such programs perpetuate the demeaning paternalism inherent in protective legislation. All
would agree that, at best, affirmative actions are and should be a temporary path to the ideal of equality of opportunity for all workers. The goal is
not, and should not be, statistical parity. The goal is freedom from discrimination.

APPLYING TITLE VII TO SEX DISCRIMINATION

Given the circumstances under which Title VII was adopted, its success in achieving an end to discrimination lay not in the law as written but
in the ability of the government and the courts to enforce it. It did not get
off to a promising start. The agency charged with enforcement was the
Equal Employment Opportunity Commission, a newly created agency reporting directly to the president. Before the 1972 amendments, the
agency's primary role was a conciliatory one. It could bring charges, but
only individuals or the attorney general could initiate complaints or bring
suit. The attorney general rarely acted, and most individual victims were
hesitant to do so, for a variety of reasons. Further, the first director of
EEOC publicly stated in 1966 that the sex provision was a "fluke" that had
been "conceived out of wedlock"—remarks that drew criticism from Rep-
resentative Martha Griffiths on the floor of the House (Baer 1978).

To these problems were added weak management, an ineffective organizational structure, and inadequate staff or budget. The organization
was plagued from its inception with personnel problems and poor performance, even after the 1972 amendments added the power to bring suit
against private employers. Only after President Carter appointed Eleanor
Holmes Norton to be EEOC chair in 1977 did the agency begin to operate
effectively. At the time she was appointed, the agency had a backlog of
130,000 cases (Abramson 1979).

Defining Discrimination

Yet despite these weaknesses, the agency was able to develop policy
guidelines that were often used by the courts in settling important and
controversial cases, particularly in race discrimination. For example,

neither Title VII nor the Executive Orders gives a formal definition of discrimination. When the issue was brought to court in the landmark *Griggs* v. *Duke Power* case (401 U.S. 424 [1971]), EEOC guidelines served as the basis for the court's precedent-setting ruling. In that case the justices adopted the EEOC view that even employment practices that appeared to be neutral on their face in terms of equal treatment and even in terms of their overt intent could be discriminatory if they had disparate effect on women or members of minority groups. The only defense available to the employer would be to prove beyond doubt that the questionable practice was necessary for the operation of the business and was in fact related to job performance (Abramson 1979).

Sex as a Bona Fide Occupational Qualification

Title VII provides that even if sex discrimination is proved, an employer has the defense of showing that sex is a bona fide occupational qualification (BFOQ). The interpretation of this provision was crucial to the effectiveness of the act; anything but a very narrow definition would essentially nullify the act as far as women were concerned. The EEOC guidelines argued that sex is not a BFOQ when the employer relies on assumptions of comparative behavior of women and men, stereotyped characterizations of the sexes, or preferences of customers, coworkers, employees, or clients. The issue came to court in the case of a male seeking a job as a flight attendant. The airlines argued that being a woman was a BFOQ for flight attendants on the basis of psychologists' testimony that anxious passengers would be more reassured by feminine attendants. The EEOC's guideline prevailed. The court ruled that the airline was in the business of transporting passengers and freight by air, not in serving food and drink or in comforting passengers. If they should decide to provide these optional services, they could be done equally well by male or female cabin attendants. Customer preference did not constitute a BFOQ (*Diaz* v. *Pan American World Airways* 442 F. 2d 385 5th Cir.[1971]). It has often been said that the decision is so narrow that the only jobs in which sex can be considered a BFOQ is a sperm donor for males and a wet nurse for females. In other cases the court has upheld this view defining as illegal the refusal to hire women, but not men, who are parents of preschool age children, or to require women to quit their jobs when they marry (Gilbreath 1977).

Protective Legislation as a Bona Fide Occupational Qualification

Another potential stumbling block for Title VII was the question of whether protective legislation could be used as a BFOQ defense, a question that ultimately spelled out the fate of such legislation. The act itself is silent, saying only that

> nothing in this title shall be deemed to exempt or relieve any person from any liability, duty, penalty, or punishment provided by any present or future law of any State or political subdivision of a State, other than any such law which purports to require or permit the doing of any act which would be an unlawful employment practice under the title.

Very well! What does that mean? Are protective laws legal or illegal? Are they a BFOQ? In the debate over amending Title VII to include sex, opponents argued that it would, in fact, eliminate such protective statutes. Congresswomen Griffiths responded:

> Some protective legislation was to safeguard the health of women, but it should have safeguarded the health of men also. Most of the so-called protective legislation has really been to protect men's rights in better paying jobs (EEOC 1964).

She was joined by Congresswoman St. George of New York, who concluded an impassioned appeal for passage, saying:

> We do not want special privileges. We do not need special privilege. We outlast you—we outlive you—we nag you to death. So why should we want special privileges?

Nevertheless, the EEOC took a cautious stand toward overriding protective legislation. In its first guideline, issued in 1966, it indicated its belief that the law was not intended to disrupt state protective laws and that these laws were a basis for the application of the BFOQ defense. Within a year it revised its position, declaring it would make no determination in cases where conflicts existed between Title VII and state protective legislation except in cases where the clear effect of the law was discriminatory. In these cases their only action would be to notify claimants of their right to sue. A third guideline, issued in 1968, reaffirmed the belief of the commission that Congress did not intend to overturn these laws but stated its own belief that some of the laws were no longer relevant because of changing technology and the expanding role of women workers in the economy. It announced that it would consider these laws as a basis for BFOQ defense but would not accept a law whose effect was clearly discriminatory rather than protective (Baer 1978).

The matter was finally resolved when the court ruled that if a job required lifting or other strenuous work, a woman must be given a chance to demonstrate her qualifications for the job. It went on to conclude that state laws did not create a BFOQ, that the earlier EEOC guidelines were not controlling, and that the laws were void under Title VII (*Rosenfeld* v. *Southern Pacific Company.*, 293 F. Supp. 1219 [C.D. Cal 1968]).

In a similar case the court went a step further, shifting the burden of proof that sex is a BFOQ to the employer. It enunciated the rule that an employer must have "a factual reason for believing that all or substantially all women would be unable to perform safely and efficiently the duties of the job involved." In this case, the court asserted, the employer had assumed on the basis of stereotyped characterizations that few or no women could meet the weight-lifting requirement and that all men could. In the matter of protecting women from risks, the court held that

> Title VII rejects just this type of romantic paternalism as unduly Victorian and instead vests the individual woman with the power to decide whether or not to take on unromantic risks. Men have always had the right to determine whether the incremental increase in remuneration for strenuous, dangerous, obnoxious, boring or unromantic tasks is worth the candle. The promise of Title VII is that women are now to be on an equal footing. We cannot conclude that women are now to be on an equal footing. We cannot conclude that by including the bona fide occupational qualification exception Congress intended to renege on that promise (*Weeks* v. *Southern Bell* [277 F.Supp. 117 (S.D. Ga.1976]).

In the ensuing years a plethora of cases, mostly class actions, were brought to court challenging hours and weight restrictions and job prohibitions. The courts struck down most sex-specific laws, and state legislators struck down the remaining ones. What statutes remain on the books are no longer enforced (Ratner 1980).

Pregnancy, Reproductive Hazards, and Title VII

One issue in which the courts' view departed from that of the EEOC was the problem of how to deal with the pregnant employee. The paradox here is apparent. Protective legislation had been consistently upheld since 1908 when the court held that the state had a legitimate interest in protecting women from injury during pregnancy. Yet the court resorted to fairly tortuous reasoning to find that employers did not violate Title VII protections by denying sick leave, disability insurance, or health insurance coverage to female employees to cover disabilities resulting from normal pregnancy.

The court did rule that maternity leave policies that mandated extended periods of absence violated the due process clause of the Fourteenth Amendment (Baer 1978). However, it found no sex discrimination in California's disability insurance plan, which excluded pregnancy disabilities from its coverage, but did cover such sex- and race-singular disabilities as hemophilia, prostate operations, circumcisions, and sickle cell anemia. It reasoned that

> there is no risk from which men are protected and women are not. Likewise, there is no risk from which women are protected and men are not (*Geguldig* v. *Aiello* 417 U.S.484 [1974]).

It repeated this language and extended the line of reasoning to a company health insurance program that covered sport-related injuries, injuries incurred while committing a crime, prostate surgery, circumcision, and hair transplants but excluded pregnancy. In that case (*General Electric Company* v. *Gilbert* 429 U.S. 125 [1976]) the majority based its decision on the logic that the only possible sex discrimination occurs when men and women are treated differently with respect to a shared situation or characteristics (Abramson 1979). Since men cannot be pregnant, the courts were saying, it is not discrimination against women to deny them health benefits for pregnancy disabilities. The plan does not discriminate against women, it simply removes one condition, pregnancy, from the list of covered conditions.

The courts continued this verbal hairsplitting in two more cases. In one case, women were required to take unpaid maternity leave during which they lost all accumulated seniority, even though seniority rights were retained for all other types of disability leave. The court rejected the loss of seniority but upheld the validity of the required unpaid leave, on the astonishing grounds that payment would constitute a benefit that men cannot and do not receive (*Nashville Gas* v. *Satty* 98 S. Ct. 347 [1977]). That logic was extended even further in a case challenging a retirement plan that required women to make larger contributions than men. In overturning the plan, the court distinguished between it and the disability plan upheld in the *Gilbert* case. The disability plan, the decision argued, distinguished between two classes of people, pregnant and nonpregnant ones. While all pregnant people were female, nonpregnant ones were both male and female, so no discrimination existed. However, the pension plan was discriminatory since all women were required to pay higher pension contributions than men (*City of Los Angeles* v. *Manhart* 46 L.W. 4347 [1978]).

Clearly some escape from this quagmire was needed. The justices had argued in *Gilbert* that the problem was that Congress had failed to explain its intent in outlawing discrimination on the basis of sex. Lacking such evidence of congressional intent, the court was reluctant to draw any inferences on its own. In addition, the *Gilbert* decision triggered considerable response from the media and from women's organizations such as the National Organization for Women (NOW) (Huckle 1981). Despite considerable political opposition, Congress responded with the Pregnancy Disability Act of 1978, technically an amendment to the Civil Rights Act of 1964.

The Pregnancy Disability Act broadened the definition of sex discrimination to encompass pregnancy, childbirth, or related medical conditions. Discrimination on the basis of these factors in hiring, promotion, suspension, discharge, or in any other term or condition of employment is defined as an unfair labor practice and is prohibited. An employer cannot

- require women to take leave set arbitrarily at a certain time in their pregnancy
- fail to grant full reinstatement rights to women on leave for pregnancy-related reasons, including credit for previous service and accrued retirement benefits as well as accumulated seniority,
- fail to pay for disability or sick leave for pregnancy, childbirth, or related medical conditions in the same manner as it pays for other employee disability or sick benefits (Trotter, Zacur, and Gatewood 1982a).
- refuse to hire or promote a woman because she is or could become pregnant,
- ask preemployment questions about a woman's childbearing status,
- protect women employees from "reproductive hazards" without scientific evidence that a hazard actually exists. They may, however, transfer a woman to a less strenuous and/or hazardous assignment during her pregnancy without guaranteeing her normal rate of pay (Trotter, Zacur, and Gatewood 1982b).

The history of Title VII has shown that the courts, and to a lesser extent the EEOC, have been reluctant to expand the definition of discrimination and the coverage of the act to apply to women in the same way they have for minorities. Where the EEOC has issued strong and clear guidelines, the courts have tended to follow their leadership. But in the absence of a strong message from EEOC, and given the unusual circumstances in which sex came to be covered in the act at all, the courts have proceeded cautiously indeed. The issue of pregnancy disability and reproductive hazards seems at last to have been resolved by Congress in the Pregnancy Disability Act of 1978.

Two other sex-related issues have caused both the courts and EEOC enormous problems. One, the issue of sexual harassment as a violation of Title VII, seems to have been settled through a series of court decisions. The other, comparable worth, remains an increasing politically and economically disturbing conundrum.

Sexual Harassment and Title VII

Phyllis Schlafly, testifying at hearings of the Senate Labor and Human Resources Committee, said:

> Noncriminal sexual harassment on the job is not a problem for the virtu-
> ous woman except in the rarèst of cases. When a woman walks across the
> room, she speaks with a universal body language that most men intui-
> tively understand. Men rarely ask sexual favors of women from whom
> the certain answer is "no."

Phyllis Schlafly obviously had never worked at the same place as Kyriaki Kyriazi.

> Kyriaki Kyriazi, a 47-year-old native of Greece, was employed by the
> Western Electric Company in an industrial engineering position. In the
> course of her work, her co-workers shot rubber bands at her, engaged in
> boisterous speculation about her virginity, and circulated an obscene
> caricature of her. Her two supervisors were aware of this behavior and
> acquiesced in it by choosing to ignore it. When she complained, she was
> advised to seek psychiatric help. She refused to do so and was fired.

Three issues have dominated controversy over sexual harassment as a violation of Title VII: What is it? How serious is it? and What is the employer's responsibility?

Unwanted, unreciprocal sexual behavior is pervasive in the workplace to an extent that is only now beginning to be realized. *Redbook* magazine published a questionnaire in its January 1976 issue, asking "How do you handle sex on the job?" Some 9,000 women responded, and nine out of ten of them reported one or more forms of unwanted attentions on the job. Most of the respondents were young, married women in white-collar jobs, probably a reflection of *Redbook*'s readership. But responses were received from women of all ages, occupations, incomes, and marital situations. These data, of course, came from a "self-selected sample"; when the authors compared their results to those from a study at Cornell University and other studies using standard random sampling techniques, they found lower, but still astonishingly high, percentages of women reporting problems (Safran 1976).

The *Redbook* article had considerable impact. The problem was much larger than anyone had yet suspected, and more research followed. Probably one of the most extensive studies was a survey of federal employees conducted in May 1980 by the U.S. Merit Systems Protection Board, which found the problem to be widespread throughout federal service: 42 percent of the women and 15 percent of the men reported having been sexually harassed at work within the previous 24-month period,

with the women much more likely than men to be victims of the most severe form of harassment. Single and divorced women were more likely
than married women or widows to be victims; job category had no relationship to harassment for women, although both women and men in
nontraditional occupations were more likely to be harassed. Hierarchical
level made no difference for women, but men in lower ranks were much
more likely to be harassed than those in management ranks. Younger
workers were more likely than older ones to be harassed; having a strong
financial dependence on the job and/or being a probationary employee increased the likelihood of harassment.

Women's harassers were more likely to be older married men, while
men's harassers were most likely to be younger, single women. Both
sexes were most likely to be harassed by a coworker, but more women
than men were harassed by a superior, and more men than women were
harassed by subordinates. These results suggest that harassment of
women was more likely to be a matter of power and intimidation, while
harassment of men may have been related to sexual attraction.

The harassment took many forms, from actual or attempted rape or
sexual assault (reported by 1 percent of the women and .03 percent of the
men) to pressure for dates or sexual favors, letters or phone calls, to such
less serious forms as sexual remarks, suggestive looks, or deliberate
touching. Harassment related to fear of retaliation was more common
among women victims than men, and occurred even when the harasser
was a co-worker (Tangri, Burt, and Johnson 1982).

A follow-up to the *Redbook* study, conducted jointly by *Redbook*
and *Harvard Business Review,* surveyed a stratified sample (by sex) of the
readers of the *Harvard Business Review* on their perceptions of sexual
harassment. The results confirm that men and women disagree strongly
on their perceptions of the problems. So great were the differences that
the authors concluded: "From the comments in the returns, a visitor from
another plant might conclude that men and women work in separate organizations."

Respondents agreed that the sexual behaviors described in the survey were widespread; almost all the behaviors described had been observed by many people. They tended to disagree, however, about how
frequently they occurred and about which behaviors constituted harassment. A high 66 percent of the men but only 32 percent of the women
agreed with the statement: "The amount of harassment at work is greatly
exaggerated." Further, top managers, mostly men, were much more
likely than middle- and lower-level managers to agree with the statement.
Harassment was considered much more serious when it came from a
supervisor than when it came from a co-worker. Top managers, in short,
seemed to be naively unaware of the extent of the problem or of its impact
on women victims (Collins and Blodgett 1981).

Nevertheless, several events in recent years have served to get their attention. Management may not understand the seriousness of the problem, but as the courts and the EEOC have brought protection from sexual harassment under the coverage of Title VII, employers have come to realize its legal and financial implications. The courts have come almost full circle on the issue, from refusing to take any action at all to leveling stiff penalties.

An important case denying recovery involved two women employees who rejected the sexual advances of their supervisor. The harassment continued until they resigned rather than face the continued abuse. The court rejected their claim of sex discrimination under Title VII, taking the position that harassment committed by the supervisor was the act of the supervisor only and bore no relationship to the employer. Since the supervisor's conduct was not the result of a company policy, the court concluded that the corporation had more to lose than to gain by the conduct and should therefore not be held liable. The court said:

> [The supervisor's] conduct appears to be nothing more than a personal proclivity, peculiarity, or mannerism. By his alleged sexual advance, [he] was satisfying a personal urge . . . (*Corne* v. *Bausch and Lomb* 490 FSupp 161 DC Az [1975]).

In a similar case, a supervisor made a sexual approach to a woman employee while the two were discussing possible job advancement for her. After she rejected the supervisor's sexual "suggestions," which were accompanied by force, he harassed her in the form of disciplinary layoffs and threats of demotion. Fifteen months after the original incident, the victim's job was terminated. The district court's response was that this was not sex discrimination, merely discrimination due to sexual activities.

> Title VII . . . is not intended to provide a federal tort remedy for what amounts to physical attack motivated by sexual desire on the part of a supervisor and which happens to occur in a corporate corridor rather than in a back alley (*Tomkins* v. *Public Service Electric and Gas Co.* 422F Supp. 553 DC NJ [1976]).

So the courts continued to hold that employers were not liable for sexual harassment under Title VII unless they had a policy permitting it, which of course no employer did. The courts also seemed to worry that if they found for the plaintiffs they would be opening the doors to a flood of cases, a concern that suggests that they recognized how pervasive the problem is (Seymour 1979).

However, *Tomkins* was overturned on appeal, and the tide began to turn. The appeals court ruled that the lower court had tolerated the supervisor's sexual demands and this created a prerequisite for continuation of, or advancement in, her job. From that point on, in a series of cases in the late 1970s, the courts ruled that Title VII is violated when acceptance of sexual advances by a supervisor is made a condition of job retention or when a supervisor takes retaliatory actions because a female employee refuses sexual advances (Sawyer and Whatley 1980). The courts have also permitted victims to bring their cases to court without having exhausted all the internal remedies the employer provides (Ledgerwood and Johnson-Dietz 1981).

In the wake of these findings, the EEOC issued guidelines in 1980, spelling out the definition of and responsibility for sexual harassment. The guidelines, derived in part from existing case law, assert that unwelcome sexual advances, requests for sexual favors, and other verbal or physical conduct of a sexual nature constitute sexual harassment when:

1. submission to such conduct is made either explicitly or implicitly a term or condition of an individual's employment,
2. submission to or rejection of such conduct by an individual is used as the basis for employment decisions affecting such individual, or
3. such conduct has the purpose or effect of unreasonably interfering with an individual's work performance or creating an intimidating, hostile or offensive working environment.

The guidelines also specify the employer's responsibility:

An employer is responsible for its acts and those of its agents and supervisory employees with respect to sexual harassment regardless of whether the specific acts complained of were authorized or even forbidden by the employer and regardless of whether the employer knows or should have known of their occurrence . . .

. . . with respect to conduct between fellow employees, an employer is responsible for acts of sexual harassment in the workplace where the employer (or its agents or supervisory employees) knows or should have known of the conduct, unless it can show that it took immediate and appropriate action . . .

. . . an employer may also be responsible for the acts of non-employees, with respect to sexual harassment of employees in the workplace, where the employers (or its agents or supervisory employees) knows or should have known of the conduct and fails to take immediate and appropriate corrective action . . .

Prevention is the best tool for the elimination of sexual harassment. An employer should take all steps necessary to prevent sexual harassment from occurring, such as affirmatively raising the subject, expressing strong disapproval, developing appropriate sanctions, informing employees of their right to raise and how to raise the issue of harassment under Title VII, and developing methods to sensitize all concerned (*Federal Register* 1980).

Under these guidelines, employers are responsible not only for be-haviors that directly affect the victim's employment, but also those that impose psychological harm. Unlike other forms of discrimination, whether conduct constitutes illegal harassment depends on the victim's perception of it. If the harassing behavior is performed by a supervisor, the employer is absolutely liable, regardless of policies or rules or of at-tempts to correct the situation. If the behavior comes from co-workers, clients, or anyone else, employers can also be held liable, but only if they knew or should have known about it and failed to take appropriate action.

In cases where the victim has suffered a direct loss (loss of a job, de-nial of a promotion) the courts have typically awarded back pay and attor-ney's fees. In cases where the damage was psychological but the victim had suffered no monetary loss, the remedy was often simply a "slap on the hand" to the employer, perhaps an injunction from making vulgar and indecent remarks to women employees. Such remedies were a small threat and had little effect in deterring employers from eliminating sexual harassment from their firms. They also provided little incentive to victims to pursue their cases. However, of late the courts are permitting victims to bring charges of assault, battery (if there is physical contact), invasion of privacy, and infliction of emotional distress and to sue for compensatory and punitive damages. These cases are then subject to trial by jury, and juries are apt to be sympathetic to the plight of a harassed worker. Em-ployers, rather than submit themselves to the trial process, frequently set-tle out of court for undisclosed, but surely substantial, amounts (Wymer 1983).

Kyriaki Kyriazi, harassed by her coworkers at Western Electric, brought suit in federal court and expanded her complaint into a class ac-tion including nearly 2,000 women employees and applicants. The court found that she was entitled to reinstatement and to approximately $100,000 in back pay. Back pay was also ordered for the other class-action plaintiffs. The exact cost to the employer is unknown, but it will exceed several million dollars (Kronenberger and Bourke 1981). However, the court went still further and ordered the three harassers to pay her $1,500 each. The company was forbidden to pay the damage awards for them be-cause

> any other result would permit Western to entirely circumvent the pur-
> pose of the punitive damages which have been awarded, and to pass on
> to its shareholders or the consuming public the consequences of the
> wrongdoings of its employees (*Kyriazi* v. *Western Electric Co.,* U.S.D.C.
> NJ [1979]).

Sexual harassment is physically and emotionally destructive to its victims. It is a wasteful, disruptive, and costly misuse of employers' resources. It is illegal, and many employers have taken steps to eliminate it from their workplaces. Yet it continues to occur wherever women and men work. Victims are entitled to both compensatory and punitive damages, and those who have suffered through the agonizing process of litigation and won their cases have often received very substantial awards. But by the time a case comes to court, both parties have lost. The guidelines are quite right when they assert that "prevention is the best tool for elimination of sexual harassment." Management must take all steps to prevent sexual harassment, not just on humanitarian grounds, nor even on legal grounds, but on the grounds of sound management practice.

Comparable Worth and Title VII

Since the passage of the Equal Pay Act of 1963 and the Civil Rights Act of 1964, and the issuance of the Executive Orders, efforts by government and by women's advocates to achieve equity have moved ahead along two fronts. One has been the effort to achieve equal pay for equal work. The other has been to attempt to reduce occupational segregation, specifically by attempting to move women into male-dominated occupations. The first effort has been fairly successful; the second has been much less so.

Only very recently has any serious attempt been made to address pay inequities in female-dominated occupations—that is, discrimination based on the "comparable worth" of jobs. The issue has recently been the subject of a great deal of research attempting to establish to what extent the pay disparity between women and men workers is the result of differences in the characteristics of the jobs or the characteristics of the individuals holding them and to what extent it is the result of sex discrimination. The results of these studies seem to confirm beyond reasonable doubt that at least some of the wage disparity is a result of discrimination.

The next questions are to what extent such discrimination is illegal and what can be done about it? Neither the problem nor the concept is a new one. As long ago as World War II, the War Labor Board required employers to pay women the same as men for jobs that were comparable, based on traditional job evaluation methods (Harriman and Horrigan 1984). The board found, for instance, that after the General Electric Company studied its jobs to determine the degree of skill, effort, and ability involved, it reduced the wage rate by one-third if the job was being performed by women. At Westinghouse Electric, the practice was the same but the rate was reduced by 18-20 percent (Newman 1976). When the war ended the board was dismantled, many women left the labor force, and employers reverted to the familiar pattern of paying women less than men.

The Kennedy administration proposed a "comparable worth" bill to the Congress in 1962; Congress rejected it in favor of the equal pay standard of the Equal Pay Act of 1963. For the next 15 years comparable worth was virtually ignored. The women's movement did not pursue it, the EEOC did not pursue it, and the unions did not pursue it. Then, in the late 1970s, it burst upon the American scene like a roman candle. The EEOC, under the aegis of Eleanor Holmes Norton, began to bring comparable worth suits to court, and Ms. Norton predicted quite accurately that this would be the most important equal employment issue of the 1980s. The labor movement began to use it as an organizing issue, and in 1981 the AFL-CIO unanimously endorsed a comparable worth resolution at its national convention (Hartmann and Treiman 1983). Unions, especially those representing public sector employees, have bargained both for comparable worth studies and for salary adjustments to remedy the inequities found in the studies. Women's groups, very late to come to political lobbying, have now begun to lobby for comparable worth legislation at every level of government. A number of state and local governments have adopted comparable worth statues, the federal Congress has held hearings and is considering several pieces of legislation (Harriman and Horrigan 1984).

Comparable Worth and the Courts

Nevertheless, the courts have been extremely reluctant to become involved in declaring comparable worth to be a form of illegal discrimination (Harriman and Horrigan 1984). Part of the difficulty goes back again to the cavalier way in which the Congress came to include women in Title VII. In the absence of hearings or testimony to the contrary, the courts have continued to assume that it was not the intent of Congress to wage battle over sex-based wage discrimination. Further, the passage of the Bennett Amendment to Title VII clouded the issue. The pertinent section of the amendment reads:

> It shall be an unlawful employment practice under this title for any employer to differentiate upon the basis of sex in determining the amount of wages or compensation paid or to be paid to employees of such employer if such differentiation is authorized by the provision of [the Equal Pay Act of 1963] (29 U.S.C. 206[d] [42 U.S.C. 2000e-2h]).

This amendment was introduced and adopted almost without discussion. Unfortunately, it can be interpreted in two ways: (1) It could mean that the amendment limits Title VII to the equal work standard of the Equal Pay Act, or (2) It could mean that an employer could raise the same affirmative defenses for unequal pay—that is, a merit system, seniority system, incentive system, or anything other than sex.

Under the first interpretation, comparable worth cases could not be brought to court at all. Even if employers deliberately and knowingly paid lower wages for jobs in female-dominated classes, since such practice would not be illegal under the Equal Pay Act it would not be illegal under Title VII. Under the second interpretation, cases could be brought to court under Title VII, and employers could use any of the four affirmative defenses to justify the unequal pay.

This confusion led to many years of debate in litigation as the courts struggled to resolve the issue and the Congress remained silent. In the first two cases that were brought to court, the court held that the Bennett Amendment limited Title VII to the equal work standard and the cases were decided on procedural grounds alone.

In the case against Westinghouse Electric Company, a similar finding was overturned by the appeals court. The union argued that job classes were segregated by sex and that, as a matter of policy, wages set for women's jobs were lower than those for men's jobs. The company did not deny the allegation but, basing its defense on the Bennett Amendment, argued that it was not illegal, that is, that Title VII did not apply. The court rejected this argument, noting that under this reasoning the law would permit the employer to discriminate against women in a way that would be prohibited against "whites, Jews or Gentiles, Protestants or Catholics, Italians or Irishmen, or any other group protected by the act" (*I.U.E.* v. *Westinghouse Electrical Corporation*. 631F.2d 1094 3rd Cir. [1980] cert. denied 452 U.S. 1979 [1981]).

The issue was finally resolved in 1981 when the Supreme Court adopted the interpretation that the amendment merely permits employers to raise one of the affirmative defenses (*County of Washington* v. *Gunther* 452 U.S. 161 [1981]). This case, originally filed in 1974, was brought by female jail matrons in Oregon whose work was very similar to that performed by male jail guards, except that they had more clerical duties to perform. The employer evaluated the female jobs at 95 percent of the worth of the male jobs, but the women were paid only 70 percent of the evaluated worth of their jobs while the men were paid 100 percent of the evaluated worth of theirs. In a five-to-four decision, the Court agreed with the appeals court that the Bennett Amendment did not limit sex-based compensation cases under Title VII to the equal pay standard. The Court expressed its unwillingness to deprive victims of discrimination of a remedy, but it also stressed that it was not endorsing the controversial issue of comparable worth and did not define "the precise contours of lawsuits challenging sex discrimination in compensation under Title VII." It did, however, indicate a broad view of the potential contours of such litigation (Harriman and Horrigan 1984).

All that the *Gunther* decision accomplished was to settle the issue of the Bennett Amendment. The Court remanded the case back to the district court to be heard on its merits. So after eight years, the only thing the plaintiffs had won was the right to bring their case before the court. Instead, the parties entered into a consent decree and Alberta Gunther and her codefendants each received $3,250 in back pay (Harriman 1983).

Whatever its limitations, the *Gunther* case did open the courtroom doors to women who work in female-dominated occupations, and a number of suits have been filed. The one that has received the most attention so far was brought by the American Federation of State, County and Municipal Employees (AFSCME) against the State of Washington. Washington had completed a comparable worth study of positions in state government in 1974 that found female jobs to be compensated at 20 percent below male jobs. The state had begun implementing the increases necessary to remedy the inequities when, in 1976, Governor Dixie Lee Ray took office. She refused to support either the concept or the implementation of the study. Nevertheless, the study was updated in 1976 and again in 1980, each time finding greater disparity. Finally, in 1983 the legislature, with the combined efforts of two clerical and one nurses' unions and a number of women legislators, adopted legislation to fund the increases (Remick 1983). In its suit, filed in 1981, AFSCME argued that the state had intentionally discriminated against women by ignoring its own evidence. The district judge agreed and awarded back pay to 1974, the date of the first study, an award that could run as high as half a billion dollars. This decision is now under appeal.

The Future of Comparable Worth

The concept of comparable worth got a tremendous boost when, during the Carter administration, EEOC chair Eleanor Holmes Norton declared it "the equal employment issue of the 1980s." The EEOC commissioned the study by the National Academy of Science to study the roots of wage discrimination. It began bringing individual and class action suits into the courts to determine the parameters of Title VII, to establish the procedures and burdens that would have to be satisfied to successfully challenge a particular employer's employment practices, and to obtain redress for women in sex-segregated jobs. One of President Carter's last acts as president was to expand the ability of the Office of Federal Contract Compliance to investigate pay inequities in federal contracts (Harriman and Horrigan 1984).

However, the Reagan administration revoked that authority and is generally opposed to the comparable worth issue. Reagan administration officials have referred to it as "radical" and even as "a looney tunes idea." Since 1981, the EEOC has greatly reduced the number of complaints it has investigated and the number of awards it has won. Early in the administration the EEOC announced its intention not to investigate comparable worth claims on a class action basis (Simpson 1983). This proposal met with a great deal of criticism and was eventually dropped. Nevertheless, it appears that the EEOC will go to court in the future on the side of the employers in comparable worth suits.

If and when cases do get to court, the eventual outcome may depend on the composition of the Supreme Court. Only two consistently liberal justices now sit on the Supreme Court. Because of the age of the sitting justices, President Reagan could have the opportunity to make two or more appointments during his second term. Since justices serve for life, his choices will have long-term consequences. Because of the controversy surrounding the issues of abortion and school prayer, Reagan will be under pressure to appoint people of conservative views. It's possible that the Court would become unanimously conservative, an outcome that would not bode well for the future of comparable worth suits. No one can predict, of course, how any justice will vote on a particular issue, and several of the current justices have voted in favor of Civil Rights issues. Nevertheless, supporters of the comparable worth issue will be watching the Court appointments carefully.

Regardless of what happens in the courts, however, the issue will not go away; it will be kept alive by the labor movement and the women's movement. As we know, the historical relationship between women and the unions has not been a particularly rewarding one for either. The unions have tended to represent men and send women to government, an approach women were willing to take. But in recent years, just as EEOC has been backing away from pursuing women's issues, the labor movement has greatly increased its interest in organizing women workers. Blue-collar employment in the smoke-stack industries, the traditional stronghold of the labor market, is declining rapidly and union membership is at an all-time low. Unions must move in to white-collar and public sector occupations in order to survive, and in fact the greatest increases in union membership in the last two decades have been in these heavily female-dominated organizations.

Comparable worth offers a perfect organizing issue for the labor movement, now faced with the problem of organizing the very women workers it has so long ignored. Since government has, in the past, also pursued the issue, organizers have a basis for comparison. Since the issue speaks directly to the economic concerns of enormous numbers of working women, it has an immediate appeal. Those unions seeking to organize and represent women—AFSCME, the American Nurses Association, and others representing clerical and service employees—have been the most actively involved. Union leaders are saying to workers: "You can go to the EEOC, and they will take it to the courts, and maybe in five or ten years you'll get something. Or you can join the union and we'll take it to the bargaining table, and we'll get it for you now" (Harriman and Horrigan 1984).

Alberta Gunther and her coworkers each got $3,250 in back pay after eight years in the courts. The women in Washington State have been awarded back pay to 1974, but by the time all the appeals are exhausted many more years will pass, and they may or may not receive the money. Union organizers can point to these problems and hold out the hope that they can do it better, that they can win higher wages with neither the cost nor the delay involved in a court battle. Using whatever methods are effective—negotiation, legislation, litigation, or strikes—they will bring the considerable resources of the labor movement to bear on the issue.

In the meantime the women's movement has also become active in pursuing comparable worth, perhaps for some of the same reasons. Social movements in general and the women's movement in particular have been slow to take up lobbying efforts. Not until 1973 was a national women's political lobby formed by the National Organization for Women and the National Women's Political Caucus, and then it was extremely controversial. The major catalyst came with congressional support for the Equal Rights Amendment (ERA), and for ten years most of the efforts of the movement were directed at the ratification of ERA (Costain 1981). Comparable worth was considered too vague, too radical, and too unrealistic even by members of the women's movement and was virtually ignored. Since the failure of ERA these groups, like the unions, have turned to fundamental economic issues that affect women workers. As a result of both union and movement pressure, comparable worth legislation and lawsuits are pending in many states and local jurisdictions; the number is growing steadily and rapidly. At the same time, several bills have been presented to the Congress.

Not surprisingly, well-organized and well-financed opposition is mounting from both political groups and employer organizations, for the political, social, and economic implications are enormous. The extent to which the advocates of comparable worth will be successful in eliminating or even reducing pay inequity in female-dominated jobs remains to be seen, but the issue is not simply going to go away as long as women remain in the labor force.

SUMMARY

Ever since the Industrial Revolution, workers have fought for better pay, shorter hours, safer and healthier working conditions, and greater job security. Much of the pressure for these changes came from the labor movement, which was primarily a men's movement. Women had the greatest need but also the least to contribute to the union movement. Reform was pursued through two avenues, at the bargaining table and through legislation. However, when protective legislation was adopted by many states, it covered only women workers. Over time the welfare of men workers came more and more to be the concern of the unions, and the responsibility for women workers fell to the state. Whatever the intentions of the reformers, the result was to increase the occupational segregation of women and to decrease their earnings.

During the 1960s, several pieces of federal legislation were enacted that addressed, directly or indirectly, the issue of sex discrimination. The Equal Pay Act of 1963 bans unequal pay for equal work, unless the difference is based on a nondiscriminatory merit system, a seniority system, an incentive system, or anything other than sex. Title VII of the Civil Rights Act of 1964, and its 1972 amendments, prohibits discrimination in all employment practices on the basis of race, religion, national origin, or sex. Executive Orders extend the coverage of these bills to federal employees and federal contractors. This legislation is supplemented by many state regulations.

Despite the reluctance of the courts to interpret the law broadly where women are concerned, this body of legislation has been used to strike down protective legislation. It has also been used to achieve equal pay for equal work, to reduce employment discrimination against women, and to prohibit the sexual harassment of women in the workplace. When the courts refused to extend protection of the law to pregnant women, Congress enacted the Pregnancy Disability Act of 1978.

Advocates of equality for women have attempted to broaden the coverage of Title VII to include pay inequities between different jobs or job categories within an organization. The courts have taken a very cautious approach to the issue, and the government has cut back on its active involvement. However, legislation is being proposed and enacted at every level of government and cases are being brought to the courts, mostly at the instigation of the labor movement and the women's movement. Each of these groups has a vested interest in pursuing the issue.

Much has changed in the political and economic environment of the workplace since the beginning of the Industrial Revolution. However, as we stand on the brink of an electronic revolution, much still remains the same. Women and men no longer work 12 hours a day, they rarely work under unsafe or unhealthy working conditions, and they are more protected against financial disaster from illness or injury or from economic fluctuations. Those changes have come about through a combination of legislation and negotiation; but women still earn less than men, and they continue to work in segregated occupations. The major change seems to be that the majority of women now work continuously throughout their lives, they perceive themselves as permanent members of the labor force (even if others fail to perceive them that way), they perceive themselves as victims of sex-based wage discrimination, and they are willing and able to pursue change through the same institutions that have brought about success for men: the law and the bargaining table.

5

Roles and Stereotypes

In the previous chapters we looked at the causes and results of the differential work experiences of women and men from several directions. We have examined the evidence that suggests that occupational segregation and the low pay of female-dominated jobs are, at least in part, the product of discrimination. We turn now to still another approach, a study of the ways in which either biology or society shapes the behavior and the beliefs of women and men. These biological and gender differences are often offered as an alternative explanation for sex differences in jobs and earnings.

The one thing that we can say with confidence about women and men is that they seem to be quite different from each other. Women and men lead lives that are very different but that are complementary in many ways. Some of these differences are biologically determined; only men can father children, and only women can bear and nurse them. When we speak of these differences, the terms we use are "male" and "female." Most of the division of labor, however, is a function of social custom or device; we call these gender differences or role differences and use the terms "masculine" and "feminine."

In this chapter we will be looking at the evidence of sex differences, at some explanations for those differences, and at the notion of psychological androgyny, an alternative way of conceptualizing sexual identity.

SEX DIFFERENCES

The seminal work on sex role differences was done by Maccoby and Jacklin (1974) in a comprehensive review and critique of the research literature. While their work has also been the subject of methodological criticisms, it is far and away the most comprehensive and reliable work available on sex differences and similarities. What they found tends to confirm some commonly held stereotypes and to disconfirm others. They found, for instance, that males on the average are taller, heavier and more muscular, and more aggressive than females but also that they are more susceptible to illness. After adolescence males excel in quantitative ability and in visual spatial ability, and females excel in verbal ability, verbal creativity, and manual dexterity when speed is a factor. For other types of creativity, general intelligence, and cognitive style, very little difference has been found between male and female abilities. In personality characteristics, such as love, sociability, nurturance, dependency, empathy, or emotionality, areas in which males and females are perceived to differ significantly, either very little difference was found or the evidence was conflicting.

Maccoby and Jacklin's work makes it clear that actual sex differences have been greatly exaggerated. It is also essential to understand and bear constantly in mind that those differences that have been found are statistical differences, not individual differences. The differences for each group tend to be spread over a normal curve, and the curves for the group overlap substantially (see Figure 5.1). What this means is that differences within groups far exceed differences between groups. Another way of saying this is that the differences between any two men—in size, in quantitative ability, or in aggressiveness—may be greater than the differences between any given man and woman. Any given woman may exceed any given man in any of these characteristics; any given man may exceed any given woman in verbal ability or manual dexterity. Thus it is essential not to particularize the results of these studies. All we can say for sure is that, on the average, males and females tend to differ on these dimensions.

However, it has been said that "circumstances that are perceived as real are real in their consequences." To the extent that the larger society believes that women and men differ significantly and that women's abilities or characteristics are of less value than men's, it is as if it were true. And, as we shall see, these beliefs do tend to persist.

ROLES AND STEREOTYPES

Because our world is infinitely complex, we must group physical and social phenomena into categories or typologies. These typologies allow us to reduce the number of individual stimuli we confront. The more successful we are in arranging knowledge into these types, the easier it is to comprehend the world in which we live. For this reason natural scientists divide the physical world into genera, phyla, and so on. Social scientists study human behavior in the forms of roles, role sets, and stereotypes. In

FIGURE 5.1
Trait Differences between Women and Men
are Statistical not Individual

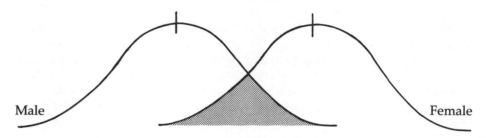

On some variables, such as verbal abilities, women on the average exceed men on the average, but some men will exceed some women.

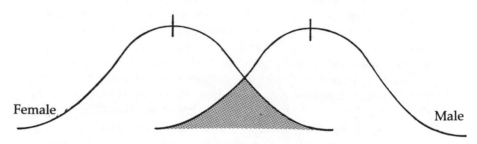

On other variables, such as physical strength, men on the average exceed women on the average, but some women will exceed some men.

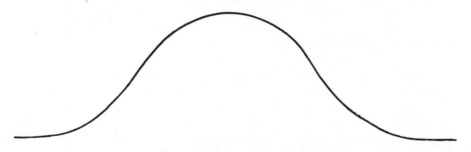

On many variables, such as intelligence, there are no sex differences.

studying sexual behavior, social scientists look for "sex roles" and "sex role stereotypes." Although the definitions and distinctions between these terms are subject to debate, we will rely on the following interpretations. A "role" is the expected and actual behaviors or characteristics that attach to a particular social "status" in our society (Duberman 1975). A "stereotype" is the set of attributes that are attributed to all individuals who occupy a particular role. Stereotyping occurs when the observed traits or behaviors of some members of a role group are attributed to all members of the group by the larger society. A stereotype exists when a broad cross section of the population agrees that certain traits or behaviors are commonly associated with a particular role.

Statuses can be either "ascribed" or "achieved." Achieved statuses are acquired through individual effort or ability; they are not assigned at birth. One achieves the status of assembly line worker, clerical, or lawyer, or of husband or father, or of friend through individual behavior. Ascribed statuses, on the other hand, are assigned at birth and include such characteristics as race, age, and sex, as well as son or daughter, sister or brother. They cannot in the normal course of events be changed.

To every status, whether achieved or ascribed, certain roles become attached, and in the case of sex these come to be known as sex roles. Roles are learned over a lifetime through the process known as socialization. Most children learn their sex roles through the process of role-taking, that is, through observation and control within the family. Thus specific details of the appropriate sex role will vary from culture to culture, religion to religion, region to region, class to class, and family to family. Further, individuals differ in the extent to which they conform to or deviate from the norms of the prevailing sex role. Hence gender roles, as opposed to gender statuses, are socially derived and are therefore capable of modification. One cannot change one's sex but one can change one's sex role (Duberman 1975).

For example, one might occupy the status of "manager" in our society, an achieved status. That status carries with it certain rights, obligations, and prestige, along with certain expectations of behavior, all of which constitute the role of manager. Managers are expected to plan, organize, direct, control, and staff the organization over which they have managerial responsibility. Managers are also expected to be knowledgeable about a number of areas concerning the specific organization, the industry, and the environment of the firm and to have some skill and ability in managing the human resources that come under their suzerainty. Managers are further expected to have certain traits: to be rational, equitable, and decisive. All of these are part of the managerial role. When we encounter a person whose job title is manager, we make certain assumptions about that person—that she or he carries all the job activities and the job privileges of a manager. We assign to that person all the personal characteristics that we associate with the role of manager. We see the manager not as an individual but as a manager. That is the effect of stereotyping.

Stereotypes usually have some basis in reality, and they serve a useful purpose in helping us to understand the social world in which we live. The difficulty is that, partly because they are rooted in reality, they are very difficult to change. Human nature being what it is, we tend to dislike ambiguity and to prefer congruity. When we observe an individual behaving in a way that is different from what we associate with their stereotyped group—for example, we observe a manager who makes inconsistent or emotional decisions—we experience something called "cognitive dissonance": two notions that we believe to be true are in opposition to each other (Festinger 1957). If our stereotype is accurate, this person who is a manager must also be rational. But our information contradicts this knowledge. We can observe that this person has the title of manager, and we can also observe that his or her behavior is quite irrational. Something is clearly wrong. Either our stereotyped belief or our observation must be in error. Do we change our stereotype of managers? Or do we disbelieve our senses? Probably neither. Instead we may conclude that this particular person is not a typical manager. He is, we say, a deviant; he deviates from the stereotypical behavior of people of the class of manager. Thus we are able to maintain both our stereotyped belief and the accuracy of our perceptions.

Roles and stereotypes have enormous power to shape our behavior. The learning of roles, and particularly sex roles, starts almost at the moment of birth. We give boys and girls different colored and different shaped clothes and toys. Boys are dressed in denim jeans, sometimes even in denim diaper covers; girls are dressed in frilly dresses. Boys get footballs, toy trucks, building blocks; girls get dolls and doll houses. We even describe newborn infants differently. Boys are "strong," "hefty," "handsome," and girls are "dainty," "sweet," and "pretty." Boys at these earliest stages are being taught to be active and self-reliant; girls are learning to be passive, dependent, and nurturing. Girls who deviate from these norms and adopt masculine behaviors during early childhood may receive positive sanctions because the society understands that when they reach puberty they will assume their "natural" role. Boys who adopt feminine roles, however, will receive negative sanctions. It will not be assumed that they will change their behaviors at puberty. Each is exhibiting deviant behavior, but being a tomboy is cute and being a sissy is not. Boys and girls who behave according to the norms for their sex-appropriate roles will be seen as acting "naturally."

The importance of all of this is that sex roles and sex stereotypes have a significant effect on how we behave, on how we view ourselves, and on how our behavior is perceived by others. It's essential to understand the

nature of masculine and feminine sex roles and sex stereotypes in con-
temporary society.

MASCULINE AND FEMININE

Sexual roles in our society are characterized by three aspects. Masculinity and femininity are seen as opposites of each other; masculine traits
are more highly valued than feminine traits; and the perception of masculine and feminine traits holds across a wide sector of the populace, regardless of sex. They do, however, vary according to race and social class.

The definitive work on sex-role stereotypes was done by Broverman
et al. (1972). These researchers measured the traits that were associated
with masculinity and femininity, the degree to which men and women
were perceived to hold those traits, and the value that was put on those
traits. They found a very high consensus for their results; across their
sample they found very few differences between women and men, between old and young, between East and West, between middle- and
working-class respondents in terms of the extent to which the stereotype
was held. Figure 5.2 shows the results of their research.

Two conclusions are self-evident. First, the number of desirable traits
associated with masculinity is more than double the number of desirable
traits considered feminine. Second, the feminine traits considered desirable are not ones that would be considered important or valuable in most
professions or occupations. Thus men are seen stereotypically as being
aggressive, independent, unemotional, objective, dominant, active,
competitive, logical, worldly, skilled in business, adventurous, self-confident, and ambitious—all traits that are related to the concept of competence. Women on the other hand are seen stereotypically as being exactly
the opposite of men on all of these dimensions. Desirable traits for a
woman are being talkative, gentle, tactful, religious, quiet, empathetic,
aesthetic, and expressive—traits associated with passivity. While much
of the management literature of late has argued for an increased "concern
for people," the feminine stereotype hardly matches the model of the en-
lightened manager. The ideal manager of that body of literature embodies
the desirable male traits into a concept called "concern for product" and
combines the two. The stereotypical male, in order to meet the ideal,
would have to learn to be more empathetic and more expressive but not
more passive. The stereotypical female, in order to meet the ideal, would
have to learn a vast repertoire of traits associated with competence and
perceived as being unfeminine.

The Broverman study found consensus across groups that differed in
sex, age, religion, marital status, and education level, but their research
was done largely with college students. To what extent do race and social

FIGURE 5.2
Male-Valued and Female-Valued Stereotypic Items

Competency Cluster: Masculine Pole Is More Desirable

Feminine Pole	Masculine Pole
Not at all aggressive	Very aggressive
Not at all independent	Very independent
Very emotional	Not at all emotional
Very subjective	Not at all subjective
Very easily influenced	Not at all easily influenced
Very submissive	Very dominant
Dislikes math and science very much	Likes math and science very much
Very excitable in a minor crisis	Not at all excitable in a minor crisis
Very passive	Very active
Not at all competitive	Very competitive
Very illogical	Very logical
Very home oriented	Very worldly
Not at all skilled in business	Very skilled in business
Very sneaky	Very direct
Does not know the way of the world	Knows the way of the world
Feelings easily hurt	Feelings not easily hurt
Not at all adventurous	Very adventurous
Has difficulty making decisions	Can make decisions easily
Cries very easily	Never cries
Almost never acts as a leader	Almost always acts as a leader
Not at all self-confident	Very self-confident
Very uncomfortable about being aggressive	Not at all uncomfortable about being aggressive
Not at all ambitious	Very ambitious
Unable to separate feelings from ideas	Easily able to separate feelings from ideas
Very dependent	Not at all dependent
Very conceited about appearance	Never conceited about appearance
Thinks women are always superior to men	Thinks men are always superior to women
Does not talk freely to about sex to men	Talks freely about sex to men

Warmth-Expressiveness Cluster: Feminine Pole Is More Desirable

Feminine	Masculine
Doesn't use harsh language at all	Uses very harsh language
Very talkative	Not at all talkative
Very tactful	Very blunt
Very gentle	Very rough
Very aware of feelings of others	Not at all aware of feelings of others
Very religious	Not at all religious
Very interested in own appearance	Not at all interested in own appearance
Very neat in habits	Very sloppy in habits
Very quiet	Very loud
Very strong need for security	Very little need for security
Enjoys art and literature	Does not enjoy art and literature at all
Easily expresses tender feelings	Does not express tender feelings at all easily

Source: Inge Broverman, Susan Vogel, Donald Broverman, Frank Clarkson, and Paul Rosenkrantz, "Sex-Role Stereotypes: A Current Appraisal," *Journal of Social Issues* 28 (1975): 59–78.

class affect roles and stereotypes? Helen Hacker (1975) studied sex role assumptions, expectations, relationships, and behaviors of the five social classes (upper, upper middle, lower middle, working, and lower class) and found some interesting changes occurring, especially among middle- and working-class families.

In the upper classes, which constitute about 1 percent of the population, emphasis is placed on preserving historical wealth, power and privilege, and the first line of defense is parental control over mate selection. Since women tend to acquire the status of their husbands, it becomes particularly important for girls to marry men of their own class, and great emphasis is put on feminine grace and beauty. Girls often attend exclusive women's colleges, so have few opportunities to meet men outside their own social class. Husband and wife roles are clearly separated. The woman's role is that of hostess and companion; she may participate in community activities as a means of finding self-expression but almost never works for wages. The man earns or manages the family's wealth. Both women and men tend to adopt feminine norms in interpersonal behavior, that is, there is an absence of overt aggression. Divorce is quite rare.

The upper middle class, which constitutes about 9 percent of the population, includes the upwardly mobile career executive and his alter ego, the executive wife. The wife is devoted to her husband's career and enhances it in a number of important ways. Husband and wife are more dependent on each other and less involved with the extended family than are the upper-class couple. The wife may hold a professional position, or she may be a full-time homemaker. In either case she will be involved in the traditional role of wife and mother.

Upper-middle-class wives are the ones of all wives most subject to role conflict. With the entry of increasing numbers of women into the labor force, these women increasingly find their traditional roles changing and being redefined. These women want recognition as wives and mothers, but they want "something more" besides. This something more may take the form of direct monetary gains from employment or indirect personal gains from the satisfactions that come from having a life and interests outside the home. The traditional behaviors of the feminine role are considered mandatory, although paid employment is permitted. And other personal attributes that are being added to the feminine role are rapidly becoming mandatory as well.

In the lower middle classes, which comprise about 40 percent of the population, women often work and their wages often lift the family's income into this class. Lower-middle-class husbands are skilled, semiskilled, and lower white-collar workers; lower-middle-classes wives might be clerical workers, school teachers, or civil service workers. Respectability and upward mobility are important values. The husband is clearly the head of the household; the wife's job, if she has one, is an extension of her housewife role. She is "helping out." However, husband and wife share many joint activities. Unlike his executive counterpart in the upper and upper middle classes, the husband has sufficient time to take an active part in family life.

The working class makes up about 40 percent of the population, but defining what it is or is not, and making generalizations about it, is becoming increasingly difficult because of the social changes that are taking place. Many workers, especially unionized ones, have high earnings and are experiencing both social and geographical mobility, including movement toward suburbanization. Nevertheless, it is possible to discern some characteristics, especially if we divide the group into traditional and modern working-class families.

The traditional working-class family resembles very much the breadwinner model. Gender roles are clearly segregated, and both sexes subscribe to an "ideology of patriarchy" and male dominance. But the husband/father's actual power in the family is often circumscribed by his lack of success in the labor force and by a lack of involvement in family affairs. The father sees his role as strictly limited to that of economic provider; sharing in domestic chores or having his wife work outside the home is a threat to his masculinity. This view of masculinity is shared by the wife. It is she who really runs the family, managing the household finances, bearing and rearing the children, and maintaining the household, much like the homemaker wife of the industrial period. She does all this, and often holds a job, while carefully maintaining the fiction that the husband is the head of the house. This clear separation of roles leaves the marriage partners rather isolated from each other and leads to a lack of closeness and communication (H. Hacker 1975).

Gender roles are learned early and well in the traditional working-class family. For girls, marriage is the chief objective, although most know that they will work at mundane jobs after marriage. There is little hope or expectation that they will receive education beyond high school. Courtship and romance are highly valued, and sex is often used as an inducement to marriage. Working-class boys and girls are kept segregated in school and social activities, and each sex tends to hold highly stereotyped views of the other. As a result they find difficulty in communication, a problem that contributes to the isolation and conflict that many experience in their marriages. As they grow older, the women continue to seek out women friends, the men to confide in other men.

However, a modern version of the working-class family seems to be emerging, particularly where husband and wife have graduated from high school or have moved to the suburbs. The increased education seems to provide not only greater earning power and with it greater self-esteem, but also greater ability to reason and to communicate. The move to the suburbs seems to break traditional ethnic traditions. In this modern version of the working-class marriage, the balance of power is more evenly weighted. There is more sharing of responsibility and a deeper emotional involvement. Wives are more likely to work outside the home, and husbands and wives tend to share home improvement projects or plans for the children's future made possible by extra income. Sex relations tend to be more satisfying, especially for the wife, partly because of improved birth control and partly because of the improved communication. For the working-class male, however, the modern marriage is a mixed blessing. More and more is being demanded of him, emotionally and sexually, than ever before. He is often being asked to redefine himself, a difficult task for the best of us, and one for which he has little guidance and few models.

The lower class is made up of people who live at or near the poverty level throughout their lives; it does not include young people at the beginning of their work lives or older people who may temporarily experience poverty. Families are often unstable. If the father works it may be at low-skilled, low-paid jobs, which are often seasonal or intermittent. Sex roles are highly segregated; husbands do not participate in household chores; fathers often rely on physical coercion to exert power. Both women and men adopt masculine behaviors in interpersonal behavior, acting out their anger and aggression.

Young people growing up in urban slums hold little hope of getting ahead by their own efforts. They live in the here and now, searching for excitement and pleasure. They see their only hope of a better life in luck, not in education or hard work. They marry at a young age and have more children than middle-class families.

Race and ethnic differences in sex-role behavior are also evident. In Latin America and in Mediterranean and Middle Eastern societies, sex roles are rigidly enforced and men and women have very little social interaction (Safilios-Rothschild 1977). Traditional values, deeply embedded in religious belief, tend to persist in these cultures, although the extent to which they are found currently depends in part, as it does in the United States, on socioeconomic status. Socialist countries such as Sweden, China, and the Soviet Union have adopted national policies of equality between the sexes, but even there old traditional values die hard (Yorburg 1974). In cultures where men and women are kept segregated, where sex roles are rigidly enforced, and where women are considered greatly inferior to men, the only possible relationship between women and men is a sexual one. Women learn from an early age to attract male attention by flirting, teasing, and dressing up. Men learn to look to women only for sex and to compete with other men for the most desirable women. In our country, groups that derive ethnically from traditional cultures tend to repeat the patterns. That is, men and women have little social interaction, their relationships are mainly sexual, and the double standard is rigidly adhered to (Safilios-Rothschild 1977).

Regardless of social class, regardless of race or ethnic background, males and females are shaped by the society, to a greater or lesser extent, into some kind of sex roles. These roles in turn have enormous influence on both their personal and working lives. As a result of the socializing influences they will have vastly different life experiences.

The Feminine Experience

The Broverman study and many others have measured a singular stereotype of women and have found it to be highly consensual over all demographic categories of age, sex, and region at the point in time at which their survey was conducted. Other researchers have looked at images of women past and images of women future and have found both consistency and change.

Chapter 2 traced in some detail the process by which male and female roles changed as a result of technological and economic change. As roles have become more segregated, women in general and women's work have tended to be increasingly devalued. Three dominant images of women's worth are apparent even from much earlier times, through the golden age of Greece and Rome and the Middle Ages, and through the history of Judeo-Christian religious teachings. They are: woman as inferior, women as evil, and woman as love object (Hunter 1976).

In ancient Rome women achieved a kind of women's liberation. They were more independent than women had ever been in any point in history and enjoyed access to education, property, and divorce. This development prompted some writers of the period to viciously ridicule all women who attempted to move out of an inferior position. So successful were these attacks that succeeding generations of historians have blamed the liberation of women for the breakdown of the family, for an increase in hedonism and debauchery, and ultimately for the decline and fall of the Roman Empire.

The image of woman as evil pervades the course of history. Early Greek mythology blamed evil on Pandora, early biblical writings blamed it on Eve. Jesus and Paul did not label women as evil per se, but through their teachings sex came to be associated with sin and celibacy with the highest form of Christianity. The natural extension of that linkage was that woman came by her very nature to be viewed as the source of evil, the temptress. From there it was a relatively short step to burning women at the stake as witches.

Despite the threat of evil and temptation that women presented, the tradition of woman as love object also goes back a very long way. It is found in the early Hebrew literature, particularly in the beautiful love

historical images

poem, "Song of Solomon." The Christian church maintained throughout the medieval period its disapproval of sex and love, but in the secular world the notion of chivalry glorified women and attributed to them qualities that improved the nature of men. The feminine role was always a passive one. Women were to be beautiful; they were to inspire men to acts of derring-do and creativity. But if they succumbed to the blandishments of their adoring knights, they lost their virginal qualities and became again associated with evil and sin. They were put on a pedestal, a rather precarious position in which to live (Hunter 1976). Women in the Victorian era, that is, at the time when the middle classes were beginning to emerge from the working classes, found themselves placed in this role of purity and passivity. The rationale for withholding the vote from women was the fear that exposure to the rough and tumble world of politics would shock their sensibilities or, even worse, corrupt their morals (Tannahill 1980).

These historical images can be found in contemporary views of womankind. Contemporary stereotypes can be broken down into several categories, including housewife, "bunny" (sex object), clubwoman, career woman, and athlete (Clifton, McGrath, and Wick 1976). The two traditional roles, housewife and sex object, produce very distinct stereotypes among both women and men. The housewife stereotype conforms very closely to the traditional sex role and to the image of woman as love object. Housewives are seen as faithful, gentle, kind, sensitive, sympathetic, dependent, cooperative, emotional, tender, conservative, casual, calm, generous, agreeable, secure, and loyal.

The "bunny" or sex object stereotype is also distinct and strongly held. A bunny is described as glamorous, good-looking, pleasure-loving, romantic, excitable, passionate, frivolous, and sensual. Housewives and bunnies are seen as having almost no attributes in common; housewives are not romantic, passionate, and sensual, and bunnies are not gentle, kind, sensitive, and tender.

A third stereotype is suggested by three other categories—club woman, career woman, and athlete. None of these emerged in the research as a distinct stereotype, but a number of common elements appeared. All three of these roles, which are relatively independent of men, are ascribed as having strongly masculine traits: active, aggressive, hardworking, alert, confident, ambitious, competitive, persistent, and independent. (Club woman was also described as argumentative and boastful by the men in the sample.) Does this finding confirm a perception of women as inferior? These traits, according to the Broverman study, are the ones associated with competence and most highly valued. But unfortunately they are traits valued only in men, not in women. Women who have stepped out of the traditional role are perceived in this study to have lost their femininity (Clifton, McGrath, and Wick 1976).

An earlier study by the Broverman group (1970) underscores the pervasiveness of the inferiority attached to the feminine stereotype. A sample of mental health professionals, psychiatrists, psychologists, and psychiatric social workers was asked to pick the traits that they thought described either a mentally healthy male, a mentally healthy female, or a mentally healthy adult (without specifying sex).

The results confirmed that even mental health professionals hold very stereotypical views of masculinity and femininity. The profile of the mentally healthy male and mentally healthy female conformed very closely to the stereotypes held by college students. But the profile of the mentally healthy adult came much closer to the stereotypical male than the stereotypical female. Being gentle, expressive, passive, and nurturant was considered normal and healthy for females but not for males or adults. Women were considered to be mentally healthy when they had adequately "adjusted" to their environment. This view puts women in the position of

> having to decide whether to exhibit those positive characteristics considered desirable for men and adults, and thus have their "femininity" questioned, that is, be deviant in terms of being a woman; or to behave in the prescribed feminine manner, accept second-class adult status, and possibly live a lie to boot (Broverman et al. 1970).

Despite changes that are occurring at a rapid pace in the life experiences of women, then, we can see that feminine stereotypes are changing very little. Women continue to be seen either as evil or as love objects, but in either case as inferior. Stereotypes of women can be differentiated from a single category (female) or from a variety of categories (housewife, bunny, career woman, athlete). Feminine roles can be distinguished by social class or by race. But the fact remains that women who adopt traditional feminine roles are seen as normal, healthy women; women who adopt nontraditional roles may be seen as competent, but they are also seen as unfeminine and deviant. As Broverman et al. said 15 years ago, women still face the conflict of being feminine and therefore second-class adults, or competent and unfeminine. What a choice!

The Masculine Experience

Some real differences exist between men and women. Men are not only taller and more muscular than women but also they are more aggressive. After puberty men's mathematical and visual-spatial abilities, on the average, exceed women's. Beyond that, a great deal of myth but little substance can be found (Maccoby and Jacklin 1974). Yet the ideology of male dominance and male superiority persists. Until the resurgence of the women's movement in the mid-1960s, relatively little serious evaluation of masculine roles and stereotypes took place. As in the study of organizations, the assumption, apparently, was that male is normal, and most of the research studied women and how women differed from men. Only recently has there been a comprehensive body of literature regarding the study of the life experiences of men. The literature is often controversial, often superficial, and often rooted in ungrounded assumptions, but one thing seems clear: The masculine role is probably as limiting in its way to men as the feminine role is to women (Pleck 1976).

Two aspects of the masculine role predominate. Roughly they correspond to Talcott Parsons's formulation of roles as either instrumental or expressive. The instrumental role includes the expectations that males will be physically active and adept and that they will achieve some form of success, however defined, in the workplace. The expressive role includes the expectation that they will suppress all expression of emotionality—that they will be "cool." Little boys, like little girls, learn their sex roles early and they learn them well. While feminist women complain, justifiably, about the limitations of behavior put on little girls, they tend to overlook the more powerful restraints put on little boys. Boys learn very early the importance of being good at sports, of being dominant, and of "acting like a man." They learn very early the negative sanctions that go with acting like a girl, that is, being a sissy. They may not always understand what it is that they are to do, but they know well what it is they are *not* to do. They are not to let anyone overpower them, they are not to be afraid, they are not to cry, they are not to do anything that girls do.

The Instrumental Role

The instrumental aspects of the masculine role include being physically and mentally strong and providing for one's family. As we saw in Chapter 2, the Industrial Revolution greatly increased the separation of men's and women's roles. Patriarchy had been a part of the social system since time immemorial. Industrialization made the breadwinner's domination over the family nearly complete. But the Industrial Revolution had two significant negative effects on masculinity: It reduced the amount of physical labor that jobs required, and it reduced the amount of time that young boys spent in the company of men. The social response to these changes was a marked increase in institutions that permitted boys to learn masculine behaviors and men to validate their masculinity. The institutions most effective for these purposes were sports, war, and boys clubs, notably the Boy Scouts.

The values of the Protestant Work Ethic regard hard work and providing for one's family as synonymous with masculinity. The American tradition of rugged individualism was and is highly regarded. Yet with industrialization the actual work that men did was increasingly less physically demanding, and their pay and benefits were increasingly standardized. Men came to feel that their masculinity was being diminished. At the same time young boys were increasingly in the company of women, both because of fathers' nonparticipation in family activities and because of the increasing number of female school teachers. It is no small coincidence that Teddy Roosevelt and his Raiders became instant national folk heroes. Roosevelt represented everything that was valued in the name of masculinity and much that ordinary men saw themselves as losing (Dubbert 1979). Since roles are historically passed down from one generation to the next, the concern that masculine values and behaviors were not being properly preserved was of no small consequence. Out of this concern came a greatly increased emphasis on the teaching of instrumental roles and an increased avoidance of expressive roles.

A number of organizations sprang up during this period that presented opportunities to express one's manhood and to teach manly virtues to the younger generation. The Young Men's Christian Association (YMCA) and especially the Boy Scouts met these requirements. The Boy Scouts were founded in South Africa. The movement was formally incorporated in the United States in 1910 and within a decade became the largest male youth organization in U.S. history. It turned the idle street gang into the active Scout patrol. It would turn "sissies, hot-house plants, little Lord Fauntleroy types, puny, dull or bookish lads, and dreamers" into boys who were "full of life and energy, full of ideas, filled with ideals and with heroes." The American scouting movement added to the Scout oath the condition "To keep myself physically strong, mentally awake, and morally straight," and added the tenth law "A Scout is Brave" (Hantover 1978).

The Scout movement attracted adult males as well as young boys. Scouting offered men the dual opportunity to teach young men the manliness and virility that had occurred naturally in earlier times and to express their own manliness that was now seen to be eroding. Young college-educated men in white-collar occupations, perhaps the ones experiencing the greatest threat to their masculine identity, were eager to validate their manhood by taking the role of scoutmaster.

Participation in sports also took on new meaning during this turn-of-the-century period. It is not altogether clear how this came about, but it probably had its roots in Victorian Christian morality, which maintained that a moral person was a good steward of mind and body. For whatever reason, a sports craze swept the country. The YMCA which had been active in this country since before the Civil War, promoted gymnastic and athletic programs to "protect against the allurement of objectionable places of resort" (Dubbert 1979). Roosevelt endlessly extolled the virtues of sports like running, rowing, football and baseball, boxing and wrestling, shooting, riding, and mountain climbing. Schools were encouraged to offer physical education and sports programs, and a link was perceived between having a healthy, active body, a good mind, and a good character. Team sports began to be popular, to some criticism. They encouraged spectatorism rather than participation, and they failed to offer the display of prowess and virility that individual sports required. Nevertheless, football and baseball games drew huge crowds and created a new breed of heroes. Even in the colleges, physical and athletic ability often took precedence over intellectual prowess in the validation of masculinity.

Sports activity, like the Boy Scouts, was attractive to men because it gave them a safe retreat from feminine influence. The sports arena became a sort of modern equivalent of the men's hut found in primitive societies. There fathers and sons could share an interest and participation in sports, and, free from the mother's interference, the boys would learn the manly virtues. The world of letters and fine arts was left to women; the world of sports was the exclusive domain of men. The rougher the game, the more manliness it represented, and football became a national obsession. Colleges were rated as much for their football teams as for their academic programs. Indeed, academic and intellectual pursuits were seen to make a man soft and weak. If a man must indulge in activities of the mind, then it was essential that he counterbalance that behavior with bruising physical activity to restore his mind and body to health.

When World War I began, it was widely assumed that a generation of youth raised on sports, athletics, and particularly football would be moral and physical giants, ready to march bravely into war to serve their country. The results were disappointing. Over one-third of the 3 million men drafted into the armed services in 1917 were found to be unfit for service. The public reaction, however, was not to reject the notion that sports participation would build men, but to resolve to do the job better. Roosevelt and others chafed at the reluctance of President Wilson to enter the war. Military training and service were enormously popular ideas; they would build men out of boys. They would bring out the best in men (Dubbert 1979). War was romanticized, glorified, idealized. It represented the quintessential display of manhood.

In the years after World War I, sports continued to be enormously popular, although increasingly men took on the role of spectator rather than participant. Team sports drew huge audiences, which legitimized the spectator role (Gagnon 1976). Boxing also became enormously popular, and men like Jack Dempsey and Gene Tunney became household words. Tunney, however, failed to achieve hero stature because he was considered unmanly. He did feminine (expressive) things like reading poetry and talking about Shakespeare. Baseball hero Babe Ruth, a poor boy who made good by his own herculean effort, was more the stuff of national worship (Dubbert 1979). Schools continued to emphasize sports and athletic programs, and boys continued to feel the need to participate in team sports. The majority of men, however, now validated their masculinity vicariously; instead of active participation in sports clubs or athletic contests, they watched while others performed.

Throughout the Depression years, many men (and women) found themselves once again living in poverty. Their role as breadwinner was once again threatened. National sports heroes helped to ease the burden of frustration and restore shattered self-esteem. And war once again broke out. Once again young men were given an opportunity to develop their character and test their masculinity; once again old men could demonstrate their toughness by sending young men into battle. Football and war, then, have become the two arenas for the validation of masculinity.

When the sons of the World War I doughboys marched off to war in 1942, the romanticized vision of war was very much intact. Good boys, normal boys, were eager to get into the war and into action. Military service was (and is) widely accepted as the *sine qua non* of masculine achievement, even though war, like work, has become highly automated (Gagnon 1976). The closer one came to actual battle, the more masculine one became. Hence the foot soldier, the marine, and later the Green Berets in Vietnam, were seen as having more courage and aggressiveness than their officers (Stouffer 1976). Those who were unable to serve for reasons of health or age were pitied. Those who avoided military service were vilified. It's no wonder that when many of the sons of the World War II veterans declined to fight in Vietnam the society reacted with such vigor. These young people, after all, had rejected and denounced the very essence of masculine verity.

Thus, enormous emphasis is put on winning—in sports, in war, in business, and in politics. Coach Vince Lombardi's aphorism is often quoted: "Winning isn't everything; it's the only thing." Young boys are trained from an early age in highly organized sports functions like Little League baseball and Pop Warner football. These organizations are often severely criticized for the pressure they put on young boys to perform and to win, but parents continue to encourage (or push) their sons to participate (Fasteau 1974). For high school boys, the importance of participation in sports is exceptionally high, particularly considering that few, if any, will regularly engage in sports as adults. Nevertheless, studies of high school students show that even the most average student athletes hold higher prestige than the most gifted intellectual students (Coleman 1976).

Participation in high school or college athletics, like military service, is a badge of masculinity that men continue to wear throughout their lives. Political candidates who can claim war duty or college football duty have a significant advantage at the polling place. An old war wound or football injury is practically invaluable. Fasteau (1974) argues that the primary reason for our continued involvement in the Vietnam conflict was not, in fact, the need to fight communism but the "cult of toughness" that made political leaders dread being perceived as unmanly and unwilling to fight. Richard Nixon never ceased to remind the public of both his war service and his football days in college, even though he was admittedly a very mediocre player in a small liberal arts college not distinguished for its football team. The Watergate tragedy was partly a result of the fact that Nixon and his advisors saw themselves as under siege by an enemy. As in a football game or a war, winning became essential, and finally obsessional. To the end Nixon felt the necessity to appear tough and strong. After a tearful interlude with Henry Kissinger on the night before his resignation, he called the secretary of state to urge him not to reveal the incident because he might appear to be soft and weak (Woodward and Bernstein 1976). In his resignation speech he compared himself to Teddy Roosevelt (Dubbert 1979; Duberman 1975).

The conventional wisdom holds that sports build masculine character, that they teach boys how to compete and how to win in the rough and tumble world, and that they teach them how to work with other people. Indeed one of the most-often-quoted books on the inadequacies of women in the business world argues that women are disadvantaged because they lack the character-building experiences of team sports and military service (Harragan 1977). Yet studies of male participation in sports fail to support the conventional wisdom. In fact, research by two psychologists shows that athletic competition may actually limit growth in some areas. The people who are highly successful at sports were probably already gifted in the requisite qualities for athletic prowess. They were already mentally fit, resilient, and strong. On the other hand, some people who apparently have all the requisite qualities fail to become great successes; these people, the researchers speculate, might be too fit, they may lack the "neurotic tie" to the sport. At the same time boys who are unsuccessful at athletics may suffer considerable loss of self-esteem (Fasteau 1974).

If very few men and boys actually play football, and if in fact it fails to build character, why does it remain a national obsession? Folklorist Alan Dundes (1978) argues that football, like the Boy Scouts, fraternities, and other exclusively male organizations, is a form of ritualized homosexual behavior. The equipment worn greatly exaggerates the male physique, enlarged head and shoulders, narrowed waist, genitals emphasized by a metal codpiece. So garbed, they are allowed to touch, pat, and hug each other in ways that are otherwise denied to men. By examining "football folk speech," Dundes concludes that football is analogous to male verbal dueling. Verbal dueling is the modern machismo version of physical dueling in more primitive cultures, where males who outmaneuvered or overpowered their adversaries further humiliated them by making them act like females—for instance, by forcing them to assume a supine position. Verbal dueling, like football, almost always takes place in the presence of others, and often includes explicit and symbolic language suggesting that the adversary is like a woman, hence not a man. Football involves such activities as "penetrating" the adversaries "end zone," "scoring," "spiking," "popping" an opposing player, "making a pass" to a "tight end" or a "split end." Football players who fail to live up to their team's expectation are accused of being female; they are called "sissy," "pussy," "cunt." Dundes concludes that on the football field

> sexual acts carried out in thinly disguised symbolic form by, and directed towards, males and males only, would seem to constitute ritual homosexuality. . . . American football is an adolescent masculinity initiation ritual in which the winner gets into the loser's endzone more times than the loser gets into his (Dundes 1978).

The popularity of football, indeed of all team sports, may also be explained in its metaphorical relationship to war. Why, for instance, is the national anthem sung at the beginning of most sports contests if not to symbolize the warlike aspects of the tournament. The national anthem is probably heard more frequently at the start of sports contests than in any other time or place. Indeed the words "play ball" have, for all practical purposes, been permanently added to the concluding notes. Some young children, in fact, are not aware that the words do not properly belong there.

What is the link between sports or physical prowess, masculinity, and money? We said that prior to industrialization work meant both physical exertion and providing for one's family. We have seen that industrialization removed the necessity for physical exertion and that it was replaced first by active and later by vicarious participation in sports and athletics. What is the link between masculinity and white-collar employment? To what extent does the provider role constitute masculinity? Again, very little is known, except that the link is a strong one. Psychiatrists, for example, report that both men and women equate moneymaking with masculinity. For some men the relationship is so strong that the loss of a job or a drop in income produces impotence. Even a relationship with a woman who earns a substantial income can be threatening to some men's libido. This reaction is not, of course, totally without foundation. Just as the man has learned to believe that his masculinity is related to his ability to earn money, so many women have learned that their future lies in marrying a man with a high earning capacity. Hence, for her as well as for him, the size of the paycheck becomes a measure of his masculinity (Gould 1976). How frequently does this occur? What mitigating variables apply? What demographic variables are significant. Very little, unfortunately, is known beyond the fact that the relationship exists.

As work has become less physically demanding, the role of the business executive has become a sort of metaphor for masculine power and competitiveness. Like sports, business success as an expression of masculinity has its roots in religion. Weber (1930) has argued that the phenomenal growth of capitalism would have been impossible without Protestantism. Certainly Martin Luther, and more particularly John Calvin, made sacred the right and obligation of men to work hard, save their money, and "get ahead." The nineteenth-century robber barons—entrepreneurs like John D. Rockefeller, Andrew Carnegie, Thomas Edison, Henry Ford, and many more—were the very embodiment of the Protestant Work Ethic, and they were the heroes of their day. These men all started with very little, had little education, worked very hard, were very devout churchgoers, and came to command huge enterprises and huge fortunes through their own industry. They were hailed for their capitalistic spirit, which was equivalent to the rugged individualism of the frontiersman. They were the captains of industry. By the twentieth century public sentiment began to fear the consequences of their excesses, and antitrust legislation gradually reined in their power. Although they are often criticized as exploiters of both workers and the environment, there remains an enormous respect, almost awe, for their independence and their accomplishments.

The twentieth century has had a paradoxical relationship to its business leaders. The electronics industry has replaced the basic industries as the frontier of entrepreneurship; stories are told of small businesses started in a garage in Palo Alto or Cambridge that grew into multibillion dollar, multinational businesses. Young men wearing beards and blue jeans become multimillionaires before they are 30. There are still enormously exciting success stories, but entrepreneurship has become secularized. We admire these success stories but not necessarily the successful men themselves. They fail to arouse the same awe as the "poor boy becomes millionaire" stories of the nineteenth century.

Further, the vast majority of businessmen are not entrepreneurs but hired managers of these modern conglomerates created by the golden boys. And the hired manager has suffered a lot of criticism over the years. From Sinclair Lewis' *Babbitt* (1922) to William Whyte's *The Organization Man* (1956), contemporary writers have decried the loss of integrity and the loss of individualism in the corporate manager. The problem is not so much that business success has lost its metaphorical meaning as that business no longer offers the same opportunities for demonstrating one's machismo.

The Expressive Role

The expressive role of masculinity should more properly be labeled the masculine inexpressive role. Bruce Feirstein (1982) spells out the issues in the introduction to his marvelously insightful and funny book *Real Men Don't Eat Quiche*:

"Real men don't eat quiche," said Flex Crush, ordering a breakfast of steak, prime rib, six eggs, and a loaf of toast.

We were sitting in the professional driver's section of an all-night truckers' pit stop somewhere west of Tulsa on I-44, discussing the plight of men in today's society. Flex, a 225 pound nuclear waste driver who claims to be one of the last Real Men in existence was pensive:

"American men are all mixed up today," he began, idly cleaning the 12-gauge shotgun that was sitting across his knees. Off in the distance, the sun was just beginning to rise over the tractor trailers in the parking lot.

"There was a time when this was a nation of Ernest Hemingways. Real Men. The kind of guys who could defoliate an entire forest to make a breakfast fire—and then go on to wipe out an endangered species hunting for lunch. But not anymore. We've become a nation of wimps. Pansies. Quiche eaters. Alan Alda types—who cook and clean and *relate* to their wives. Phil Donahue clones—who are *warm* and *sensitive* and vulnerable. It's not enough anymore that we earn a living and protect women and children from plagues, famine, and encyclopedia salesmen. But now we're also supposed to be *supportive*. And *understanding*. And *sincere* . . ."

Contemporary men do face a dilemma. They are increasingly being required to demonstrate their "feminine" side, that part of their nature that includes the expression of emotion; yet the society continues to expect of them the instrumental behavior of "real men." We know that there are no biological differences between women and men in their capacity to experience emotional feeling. The differences lie not in the extent to which women and men experience an inner life, but in the extent to which they reveal it to themselves and others. Since the male role requires that men not reveal themselves, men are under constant pressure to suppress something that is a natural part of their makeup. The inexpressive male who cannot or will not reveal himself to others becomes insensitive to both his own inner life and to the emotional expressions of others. Men who don't reveal themselves to others are not the recipients of others' disclosures, particularly of other men's disclosures, and hence "their concepts of the subjective side of other people—of other men as well as women and children—are often naive, crude, or downright inaccurate" (Jourard 1974). But at the same time contemporary men are constantly being admonished to "get in touch with their feelings," to become compassionate, sensitive, and caring.

A study of a relatively homogeneous sample of white, young, single, heterosexual, middle- and upper-middle-class people in the greater metropolitan and suburban New York area demonstrated the extent of the paradox. Over three-fourths of the respondents reported feeling pressures to inhibit their feelings. Surprisingly, the greatest need to monitor feelings came from women. These women experienced the traditional feminine prohibition against displaying anger or annoyance, but they also expressed pressure to inhibit feelings of love and affection. They did so to avoid rejection or hurt, but also because the men in their lives disliked displays and discussions of this kind. The men, on the other hand, experienced contradictory pressures. A number of men reported feeling pressured to express anger and annoyance, since these were considered traditional masculine behaviors. An equal number, however, reported feeling pressured to express love and affection in sexual relationships and compassion and tenderness in nonsexual ones. Men also reported feeling pressured to engage in sexual activity to prove themselves and enhance their status through conquest. Both women and men admitted to emotional pretense. The women often reported expressing less emotion than they actually felt. The men reported expressing more emotion than they actually felt, as a way of gaining sexual intimacy (Davidson 1981). Men in male consciousness raising groups report having pretended to be open and confiding with women as a "line," a "come on" that says "see what a sensitive, compassionate person I am."

Some men can and do, however, express these most intimate of feelings to the women in their lives. A study of male college students found that they were more likely to reveal intimate information, particularly about personality and body topics, the most sensitive of all, to a woman friend than to a male friend, sibling, or parents. Their relationships with their male friends were dominated by a competitiveness that foreclosed intimacy (Komarovsky 1976).

Feelings have been described as "the real male terror" (H. Goldberg 1972). To a greater or lesser degree, men block all feelings. Dependency is avoided, sometimes to an extreme; men are expected to be winners not losers, to "make it on their own" without help from others. Passivity is related to dependency; men are expected to be active, to do something, anything, but not to be idle. Leisure becomes associated with passivity, then with laziness, so men fill their nonwork time with activities and feel uncomfortable if they are not busy all the time. Even such supposedly stress-reducing activities as sports or exercise programs become competitive. Active, independent males, of course, cannot ask for help, even for directions to the nearest gas station, without threatening their masculinity. If the problem becomes asking for help on a major understanding, or for help with a mental or physical problem, it is even more threatening. Men who express fear are called by feminine names; they are "sissies," "gutless," they have "no balls."

Sadness also is incongruent with masculinity, and crying is totally prohibited. For example, Edmund Muskie, U.S. senator from Maine and Democratic vice-presidential candidate in 1968, was the front-runner for the Democratic nomination in 1972. Then, on the eve of the New Hampshire primary, Muskie stood on a platform, exhausted from the campaign efforts, and tried to respond to a newspaper article that unfairly criticized his wife. Overcome with frustration, he had to stop and brush away tears. That gesture was broadcast on every radio and television news program and reported in every print medium. Editorial writers proclaimed him unfit for the office of president, and his candidacy was dead. Clearly, the country would be unsafe in the hands of a man who would cry, even if he cried over a vicious attack on his wife.

The one emotion that men are often allowed to express is anger, but even here there is a taboo. While little boys are expected to be aggressive, the expression of it is expected to be directed impersonally, against strangers, enemies, or competitors. At home or in school, in personal relationships with family and friends, they are expected to be polite, considerate, and conforming. If they are aggressive to other boys or, worse, to girls, they are called bullies. From boyhood on, males are expected to treat girls and women as fragile and delicate creatures dependent on men for protection. The male is allowed to get angry at a woman only if she gives him some "righteous" cause for doing so, that is, only if she behaves in some unfeminine way. This repression of anger, according to Goldberg, has the effect of stifling spontaneity and creating emotional distance between women and men. At the same time, the male is not allowed close relationships with men, because men are his competitors and it's important that he not reveal his weaknesses or in any way make himself vulnerable to them. Of course, he must never touch or be touched by other men, and he may only touch or be touched by women with whom he has a sexual relationship. Touching means sex, and touching other men means homosexuality (H. Goldberg 1972). One outcome of this connection is that many men have no close relationships with men and only sexual ones with women (Safilios-Rothschild 1977).

Even gestures of pleasure may be seen as unmasculine. Expressions of high spirits, of freedom and spontaneity, are childlike behaviors, and real men are serious, they are stable and settled, they are goal-oriented. Impulsiveness, spontaneity, even loud and uninhibited laughter are irrational. Would Flex Crush laugh out loud? Would he jump in the air, pour champagne over the coach's head, swat his teammates on the fanny with a towel when his team won the game?

Finally, the masculine role requires men to be objective and rational, so abstractions or paradoxes may be threatening. The masculine role requires men to see the world in absolute terms, as black and white, as good and evil, as masculine and feminine. Grey areas or logical paradoxes create anxiety and distrust. Does Dirty Harry worry about the civil rights of the criminal he is chasing?

Inexpressivity leaves men with two roles to play in their relationships with women: the cowboy and the playboy. The cowboy type, epitomized by John Wayne, or more recently perhaps by Sylvester Stallone, is the rugged "he-man," strong, resilient, resourceful, capable of coping with overwhelming odds. He loves his girl and his horse (or his motorcycle) but does not express his love, since to do so would conflict with his image. The playboy, epitomized by James Bond, is like the cowboy in that he is resourceful and shrewd and treats women with detachment and independence. Unlike the cowboy, however, he is unfeeling. Instead of hiding genuine feelings of love and affection, he manipulates women for his own purposes without either affection or remorse (Balswick and Peek 1971).

The Origins of Male Inexpressiveness

The origins of male inexpressiveness are unclear, and there are at least two schools of thought. The first postulates that it has its roots in homophobia, the fear of homosexuality. Homophobia, in turn, stems from Christian prohibitions against the enjoyment of sex. The second approach argues that it is actually an instrumental role used to maintain male dominance and power over other men and especially over women.

Homophobia is "the irrational fear or intolerance of homosexuality" (Lehne 1976). It is generally associated with the fear of male homosexuality, and should more correctly be called "homosexism," or sexism between individuals of the same sex. Homophobia is related to stereotypes about homosexuals that are not grounded in reality, stereotypes that suggest that homosexuals are afraid of the opposite sex, that they act like the opposite sex, that only certain occupations are appropriate for homosexuals, that homosexuals molest children, and that homosexuality is "unnatural." Although a good deal of research evidence contradicts these beliefs, homophobia persists and is generally a characteristic of individuals who are otherwise rigid and sexist.

The roots of homophobia go back to the beginning of Christian history. The Bible (particularly the New Testament) contains some prohibitions against homosexuality, and indeed against many forms of heterosexual behavior. The church, from the beginning concerned for social control and stability to insure its continued survival, was troubled by man's sexual drives and appetites. St. Paul, for instance, allowed that marriage could be good, but truly strong and good men would remain celibate. St. Augustine, like St. Paul and other leaders of the day, felt that sexual intercourse was fundamentally disgusting, degrading, shameful, and unclean. Therefore celibacy was the desired state, but those who were too lustful to remain celibate should use sex without passion for the begetting of children. Sex within marriage was permitted, although not considered an integral part of marriage. Contraception was the major sin, more serious even than abortion.

St. Thomas Aquinas, more than any other Christian scholar, extended Augustine's views of sexuality in general to homosexuality, and made it responsible for the fire and brimstone that brought down Sodom and Gomorrah. His case was based on Augustine's proposition that sexual organs were designed for and could only legitimately be used for procreation (Tannahill 1980). Prohibitions against other sexual behavior and against contraception and abortion have generally been relaxed except among practicing Catholics, but homophobia has persisted.

As religious beliefs have waned, the social sciences, particularly psychology, have taken their place in justifying homophobia. Psychology and psychiatry have consistently regarded homosexual behavior as deviant and have argued extensively as to whether it constituted mental illness. Although the American Psychiatric Association recently removed homosexuality from its list of mental illnesses, the majority of Americans continue to look on it as a pathological condition capable of being "cured." Freud viewed it not as a mental illness but as a form of arrested psychosexual development. He believed that homophobia was rooted in "latent homosexuality," which is present in almost everyone. Since latent tendencies are by definition incapable of demonstration, it would be hard to prove or disprove his theory (Lehne 1976).

For whatever reasons, homophobia is pervasive. A majority of people believe that homosexuality is "bad for society," and homosexual activities are still illegal in a great many states. Arguments against removing occupational discrimination against homosexuals center on the fear that they will "corrupt" their fellow workers, especially in occupations that require sharing living quarters, like firemen or the military. Another concern is that removing the sanctions would allow homosexuals to molest or convert children. While neither of these fears is supported by evidence, they continue to be held by a fairly substantial proportion of the population.

Individuals who are highly homophobic also tend to be more status conscious, more authoritarian, and more sexually inflexible than low homophobia individuals. Homophobic individuals tend to support political repression and a double standard of sexual morality and not to support equality between the sexes or civil rights for women and minorities. Homosexist individuals (those prejudiced against homosexuals) share a belief in the importance of rigid sex roles for the continuation of society, and they believe in the acceptability of authoritarian techniques to enforce their social beliefs.

Homosexist individuals, even those whose lives are not generally affected by homosexuality, are often also homophobic. Such prejudice persists, perhaps, because homophobia is used as a technique of social control to enforce norms of male sex-role behavior. Since men devalue homosexuality, then homophobia becomes a norm that can be used to control men in their male roles. Any man can potentially (latently) be a homosexual, and as long as there are social sanctions against homosexuality, the fear of being labeled a homosexual is powerful enough to insure conformity with male roles. When homosexuality is made a crime, there is no way in which an accused can defend himself; there is no way to prove that one is not a latent homosexual and therefore a criminal. The charge of homosexuality can then be brought against individuals when evidence is lacking to convict them of other crimes of which they are suspected (Lehne 1976).

The irony of homosexism is that it is not just homosexual males (or females) who are its victims. All males, and all females, have their behavior controlled through the negative social sanctions that await them if they deviate from traditional sex-role norms. Men are reluctant to enter into close relationships with other men, and when they do they are afraid to express their love for their men friends. Men are reluctant to enter into feminine activities or female-dominated occupations for fear of being labeled homosexual.

An alternative hypothesis to the homophobia explanation, however, argues that male inexpressivity is a tool that men use to maintain power. These two explanations are not, however, mutually exclusive. In itself, male inexpressiveness is of no particular value in our culture, but it is an instrumental requisite for assuming male roles of power. In other words, little boys learn to be inexpressive, not simply because of social expectations, but because the culture is preparing them to become decisionmakers and wielders of power (Sattel 1976). There are three points to consider in this argument.

First, inexpressiveness in a role is determined by the corresponding power (actual or potential) of that role. The more powerful the role, the less free the male is to express his feelings. It's clear that inexpressivity in males is situationally variable and that males can unlearn inexpressivity with females, particularly their wives (Narus and Fischer 1982; O'Leary and Donoghue 1978). It's not clear, however, in what way power affects the equation.

Second, male inexpressiveness may represent an effort to control a situation and to maintain position. Communication is by definition a two-way process. If one person refuses to enter into a dialogue, the second cannot continue. Hence the nontalker has controlled the substance and nature of the interchange. He has controlled not only what is *not* said but what *is* said.

Third, male inexpressiveness is an intentional manipulation of a situation when threats to the male position occur. Silence and inexpression are the ways men learn to consolidate power. By revealing only strategic portions of oneself, one never reveals the extent of one's resources, efforts, or rewards. Men talk about issues and ideas, not personal concerns, not because they are uninterested in the latter but because revealing themselves would give away power to the competition.

Inexpressiveness in males is probably a function of both homophobia and power building. Its cause is not as important as its effect, which is not only to cut men off from awareness of and sensitivity to the feelings of others but also to cut them off from themselves.

Sex roles and sex role stereotypes, then, characterize women and men as being polar opposites of each other. Literally from the moment of birth on, males and females are subjected to social approval or social sanctions, according to the extent to which their behavior corresponds to social expectations. But in spite of these forces, not all individuals conform to sex-role expectations, and not all conform to the same extent. We turn now to the study of individual adaptation to sex roles and particularly to some of the consequences of sex typing.

PSYCHOLOGICAL ANDROGYNY

As the Broverman studies demonstrated, society has historically considered stereotypical masculinity to be an indication of good mental health for males and femininity to be the mark of a mentally healthy female. Psychologists have conceived of masculinity and femininity as bipolar ends of a single continuum. A person could be one but not the other. Personality tests that measured sex role gave one score. A man who tested as feminine, or a woman who tested as masculine, were considered sexual deviants and might very well be treated for their disorder.

However, philosophers, poets, and playwrights have long recognized that every individual has both masculine and feminine traits and qualities. In literature as in life, the most independent and inexpressive male could be touched by the love of a child or moved by the plight of an animal; the most helpless and frivolous woman could cope with danger or save her family from disaster when the occasion arose.

In recent years psychologists have recognized these anomalies and have responded to the rhetoric of the women's movement that the bipolar system of sex role differentiation "has long since outlived its usefulness, and . . . it now serves only to prevent both men and women from developing as full and complete human beings" (Bem 1975). Instead, they have recognized that individuals should be "encouraged to become *androgynous* . . . they should be encouraged to be both instrumental and expressive, both assertive and yielding, both masculine and feminine—depending on the situational appropriateness of the various behaviors" (Bem 1975).

The concept of androgyny required new methods of measurement, and several have been developed. Probably the most frequently used is the Bem Sex Role Inventory (BSRI), which contains a list of 60 positive traits that have been divided equally into masculine, feminine, and neutral on the basis of sex-typed social desirability. Individuals' sex role orientation is determined by their endorsement of masculine and feminine personality characteristics (Bem 1974). Individuals are considered masculine or feminine if they score above the mean on just one scale, "undifferentiated" if they score below the mean on both, and androgynous if they score above the mean on both (Bem, Martyna, and Watson 1976). Another frequently used measure is the Personality Attributes Questionnaire (PAQ) (Spence, Helmreich, and Stapp 1974). Although measurements and definitions have varied over time, the similarity of results suggests that androgyny is an important concept in understanding sex role behavior.

Androgynous individuals differ from sex-typed individuals in one important aspect. They seem to have a larger repertoire of behaviors; they are able to adapt their behavior to the situation, even when doing so requires behaving in ways that might be considered inappropriate to their sex role. In a series of experiments with students at Stanford University, for example, researchers found that masculine and androgynous individuals were very much alike in terms of independence from social pressure, a masculine behavior. In a standard test of conformity, these masculine and androgynous subjects conformed in significantly fewer test trials than did the feminine ones (Bem 1975). On the other hand, feminine and androgynous individuals were more nurturing, both toward an infant and toward a fellow student with a personal problem, than were the masculine ones (Bem, Martyna, and Watson 1976). Androgynous individuals of both sexes were able to perform cross-sex behaviors with little reluctance. Sex-typed people avoided a wide variety of simple, every-day activities (nailing two boards together; winding a package of yarn into a ball) when those activities were stereotyped as more appropriate for the other sex. They also reported more discomfort and temporary loss of self-esteem when they were required to perform such tasks (Bem and Lenney 1976).

Androgynous people, whether male or female, tend to be alike; sex-typed ones tend to be different. Androgynous males have been found to be high in both the instrumental and expressive domains; androgynous females are high in both independence and nurturance. On the other hand, feminine males are low in independence and masculine males are low in nurturance. Feminine women are low in independence, and masculine women are low in nurturance.

A major tenet of the androgyny literature has been that androgynous individuals are better adjusted mentally than sex-typed people, but this claim has not been entirely supported by the evidence. Instead, it appears that perhaps it is masculinity, not androgyny, that contributes to adjustment. In other words, androgynous women and both androgynous and masculine men all report high adjustment (Silvern and Ryan 1979).

Feminine women appear to have lower self-esteem than androgynous or masculine women and to be more introverted but not to differ particularly in physical or mental health. Contrary to popular belief, younger women do not seem to be any more likely to be androgynous than their middle-aged sisters (Hoffman and Fidell 1979).

Androgyny is as important for its impact on life choices as for its effect on behavior. And indeed sex type and life choice seem to be related. Feminine-typed women tend to have conservative attitudes about the role of women, to like housework (more than any of the other types), and to take full responsibility for child care and homemaking. They tend not to be employed outside the home, they are less educated, and are less economically advantaged than the other types. Masculine women, and to some extent androgynous women, seem to display an almost opposite pattern. They tend to exhibit a feminist pattern in their choices: to have higher education, to work outside the home, to have higher socioeconomic status, and to have more liberal attitudes (Hoffman and Fidell 1979).

As we move to the study of management and organizational behavior, we will return repeatedly to the concept of androgyny. Again and again we will see that it is sex role orientation, not sex, that seems to be significant in the way in which individuals behave and the way in which they perceive and evaluate the behavior of others.

CONCLUSION

To a greater or lesser extent, each of us is shaped by the larger society of which we are a part into attitudes, beliefs, and behaviors based upon our biological sex. Those attitudes, beliefs, and behaviors, in turn, serve to form the shape of our lives, affecting not only the roles we adopt but also our attitudes toward those roles. They affect not only the choices we make on a daily basis but also the choices we make about careers and marriage, the two most important arenas for self-expression for most of us. They shape, as we will see throughout the rest of this book, the way in which we present ourselves to the larger society, our motivations, our satisfactions, and our ambitions. They affect not only the way we perform but the ways in which our performance is evaluated by ourselves and others. They affect not only our expectations of ourselves and others, but the expectations that others have of us.

Sex role theories are often used to explain the differential experience of women and men in organizations. They are used to support the argument that the problem is not discrimination but socialization. Women, taught from the cradle on to be passive, dependent, and nurturing, fail to make the kind of educational or career choices necessary to achieve success or fail to exhibit the kind of behavior necessary to be successful in male-dominated occupations. This explanation lays the problem anywhere but on the organization. Women can be blamed for failing to take the initiative to overcome the effects of historical discrimination; society can be blamed for socializing women and men into these roles. The solution is to train women to be more like men, confirming once again the "male is normal" hypothesis.

Sex roles and sex-role stereotypes should not be viewed as hopelessly deterministic. What has been learned can be unlearned; changes in social values follow changes in behavior, albeit slowly. Nothing has been more apparent in recent years than the extent to which women's lives are changing. What is less apparent, but certainly still visible, is the extent to which men's lives are also changing. If change persists, roles and stereotypes will adjust. What is seen as unusual or inappropriate behavior in one generation tends to become the norm that governs the next one. We are already seeing an erosion of the feminine stereotype, with more women incorporating masculine traits into their personalities without relinquishing their positive feminine traits. Perhaps soon we will also see an increase in the number of men who can maintain the positive qualities of masculinity and at the same time internalize the best of what is feminine.

But sex roles and sex role stereotyping, which certainly do exist, cannot explain away the discrimination that continues to exist. Androgynous women and masculine women, willing and able to assume roles that include the positive masculine traits, still find themselves the victims of subtle, and sometimes not so subtle, discrimination. There is certainly a need to change stereotypes so that they more accurately reflect the reality of contemporary lives; but simply changing stereotypes will not bring an end to sex discrimination. Much of the responsibility for that lies within the organization.

6
Working Together

The relationships among and between the sexes have been the subject of confusion, concern, and conjecture for as long as civilization has existed. In song, poem, novel, and drama, as well as in all of the social sciences, writers both scientific and creative have explored the dynamics of friendship, family, and love.

The entertainment media have tended to glorify men's friendships and to ridicule women's friendships (with some notable exceptions in both cases). On the other hand they have represented male-female relationships in every conceivable form and from every imaginable standpoint. The rapidly growing body of social science literature is small by comparison; it attempts to separate myth, stereotype, and legend from reality. Unfortunately from our standpoint, little is yet known or understood about these vastly complex relationships, and even less is known about the impact and importance of these relationships on organizational behavior.

Considerable research has examined the operation of informal relationships within formal organizational structures, but the vast bulk of this research ignores the issues of sex and gender. By simple observation we are aware that, since men and women have typically been segregated in the workplace, the norms of the social world have tended to govern their interactions. Women relegated to low-paid, dead-end jobs have tended to put a high value on their friendships with co-workers, but so also have men in low-level jobs. Men in careers with higher mobility have tended to compete with their male peers, but women in these same career fields have sought encouragement and support from women peers. Women have often served as "office wife" to men managers, but women managers have been denied the same loyalty and attention from their female subordinates. Social as well as organizational taboos have discouraged romantic or sexual relationships between people on unequal status levels, but office romances have continued to occur. For the most part these observations have been assumed to be reliable; very little serious research has attempted to validate or analyze them or to assess their implications for the organization.

Now as women increasingly move into nontraditional roles, many assumptions and practices are being challenged, and these observations take on new significance. New questions are being raised? What differences exist between men's friendships and women's friendships? What happens to women's friendships if they find themselves competing, not for the attention of men, but for a limited number of promotional opportunities? What is the nature of the relationship between women of differing age and status? What is the nature of the relationship between women and men who are equal, or relatively equal, in status or organizational level? What problems do sexual attraction or romantic involvements create for managers? For employees? Does it make any difference? Why has it not been studied?

The literature on friendships, romance, and sexual activity in organizations remains sparse; much of what exists tends to be anecdotal and speculative. Social scientists have studied the nature of male/male and female/female friendships but not the importance of these friendships for organizational behavior. Very little is known about nonromantic friendships between women and men, in or out of the organization. Some research is currently being done on romantic and sexual liaisons in the workplace, although efforts at serious study have been hampered by the sensitivity of the subject. Drawing on the available body of knowledge, this chapter will look at relationships between women and men, between women and women, and between men and men. It will attempt to describe the nature of these relationships and their implications for management.

MALE/FEMALE RELATIONSHIPS

Whenever women and men interact with each other, whether at work or at play, there is some level of sexuality involved. How they choose to deal with that sexuality is determined by a great many factors, but some way is always agreed upon, usually tacitly. Appropriate and mutually agreeable sex roles are adopted, virtually unconsciously. Organizational sex roles are often fairly direct extensions of these social roles; like social roles, they are characterized by separation and by reciprocity. Organization roles have been so clearly in conformity with social expectations that very little attention has been devoted to them.

On the other hand, sexual or romantic relationships at work have traditionally been seen as inappropriate and unprofessional, especially when they involved individuals with different status or power within the organization. These taboos have been so strong that little, if any, research has been devoted to the problem of sexual attraction among co-workers.

As social and organizational changes disrupt traditional status hierarchies, they also disrupt traditional role relationships. We need to understand better the nature of both the nonromantic, nonsexual relationships between women and men in organizations and the consequences of romantic, sexual attraction and relationships.

Male and Female: Nonromantic Relationships

The separation of roles has been perpetuated by their reciprocity, which is inherent in the formal organizational roles to some extent and to a much greater extent in the informal system. In the formal system, male roles tend to have reciprocal female roles, and the higher the status of the male role or occupation, the higher the probability that there will be a reciprocal female role or occupation. Ergo, doctors have nurses, lawyers have legal secretaries, and managers have executive secretaries or administrative assistants. In these reciprocal roles, status and behavior expectations are quite clearly understood.

The metaphor of the office wife, often used to describe the role of secretary, is a case in point. Secretaries tend to take their status from the man they work for, in the same way that women have traditionally taken their status from their husbands. Secretaries, like wives, form attachments with a particular man; they treat him in a differential manner and remain loyal to him over a long period of time. Secretaries often derive their rank and level of reward from the position of their bosses, not from their own skills or abilities. The higher the boss's rank, the higher the secretary's rank. A secretary achieves promotion by being assigned to a boss who gets promoted. In return, the boss receives a measure of status from his secretary. As with a corporate wife, the secretary has to be well dressed and well educated and make a pleasing impression, for her behavior reflects on her boss (Kanter 1977).

But in addition to these reciprocal characteristics of formal organizational roles, men and women tend to enact a reciprocal set of social roles in the informal structure of the organization. These roles also are an extension of socially sanctioned male-female roles played out in the larger society. One typology of roles rather humorously, but at the same time quite accurately, describes these interactive roles (Bradford, Sargent, and Sprague 1975).

The Macho and the Seductress

The male in this role is constantly asserting his male potency. Interactions with women usually have a sexual component to them. He asserts his dominance by calling attention to the woman's sexuality by commenting on her dress or appearance, then minimizing or denigrating her competence in other areas. His message is that she is a sexual object, not a competent person. The female reciprocal role, the seductress, is played by the woman who constantly asserts and reaffirms her sexual desirability through her dress, manner, or behavior. She exerts a certain power over the men by her ability to confer or withhold sexual favors. A woman may not consciously or deliberately play this role; it may be assigned to her by the men in the organization if she is seen as sexually attractive and potentially available (Kanter 1977). Both participants in these roles may gain satisfaction by reaffirming their sexuality.

For the seductress, attention is focused on her female status, rather than on her status as a competent member of the organization. Tension is generated between other women and as well as other men. She is recognized for her social role, not for her organizational role. When the woman is an unwilling or reluctant participant, she may also lose self-esteem.

The Chivalrous Knight and the Helpless Maiden

Men in our society have learned well their roles as the provider and protector of women. Their masculinity often depends on being polite, kind, and gentlemanly. They open doors for women; they help women out of cars and across the street; they refrain from using profane language around women; and they even avoid conversations about serious concerns like politics and business. They are polite, tolerant, and respectful toward women. Further, they are taught such behaviors at an early age and are frequently rewarded for them. Little wonder, then, that in the work world, they tend to treat women in the same way. They protect them from tasks that require technical ability, skill, or responsibility. They protect them from any events that might create a conflict between their jobs and their marriages, like raises, promotions, transfers, or travel. The woman who plays the reciprocal of the helpless maiden, like the seductress, may find it useful in the short run. She may be protected from onerous duties or, more importantly, she may be protected from making serious mistakes.

The helpless maiden may also be protected from taking necessary and useful risks. She may surrender the opportunity to become, and to be seen as, a competent person. The woman who exploits the role of helpless maiden, by feigning helplessness or ineptness, or by crying or flirting, may be able to manipulate males to do her bidding, but in the long run she will pay a price. The very beliefs that a man may hold about women may make it impossible for him to avoid being manipulated. If he confronts her, challenges her, it has to be on the basis that she is competent enough and strong enough to accomplish on her own, without dependency on him. Yet he believes that only men are strong and competent and that his masculinity is dependent on being strong and protective. It's little wonder that these men often find themselves angry and frustrated.

The Protective Father and the Pet

This relationship is akin to a father-daughter relationship. The pet is not seen as sexually available, yet she serves as a kind of cheerleader or mascot for the older male, often of high status, and his companions. Pets are valued for their support of male humor and displays of prowess. They are expected to observe and approve from the sidelines but not to participate. Occasional displays of competence are tolerated, even approved, because of their rarity. The pet may get a certain amount of visibility in this role, but the attention is again on her femininity, rather than on her competence.

Young women may sometimes confuse this role set with a mentor/protégé relationship. (See Chapter 11 for a full discussion of the mentor/protégé relationship.) Unfortunately, the protective father often lacks the organizational power necessary to be an effective mentor. Not recognizing his powerlessness, the woman may welcome the attention of an older man in the organization who seems to take an interest in her career and introduces her to other important people. The protective father, rather than sponsoring her continued achievement, is mainly involved in protecting her, sometimes to the point of overprotection. The mentor encourages his protégé to take risks, to express opinions, and to develop competence and independence; the protective father values his pet for her childlike qualities and encourages her to be dependent on him.

The Tough Warrior and the Nurturant Mother

The tough warrior is the inexpressive male whom we saw in Chapter 5 who is often characterized in the movies by actors such as Clint Eastwood or, earlier, Humphrey Bogart. He is independent and self-sufficient, suppressing all emotions; he may carry this role to such an extreme that he becomes isolated from peers or subordinates, to the dysfunction of the performance of his duties. The nurturant mother becomes a source of solace and support. She fills the Madonna role, she is not seen as sexually available and is not subject to sexual pursuit. Instead, she serves as the confidante, the counselor, and the nurturer (often in a real sense, as in bringing the coffee).

While this role is relatively safe, it, too, has negative consequences. The mother is rewarded for service, rather than for action, and she is perceived as being an "emotional specialist," a stereotypically feminine characteristic that may be interpreted as being sentimental or irrational (Kanter 1977). Further, since mothers are often seen as being dominant and controlling as well as nurturing and supportive, the woman in this role must suspend criticism and deal in support, approval, and encouragement, thereby suspending her ability to use critical or evaluative skills.

The most serious outcome of these feminine roles is that they emphasize the woman's feminine role over her organizational role. They all have the effect of suppressing her competence as well as her confidence.

Either party can, of course, refuse to play the reciprocal role, but it's not always easy to do so. The feminine role expectancy includes being compliant and cooperative; the masculine role includes being sexually aggressive. When the macho male flirts, the expected feminine response is to flirt back. When the seductress flirts, the expected masculine response is to escalate the flirtatiousness. Women sometime engage in a pseudoseduction plot, manipulating male colleagues by subtly suggesting that they are sexually interested and available but yet always avoiding any sexual activity (Hively and Howell 1980). Other women, who proclaim that they only want friendship with a man, feel rejected and offended if he doesn't indicate at least some sexual or affective interest (Safilios-Rothschild 1977). Refusing to respond to these behaviors requires overcoming long years of social conditioning.

The situation gets even harder when the intent is to be genuinely helpful. When the chivalrous knight, with only the kindest of intentions, assumes that the woman couldn't, and wouldn't want to, understand the budget, it's very difficult indeed to risk offending him by refusing to play the helpless maiden. The alternative that seems safest may be the mother role, but this may not be available to young women.

The best alternative is to abandon situationally inappropriate modes of behavior and to insist upon sex-neutral organizational roles, but that, too, is no simple task. The traditional male/female organizational roles are to a great extent a mere extension of the social roles that have evolved as an intrinsic part of the industrial/Victorian era. So long as these roles were accepted and acceptable to all, few problems arose. They represented comfortable and familiar ways of interacting in a nonsexual way.

But in recent years the old social order has been challenged. Many women are moving into nontraditional occupations. Some of them wish to adopt nontraditional sex roles as well. Recognizing that the traditional roles restrict their behavior and limit their options, they actively seek to abolish the remnants of patriarchy that persist in organizations.

Other women, however, have achieved new organizational positions but have no desire to discard old social roles that they find comfortable and effective. Many men feel highly threatened by the "new" women who demand equal treatment and deliberately cling to old behaviors that keep women in a submissive and passive role. Other men, however, genuinely and sincerely wish to help and not to hinder; but they face a real dilemma. If they hold open the door for a woman, she may be offended, but if they don't hold open the door she may be offended. Common sense says that whoever gets to the door first, or is carrying the smalles load, would open the door, but common sense often doesn't always prevail in social situations. If a man compliments a woman on her appearance, is it a harmless, friendly gesture; is it a sexual approach; or is it a subtle put-down, emphasizing her feminine characteristics rather than her competence? If he doesn't express some sexual interest in her, will she feel rejected and insulted? If he compliments her on her work, is he being patronizing? If he criticizes her work, is it a valid critique or a sexist attack? If he invites her to join him at an important business lunch, is he acting as a mentor or as a protective father? If he includes her in an important business trip, is it business or monkey business?

The problem is real for both women and men. The old roles are no longer appropriate, but new ones have not yet emerged. Roles function in our society to provide order and stability. But roles must be consensual. To perform their function, a significant proportion of the members of the culture must agree on at least the basic elements. And this is where we are at present. Many people, but by no means all, have rejected the existing role expectations for masculine and feminine behavior at work, but no consensus exists as to what new role expectations should replace them. In the meantime a lot of confusion, pain, embarrassment, and anger are occurring.

Male and Female: Romantic Relationships

As long as the sexual segregation of organizations kept women in subordinate positions, the issue of overt sexual involvement was kept at bay. It's true that women have often been treated as sexual possessions in an organization and prized for their sexual attractiveness. Many workplaces are characterized with a great deal of sexual energy, if not of sexual activity. Clearly, the office romance has always existed, as has the problem of sexual harassment. But taboos against sexual relationships between high-ranking males and low-ranking females also existed and were highly consensual. If these taboos did not prevent office romances, they did serve to keep them discreet.

In recent years women have increasingly moved into occupations and organizational levels formerly dominated by men. Taboos that once prevented a male manager from a sexual liaison with his secretary no longer apply when differences in status and power are reduced. Further, the propinquity of working relationships, plus the shared emotions of working together, may arouse a powerful attraction. When two people work together on tasks that involve high levels of ability, close coordination, and intense competition, a good deal of emotional energy is generated. When the co-workers are women, they may develop a strong friendship. When the co-workers are men, they may alternately enjoy a sense of comradeship or compete with each other for dominance in the situation. If the co-workers are a man and a woman, a number of outcomes are possible. They may experience differing emotions. She may feel a strong sense of friendship, as she would toward a woman colleague, while he experiences a sense of competition. However, since for many people the only experience in relationships with the opposite sex is sexual, one or the other or both may experience a strong sexual attraction.

Sexual attraction, of course, may or may not present problems for the individuals involved or for management. For the individual, one potential problem is the fear that social-sexual behaviors will be misinterpreted, rejected, or perceived as inappropriate. Although after the completion of school or college the workplace often offers the primary setting for making new acquaintances, it differs in several ways from exclusively social settings. Most people are there, in fact, to do their jobs and to earn a living. They typically plan to work there for an extended period, hence any awkwardness associated with sexual advance, or perceived sexual advance, is apt to have long-term consequences. Further, status hierarchies affect the ability of individuals to initiate or respond to sexual overtures. As a result, those who would initiate social-sexual behaviors tend to do so in ways that are indirect, ambiguous, and susceptible to multiple interpretations (Gutek, Morash, and Cohen 1981).

For managers, sexual attraction is a cause for concern because of its potential to disrupt the workplace. Little research is available about the nature or the extent of sexual behavior at work, and accurate data would probably be difficult to get. One major study involves a descriptive model of organizational romance. It is based on responses to a questionnaire distributed in the waiting areas of two metropolitan airports to people who had experience as a third party observer of romantic relationship between two people in the same organization (Quinn 1977). It tells a great deal about the sensitivity of the subject that these essentially anonymous people, killing time between flights, were the only subjects available to talk about office romances. The respondents were predominately white and middle class, and over two-thirds were males. Despite the limitations of the methodology, the model offers a useful way of looking at office romances; it presents four formative aspects of organizational romances and four types of organizational impact.

The four formative aspects are proximity, perceived motives, types of relationships, and work group characteristics. On-going proximity—having work stations in nearby locations and/or performing tasks that require either professional or social interaction—was a factor in most of the cases. In only a few cases did occasional or temporary contact lead to romance.

The motives of the lovers, as perceived by the third-party observers, can be classified into three categories: job motives, ego motives, and love motives. Job motives included such instrumental rewards as advancement, job security, increased power, financial rewards, and easier work. These motives were rarely attributed to males, since women rarely have the power to confer these rewards. Ego motives included excitement, ego satisfaction, and adventure. People with sincere motives were those who were genuinely "in love" and who were seeking companionship and a spouse. As noted above, in our mobile and work-oriented society, where people are increasingly cut off from family and other social institutions, the workplace tends to become the primary setting for meeting people (Driscoll and Bova 1980; Driscoll 1981).

When the motives of male and female partners were compared and evaluated, three types of relationships appeared:

- "The Fling" occurs when both male and female have ego motives. It is characterized by a high level of excitement on the part of both participants, who often believe that the relationship is going to be of short duration.
- "True Love" occurs when both participants have love motives. It usually, but not always, occurs between two unmarried people and leads to marriage.
- "The Utilitarian" relationship occurs when the male has ego motives and the female job motives. He meets his needs for excitement or ego satisfaction while she meets her needs for advancement, job security, or increased power.

Even if proximity and motive are favorable to the start of a romance, certain characteristics of the workplace may serve as a deterrent. The important work group characteristics, which are often interrelated, are: rules and expectations, closeness of supervision, closeness of interpersonal relationships, and intensity or criticalness of the work or mission. Many organizations have explicit rules against romantic entanglements, more or less strictly enforced, and others have no written rules but rather firm expectations. On the other hand, in some organizations the expectation is that sexual activity will occur, and women are hired more for their sexual attractiveness than their work skills. Close supervision and the existence of other intimate relationships (a spouse or steady relationship) tend to act as deterrents, and the work group sometimes expresses disapproval, especially if the members feel that the image or reputation of the group is threatened. In these cases, the lovers may respond to pressure by breaking off the relationship or by becoming more discreet. Finally, intensity or criticalness of the work or mission is usually, but not always, a deterrent. Relationships may flourish because there is not enough work to do and people are bored. However, on occasion, great pressure that includes long hours and intense concentration leads to romantic involvement (Quinn 1977).

The inclination, or even the opportunity, for a sexual liaison does not, of course, necessarily mean that a romantic involvement will occur. However, the man and woman who work closely together always suffer the suspicion that they may be romantically or sexually involved and inevitably suffer the consequences of that suspicion. It is clearly a fallacy to assume automatically when a woman and man are seen enjoying each other's company that, first, there is a sexual attraction between them and, second, that attraction always leads to bed. In reality, a series of stages lies between attraction and sexual consummation, a developmental sequence that varies in duration:

- *Curiosity:* the couple are interested in getting to know each other.
- *Exploration:* when proximity occurs and curiosity is aroused, the couple look for ways to spend more time together, either socially or professionally.
- *Friendship:* the couple finds mutual interests, begins to share thoughts and feelings. They make time to be together.
- *Intimacy:* The couple takes the risk of revealing to each other their vulnerability, admitting weakness, failures, ambitions, and expectations.
- *Sexuality:* Strong sexual desires and passions are aroused; the intimacy is consummated.
- *Commitment:* The pair decide to build a future together (Josefewitz 1982).

Most relationships stay within the first two stages. And of course the first four stages could be used to describe same-sex friendships as well as mixed-sex ones. It is possible for people to have intimate friendships, even to be sexually attracted to each other, without having intercourse. Nevertheless, their attraction, whether consummated or not, will not go unnoticed and will have consequences for the individuals and for the organization (Bender 1979). The impact on the organization will depend upon a combination of four factors: visibility of the relationship, behavior changes in the participants, reactions of other members of the organization, and the overall impact on the system (Quinn 1977).

In most cases, couples try to keep their relationships secret from their co-workers, either because of rules forbidding fraternization or because of the fear of gossip or general disapproval. However, in most cases efforts at secrecy are doomed to failure. Work groups are highly sensitive to even slight changes in behavior, especially when sexual behavior may be involved. Being seen away from work together, having longer or more frequent conversations, or lunching together may arouse curiosity and gossip, even in the absence of direct evidence like being caught in the supply closet. Of course, if one or the other of the couple is operating out of ego motives, it will be necessary to reveal the relationship, which is sometimes done quite subtly but nonetheless effectively.

Behavior changes can be positive or negative. Some people become energized; they are happier, easier to get along with, more willing to work. Others change for the worse; they become preoccupied, make sometimes costly errors, increase their absences or tardiness. They may become either indifferent to or highly sensitive to criticism. In a utilitarian romance, changes of power may occur. The male in the higher position is able to give the female her desired rewards, favorable treatment, increased power, or advancement; at the same time he may become less accessible to other subordinates.

Reactions of other members of the organization may run the gamut from approval and encouragement to strong disapproval and punishment. If the couple are each unmarried and no power shifts are involved, others may enjoy a vicarious romantic relationship or at least remain indifferent. But if the affair is not perceived as legitimate, or when competence and power changes are pronounced, members begin to develop strategies for coping with the relationship (Collins 1983). These might include anything from counseling or advising one or both members on the negative effects of their behavior, to blackmail, ostracism, and quitting.

A number of points can be made in summarizing the sexual element of contemporary organizational life. The workplace is increasingly a primary setting for establishing new relationships, both of the same sex and the opposite sex. As women increasingly move into new levels of the hierarchy and into nontraditional female occupations, the old rules and taboos against organizational romances are no longer effective. Competent, ambitious people find each other attractive, and when women and men are together that attraction often turns to sexual desire, and that desire is sometimes but not always consummated. Whether or not a couple is sexually active, any changes in their behavior or performance will be noted by other members of the organization. They will be the subject of office gossip and, if others in the organization feel resentful or disapproving, they may be subject to negative sanctions. Although there is the possibility for the development of sincere love relationships leading to marriage, a consequence that would meet with organizational approval, there is also the possibility that the attraction will cause problems for the couple and have negative impacts on the organization, in the form of disruption, loss of productivity, and even increased turnover.

A corollary to this concern is that people may avoid working together for fear that a mutual romantic attachment might develop, that a nonmutual, nonreciprocated attraction might cause embarrassment to one or the other, or that even in the absence of any involvement, speculation or gossip will hurt their careers or reputations. To the extent that such fears discourage males from working with competent females, there can be serious damage to the females' careers and serious loss of productivity to the organization.

Management is not very good at dealing with these situations. In the past, when rules against fraternization or taboos discouraged it, management might have taken steps to end a romance that became public knowledge, usually by firing, transferring, or demoting the woman. That remedy is still frequently used, but in cases where the couple are on equal levels or the woman is higher in rank, it's less likely that she will be the one punished (Collins 1983). The most frequent managerial response is no response, but there are times when management cannot or should not ignore the matter. In those cases, several specific remedies should be considered:

- reevaluating and clarifying fraternization and nepotism policies, communicating them clearly to members, and applying them consistently and fairly;
- making counseling or other resources available to members having difficulty dealing with feelings of attraction;
- raising the topic as a legitimate issue as a part of team-building efforts (Driscoll and Bova 1980);
- treating the relationship as a conflict of interest rather than a moral issue;
- persuading the couple that the person least essential to the company (in reality usually the woman) or both should leave the organization and helping the ousted person find other employment (Collins 1983).

None of these remedies is easy to implement. The nepotism/fraternization policy issue becomes increasingly complex as cohabitation, homosexuality, and singleness become increasingly common lifestyles. The company must create policies that are realistic and enforceable and that provide the protections against abuse that such policies were designed for originally (Bender 1979). The other remedies require that management acknowledge and discuss the issue of sexuality in their organizations, and most of them are poorly equipped for such a task (Jamison 1983).

Individuals can take some steps to avoid having sexual attraction interfere with their working relationships. First of all they must recognize that their actions will not go unnoticed. Women and men who work together, especially if their work requires meals or travel together, must be like Ceasar's wife. They must not only avoid sin they must avoid the appearance of sin. Women can refuse to play the seductress and to play out the pseudoseduction plot. Both men and women must be sensitive to the concerns of spouses and recognize that, legitimate or not, there will inevitably be some curiosity, at the least, about a work partner who is a potential sex partner. To what extent husbands or wives should be or can be considered in adjusting one's work behavior has to be an individual decision, but it is unrealistic to ignore the fact that jealousy can be aroused and can be a serious problem (Bender 1979). Good working relationships often require social as well as task-related interactions. But couples who spend time alone together increase the likelihood that they will be the subject of gossip. Three's a crowd, according to an old axiom, and a crowd may protect reputations.

So far we have been talking about ways to avoid gossip. But what happens to couples who feel a strong attraction but who cannot or choose not to consummate the relationship. The conventional wisdom of psychology suggests that couples can resolve this problem, like any problem, by acknowledging it and talking openly about it. However, such an approach seems fairly unrealistic. Women are so thoroughly socialized to be sexually passive that few women would be willing or able to broach the subject of sexual attraction to a male co-worker. Men who are taught to be sexually aggressive have little experience in articulating feelings of any kind, much less feelings of sexual ambivalence or restraint. Either party, however, may find some help in talking the situation out with a trusted same-sex friend, preferably one who is not a member of the organization.

FEMALE/FEMALE RELATIONSHIPS

There are two opposing paradigms of women's relationships with other women, and to at least some extent each is grounded in reality. On the one hand, women are seen as having close, supportive, long-lasting and intimate nonsexual relationships with other women, and on the other hand women are often viewed as treating other women with distrust, suspicion, or outright dislike; women can be friends or foes. In some ways these two types of relationship are analogous to the female stereotypes of woman as "Madonna," that is, as supporting and nurturing, and woman as evil. In organizational settings, we can see both of these types of relationships existing and to some extent being detrimental to the advancement of women.

Women as Friends

Studies of children's relationships show sex differences from preschool age on. Little boys are more sociable and more affiliative than little girls, in the sense that they interact more frequently in a positive social way with other children in their age groups. Girls have fewer of these interactions, but they are more likely to like the people with whom they interact, even if their friends' behavior occasionally disappoints them. In the early school years girls focus their play in intensive relations with one or two "best friends," while boys play in larger groups. At junior-high-age young girls establish a closer degree of intimacy in their friendships and reveal more personal secrets than do boys; possibly because of this self-disclosure they may be less likely than boys to accept a newcomer into their "inner circle," although they may be friendly toward her (Maccoby and Jacklin 1974).

At least through college age, this pattern of intimacy in friendship continues. Women and men tend to have equivalent numbers of friends and to put the same value on friendship, but their interactions are quite different. Women prefer getting together with friends "just to talk" and talk centers on feelings, problems, and personal relationships. Men prefer activities such as sports, and when they do talk it is about shared activities and interests. While members of each sex describe themselves as putting an equal value on intimacy and as having an equal number of intimate friends, it appears they may have different standards for assessing intimacy. The women's interactions with a best friend are more personal and involve more self-disclosure (Caldwell and Peplau 1982).

The question raised by these studies is not so much about the nature of women's friendships as the nature of men's. Women tend, at least through college age, to continue the pattern of intimate friendships with their best friends, although by college age they seem to have expanded the scope of their acquaintances.

Unfortunately, little is known about the extent to which these patterns continue into adult life. Most studies of adults have concentrated on self-disclosure in mixed-sex dyads, usually in marriage, and rather surprisingly have found few differences (Maccoby and Jacklin 1974). Conflicting data on adult same-sex friendships suggest that there may be significant differences in terms of both the number and the intensity of relationships depending upon age, employment, and marital status (Wright 1982; Caldwell and Peplau 1982). The media often portray women continuing childhood patterns, not only sharing intimate secrets with other women but conspiring with them against men, usually their husbands. Thus Lucy continually plotted with Ethel to manipulate Ricky in "I Love Lucy"; Laura (Mary Tyler Moore) and her next-door neighbor Milly shared every aspect of their suburban lifestyle and often conspired against their husbands on the "Dick Van Dyke Show." Later in her own show, Moore again had a confidante and sometimes conspirator, her best friend Rhoda. To what extent these depictions reflect reality for adult women is unclear. Much more attention has been focused on the hostility between women.

Women as Foes

Women, it is frequently argued, must depend on men for their support, survival, and status. Men are valued for their ability to provide and protect, and women must compete with each other for the attention of, and ultimately marriage to, the most desirable men. This perception is also reflected in the media, most often perhaps in both daytime and night-time soap operas, where men are constantly portrayed as sex objects over which beautiful but desperate women compete in the most aggressive and manipulative ways possible. If this view is accurate, then it would support the suggestion in the reseach literature that the "best friend" sharing of intimacies begins to disappear after puberty.

A psychoanalytic view posits that there are indeed barriers between women and argues that they are rooted in the mother/daughter relation-ship (Caplan 1981). As young girls become conscious of gender identity and the rules of behavior that are governed by one's sex, they recognize their similarities to their mothers, both physically and in the way they are viewed by society. How they are viewed, of course, is as nurturant, and little girls recognize very early that they will be valued primarily for their success in filling this role. This recognition plants the seeds for feelings of both alliance and hostility between mother and daughter, which in turn generalizes to all relationships between women. The barriers between women come from several sources:

1. The nurturant role is so hurriedly and so thoroughly taught to young female children that they may be pushed out of the nurtured role before they are ready, leaving them feeling insecure and inadequately loved. When they become mothers of daughters themselves, they may rely on their own daughters to supply the nurturance that they crave. In a more general sense, women come to expect nurturance from other women. Their husbands typically maintain a certain amount of emotional distance and fail to provide the kind of nurturance that they desire. In modern times, geographic mobility may cut them off from extended families and networks of friends, making them more dependent on their husbands than ever. And since social norms restrict their freedom to talk about their husbands' failings, their freedom to turn to other women is impaired. Added to this is the feeling that women belong to an inferior class so are not the first choice of nurturance. When a woman does turn to a woman friend, it is with a real sense of need and also with a conviction that the woman ought to be available to nurture her. If the woman is not, in fact, there for her, the rejection produces a real sense of rage.

The nurturant role can also explain the jealousy between women. Women are taught that their activities are restricted to their ability to "look attractive, act nice, be helpful, and take care of others." They are prohibited from doing anything active, productive, or pleasurable out-side those limits. Further, they must rely on a man to take care of them, but they cannot approach or request a commitment from him directly. They must achieve a commitment by being as conspicuously attractive, nice, helpful, and nurturant as possible. The only things that can get in the way of success are failure to be as attractive, nice, helpful, and nurturant as you might be, or another woman, or both. Women come to direct their anger and fear both at themselves and at other women and not at the men they compete for.

The restriction of female activities to nurturing also results in women avoiding substantive conversations with other women, since it may seem masculine to talk about business or world affairs. It may also result in women using the role as a kind of crutch, substituting vicarious experience for real experience in the role of confidante or advisor. This role may mask jealousy or disappointment, which, again, tends to get turned toward the other woman.

2. The devaluing of women, so pervasive in our society, causes both women and men to place less value on the friendship, judgment, and opinions of women than of men. Women spend time with other women only when there is no chance to spend it with a man. Since women tend to put a low value on their own worth, they tend to put the same low value on the worth of others like them. This devaluing of women explains the oft-heard statement by women that "I really don't like women; I prefer the company of men." Perhaps what they are really saying is that they want to be like men, superior to women.

3. Constraints are placed on the behavior of girls that are not placed on boys. Limits are placed on physical activity, sexual play and exploration, and the expression of anger and aggression. These behaviors are suppressed because they are inconsistent with the nurturant role. These restrictions are carried into adult life, where women who deviate from them, women who break the rules, receive negative sanctions and are ostracized by other women. These sanctions are fueled by fears that untraditional behavior will be seen as potentially possible for all women, which might be threatening to men or, even worse, might be attractive to them.

4. The fear of homosexuality, or the fear of rearing a homosexual child, limits the physical interactions between a mother and daughter in ways that don't apply to mother/son, father/son, or father/daughter relationships. There is, of course, a certain amount of unconscious sexual content in the daily interactions of parents and children, especially small children. Despite incest taboos, the norm of heterosexuality and the higher value put on male children permit a good deal of physical intimacy and eroticism between a mother and her infant son. Between mothers and daughters, however, the homosexual taboo may limit these expressions. Fathers, on the other hand, are in general less nurturant and spend less time in caring for children of either sex. So while the fear of homosexuality might inhibit his relationships with a male child, the issue is moot since he doesn't take care of the child anyway. And the daughter, who receives less nurturing from her mother and might benefit from heterosexual contact with her father, is denied it.

The preference for heterosexuality may also explain hostility between adult women. Sex role behavior prescribes that males be inexpressive and females expressive, and this is seen as a sort of divine plan occuring in nature. It follows from this that relationships between females will acquire a level of emotional intensity not found in male/male or male/female relationships. Both women and men subscribe to this myth of the greater emotionality of women and fear the emotional energy generated in relationships between women. While a man may tolerate a woman's emotional outbursts, a woman may respond with an equally intense outburst of her own. The result is the petty, childish bickering often associated with female behavior. Even mature and responsible women fear that being around another woman will arouse feelings and fears with a greater degree of intensity than would occur with a man. In order to avoid arousing feelings that they cannot suppress, they may avoid close relationships with women altogether.

5. The very similarity between women, both physical and emotional, is a source of hostility between them. Because of this similarity, women see other women as a kind of mirror image of themselves, expecting to find in them a response to their own needs for nurturance. When they fail to find it, they become angry and hurt. Daughters look at their mothers and say "That's me in thirty years," and to the extent that what they see is limited and repressed, they experience disappointment and resentment. The similarity exacerbates the feeling that children generally have that their parents can read their minds. Since the mother spends the most time with the children, and since she is most like the girl child, the child may experience feelings of intrusiveness and loss of privacy. She may find it particularly difficult to break away from her mother at adolescence (Caplan 1981).

These five sources of hostility are said to create barriers between all women, not just mothers and daughters. One could question the Freudian determinism of the argument, but there is a certain compelling logic about it nonetheless. There is little evidence that this hostility is universal, but that may be irrelevant. To the extent that such hostility does exist, this psychological explanation for it is probably as good as any. It does seem to explain why the "best friend" behavior of prepubescent girls sometimes turns into suspicion and hostility at adolescence.

Women in Organizations

In organizations, evidence supports both paradigms of female relationships. Women tend to form very close, stable relationships with their co-workers, but they also experience conflict and competition with female peers, subordinates, and superiors.

Women as Friends

Often women in organizations, particularly clerical workers or others in occupations with little opportunity for upward mobility, form very cohesive peer groups. For women in these occupations, peer group acceptance is often more important than other aspects of their job and a more important reward than intrinsic factors. This behavior is sometimes threatening to out-groups in the organization and leads some to conclude that "women always stick together." The behavior tends to support the stereotype of women as having a few close "best friends."

This behavior, however, may be a function of the blocked upward mobility of these occupations, rather than of their being female. People get "stuck," that is, reach the top of their career level, in organizations for a variety of reasons, but women are stuck almost from the beginning. Their career ladders tend to be short, and the differences in pay and other rewards between the bottom and the top are relatively small. For stuck employees, peer group norms are likely to develop around and support the generally lower level of aspirations. For one thing, these people stay together on the job longer than people who are moving upward, so the group membership is fairly stable and very important.

Powerful others in the organization have little to offer stuck employees in terms of rewards, and so group members tend to focus attention on each other, rather than on higher status people. In fact group solidarity is often maintained by criticizing or ridiculing higher level groups or individuals. These groups can be compared to adolescent gangs that develop norms of mutual aid and loyalty. Pressure to remain loyal to the group is sometimes so strong that the offer of a promotion may create a very real dilemma. Promotions for clerical workers often carry small rewards, either intrinsic or extrinsic, and accepting the promotion often means exclusion from the group. Since for women, especially, there may be no comparable group at the next level, the result may be isolation (Kanter 1977).

The existence of these groups can be explained as a function of rewards; women fail to find intrinsic rewards in the kind of work that is permitted to them and turn instead to the rewards that come from group membership (Kanter 1977). However, it may also be that women form and maintain these close-knit groups because they are seeking (and finding) nurturance. If, in fact, women fail to find the desired level of emotional intimacy and support in their primary relationships with their husbands, they may find it instead in their secondary relationships with their co-workers. And since these relationships endure over long periods and absorb a substantial portion of time, and since women's relationships tend to be intense, it's not at all surprising that these groups become extremely important and at least potentially satisfying.

Women as Foes

On the other hand, many upwardly mobile management or professional women report conflict and competition among women peers, indifferent or hostile reactions from clericals, and hostility from senior women in their organizations, all of which would support the notion of a general level of hostility among women. A number of explanations can be offered.

If it's true that women look to other women for support and nurturance and feel angry and frustrated when they fail to get it, then surely women who find themselves virtually isolated in organizations could be expected to experience such feelings. As women break into new occupational areas, they find themselves both isolated and visible. They must be not only highly competent but also able to understand and participate in the political and strategic processes of the organization. Change tends to occur very slowly in organizations, and managements may move very cautiously in appointing and promoting women, waiting to see the results of each step before proceeding with another. So while there may be many promotional opportunities for men, there may be far fewer for women. The political reality may be that the only real competition that an upwardly mobile career woman encounters is that presented by the other women at her level. She then finds herself in the position of needing and wanting support and friendship from the only people around who are not in a position to give it to her.

If the young woman executive looks to her secretary for support or encouragement, the chances are she may not find it there either. It's almost a truism that clerical women are less helpful to women than to men bosses. The reasons are numerous and probably have more to do with the devaluing of women than with a need for nurturance.

First, people in general prefer to work for people with power. For women, especially, often the only avenue to advancement is to attach oneself to a powerful and upwardly mobile employer. If a female secretary perceives her female boss as being less powerful or less promotable, there is little incentive to provide the level of support and services that she would to a similarly placed male.

Second, there is a traditional role involved in the boss/subordinate relationship that requires that the boss be dominant and the subordinate submissive. This relationship is possible between a male boss and a female secretary, even if the woman is considerably older than the man. The woman playing the office wife or mother not only provides direct job services but may serve as both his listening post and spokesperson, giving and receiving information that is important to him. However, among women, the only basis for dominance/submission is the mother/daughter relationship, one that is often filled with conflict. In effect, the subordinate woman responds to her female manager as she would to her mother;

she may, for instance, withhold information from her and spread gossip about her. The situation tends to be further exacerbated if there is a considerable age difference between the two.

Third, clerical women may feel that the woman manager's position or behavior is sex role deviant or inappropriate. She may feel that the woman is neglecting or abandoning her role as wife or mother, which she may then translate as a denigration of those roles. If, for instance, the clerical woman has subjugated her own abilities or ambitions to devote her primary energies to her family, she may feel very strong resentment toward a woman who opts to put a career first before marriage or motherhood.

Fourth, women in professional or managerial positions often choose not to become a part of the clique in the secretariat ranks. They recognize a need to distance themselves from the clerical ranks in order to achieve legitimacy in the organization. However, this may mean that they must reject offers of friendship from the very women that they count on for administrative services. If they are also isolates in the organization without a peer group at their own level, they will seem very aloof to their subordinates.

Finally, the woman's work is often seen as simply less important and less urgent than a comparable man's. So that, for instance, in a situation when male and female managers must share the services of a secretary, clerk, or typing pool, the clericals may exercise their discretion by doing the man's work sooner or better. For all these reasons, and probably many others, women in nontraditional roles often find themselves abandoned or sabotaged by the people they most expect to support them.

The Queen Bee Syndrome

Women at entry and middle management levels find that they meet with competition from women at their own level and antagonism from women at a lower level. Often in their search for support, they turn upward in the organization to the women who have "made it," the one or two women in upper management, only to find that there, too, they are unwelcome. The values of the women's movement would argue that these women, of all women, having struggled against enormous odds to achieve success in a male-dominated culture, would turn and offer a helping hand to ease the journey for younger women. Often they do, but often they don't. Some of these women respond with an attitude that says: "If I can do it, anybody can. I didn't need a whole movement to help me and neither do they." This response has been referred to as the Queen Bee Syndrome, and several reasons are advanced for its occurrence.

First of all, these women have been co-opted by the system. In order to survive and flourish they have taken on the attitudes, behaviors, and protective cover of the male culture.

Second, these women enjoy a very special position, with a great many rewards, since they enjoy not only the benefits and perquisites that come to all successful people but also the attentions that come from being the only woman in an all-male group. They see other women as competitors and as threats to their privileged position. They certainly don't want other women to enjoy the fruits of success without having to go through the same struggles that they did. Surprisingly, women identified as queen bees reveal attitudes toward work and family more like those of traditional women and men and less like feminist women. They tend, for instance, to agree with the statement: "Women have only themselves to blame for not doing better in life" and to disagree with the statement: "Special courtesies extended to women tend to keep them helpless and in their place" (Staines, Tavris, and Jayaratne 1974).

It would be a mistake, however, to conclude that "queen bee" behavior is a sex-related trait. Many men take the attitude that success is a product of individual effort and achievement, take pride in the fact that they have worked very hard to reach success, and take pleasure in seeing that younger people struggle just as hard or harder than they did. Maccoby reports in *The Gamesman* (1976) that 40 percent of the male managers he interviewed believed that "the fittest should survive." On the other hand, in a study of attitudes toward women as managers, women with high levels of education, regardless of salary or organizational level, reported very favorable attitudes toward women managers (Terborg et al. 1977). These results would seem to predict that the Queen Bee Syndrome is not as prevalent as expected. The important point, however, is not that this is a characteristic unique to relationships between women but that it is one dimension of the very complex set of interactions that working women engage in with other women.

The conclusion we come to is that the structure of most organizations encourages women to remain in low-opportunity positions and rewards them for doing so with important and satisfying peer group relationships. The woman who seeks achievement in the nontraditional occupations may find herself alternatively cut off from and in competition with other women, at her own level, at the subordinate level, and at the top management level.

MALE/MALE RELATIONSHIPS

Men's relationships with other men have always been seen as being characterized by warmth, good fellowship, laughter, and caring. Men are generally assumed to prefer the company of other men and to have significant and long-lasting friendships. As we saw in Chapter 5, organizations like the Boy Scouts and the YMCA were very successful in the early part of the century because they gave men a legitimate reason to spend a good deal of time away from the influence and domination of women. Throughout history men have cherished and protected their right to participate in all-male groups. The hunting party of tribal societies may have been organized for the purpose of providing food, but some sociologists maintain that it was more important as a social phenomenon, since, for one thing, the women and children had to continue to gather food while the hunting party was away. The hunting party has almost exact replicas in the hunting, fishing, and camping trips that some men enjoy for recreational purposes today. The men's hut in tribal societies was a place where women were excluded, and where the men could both talk "men's talk" and discuss the important issues facing the tribe. Today men withdraw to their clubs, lodges, and sometimes the neighborhood tavern for the same purposes.

One of the most visible vestiges of the men's hut is the Bohemian Grove in northern California, where for two weeks every summer men of great wealth and influence from all over the country, and even the world, gather in secrecy to do whatever it is they do. Women are excluded entirely from the camp, although apparently not from the nearby towns and resorts. Reports from the Grove suggest that during the encampment, these men, heads of state and captains of industry all, dress and behave in a variety of bizarre ways, drink and eat lavishly, participate in a variety of musical and dramatic entertainments, and discuss major political and economic issues.

This preference for and enjoyment of members of one's own sex has been called homosocial behavior (as opposed to "homosexual" behavior) because it does not necessarily involve explicit erotic sexual interaction. Sociobiologists assert that the tendency for males to congregate in groups began with the hunting party and with the need for males to cooperate in order to protect not only themselves but also their women and children. Because those who were successful in forming and maintaining groups were the ones who survived, the tendency to group behavior has become part of the genetic code so that now "male bonding" is an innate quality in males (Tiger 1969). The evidence to support this conclusion, however, is based largely on animal studies (Tavris and Offir 1977).

Whatever the origins of homosocial behavior, men can and often do satisfy most of their needs with other men, including intellectual, physical, political, economic, occupational, social, power, and status needs. Men, it has been argued, need women only to satisfy their need for paternity, "the ultimate claim to masculinity." The homosocial world gives men access to unequal power and resources in the society. The ultimate homosocial world, perhaps, is the Mafia, a family without women, characterized by territoriality, dominance, resource acquisition, and loyalty. The upper-class male club is simply a refined version of the Mafia (Lipman-Blumen 1975). Thus the Bohemian Grove encampment could be seen as a sort of metaphorical mafia.

Nevertheless, masculinity in our culture is characterized by inexpressiveness, and the inexpressive male has a pattern of friendships that is quite different in character from that of women. Men may have a wide circle of acquaintants but few if any real friends (Fasteau 1974).

Among even very young boy children, the attraction of group membership and the lack of intimacy is apparent. Boys, as opposed to girls, have more social interactions with children their own age. Unlike girls, they don't seem to care very much whether they like their playmates. The important element is the game, and when they have the chance to choose partners or teammates, they will choose on the basis of skill or ability rather than personal attraction. Among very young children, boys tend to form more intense relationships than girls, in that they always seem to play with the same children and to avoid others. Later, however, by about age 7, the pattern drifts substantially. At this age girls focus their attention on one or two best friends, but boys play in larger groups and form gangs. By junior-high-age boys are more likely than girls to welcome a newcomer into their group, which seems to suggest that their friendships involve less self-revelation (Maccoby and Jacklin 1974).

At college age, both quantitative and qualitative differences between women's and men's friendships are apparent. Men and women tend to have about the same number of friendships, but the evidence as to the intensity of the relationships is contradictory. One recent study rejected the notion that women's friendship's are face-to-face while men's are side-by-side, and found that, in fact, women's and men's friendships are equal in terms of intensity and duration (Wright 1982). However, the preponderance of the evidence shows that women prefer to spend their time with their friends talking, while men prefer to spend it doing active things together, suggesting that men would be less prone to self-disclosure (Caldwell and Peplau 1982). College males report very little intimacy and a good deal of competition with their male peers. When they do reveal themselves, they are more likely to disclose to their closest woman friend than to anyone else, including either their male friends or their parents (Komarovsky 1976). Even men who report fairly intense and long-lasting relationships tend to emphasize external interests and mutual activities. They also tend to see their friends in a differentiated way—different friends for different activities or interests (Wright 1982).

When men reach adulthood, this friendship pattern seems to hold constant. Successful male managers have defined friendship pretty much in the same way that the student populations did: a friend was someone you could rely on, someone you could trust, someone who would warn you of danger and protect you from misjudgment. Most of the managers reported themselves as wanting to have friends, but very few gave wanting to help others as a goal in life. Perhaps not surprisingly, few of them had any real friends ("only acquaintances," one said). They seemed unable or unwilling to give or take the kind of criticism that would constitute friendship, relying instead on a value system that encouraged uncritical admiration and support (M. Maccoby 1976).

The camaraderie of men in all-male or predominantly male work groups, as reported by the men themselves, is similar to that observed in other settings. Groups of comparative strangers rely on stories about sexual adventures and exploits, off-color jokes, stories about either work or sports prowess, and stories about capacity for food and drink. When a woman is present the men, rather than tempering their inclination to tell these stories, may become more boisterous, show off for the woman, and increase the degree of sexual or business prowess contained in their "war stories." Men will occasionally use sexual innuendos, locker-room humor, or business successes to test the woman's acceptance of the dominant male culture or to underscore the woman's exclusion from the group (Kanter 1977).

It's clear, then, that males do seem to prefer the company of other males and to turn to them for gratification of most of their needs. However, they apparently often fail to find their needs for friendship or intimacy satisfied. This estrangement has been called "the lost art of buddyhood" (H. Goldberg 1976). Men are constantly "checking each other out," comparing themselves with other men, competing not only in sports or business but for the attention of women. They are often fearful that a friend might do better at something like career or sports, which would spell the end of the friendship.

As a consequence, men are blocked on both sides from friendship with other men. They cannot share their failures, for fear of being seen as weak, and they cannot share their success, for fear of being boastful or of inciting jealousy. The only safe conversational topics are cars, sports, and politics; the only safe friends are women. To make matters worse, close friendships among men are often looked at with suspicion. The need for a buddy is often perceived by others as adolescent or immature, or worse as a sign of latent homosexuality. Wives often resent the time spent with a buddy and interfere whenever possible. Friendships become acceptable only when they involve some business trade-off or when they are directed toward some external goal.

It's less clear why this estrangement occurs. The barriers to intimacy between men include competition, homophobia, aversion to vulnerability and openness, and a lack of role models (Lewis 1978). The strain of competition is greatly exacerbated by the pressure to compete in athletics, which imbues in both athletic and nonathletic boys the importance of winning, of constant high levels of performance, and of being a high individual performer within the team (Stein and Hoffman 1978). The values of both group loyalty and team performance and individual identity within the group are fostered by the military, particularly in basic training. The inferiority of women and the danger of homosexuality are also highly stressed in the military, making any real friendships nearly impossible. In Latin and Mediterranean cultures, where the natural expression of feelings is more accepted, men have more latitude in expressing emotions toward male friends. But to avoid any suspicion of homosexuality, they counter this behavior with almost continuous preoccupation with the pursuit and conquest of women (Safilios-Rothschild 1977).

Tiger (1969) and others may argue for the superiority of male friendships. Men may, in fact, have a biological propensity or predisposition to male bonding. They may have an inherent need for real social contact with other males. If that is so, it would seem that for many, the need is far from being met.

SUMMARY

Women and men differ biologically and socially. They also differ in the nature of their social interactions. Men and women tend to interact with each other in ways that enact their stereotypical roles and at the same time reinforce their differential power and status. They often bring these social roles into the organization and adapt them to organizational roles in nonsexual ways. However, increasingly organizational taboos against office romances are being relaxed, as are sexual mores in general. And increasingly the office romance, or the potential office romance, is causing problems not only for individuals but for management as well.

Women's relationships with other women have been the subject of a good deal of study, mostly by psychologists. Women are capable of, and often have, close, intimate, and enduring friendships with other women, relationships that are often characterized by a high degree of self-disclosure. But women also often find themselves in competition with other women, for nurturance, for the attentions of men, and more recently for job opportunities. Women in organizations often supply much needed help and support for each other, but they also often provide antagonism or outright hostility.

Men from the youngest ages tend to have wide circles of acquaintances, and their preferred method of interacting with them is in sharing of interests or activities. They put a high value on membership in these groups, whether they are exclusive clubs or street gangs. Acceptance by the group and loyalty to the group are essential. Some evidence exists for the theory that men have an innate need to have some sort of relationship with other men, but the exact nature of the need or the ideal kind of re-lationship is unclear. Men may crave a more intimate, sharing, and sup-portive relationship with a true friend or buddy, but social and sexual norms of competitiveness and homophobia make that virtually impossi-ble in adulthood.

Men come to the workplace, a primary arena for the validation of their masculinity, with a need to belong to the dominant group and perhaps with a need for intimate friendship. Their work relationships tend to follow the pattern established in social roles. They compete within the group through "male verbal dueling," taunting each other with tales of their sexual conquests, their sports achievements, and their business successes. They avoid friendships with other men that might involve self-disclosure or that might be perceived as having a homosexual potential. They form safe, cohesive groups that exert power within the organiza-tion, and they use the power of these groups to control the culture and to exclude and isolate individuals who constitute a threat, such as women and minority group members.

Men's relationships to other men at work are not, as most of the liter-ature of organizations implies, devoid of sexual content. Men in organiza-tions, like men everywhere, are constantly in the process of competing with, comparing themselves with, and seeking validation from, other men. The entry of women into the "men's hut" means that men must now compete with women as well as with men. The nature of the contest and the value of the outcome is greatly changed, in much the same way that the value of prizefighting would be changed if women competed with men in the ring. Or if women played football. Or if women were allowed into combat in the army. The value of these activities, in allowing men to exhibit their prowess in order to win the respect, admiration, or friendship of other men, and in order to validate their own masculinity, is lost. After all, how can you validate your masculinity by going 15 rounds with a woman? And what would happen to your masculinity if you lost?

7
Communication

Whenever conflict arises, whenever carefully laid plans go awry, whenever hopes are frustrated and dreams shattered, someone is sure to attribute the problem to a breakdown in communication. And indeed there is always some truth in this attribution. But the statement is often so vague as to be meaningless. What is communication and why is it important in organizational life? Why does miscommunication occur so often? How does it occur? And, of course, how do sex and role contribute to communication or miscommunication?

Communication is the process of exchanging meaning. More specifically, communication consists "of a *sender* transmitting a *message* through *media* to a *receiver* who *responds*" (Kotler 1980). Communication is the essential life blood of organizational life. Organizations require, almost by definition, both differentiation and coordination. An organization can be defined as two or more individuals working toward accomplishment of some common goal. The term "organization" implies some division of labor (differentiation) both horizontally and vertically. Differentiation, in turn, requires some means of coordinating and controlling the activities of the various members and units of the organization (coordination). That coordination, in turn, requires the ability to exchange meaning. It requires communication.

Communication requires three sets of behaviors: sending, receiving, and responding. Miscommunication can occur in several ways. One, the sender simply neglects to send, that is, the person with some vital piece of information neglects to transmit it to the relevant others in the organization. Two, the sender sends the information, but the receiver fails to receive it. Again, two errors are possible. Either the receiver receives no message at all, or, usually worse, the receiver receives a message but misapprehends it, that is, the meaning that the receiver attaches to the message is not the same meaning that the sender intended. Third, the receiver can fail to respond, or, once again, the response can be misunderstood. In any of these cases, the results may be costly for the individuals and for the organization.

Let's take an example. Mary Jones is production manager for the Sicilian Pizzeria and Gelateria. Jim Smith, a catering salesperson has sold a large order of anchovy pizza and kumquat gelato for the Republican fund raiser on a Sunday afternoon in the suburban town of Griede. He processes the order so that it comes to Jones's attention two days before the scheduled event. She is temporarily awaiting a shipment of anchovies from Peru, kumquats are out of season, and the delivery person is getting married on Sunday and has been promised the day off. Clearly, a case of failure to communicate. Smith will no doubt argue that he should have been told that these products and services were not available at this time. Jones will argue that he should not commit the firm to extraordinary orders without checking first to see that they are feasible. Each, of course, is partially right, but that doesn't undo the damage that is done to the firm or to each of them.

Sometimes, of course, messages are sent and not received. In this case Jones has issued a routine memo to all department heads indicating which gelato flavors would be available for the next six weeks and which would be in short supply. But the memo is piled on the desk of Smith's boss; salespeople don't have time to read a lot of paperwork. Instead, Smith had called Jones's office and talked to her secretary, who said he thought for sure they could manage it. Smith didn't ask him to check with Jones, and he didn't. Smith perceived his question as a formal request and the answer as an assurance that his order could be filled. The secretary, who was a temporary from Western Girl, perceived Smith's question as a request for his opinion, gave his opinion for what it was worth—not much—and saw no reason to pass on the information to Jones. In this case, the miscommunication is more complex, but the result is the same: an unhappy customer, an angry salesman, and a frustrated production manager.

This example is highly simplistic, of course. The dynamics of the communication process involve the shared meaning of a great many symbols, both verbal (written or spoken words) and nonverbal (all message carriers other than words). And in both verbal and nonverbal communication, sex differences confound and increase the problems of clear communication.

VERBAL COMMUNICATION

Language provides some powerful evidence of the inequity that exists in our society between the roles of women and men. Women experience discrimination in language in two ways: "in the way they are taught to use language and in the way language use treats them" (Lakoff 1975). In both of these ways, women are relegated to such subservient functions as sex object or servant, and for this reason certain words have different meanings when applied to men or to women. These different meanings rely exclusively on the different roles played by the sexes in our society.

Women and men use language differently. Men speak in forceful ways that are considered unfeminine for women. Women use words, phrases, or intonations that would be considered effeminate if used by men. The implications of this are that women in our society are caught in a double bind. If they talk like men, forcefully or emphatically, they are labeled as unfeminine; if they talk like women they are ridiculed as unable to think clearly, as unable to take part in a serious discussion, even in some sense as less than fully human.

Lakoff (1975) believes

> it will be found that the overall effect of "women's language"—meaning both language restricted in use to women and language descriptive of women alone—is this: it submerges a woman's personal identity, by denying her the means of expressing herself strongly, on the one hand, and encouraging expressions that suggest triviality in subject matter and uncertainty about it; and, when a woman is being discussed, by treating her as an object—sexual or otherwise—but never a serious person with individual views. The ultimate effect of these discrepancies is that women are systematically denied access to power, on the grounds that they are not capable of holding it as demonstrated by their linguistic behavior along with other aspects of their behavior: and the irony here is that women are made to feel that they deserve such treatment, because of inadequacies in their own intelligence and/or education. But in fact it is because women have learned their lessons so well that they later suffer such discrimination.

The Ways in Which We Speak

Clearly, great differences exist between individual women and individual men in their speech patterns. If there is such a thing as "men's speech" and "women's speech," considerable similarities would be found between the two. Nevertheless, some generalizations are allowable about sex differences in content, linguistics, and syntax.

1. Women's speech tends to be more person-centered, more concerned with interpersonal matters, to deal more with the feelings of both the speaker and the listener, to be more polite, and more indirect. It employs more fillers, qualifiers, disclaimers, and other softening devices to avoid strong or direct statements.

2. Men's speech tends to be more concerned with external things and to involve more factual communication. It is more literal and direct, employs stronger statements and stronger language, and tends to exert power over the listener (Eakins and Eakins 1978).

Many of the words that women use are different from the words that men use. For example, women use adjectives that discriminate in great detail about nuances of color or feeling—words like *mauve* or *puce* that men would not only never use but that they consider to make trivial and irrelevant distinctions. Women also use certain adjectives that would be ludicrous (or effeminate) if used by a man, words like *adorable, lovely, charming, divine* (Lakoff 1975). Women also make greater use of "intensive" adverbs such as *so, such, terribly, quite,* or *awfully,* as in "The dinner was *so* delicious." They also tend to use emphatic forms like *fantastic, ghastly, amazing,* and reduplicative forms such as *itsy-bitsy* or *teeny-tiny* (Key 1975) except in the company of men (McMillan et al. 1977). The effect of these syntactical differences is that men's speech has more strength and impact, they get listened to and heard more often, and they get reinforcement for their position of power.

The expletives, exclamations, and expressions used by women often take forms that are considered meaningless, such as *Oh, dear* or *Oh, fudge.* Men in similar circumstances are morely likely to use stronger expletives—*Oh, shit* or *Oh, damn.* The male language expresses feelings a great deal more forcefully. There is clearly a difference between "Oh, dear, I've pricked my little finger" and "Oh, shit, I've cut my hand," although both might describe the same injury. This double standard of language permits men to use the full range of vocabulary, including sexual and profane terms, except in front of women and children, but denies the same freedom of expression to women. Linguist Mary Ritchie Key (1975) reports being advised not to use the word *damn* in a linguistic example because "it made me sound like a feminist." Obviously many people of both sexes feel little need to express themselves using profanity or expletives. Indeed, many will argue that those who must rely on these terms suffer a paucity of language. However, the point here is not that women should be as free as men to curse and swear, but that women are denied the opportunity to express thoughts and feelings with the force and energy that is permitted to men. Women are not seen as feminine if they permit themselves the luxury of strong expressions of feelings.

Women not only use different words from men, they also use different syntax. Women are more likely to use "tag lines" or "tag questions," lines midway between an outright statement and a yes-no question—less assertive than the former, more confident than the latter—for example, "John is there, isn't he?" Another syntactical form is a difference in patterns of intonation in women's speech—a declarative answer to a question that has the rising inflection of a yes-no question and is uttered hesitantly, as though one were seeking confirmation for his answer. "What time is dinner?" "Oh . . . around six o'clock . . .?" The answer is really saying "We'll eat at six o'clock if that's all right with you." These patterns are part of a pattern of politeness associated with femininity. They avoid forcing an opinion on the listener and leave the door open for either agreement or contradiction. However, they have the effect of making women seem indecisive and unsure of themselves. They can also be used on requests. A direct order, "close the door," can be turned into a compound request with the addition of particles, "won't you please close the door?" The more particles that are added, the more polite the request, and the more polite, the more powerlessness is conveyed, and the more characteristic it is of women's speech (Lakoff 1975; Key 1975). Both women and men expect women to use these polite forms, whether they are attempting to achieve feminine or masculine goals, and whether they are speaking to women or men (Kemper 1984).

Men also use tag questions, however they more often use them to add force or emphasis, as in "You aren't going to stand in my way, are you?" (Eakins and Eakins 1978). Men are expected to speak like women and use polite forms of address when speaking to women or attempting to accomplish feminine goals, but on masculine tasks, especially when speaking to men, they are expected to be impolite (Kemper 1984).

Women also use more "modal constructions." A modal construction occurs when a speaker expresses possibilities, probabilities, or doubtfulness about events that did or will take place. The modal class words are *can, could, shall, should, will, would, may, might,* or verb auxiliaries such as *have* and *been.* An example would be a statement such as "I think I may have gotten a higher score than Arnold" (Key 1975).

McMillan et al. (1977) tested three hypotheses based on the work of Lakoff and Key: that women use more syntactic categories than men that connote uncertainty, that they use more linguistic categories that connote uncertainty, and that men interrupt women more frequently than women interrupt men. They found support for all three. Their conclusions show that:

- Women do not use more intensifiers in the presence of men, which probably reflects women's subculture; but
- Women use three syntax categories—modal construction, tag questions, and imperative constructions in question form—more frequently in the presence of men, supporting the uncertainty interpretation;
- Men use each syntactic category slightly more often when women are present; and
- Men interrupt women more than they interrupt other men.

Women's speech is also made more uncertain and hesitant than men's by the use of qualifiers and fillers (Eakins and Eakins 1978). Qualifying, softening, or mitigating words and phrases are often added to statements to soften or blunt their impact. They are used to avert or avoid negative reactions to our words and have the effect of making statements less absolute in tone. They are found sometimes at the beginning, sometimes at the end, and sometimes sprinkled through the statements. Such words and phrases as *well, let's see, perhaps, possibly, I suppose, I think, it seems to me,* and *you know* all have this effect. The statement "That's not true," for instance, has a very different impact from the statements, "Well, I don't think that that's true," or "Well, I really wonder if that's true." We can further qualify a statement by adding such softeners as *rather, somewhat, sort of,* and *to some extent.* We might say "Well, I wonder if to some extent that's not always true."

Another type of qualifier is the disclaimer. These mitigators usually come at the beginning of a sentence and are used to explain, excuse, or ask forbearance of the listener. They include such phrases as "I hope you won't be angry, but . . .," "This may sound a little silly, but . . .," or "I don't know much about it, but . . . ." Once again, research is scanty as to the differences between women and men in their use of disclaimers, but what is available shows that women do, in fact, tend to use these forms more frequently than men, particularly the forms that indicate poor logic, ignorance of the facts, or tentativeness and hedging (Eakins and Eakins 1978). While it's clear that these disclaimers have a positive effect in softening the impact of negative messages and seeking concurrence of opinion, it is also true that they tend to make the speaker seem less knowledgeable or less self-assured. Disclaimers like "Well, I don't really know very much about this, but I wonder if . . ." may make the listener prejudiced against an opinion even before it is expressed.

Fillers are words and sounds like *well, you know, I mean,* or *like*; in male-female conversation women use more of them than men do (Eakins and Eakins 1978). Women also use fewer of them in female-female conversations, suggesting that women are more fluent, more at ease, and less hesitant talking to other women than they are talking to men.

Men and women vary not only in their choice of language but also in their conversational behavior. Differences have been found in turn-taking (who speaks when), expressivity, the selection of topics, and the use of humor (Eakins and Eakins 1978).

Women tend to listen more and to provide "stroking behavior" by nodding more frequently or issuing an "Mmhmm" sound, a sound that seems to express agreement or support without any attempt to break in. On the other hand, when women switch from this generally passive mode to a more directive, controlling form of talk, the men will generally not respond in the same way; not only will they not provide stroking behavior, they may not take the women seriously or respond at all.

Not surprisingly, men have been found to take more turns and to talk more in mixed groups, in part because they interrupt women more often and answer questions not addressed to them. Turn-taking violations may take several forms: overlaps—two people speaking at once because the second speaker has started before the first one finished; interruptions—two people speaking at once before any signal that the first is near the end of the statement; and delayed minimal response.

In same-sex conversations turn-taking violations seem to be fairly equally divided, but in male-female conversations practically all the overlaps and interruptions are by male speakers—a general disregard by males for female speakers. In a study of turn taking among university faculty members, this pattern was quite evident. Males interrupted more than females; the female who interrupted the most did so to other females. The person most often interrupted was a woman, the one person without a Ph.D. degree; the person interrupted least was the department chair. These observations would suggest that status had a good deal to do with turn taking (Eakins and Eakins 1978).

Lapses occur in a conversation when one member falls silent. In male-female conversations, women have been found to fall silent more frequently than men. These silences came in response to one of three male conversational behaviors: overlap, interruption, or delayed minimal response. Minimal responses are those that do not count as a turn, the stroking behaviors such as *Mmhmm* or *Oh* or *Yeah,* but display continuing interest or participation in the conversation. Displaying or postponing these minimal responses, on the other hand, may signal disinterest, inattention, or lack of understanding. Silence following a delayed minimal response suggests that the speaker is uncertain about the listener's continued participation in the conversation. These silences are found much less infrequently in same-sex conversations (Eakins and Eakins 1978).

The content of conversation also differs along gender lines. Women's conversation tends to be more expressive or relational, while men's contributions are more instrumental and goal-oriented. These styles generally reflect social roles in which men tend to be more instrumental and women more nurturing. In mixed-sex groups women seem to take concern for group maintenance, for relief of tension, and for ego protection of other members. In choosing conversational topics, women choose to talk about persons about twice as often as men do. Men's preferred conversational topics are business and money, followed by sports and amusements. Women's preferred topics are men and clothes (Eakins and Eakins 1978).

A final sex difference in conversation has to do with the use of humor. The limited available evidence suggests that women are less able than men to tell amusing narratives, especially in mixed-sex groups. A study of the use of spontaneous humor has shown that wit and laughter in organizations may be distributed by status, with those at the lower end of the spectrum making many fewer witticisms and jokes than those with more authority. Further, a kind of pecking order prevailed in which jokes or witticisms were never directed at persons higher in authority or rank. Women rarely made jokes, but they laughed hard at the jokes told by the men (Eakins and Eakins 1978).

The Ways in Which We Are Spoken About

Language communicates messages at a number of different levels simultaneously. It conveys not only the substantive message contained in the meanings of the words themselves but also a great many social and cultural messages about the speaker, the listener, and the subject of the words. Thus, language tends to reveal a great deal of the disparity that exists in the social attitudes toward masculinity and femininity. These values are revealed in the euphemisms that we use for the sexes, the differences in meaning attributed to seemingly parallel terms, and in the use of names, titles, and pronouns.

Several years ago a county sheriff in California was running for reelection. In a campaign speech to a women's group he made several references to the positive advantages he had brought to the "girls" and the "ladies" in the sheriff's department (sworn officers). When a listener suggested to him that these terms were offensive to some voters, he asked what terms he should use instead. "Why don't you just say women?" he was asked. With that the sheriff grew red in the face, drew himself up to his full height, puffed up his chest, and responded heatedly "I was raised to respect the fair sex. If I had ever called my mother a woman, my father would have whipped me."

The word *man* has very positive connotations in our society. It is a compliment to a male person to say "he is a real man"; "he took it like a man"; "he is a man's man" (whatever that means). Little boys are admonished to "be a man" and are praised when they are called "little man." The word *man* in this context symbolizes strength and maturity. Women, however, are rarely complimented by a phrase like "she is a real woman." The word *woman* in this case suggests sexuality, rather than strength. We might say, instead, "she is a real lady." Lady, then, becomes a euphemism for woman, a polite substitute for offensive and undesirable terms like *broad* or *dame*. The parallel term *gentleman* is used far less frequently than *lady*. It is not a euphemism for man, which has no negative connotations and therefore needs no substitute. Lakoff (1977) argues that lady is often used as a euphemism for woman in the same way that *Afro-American* is substituted for *nigger.*

The word *girl* is also often used as a euphemism for woman. It is often applied to women of all ages, as in "my office girl" or "the girls in the bridge club." Many women assert that they find the term flattering, and indeed a compliment is usually intended when comments are made about a woman's youthful appearance. Feminist women, however, take offense to the term on the grounds that it suggests immaturity or helplessness. For the sheriff, however, *girl* is quite obviously like the word *lady* in that it removes the suggestion of sexuality that is present in the word woman.

Some interesting research supports the notion that these words are used euphemistically. Respondents reported that they would expect a *woman* to have interesting and important things to say; *ladies* were seen as more frivolous, having more wealth, and concerned mostly with social or charitable interests. However, older respondents in particular preferred the term to *woman. Lady* signified dignity, respect, and refinement, it brought better treatment, and it was seen as a desirable thing to be. *Woman,* by contrast, seemed earthier and more common. Younger women, and to a lesser extent younger men, however, saw *woman* as being less pretentious, less prudish, and less stilted (Eakins and Eakins 1978).

In addition to euphemisms, language tends to offer a semantic reflection of the general sexual polarization that characterizes the society. Words that seem to be pairs or couplets actually have quite different implications in use. The words themselves are neutral, neither pejorative nor oppressive; their meanings are anything but parallel. The words *mannish, manly, womanly,* and *womanish,* for instance, tell a great deal about how the society views masculinity and femininity. To be manly is to have the positive qualities of a man, and the word usually applies to a man. But to be mannish is quite another thing; the word typically refers to aberrant women. Womanly, on the other hand, suggests feminine traits of decorum and modesty; but womanish is usually used to describe a man as weak, effeminate, or petulant (Miller and Swift 1976). Eakins and Eakins term this the "my-virtue-is-your-vice" school of sexual appraisal. Other examples include *bachelor* for an unmarried male, whether or not he has been previously married, *spinster* for a never married woman, and *divorcee* for a previously married female. (There is no comparable male term to divorcee, although a previously married man may be referred to as a divorced man.) The word *sir* implies respect for a male; the parallel term *madam* may suggest the keeper of a brothel and give offense. A man who is a *wizard* is clever, even magical, but not so the woman who is referred to as a *witch.* A *brave* is seen as strong, youthful and courageous; *squaw,* like *witch,* is often used disparagingly to suggest women that are old, ugly, or aggressive. Still other examples are *king/queen, governor/ governess, patron/matron,* or *prince/princess.* A *master* is one who holds mastery, one skilled in an art of profession, but a *mistress* is normally used only in a sexual sense, that is, as a woman who has a sexual relationship with a man to whom she is not married.

Adjectives sometimes have different meanings when applied to women and to men, and different adjectives are applied to equivalent characteristics. A woman is *brainy* (not usually a compliment) but a man is *smart. Smart* applied to women usually refers to her appearance rather than to her intelligence. She is a *hooker,* a *slut,* or a *roundheels*; he is a *Don Juan,* a *Playboy,* or a *Casanova.* He is a *hard drinker,* she is a *lush.* He is a *man of the world*; she *has been around.* He is *self-confident*; she is *conceited.* He is *exacting*; she is *picky.* And so on. The language discriminates between masculine and feminine traits and behaviors and tends to put negative connotations on the female words.

Names and titles are different for women and men. Women typically give up a good deal of their identity when they marry. The traditional marriage ceremony reflects this when the couple are declared "man and wife." He retains his status as man, she exchanges her status as woman for that of wife (Lakoff 1975). Up until that moment she has been known as Miss, now she will be known as Mrs.; he remains Mr. She may give up the surname that she has previously been known by and take up the name of her husband; for many purposes she will take on her husband's full name, that is, she will become Mrs. John Smith. However, much more frequently than her husband, she will be called by her first name or by familiar titles (honey, doll, blondie) by those whom she meets quite casually (Eakins and Eakins 1978). Men on the other hand are often referred to by last name only, a form of familiarity that is considered rude and disrespectful when applied to women (Lakoff 1975). Throughout her life she will be identified with respect to her relationships to others: Harry's daughter, John's wife, Mary's mother. Even after her death she will continue to be known as Mrs. John Smith or as John Smith's widow. Men, by contrast, are rarely identified as Mr. Jane Doe, husband of Jane Doe, or as Jane Doe's widower.

Even women with considerable personal accomplishments are often identified as their husbands' possessions. At center court at Wimbledon, the sportscaster drones out the names of Mrs. Cawley, Mrs. Lloyd, or Mrs. King, even though all three women were winners before their marriages and their husbands are best known through their association with their championship wives. Marie Curie is frequently referred to only as Madame Curie, but Alexander Graham Bell is never called simply Mr. Bell (Miller and Swift 1976).

Occupational and organizational descriptors differ. The domain of most occupations is assumed to belong to men, so that when women enter they must be identified. We do not specify a male pilot or man astronaut, but the woman who becomes a doctor or a race driver must be semantically differentiated by the use of a "marker." She becomes the *woman* (or, worse, the *lady*) doctor or the *female* driver. In the same way, in those rare instances where the occupation is a female-dominated one, we may designate the occupant as a *male* nurse or *man* teacher. Unfortunately, these terms tend to demean the individuals and trivialize their accomplishments. Sally Ride tried valiantly but vainly to keep the press's attention on the mission of the space shuttle and on her accomplishments as an astrophysicist and astronaut, rather than on her cooking and housework or her plans to have children. Nevertheless, she was routinely and consistently distinguished as the *lady* astronaut.

Another kind of differential nomenclature is adding suffixes such as *-ess, -ette,* or *-trix* to distinguish male from female occupations. A man who writes poetry is a poet, a woman who writes poetry is a poetess. Other examples include *singer/songstress, sculptor/sculptress, author/ authoress, steward/stewardess, waiter/waitress, aviator/aviatrix, drum major/drum majorette* (Eakins and Eakins 1978). The effect of these modifications is to feminize the titles and by so doing to detract from them a sense of competency or power. It weakens them and makes them appear trivial. In most cases the differential titles cannot be justified on the basis of semantic necessity or clarity. It may be necessary to distinguish an *actor* from an *actress* on the basis of gender, but in few other cases does the distinction connote any meaning other than those that diminish.

A final and most difficult area of language differentiation comes in the use of exclusionary language, the exclusive use of the noun *man* and of masculine pronouns and possessives. Linguists argue that the term *man* is a grammatically correct generic term for *mankind* that includes both women and men. The difficulty, of course, is that it is nearly impossible to distinguish this meaning from the more common meaning of the word as the opposite of *woman.* Research provides some convincing evidence that when the word *man* is used generically people tend to think male and not to think female. Surprisingly, terms like "Urban Man," "Industrial Man," "Economic Man" tend to evoke rather negative images, suggesting strong images of power and dominance. When the terms are replaced with gender-free words like "Urban Life" the responses are quite different.

Studies of children from preschool through high school all show that the word *man* produces a masculine image, almost no matter the context. When the wording is changed to substitute such words as *people* and *humans* the image that is aroused includes both men and women (Miller and Swift 1976). These semantic differences apparently cause little problem for children. They learn relatively early that the word *man* has a dual meaning and learn to make the distinction when necessary. However, in the absence of clear indications to the contrary, they tend to apply the specific meaning of the word rather than the generic one. The fireman, the postman, the policeman are all perceived as males, not as either males or females. Hence the use of markers or exclusionary language reinforces occupational stereotypes and affects occupational choice, even of very young children (Rosenthal and Chapman 1982).

An even more pervasive problem arises when it comes to the issue of pronouns. The rules of English grammar assert that *he* must be used when the referent is singular and indefinite or unknown. Grammatical purists argue that substituting "he and she" is a form of sexism, since the use of *he* alone loses its sexist connotations if used consistently. This argument asserts that if you never qualify the generic pronoun it will always be understood to stand for "he and she," but insisting on the distinction has the effect of making women a special category, excluded unless they are specifically mentioned. The difficulty, of course, is that the generic term and the specific term are identical, so women are already excluded (Miller and Swift 1976). The other, more equitable, approach would be to use "he or she" in all cases except when one or the other is specifically excluded (Eakins and Eakins 1978). The generic use of *he* might be acceptable, even if it is exclusionary, if it were used consistently. But that is not the case. Indefinite referents such as *manager, engineer,* or *astronaut* would then appropriately take the masculine pronoun *he.* But to be consistent it should then be used also with such equally indefinite referents as *secretary, nurse,* or *housewife.* (If generic terms are indeed acceptable and nonexclusionary, then the marriage partner who cares for the home and children and does not seek paid work outside the home would be called a *housewife,* regardless of gender, and there would be no need for the word *househusband* [Persing 1977].) If the language were truly consistent, the deity would surely be referred to as *he* but so also would ships and hurricanes. If we can't have equity, the very least that we should insist upon is consistency.

Verbal communication distinguishes men and women in two ways: the way we talk and the way we are talked about. So far in this chapter we have seen that women and men talk differently. The many differences in semantic, linguistic, and grammatical patterns show that men's speech tends to perpetuate masculine positions of power and dominance. Further, semantic and linguistic distinctions in the words that are used to describe and define women and men also reflect cultural stereotypes and biases. Because language is such a powerful force in shaping and controlling society, it is essential that these language differences be addressed and inequities reduced if there is ever to be anything approaching equality between the sexes. Some linguists argue that it is nearly impossible to change language, and there is no question that change will come only with great difficulty. However, it is possible to insist on certain fundamental rights. Women can insist that written language, at the very least, be free from exclusionary language. They can reject the euphemisms that demean womankind. They can insist upon being recognized as autonomous individuals, professionally independent from the possession of the primary males in their lives. And they can continue to insist on the same semantic rights and privileges as their brothers.

NONVERBAL COMMUNICATION

Defining verbal communication is fairly straightforward. The term refers to words and their linguistic or syntactical usage. Defining nonverbal communication is somewhat more difficult. In a general sense, it refers to all of the ways in which meanings are exchanged other than words. We cannot claim a clear distinction between the two, for verbal communication is often influenced by the nonverbal: "It's not what you said, it's how you said it." The words themselves, particularly spoken words, take on different meanings depending on such things as facial expression, tone of voice, or posture, and the nonverbal message greatly overpowers the verbal one (Argyle et al. 1970).

There are some important distinctions between verbal and nonverbal communication. Language, that is, verbal communication, is used most often for communicating information about events external to the speakers, whereas nonverbal codes are used to establish and maintain interpersonal relationships (Argyle et al. 1970). Another distinction is that nonverbal communication need not be, and often is not, either intentionally sent or consciously received (Donaghy 1980). It is like verbal communication, however, in that nonverbal cues differ in use and in meaning between women and men. To an even greater extent than verbal cues, they reflect differences in status and power between the sexes (Henley 1973-74).

The study of nonverbal communication is particularly important to the study of women and men in organizations because of the implications it has for social control. Since we most often respond to nonverbal behavior unconsciously, and since people in dependent positions have been found to adapt their behavior to the nonverbal messages of dominant ones, the result is a self-fulfilling prophecy that keeps women dependent. For instance, when a woman or a minority is expected to perform less well than others in a situation like a job interview, and the dominant person (the interviewer) communicates that expectation in a number of nonverbal ways, the submissive individual adapts to the expectation, does in fact perform less well, and the prophecy is confirmed. The problem is then compounded when research focuses on the reasons why members of the stereotyped group perform less well, rather than on the interactions—a line of inquiry that has been referred to as "victim analysis" (Henley 1977).

Significant Elements of Nonverbal Communication

The elements of nonverbal communication that have significance for women and men in organizations include physical appearance, posture, facial expression, eye behavior, body movement, touch, and space.

Physical Appearance

Physical appearance refers not just to clothing but to all the rather static characteristics of the body as well, including height, weight, the color, style, length, and thickness of hair, the presence or absence of facial hair, the color, texture, and condition of skin, the color and shape of eyes, and much more. Most healthy people take a good deal of interest in their physical appearance; it reflects to a large extent how we see ourselves and how we would like others to see us. In a larger sense, each of us has an overall self-image—an image of the kind of person that we are that we would like to pass on to others. An important part of this self-image is the body image—the picture we have of our own body and its appearance. Since most of us are aware that initial impressions are formed largely on the basis of physical appearance and tend to be fairly long-lasting, we take a good deal of care about our appearance.

The feminine stereotype depicts women as being more concerned than men about their bodies, their clothing, and their appearance in general, and, as is often the case, there is both truth and reason to the stereotype. Women are subject to a great deal more observation than men; their figures, their clothing, their general attractiveness are the criteria by which they are most often judged. Not surprisingly, then, women are more conscious than men of their visibility, of the fact that they are being observed. This difference in visibility translates into a power difference and also into a sex difference. In a situation where one person is observing and the other is being observed—as in an interview situation, for example—the observer (or perceiver) comes to dominate the situation. Since women are judged by their dress and appearance, and men tend to do the judging, women are cast in many male-female dyads as the observed and men as the observer, and the males are able to assume dominance over the situation (Henley 1973-74).

Posture

Posture refers to those positions in which we place our bodies for a relatively long period of time, and in this sense is distinct from movement (kinesics). Our body is active at all times, that is, we are always in some position, either standing, sitting, or reclining, whether or not someone else is around. The postures that we assume tell a great deal about us, and society imposes sex role requirements. On the other hand, status also dictates acceptable and unacceptable postures, so that once again sexual differences translate into power differences.

Men and women adopt different postures. In general men's stance tends to be more open than women's. Women tend to stand or sit with their legs close together and often crossed; men tend to stand with their legs apart and to sit with one foot on the opposite knee. Women tend to tilt their heads to the side, indicating coyness or submissiveness; men tend to tilt their heads forward, signaling aggressiveness. Women keep their arms close to the trunk or crossed over the chest, while men move the arms away from the body, sometimes with hands clasped behind the head. Men in general tend to adopt more relaxed and informal positions, that is, to slouch or recline. These posture differences are not trivial. One of the earliest lessons that female children learn is to walk, stand, and sit "like a lady," and they learn the lesson well. Female clothing adds to the lesson, since dresses restrict movement and increase the problem of maintaining decorum. Women who assume masculine postures are seen as unfeminine and unattractive but may also be seen as sexually uninhibited.

In situations of nonequal status, people of higher status are allowed a great deal more relaxed posture than their subordinates. The boss can slouch on the subordinate's desk, but the subordinate doesn't slouch on the boss's desk. In meetings, people of high status will recline in their chairs, sit on the floor, turn sidewise, or assume whatever level of casualness makes them comfortable. But low-status people will sit straight in their chairs and remain more decorous. They make take their cues from the higher status individual, and follow their behavior up to a point, but they will always remain more formal than their superiors.

The comparison is obvious. Acceptable, role-appropriate feminine posture is the posture of submissiveness and vulnerability. The postures of dominance and self-confidence, embodied in more relaxed stances, are seen as inappropriate to femininity. Women who adopt them may be seen as sexually available, rather than as powerful.

Facial Expression

The face can convey a number of messages simultaneously, and it may convey them very rapidly, almost subliminally. Our facial expressions tend to convey messages about our emotions, rather than our status, and can reflect happiness or sorrow, approval or disapproval, acceptance or rejection. Most of us learn to a greater or lesser extent both to follow certain social conventions with our facial expressions and to conceal certain feelings. We learn, for instance, to look solemn at solemn occasions and to smile at happy ones; we learn not to show undue pleasure at another's pain or discomfiture.

Men and women differ a great deal in their use of facial expressions. Women are more prone than men to reveal their feelings in nonverbal ways, just as they are in verbal ways. For men, the "strong silent type" characterized by the John Wayne cowboy image requires remaining inscrutable, and the ability to maintain a "poker face" is greatly admired. The same inexpressiveness from a woman is perceived as unattractive and unfeminine.

One of the most frequent facial expressions is the smile, and a major sex difference occurs in smiling. Women smile more than men do. However, it is not at all clear that they are happier than men. A smile can mean many things: happiness, greeting, appeasement, approval-seeking, warmth, and liking. It can be a buffer against aggression, a release of aggressive tension, or a counterforce to aggressive or hostile words. To a great extent the meaning is derived by the context (Frieze et al. 1978). Women are expected to smile a lot and are considered deviant if they don't. Their smiles may really mean merely conformity to convention, approval-seeking, or submissiveness; the smiling woman may be expressing not her pleasure or happiness but her inferior status in the situation. In this respect, the woman's smile has been compared to the servant's shuffle (Firestone 1970).

Eye Movements

Looking at someone with whom you are interacting may be a sign of liking or approval, but a stare may be an aggressive threat (Frieze et al. 1978). Eye contact is one of the most studied aspects of nonverbal communication and one of the areas where greatest sex differences are found. Women look more at others than men do; they look more at each other while speaking, while being spoken to, and while exchanging glances. Regardless of the gender of the receiver, they look more often and they look longer at the other person. Why? Is it because they are generally more open to emotional expression and interpersonal relationships? Or is this another manifestation of women's greater submissiveness?

The preponderance of evidence suggests that the differences are related to status. Among unequals the subordinate is more likely to be the one seeking approval, and people have more eye contact with those from whom they are seeking approval. Women may get important feedback on their own behavior by seeking nonverbal information from the facial expressions of men, a source of information not particularly valued by males. In conversations, speakers tend to look away while listeners tend to look at the speaker; and men tend to talk more frequently and longer and to interrupt more often than women in mixed-sex conversations. Hence women would tend to look more at men. Further, there is more eye contact when the person being addressed is of high status or when the speaker has a positive attitude toward that person. Perhaps the reason that women seek eye contact more than men has to do with the fact that both women and men perceive women to have lower status (Eakins and Eakins 1978).

Prolonged eye contact, however, may express something quite different. Instead of some mutual expression of warmth or understanding it may represent a struggle for dominance. The first person to look away has demonstrated submission. Most children are familiar with the meaning of a parent's or teacher's prolonged gaze when he or she is caught in some inappropriate and unacceptable behavior. Usually (although not always) the child senses the gaze of the adult, perceives the meaning of the glance, casts down its eyes, and stops the behavior. The threat is implicit but clear; failure to change the behavior will result in punishment. Once again, the evidence suggests that women tend to show submission by averting their gaze, particularly when they are stared at by men.

Contradictions are clearly operating here. Looking at someone may be seen as a sign of either dominance or submission; looking away can also signal either dominance or submission. Eakins and Eakins reconcile the disparity by showing that the two types of eye behavior characterize dominance and submission in different ways: dominant staring and looking away, and submissive watching and averting the gaze. Staring can be used by a superior in some situations to communicate power and assert dominance. But in other situations it may not be needed. When the superior's power is secure, it becomes unnecessary to express dominance or scan an inferior's face for approval or feedback. Instead, the superior can look away or gaze into space. On the other hand, an underling can communicate submission and attentiveness, as well as gather feedback, by careful watching. But in some cases, as when receiving a fixed stare from a dominant person, the subordinant signals submission by averting the eyes.

Body Movements (Kinesics)

Movements of various parts of the body—arms, hands and fingers, leg and foot, head and shoulders, or the torso—can communicate universal messages or can be unique to the individual. Certain hand or finger gestures, called emblems, are generally and easily understood. For instance, a hand gesture with fingers curled and thumb extended and pointed sideways to the body indicates a request for a ride; the same hand with the thumb pointing downward indicates disapproval, and the same hand with the thumb pointed upwards and the hand moved forward away from the body conveys approval. Other movements that emphasize the words being spoken, called "illustrators," include raising five fingers while you enumerate five points in an argument. Other body movements, called "regulators," help to facilitate interaction between individuals by nodding, gesturing, shifting the torso. We often demonstrate our emotions through such body movements as clenching our hands, squirming, or pacing; these are called "affect displays." Still other body movements are called "adapters," unconscious habits that are unique to the individual; they have usually been adopted first as a method of achieving comfort or convenience but have become habitual over time. Examples are such things as stretching or pushing the hair back from the face. These adaptors may have little significance to strangers but may convey subtle messages to the sensitive observer or to closer acquaintances (Donaghy 1980).

Sex differences in kinesics seem to be less pronounced and less significant than in other nonverbal behaviors. One study found that men shift their posture more frequently than women do, make hand gestures of longer duration than women do, and move their feet somewhat more (Frances 1979). Women tend to tilt their heads to the side (Key 1975). Peterson (in Eakins and Eakins 1978) reports that men used more hand gestures than women, regardless of the sex of the conversation partner. Males used an equal number of gestures when conversing with women or men, but women used more gestures in their conversations with women than with men. Women tended to use more adapters, particularly arranging or playing with their hair or touching ornamentation. Men used sweeping gestures, used their arms to lift or shift body position, used a closed fist, and stroked their chins more than did females. Gestures that were used exclusively by females included tapping with the hands; exclusively male gestures included stretching the hand and cracking the knuckles and pointing. Both females and males tended to use a greater number of gestures with the opposite sex than with the same sex.

These differences in gestures tend to support the notion that males and females use nonverbal methods to display gender traits, although alone they are less compelling than some other modes. Women's lesser use of gestures can be seen as a function of passivity or submissiveness. Men's greater use of gestures, including such power gestures as pointing or sweeping hand gestures, may reflect their greater dominance.

Touch

Of much greater significance is the differential use of touch. Perhaps the earliest form of human interaction is the holding, caressing, and touching of an infant by its parents. Touching has different meanings depending on who initiates or returns the touch, the part of the body being touched, the environment in which the touching occurs, and the length or duration of the touch. Certain forms of public touching—handshaking, backslapping, dancing, or casual bumping—are usually of short duration and may be fairly impersonal. More prolonged or more intimate forms of touching are generally reserved for nonpublic places. Touch may also involve not another person but ourselves—as in stroking one's own face—or an object.

For our purposes here, however, we are primarily concerned with interpersonal touching, for it is here that the greatest sex differences are displayed and the strongest messages of power and dominance conveyed. Both sex and status differences occur in who touches whom. Men may touch other men only in public and only very briefly—with a handshake, a back or arm slap, a mock punch. Women often hug or kiss each other, albeit briefly, in public and are generally allowed a great deal more touching than are men. Men touch women a great deal more than women touch men; they help them out of cars, guide them across streets and through doors, playfully touch them on their hair or other parts of the body, and in many instances treat them in the same way they treat objects or possessions (Eakins and Eakins 1978). Women, even as children, are generally touched a great deal more than men and boys are.

Henley (1973-74) argues that the differences in behavior are as much a matter of status as of sex. People with high status touch lower status people in situations where it would be considered presumptuous to reciprocate, much less to initiate, the touch. Status, not sex, explains why women and girls are touched more frequently than men and boys; the touching serves as a reminder to observers of the higher status of the toucher. Nonreciprocal touch is more likely to be initiated by the one who is older, male, and higher in socioeconomic status. Nonreciprocal touch in a situation of unequal status serves as a status reminder, a sort of "power put-down" that reduces the perceived dominance of the person being touched, rather than increasing the perceived power of the person doing the touching. However, in an equal relationship, the touch is seen as a gesture of solidarity, closeness, or support (Summerhayes and Suchner 1978).

Since males in general have higher status than females, the effects of messages of power and dominance in touch are compounded. The supervisor may approach the secretary's desk and lay a hand on his or her arm or shoulder while she or he talks. In this gesture, the status of the secretary is diminished. The secretary, however, is unlikely to approach the boss's desk and touch him or her while he or she has a conversation. And even if she or he did, the status of the secretary will not be raised appreciably, regardless of sex. However, sex cannot be ignored. In most cases the boss is male and the secretary female. She accepts the touch of her male superior as normal behavior; it's part of the power that he possesses. If the situation were reversed, however, the male secretary would be unlikely to touch his female boss, but it is also unlikely that she would initiate touch with her male subordinate. If she did, it would be perceived as a gesture of sexual intimacy, rather than of power. Since touch as a gesture of power or dominance is seen as inappropriate for women, their touch is often interpreted as a sexual gesture by men (Henley 1976).

The study of touch between women and men is, in fact, often seen and studied as a sexual gesture. Henley rejects that approach since it has never been adequately demonstrated that men have higher sexual interest or motivation than women or that they perceive touch as a more appropriate sexual gesture than women do. However, she views touch as a symbol of intimacy as well as of power—"the nonverbal equivalent of calling another by first name" (Henley 1973-74). When it is reciprocal, it indicates equal status and camaraderie. When it is not reciprocal, however, it indicates status. But even in reciprocal sexual relationships, for instance between a dating couple, male dominance may be demonstrated by the fact that it is the male who is expected to initiate intimate touch.

Space (Proxemics)

The study of space involves three aspects: personal space, territory, and social space. Personal space is the psychological space that surrounds us and that we consider to be our own. It varies in size with the nature of the people and the situation we are in; for example, the amount of personal space we require in a classroom may be quite different from what we require at a movie theater, in a crowded tavern, or walking down the street. However, whatever our personal space, we tend to be protective of it and to resent invasion of it by others. Territory is similar to personal space, except it refers to physical rather than psychological space. It is the space that we have staked out and claimed as our own, sometimes with a territorial marker. Primary territories are the exclusive domain of the owner—a home and particularly one's bedroom; secondary territories, the living or dining room of the home or private clubs, can be used only by a few select people. Public territories—restaurants, parks, libraries, and streets—are available to anyone for temporary use. Territories are often staked out with a marker, any object that signifies our possession: a fence around our property, our books and notebooks spread over a library table.

Social space is conversational distance, the distance between ourselves and others around us. It can be divided into four categories: Intimate distances—0 to 18 inches; casual/personal distances—1.5 to 4 feet; social/consultative distances—4 to 12 feet; and public distances—from 12 feet out. As the titles suggest, the nature of interaction will change based upon the distance from the person with whom we are interacting. We will not attempt to discuss intimate matters at social/consultative distances;

we will either change the nature of the conversation or the distance. The social space is a matter of negotiation between the parties and will vary depending on age, sex, culture and ethnicity, and subject matter (Donaghy 1980).

Both territory and personal space are associated with status, and behavior reflects the lower social status of women. The amount of territory that one controls and the extent to which it can be violated is an indicator of status. High-status people have bigger homes, bigger cars, bigger offices and desks, all of which tend to keep them at a greater distance from others. Even people who frequently occupy a particular public place—a church pew, a park bench, a particular seat in a classroom—come to think of it as their own and will protect it against invasions.

In organizations, higher status individuals are accorded larger offices. This symbol of status is so important that some organizations have devised formulae that determine the number of square feet allocated to each hierarchical level. Further, the extent to which the space can be violated is also a mark of status. A private office connotes greater status than a shared office or open workplace. A private secretary to limit access, both in person and by phone, further enhances status. The high-status person may work in a private office that cannot be entered physically or by telephone without the permission of a gatekeeper, or at the very least without first knocking and receiving permission to enter. The high-status person, on the other hand, may enter the territory of the lower status person without permission.

High-status or powerful people also, perhaps unconsciously, violate the personal space as well as the territory of lower status persons, but the privilege is not reciprocated. The boss may come close to the secretary, even touch him or her, when asking a question or giving a direction; the secretary could not and would not approach the boss at the same distance. Animal studies show that among other mammals and primates, the same principle applies. Dominant animals tend to control larger territories in which to hunt for food and also may have greater choice of food and sexual partners. The dominant animals also appear to have greater personal space, space that is protected if necessary by violence. Lower ranking animals, however, will give up their territory and their personal space when approached by higher ranking ones (Frieze et al. 1978).

These status differences are reflected in sex differences in a number of ways. Women tend to control less territory than men and their personal space tends to be smaller. In the house, mothers are less likely than fathers to have a special room that is off limits to other members of the family. A den or workshop may be reserved for the father; the kitchen is generally regarded as the woman's private space, but it usually can be entered by anyone. Men often have a special chair reserved for them (such as Archie Bunker's chair) and usually sit at the head (the end) of a rectangular dining table. Women, in fact, often have no place in the home that is exclusively theirs, where they can work undisturbed and in privacy (Frieze et al. 1978). In the workplace it is often the man who has the private office, the woman who has the public or shared space.

Women generally also have less personal space. Women stand closer to each other and other people stand closer to women. When women and men approach each other on the street, women more frequently than men move out of the way. As noted above, women tend to sit in postures that command a smaller amount of space. They condense; they sit or stand erectly, and keep elbows close to the body and legs crossed. Men expand; they sprawl, keep their arms away from the body on the arms of chairs or behind the head, and keep the legs apart or put one foot on the other knee (Eakins and Eakins 1978). When men intrude on the personal space of women, women tend to yield the territory; it is perceived as a legitimate expression of dominance. However, when women intrude on the personal space of men, it is likely to be perceived as a gesture of intimacy or sexuality.

As with the other nonverbal cues—physical appearance, facial expression, eye movements, posture, body movements, and touch—behaviors associated with space and performed by high-status persons and males are perceived as appropriate gestures of power and dominance, but the same behaviors performed by women are seen as inappropriate and may be interpreted as sexual in nature. Henley argues that power is exercised along a continuum, from least to greatest application of force. The continuum includes at least the following points: internalized controls, environmental structuring, nonverbal communication, verbal communication, mild physical sanctions, long-term restraint and ramifications, weapons, death, and war. Usually the mildest form of force that is effective will be used. Nonverbal communication marks the dividing line on this continuum between overt and covert control (or overt and covert resistance). Men make greater use of gestures that indicate both intimacy and dominance, and the argument that these are an indication of sexual attraction does not sufficiently explain their reasons for doing so. When women and other powerless people attempt to usurp nonverbal symbols of power, they are often ignored, denied, or punished by others, rather than accepted, and this denial often takes the form of attributing the gesture to sexual advance rather than dominance. Hence a good deal of women's behavior that is interpreted as self-limiting may in reality be the end of a sequence in which assertion was tried and suppressed on the nonverbal level.

Women have been found to be particularly apt at reading these nonverbal messages and tend to respond by adapting their behavior to the males' characteristics. The result is that behaviors that seem meaningless or trivial have the effect of sustaining the social control of women in submissive roles (Henley 1977).

SUMMARY

Communication is the life blood of organizational life; without it activities would grind to a halt almost before we could measure the passage of time. Communication is both verbal and nonverbal, it carries both direct and indirect messages. In our roles as senders of communication, we reveal a great deal about ourselves and our perceptions of our receivers. In our roles as receivers we are affected by both the sender and the message.

All the available evidence suggests that there are significant differences between women and men in both verbal and nonverbal communication, in the way that they send and the way that they are received. Women as senders tend to convey messages of passiveness and powerlessness. In language, women and men use different words, and masculine language is considered unfeminine and inappropriate for women. Also in language, different words are used to describe women and men, and apparently parallel words have very different connotations. In conversation, men and women tend to talk about different subjects. Women tend to listen more and give more encouragement while men tend to talk more and to interrupt more. Women and men send different nonverbal messages; feminine behavior conveys messages of submission while masculine behavior conveys messages of dominance. When women do use status or power behaviors they are often misinterpreted as sexual messages.

Thus our language, both verbal and nonverbal, tends to perpetuate stereotypes and to sustain the image of the high status and power of males and the submissiveness and sexuality of females. Communication problems present a particularly difficult dilemma for the woman manager. If she uses verbal and nonverbal language consistent with her status, her behavior may be perceived as inappropriate for her sex, or it may be interpreted as a sexual advance. But if she uses stereotypically feminine language and behavior, she may be perceived as passive and dependent, appropriate to her sex but not to her position. Either way her effectiveness is impaired.

There are no easy solutions. Managers can start by removing exclusionary language from all written organizational documents and materials. They can exclude the word "girl" from the organizational lexicon unless it refers to young female children. They can insist upon sex-neutral terms wherever possible and nonsexist language at all times. They can be aware of sexually discriminatory assumptions and sexist connotations in seemingly innocent usages. They can educate employees to the significance of these distinctions. If women are ever going to receive equal treatment with men in organizations, they must receive equal treatment in language.

8

Motivation and Rewards

An axiom that feminists are fond of quoting says "Unfortunately, a woman must work twice as hard and be twice as good as a man in order to get half as far. Fortunately, that's not hard." Unfortunately, there is a lot of truth in the statement.

In this chapter we will be looking at the related issues of motivation and job satisfaction. Theories of motivation can be grouped into two categories, *content* (or needs) theories and *process* theories. Content theories focus on the job itself. They consider the psychological needs that individuals bring to the job and attempt to motivate workers by designing jobs that provide opportunities to achieve need satisfaction. Process theories attempt to explore the internal process by which individuals translate the opportunity to achieve desired rewards into enhanced performance.

Content theories are based on the work of Abraham Maslow (1943), who posited a "hierarchy of human needs," which progressed from physiological needs, through safety needs, affiliation needs, esteem needs (from self and others), and finally to something called "the need for self-actualization." According to the theory, only unmet needs have a motivating effect, and needs are arranged in a hierarchy of "successive prepotency" that individuals climb in their search toward even higher and more abstract needs.

Although Maslow's theory has come in for a great deal of criticism (Miner 1980; Yankelovich 1981) and has never been empirically validated, it has nevertheless served as the basis for a good deal of motivation theory and management experimentation (Argyris 1957; Herzberg 1966; McClelland 1965; McGregor 1960). Since a satisfied need is not considered to be a motivator, these theories concentrate on rewards that are intrinsic to the job itself: the opportunity for personal growth, for recognition, for a sense of achievement in the task itself. They discount the motivating power of extrinsic factors such as pay, benefits, working conditions, relations with supervisors or with co-workers. The application of the theory involves re-designing jobs, through job enlargement, to provide the opportunity to achieve the higher level needs in the workplace.

It's important to note that content theories, while popular and intuitively appealing, are certainly not universally accepted. Much research has shown that although work is certainly an important part of the lives of most people, it is not the "central life interest" (Dubin and Goldman 1972; Yankelovich 1981).

Process theories differ from content theories in that they are more concerned with the internal psychological aspects of motivation, with the relationship between rewards and effort. They are more concerned with the manipulation of extrinsic rewards than with altering the content of the job to provide intrinsic rewards. An early example, Expectancy Theory, was initially formulated in the mid-1960s, has undergone a number of re-finements, and now includes a number of somewhat different models (Mitchell 1974). Its primary premise asserts that workers have a prefer-ence for various rewards associated with the performance of their jobs, they have an expectancy about the likelihood that increased effort will lead to an intended behavior, and they have expectancies about the likeli-hood that certain outcomes will result from their choice of behavior. Em-ployees in a given situation will choose those actions that are determined by their preferences and their expectations. For example, an individual—Mary Smith—wants to be promoted to a higher level in the organization, she understands that in order to achieve the promotion she will have to improve performance in the present assignment. She believes that by in-creased diligence and concentration her performance will improve. The behavior, according to the theory, that Mary Smith chooses will be a func-tion of how much she desires the promotion, the perceived likelihood that the increased effort will produce the desired improvement, and the likelihood that, if the improvement occurs, that promotion will in fact be forthcoming.

Equity Theory, also a process theory, argues that people want to maintain balance, or "distributive fairness" (Adams 1963). According to this theory, employees compare their inputs (skill, effort, expertise, ex-perience) and their outcomes (pay or other rewards) with others whom they consider comparable. Equity exists when the individual perceives that the ratio of his or her inputs to outputs is equal to that of the compari-son person. If equity fails to exist, the theory asserts, the individual will choose one of several alternatives to restore equity. Alternatives include changing inputs—by increasing or decreasing effort, for instance; chang-ing outputs—by requesting a raise, or sometimes by stealing from the company; or by changing the reference person.

Little research on either content or process theories has considered the importance of sex differences in motivation. Although some of the experimental work has been done on women subjects and some on men subjects, the researchers rarely considered the extent to which gender might play a part in the responses. As noted in Chapter 1, researchers often make stereotypical assumptions about the roots of observed behaviors, employing a gender model for female behavior and a job model for male behavior (Feldberg and Glenn 1979). Women's work behavior is assumed to result from the fact that their feminine role, as opposed to their work role, is their primary role, an assumption that leads to the conclusion that women are motivated only by extrinsic rewards, including both pay and the social aspects of the job. Higher level needs, to the extent that they exist at all, are presumably met in their roles as wife or mother. Men's work-related behavior, on the other hand, is assumed to arise from characteristics of the job itself. Work for men is seen as both the implementation of the breadwinner role and the expression of the primary masculine role. Their jobs, then, must be designed to provide both intrinsic and extrinsic rewards.

This chapter will consider this stereotypical assumption. It will examine the evidence that supports or refutes the notion that women and men differ significantly in their attitudes and expectations about work or in their work motivation. It will look first at the aspects inherent in process theories, specifically at the extent to which sex affects perceptions about work and its rewards. It will then turn to an examination of Content Theories, specifically the work of McClelland (1965) and his followers on achievement, affiliation, and power motives and their corollaries. Finally, it will look at Attribution Theory, a further refinement of content theory that looks at the effect of attribution of causation to success or failure on motivation.

JOB ATTRIBUTES AND REWARDS

Expectancy Theory asks what rewards employees value from their jobs and the extent to which these preferences affect work behavior. Controversy continues strong as to whether intrinsic or extrinsic factors have a higher motivational value. A detailed analysis of that debate is beyond the scope of this work; what we are concerned with here is the extent to which men and women differ in their preferences and the extent to which stereotypes are supported. We ask whether men and women differ in their preference for job attributes or organizational rewards and, if so, what variables, if any, mitigate those preferences.

First of all, however, it might be worthwhile to establish that the stereotype does in fact exist. Male college recruiters, who might be expected to have a fairly clear idea of the expectations of graduating seniors, were asked their perceptions of the rewards or job characteristics male and female job applicants most desired. Students, in turn, were asked to state their actual preferences. Recruiters did, as expected, perceive greater differences between male and female applicants than actually existed; actually no major differences were found between male and female applicants. But the surprising outcome was the extent to which the recruiters erred in their perceptions of both male and female graduates. The recruiters consistently assessed both male and female applicants to be more intrinsically oriented and less extrinsically oriented than they in fact were (Giles and Field 1982).

Evidence for the persistence of stereotypes was also apparent in a study of the preferred job attributes of all applicants to a public utility firm over a 30-year period. Men and women did differ somewhat in their preferences. "Security" proved to be the most important attribute for male applicants, consistent with the breadwinner role. For women, however, the first choice was "type of work"; the stereotypical values of "co-workers" and "supervisor" ranked fourth and sixth. Pay ranked fifth for men and seventh for women. However, while applicants rejected stereotypical values for themselves, they attributed them to others. Both male and female applicants indicated that they believed others would rank pay first (Jurgensen 1978).

Stereotypes do persist. And, as we have noted previously, stereotypes tend to have a basis in reality. Global surveys of sex differences in reward preferences have tended to support the stereotypes, but these differences tend to diminish considerably when other factors, such as hierarchical level, age, or tenure on the job, are considered. Women and men have been found to differ in the importance of intrinsic values, with men putting more emphasis on self-expression and the importance of extrinsic factors and women placing more value on social factors (Taylor and Thompson 1976). There is evidence, however, that the male-female gap is closing. A 1972 study found sex differences along very stereotypical lines. Men rated both extrinsic and intrinsic rewards higher than women; women rated relationships with co-workers and supervisors higher. A replication of the study in 1978 showed that differences had decreased substantially. Women still showed a preference for those characteristics that deal with comfortable and pleasant working conditions, but now rated professional development and intellectual stimulation higher than men. Both women and men in the second study ranked feelings of accomplishment as their highest priority. Overall, no clear male or female preference for any particular class of job characteristics emerged (Brenner and Tomkiewicz 1979).

Kanter (1976) has argued that these perceived sex differences in the workplace are really a function of power and opportunity structures in organizations, rather than of sex. She asserts that people in low-mobility or blocked mobility situations tend to limit their aspirations, seek satisfaction in activities outside of work, dream of escape, and create sociable peer groups in which interpersonal relationships take precedence over other aspects of work.

These behaviors and preferences are equally characteristic of women and men. Because women are so frequently placed in low-status positions, the behaviors are attributed to their sex, rather than to their position on the hierarchy, and once again the stereotype is reinforced. If Kanter is right, we should see differences in preferences for organizational outcomes disappear as women move into higher level positions or higher status occupations. Most, but not all, of the evidence supports that notion.

Differences in reward preferences between occupational levels were found in a study of six different organizations, but sex differences were also found at the highest level. High-level men put more importance than women on extrinsic rewards (compensation, direct economic benefits, and indirect economic benefits) and also on the intrinsic reward of esteem (Reif, Newstrom, and St. Louis 1976).

Sex differences were also found in a study of data drawn from a national probability sample, but on only one of the five variables tested. The only variable on which any significant male-female value difference occurred was in the "convenience aspects" of work: convenient travel to work, good hours, freedom from conflicting demands, pleasant physical surroundings, amount of work not too great, enough time to do the work, and opportunity to air personal problems. Women in every occupational category, regardless of their marital status or whether they were a secondary earner in the family, placed a higher value than their male counterparts on this variable. The only exception was women with preschool children, who placed greater importance on pay and benefits than on convenience aspects (Walker, Tausky and Oliver 1982).

Considerable research, however, supports Kanter's assertion that hierarchical level, not sex, is the determining factor (Brief, Rose, and Aldag 1977). Male and female accountants in a "big eight" firm showed no significant differences on any of the components of work motivation measured. Males and females alike were motivated by both intrinsic and extrinsic factors (Kaufman and Fetters 1980). Male and female retail sales managers demonstrated no sex differences in motivation (Brief and Oliver 1976). No sex differences in perceptions of job outcomes were found among employees of the purchasing division of a large organization, when job level was held constant (Rosenbach, Dailey, and Morgan 1979). Women in male-dominated occupations were found to have values very similar to men, putting high emphasis on instrumental success values such as power, recognition, and salary. By contrast, women in female-dominated or sex-neutral occupations did put less emphasis on these instrumental success values, but there were no differences between these groups in the socioexpressive success values (Greenfield, Greiner, and Wood 1980).

The evidence is confusing and contradictory, but it appears to be safe to conclude that any global perceptions of sex differences in preferences for occupational rewards or job attributes are unfounded. Although there may be some differences, they are mitigated by occupational and organizational status. Other variables—age, sex, education, marital and family status—have not been adequately explored to date and will surely affect these values as well. It is clearly unwarranted to make any assumptions about the desired rewards or preferred job attributes of women workers as a class.

ORGANIZATIONAL COMMITMENT/JOB INVOLVEMENT

If preferences for organizational rewards or job attributes are a function of occupation or hierarchical level, then we could conclude that stereotypes that predict women to be less motivated than men are unfounded. But the stereotypical thinking incorporates that view by arguing that women, because work is not their primary role, are less committed to their jobs or careers and less involved in their work. That is, the stereotype would use expectancy theory to argue that while women in similar occupations or at similar organizational levels may desire the same rewards from work as their male counterparts, they have less job involvement or work commitment. If that were true it would be possible to say that the desired rewards were less motivating for women, since the strength of their desire for the rewards is weaker.

Considerable research has substantiated global differences between women and men in terms of work involvement, commitment to work, or the centrality of work. But again, a more careful analysis indicates that a number of other variables greatly reduce the importance of sex differences, including hierarchical status, career salience, family status, and age.

Once again, controlling for hierarchical level apparently reduces the difference between women and men in commitment (Golembiewski 1977b), although some researchers have gone farther and have argued that there are neither sex nor position differences (Bruning and Snyder 1983). Surprisingly, organizational commitment is lower among women who feel that they have received preferential treatment because of their sex than among women who perceived themselves to have been judged on ability alone (Chacko 1982). However, it appears that for women, but not men, the longer they stay in an organization the greater their job involvement, irrespective of their occupation or organizational level (Gomez-Mejia 1983).

The assumption is often made that married women or women with children have less job involvement or organizational commitment. Again, the evidence is contradictory and suggests that the relationship is more complex than a simple married/not married equation. Being married or being a secondary wage earner in the family seems to have little bearing on one's commitment to work (Walker, Tausky, and Oliver 1982), and both women and men with employed spouses appear to have less job involvement and organizational identification than those who carry the breadwinner role alone (Gould and Werbel 1983). But one study has found that the presence of preschool children in the home reduces the work involvement of women (Walker, Tausky, and Oliver 1982) while another found higher involvement for both women and men with children (Gould and Werbel 1983).

Men and women in dual-career (as opposed to dual-earner) marriages have been found to be very alike in the degree of commitment to and importance of their careers. Those women who had planned a dual-career lifestyle before marriage were higher on career salience than those who had not, but the same was not true for men (Sekaran 1982). Despite their comparable career commitment, however, women in dual-career families apparently do not perceive themselves as being as high on job commitment as do their husbands (Sekaran 1983).

What we know so far about job involvement is that stereotypes that assert that women, especially married women and married women with children, are less committed to their work or place less importance on their careers are greatly oversimplified. In fact, women may have more job involvement and men less than what is usually assumed. The importance of job or career for both men and women is a function of occupation or organizational level, marital status, spouse's employment, spouse's commitment to job or career, the presence or absence of children in the home, and the relative contribution of each to the household. Based upon the obvious complexity of these factors and the infinite number of possible interactions, any assumptions about job involvement, work commitment, or motivation based on gender or marital status alone are clearly unfounded.

Job Satisfaction

Job satisfaction is concerned with expectations and outcomes. It is a measure of the degree to which valued and expected rewards, extrinsic or intrinsic, are realized on the job. The relationship between job satisfaction and performance is a complex one, still largely unexplained by theory or research. While a positive correlation between the two can be demonstrated, neither the degree of interaction nor the direction of causation is clear (Petty, McGee, and Cavender 1984). Appealing as the idea may be, it has never been satisfactorily demonstrated that "a happy worker becomes a productive worker." Job satisfaction is, however, demonstrably related to absenteeism and turnover, problems that are perceived as having greater impact on women workers. Equity theory would argue that women, if they failed to receive expected rewards, would seek to achieve distributive fairness by reducing their inputs, that is, by absence or withdrawal.

Although the results of job satisfaction studies are somewhat contradictory, one conclusion stands out: Women workers to a very significant extent receive smaller rewards, both intrinsic and extrinsic, than corresponding males in their organizations, yet they are equally satisfied or marginally less satisfied (Weaver 1978), and the factors that contribute to dissatisfaction differ remarkably little (Andrisani and Shapiro 1978). Satisfaction with the job seems to be closely correlated with life satisfaction for both women and men (Kavanagh and Halpern 1977) and, as Kanter predicted, what sex differences in satisfaction do appear diminish when hierarchical level (Golembiewski 1977a; Forgionne and Peeters 1983) or occupations (Smith and Plant 1982) are included in the research. Men seem to become more satisfied with age, but for women, perhaps because their work is sometimes less continuous, length of time on the job rather than age seems to be a major factor (Hunt and Saul 1975).

An early 1970s study of sex discrimination in pay and job satisfaction, based on data from a national probability sample, found that women workers were in fact victims of discrimination when it came to the assignment of organizational rewards. They were discriminated against dramatically in terms of income, and somewhat less so in terms of the "quality of their jobs." However, even though 95 percent of women workers were found to be the victims of objectively measured discrimination, only 7.9 percent reported themselves dissatisfied with their jobs (Levitan, Quinn, and Staines 1971).

A decade later, a decade in which women's awareness of discrimination had ostensibly increased dramatically, very little had changed. A study of college students in management courses found that women students expect lower pay than men students, not only at the entry level but at the peak of their careers as well (Major and Konar 1984). In another study, women workers who reported fewer positive features and more negative features in their jobs than men nevertheless did not report greater "tedium" in their jobs than the men (Pines and Kafry 1981b). Even women who, five years after college, were earning less than the males in their cohort were remarkably complacent. Men at higher levels of the organization received higher pay than females and, not surprisingly, were more satisfied than the women with the pay and promotional aspects of their jobs. At lower organizational levels, however, the situation was reversed. Females, again receiving lower pay, reported themselves *more* satisfied than males at the same level (Fairhurst and Snavely 1983b; Varca, Shaffer and McCauley 1983).

One explanation for the anomaly of high job satisfaction among women with low-paid and low-status work comes in viewing their occupational choices. People who have achieved success as they have defined it for themselves report high levels of job satisfaction, even though their achievements may not spell success to others (Lewin and Olesen 1980). Women in male-dominated professions receive more promotions and more pay—more of the traditional symbols of success—than those in female-dominated professions, yet, surprisingly, women in traditional female careers feel that their work is more important and feel more satisfaction from their work than women in male-dominated professions (Greenfield, Greiner, and Wood 1980).

For many women the significant choice is not between jobs or careers but between paid work and full-time homemaking, hence they compare their inputs and outputs not to male co-workers or even to female co-workers but to women who are out of the paid labor force. Among working-class women, for instance, even low-status work makes an important contribution to self-image. The workplace provides a source of friendship and camaraderie that is an important source of job satisfaction and is not available to the homemaker. Further, a job has clear requirements and clear payoffs—both in money and in a sense of accomplishment—and results in an enhanced self-esteem. Housework, by contrast, tends to be lonely work, and relatively few women feel competent at it. As a result, many women who find themselves relatively incompetent at housework are able to find a source of self-esteem and competence in having a paid job (Ferree 1976a; Ferree 1976b). Among women who work by choice, full-time workers encounter considerable stress and role conflict, which tends to lower their job satisfaction (Andrisani and Shapiro 1978); yet, surprisingly, they report more job satisfaction than those women who voluntarily work part time. The most satisfied women appear to be those who choose to be full-time homemakers and who are involved in volunteer activities (Hall and Gordon 1973). On the other hand, the unhappiest women are the full-time homemakers who want to work but don't. These women have low self-esteem, feel they are "pawns of fate," and mask their loneliness and worry in drugs (Fidell and Prather 1976).

The evidence, then, tells us that there are few differences between women and men in terms of job satisfaction, even though women's jobs tend to have many fewer rewards and many more negative features. Women workers seem to compare themselves with other women workers or with full-time homemakers, rather than with men workers, and hence fail to internalize the disparities. Also, women have preferences for some activities over others, and their satisfaction is a function of the extent to which their preferences and activities agree. Hence even employed women who experience a good deal of role conflict and stress report themselves more satisfied than full-time homemakers who would rather be working. There is an important implication to this, since these people also report higher self-esteem and more positive self-image. These in turn translate into self-perceptions of potency and spontaneity, attributes that are related to a number of variables associated with managerial success: self-assurance, initiative, decisiveness (Aldag and Brief 1979). The important question, then, would seem to be not so much what the actual rewards are for working women but in how they perceive those rewards and what they consider to be the alternatives.

To recap: we have shown that stereotypes predict that women and men will value different organizational rewards, that they will differ in their job involvement or their commitment to their organizations, and that they will differ in the degree and source of job satisfaction. The evidence shows that there are no clear sex differences on any of these dimensions. While some research tends to support the stereotypes in their broadest forms, clearly such mitigating variables as occupation and organizational level greatly override the effects of sex. Variables such as age, education and length of time on the job, income, marital status, spouse's employment, and presence or absence of children affect outcomes not only individually but also interactively. Much more research will undoubtedly be conducted to explore the dynamics of motivation, but in the meantime it is quite safe to conclude that organizational policies or decisions based on stereotypical assumptions about gender differences are clearly risky.

ACHIEVEMENT MOTIVATION

Achievement motivation theory is a narrow version of need theory. Rather than attempting to identify the whole range of human needs and the factors associated with jobs that satisfy those needs, achievement motivation theory concentrates on only three motives: achievement, affiliation, and power. The theory was first articulated by McClelland (1965), who developed a thematic apperception test (TAT) to measure the presence of these three motives. This projective test asks subjects to look briefly at each of a series of pictures and then write a brief paragraph about it. Each of the pictures shows an ambiguous situation involving men alone or women and men in a work situation. The subject is asked to write a brief statement of what is going on in the picture. The assumption underlying the test is that subjects will project their own motivations onto the figures in the pictures. Hence, the responses are scored for clues to the presence of the three motivations.

According to McClelland, all motives are learned, and over time each individual arranges his or her own motives in a kind of hierarchical order that then influences subsequent behavior. In the developmental process positive or negative feelings become associated with certain events, and if pleasure is associated with achievement situations, ultimately the person develops a strong achievement motivation. As achievement moves to the top of the motivation hierarchy it takes only minimal cues to arouse the expectation of pleasure, and weaker motives take on a distinctly secondary role. At that point an achievement cue, such as a challenging task, is associated with pleasure. The achievement motivation is aroused by the task, and the individual responds by striving for success.

McClelland viewed achievement motivation as closely linked to the Protestant Work Ethic and essential not only for personal success but also for economic progress. He was concerned with the process of how male children acquire this motivation. Unlike Maslow, who believed that human needs were inherent and immutable, McClelland has argued that achievement motivation is learned, and he specifies three situations in which it might develop, situations where a person achieves success through his own effort and ability (rather than through chance), characterized by intermediate levels of difficulty and risk, and in which clear and unambiguous feedback is received on the success of the individual's efforts (Miner 1980).

When it comes to the topic of achievement, sex roles and stereotypes once again influence both perception and reality. McClelland failed to find a consistent pattern of achievement motivation among women. In some cases women were found to be low in achievement motivation, which was consistent with the feminine stereotype and with the expectations of the researchers. However, in other cases women subjects were found *not* to differ from males on achievement motivation. So pervasive is stereotypical thinking that the researchers concluded not that the stereotype or the expectation was wrong but that the test was not valid for women. As a result, most of the research was conducted only on male subjects.

The feminine stereotype would suggest that women are more motivated by affiliation than by achievement, and indeed some evidence supports this conclusion. However, the affiliation motive—the desire to earn love and approval—may or may not have a negative effect on performance. As we will show later, sometimes women, to a greater extent than men, will exhibit a Motive to Avoid Success. To the extent they associate success with such negative consequences as jealousy or loss of femininity, they will decrease their performance on tasks where success might invoke these consequences. However, there are a number of contingencies that affect the arousal of Motive to Achieve Success and its effect on performance. Another view of the matter reasons that when women do perform well, particularly on such tasks as school work, they do so because they are motivated by affiliation motives rather than by desires for mastery of the task. They work for good grades, for instance, because they are rewarded by approval, but they tend to become less involved in the task itself (Hoffman 1972). Those who assert this view see the roots of the motive in early childhood socialization.

A contrasting view argues that women are, indeed, motivated to achieve, but that the areas of achievement are different from males because of cultural definitions of femininity. Women are motivated to develop skills, but the skills for which women are valued are their social skills. Women express their achievement motivation by achieving in social settings, a primarily female setting. But since they rarely achieve in traditional masculine spheres and experience negative sanctions when they do, and since women's spheres are historically devalued, their motives are misinterpreted and their behavior is attributed to affiliation motive rather than to achievement motivation (Stein and Bailey 1975). Still others assert that women often fuse the affiliation and achievement motivations, expressing pleasure and reward both in achievement per se and also in achieving in activities that "make other people happy" (Hoyenga and Hoyenga 1979). This view is certainly the least deterministic of all of those concerning achievement in women and perhaps best explains the conflicting evidence of other studies.

Some of McClelland's followers became interested in some ancillary issues, for example, Motive to Avoid Failure and Motive to Avoid Success. Motive to Avoid Failure, a theory proposed by Atkinson, posits that the fear of failure leads one to avoid activities that might result in failure but also that contribute to success (Atkinson and Raynor 1974). Motive to Avoid Success was proposed by Horner (1972), a student of Atkinson's, and posits that some highly able individuals are ambiguous about success and will seek to avoid it. Horner found that Motive to Avoid Success (or Fear of Success) was a great deal more common among women than among men and helped explain women's failure to demonstrate n-Ach. Her work has been highly controversial. Most recently, McClelland himself has contributed to the study of power motivation. His research has led him to conclude that achievement motivation is related to entrepreneurial success, but managerial success—particularly in large, complex organizations—is more closely associated with power motivation than with achievement motivation. We shall look at these three topics in succession.

Fear of Failure

For some individuals, the Fear of Failure becomes the primary motive and hence suppresses n-Ach. Fear of Failure theory views achievement motivation as a function of three factors:

- the individual's unique motivation to achieve,
- the individual's expectation that success will be achieved on a particular task, and
- the attractiveness of success on that task.

Like McClelland, Atkinson considers a 50-50 chance of success as the most motivating. Higher or lower probabilities make the task less attractive and do not arouse achievement motivation. The person with a high Fear of Failure, however, associates stronger negative feelings with failure than positive feelings with success. The motive to avoid failure becomes the primary motive and extinguishes the motive to achieve. Given an achievement situation, such as a challenging task, this person's expectation of success is low and negative feelings associated with failure arouse a motive to avoid failure. The behavioral response is to avoid situations or activities that might lead to success. Fear-of-failure individuals tend to prefer situations where the chances for success for either very high or very low. When the chance of success is very high, there is little likelihood of failure, and when the chances are very low, failure is avoided because the task was too difficult, that is, no one could have succeeded. In either event, the individual inhibits his performance and trades the chance to succeed for the chance to avoid failure (Miner 1980).

Not surprisingly, Fear of Failure has been found to be more common among men than among women. Because of the very high expectations of success that are placed on men in our society, the penalties for failure are high. Men who have inadequate experience with success tend to develop a high Fear of Failure.

Fear of Success

The Motive to Avoid Success (MAS, often identified as Fear of Success or FOS) was first described by Horner (1972) as "a latent, stable personality disposition acquired early in life in conjunction with standards of sex-role identity."

According to expectancy theories of motivation, as noted above, the arousal of motives is a function of both the expectations an individual has about the consequences of his or her actions and the value the individual puts on these consequences. Horner's theory posits that when an individual anticipates that the consequences will be negative, anxiety will be aroused. The anxiety, in turn, inhibits the action expected to give the negative consequence. From this she proposes that, since for women success often has negative consequences, most women have a motive to avoid success. Motive to Avoid Success is distinguished from a motive to fail. Women, Horner argued, don't seek failure. To the contrary, they seek achievement; but success carries the expectation of negative consequences and arouses anxiety that inhibits achievement motivation. If MAS does, in fact, occur, it would presumably be more characteristic of high-ability, high-achievement-oriented women, since these are the ones most likely to want and to get success.

To test her theory Horner developed her own Thematic Apperception Test. She used a verbal cue describing a high level of accomplishment in a mixed-sex competitive achievement situation. For females the cue was "After first term finals, Anne finds herself at the top of her medical school class." For the men, the cue was the same but the name was changed to John. She tested only for the arousal of FOS in same-sex subjects. FOS was considered present if the subject's responses to the success of someone of their own sex showed evidence of conflict, expectations of negative consequences, denial of effort or responsibility for achieving success, denial of the cue itself, or some other bizarre response.

Horner's own research found very dramatic differences between women and men in their levels of FOS; fewer than 10 percent of the males, but over 65 percent of the females, showed evidence of Fear of Success. Partly because of these dramatic findings, which were printed in an article in *Psychology Today,* and no doubt also because the theory has a kind of intuitive appeal, it has been widely cited and frequently replicated, with mixed results. Consequently, it has also been fairly highly criticized (Tresemer 1976).

Most of the studies have used students as subjects and have then generalized their conclusion to the population at large. One exception was a field study involving a matched sample of male and female managers, in which subjects responded to both same-sex and opposite-sex stimulus persons. The results did not confirm Horner's findings. No significant differences between women and men on FOS were found. Both males and females expressed anxiety toward success. Women expressed anxiety about conflict between career and family and about "ill feelings of others." Men expressed concern about the sacrifices associated with success, for example, stress, and about alienating co-workers (Wood and Greenfield 1976).

Much of the criticism of the Fear of Success theory and research, however, has to do not with the nature of the subjects but with the difficulties of measurement. Considerable evidence suggests that FOS is a situational, rather than a motivational, factor. For example:

- Situations where the individual is deviating from societal norms, which of course is what women are doing when they succeed in traditional masculine domains, elicit greater Fear of Success. In these situations FOS may represent ambivalence about success, but may or may not inhibit performance (Condry and Dyer 1976).

- Role overload (for example, a family, a job, and graduate school) and reaction to role deviance, rather than Fear of Success, may occur for both women and men (Bremer and Wittig 1980).
- Women with a traditional feminine sex-role orientation appear less highly motivated toward high achievement than androgynous or masculine women, regardless of the nature of the task (Orlofsky 1981; Major 1979). Specifically, Fear of Success is related more to the absence of masculine traits than to the presence of feminine ones. The traits most strongly associated with low fear of success are high self-confidence, decisiveness, analyticity, and independence (Cano, Solomon, and Holmes 1984).
- The complexity or difficulty of the task has an effect on the presence or absence of FOS. FOS-present women performed better when the task was relatively easy and success was ascribed to chance or luck, while FOS-absent women performed better when the task was of moderate difficulty and success was associated with ability or competence (Patty 1976).
- College women high on FOS were more likely to choose traditional female careers and to have little ambition to make a significant career contribution, whereas women without FOS were likely to choose nontraditional occupations (Anderson 1978).

All of these findings support the notion that FOS may be a situational, rather than a motivational, variable and that what the subjects may be responding to is not Fear of Success but fear of the consequences of role deviance. An important implication, however, is that if in fact Fear of Success is a situational factor, then it is not a stable personality factor, as Horner asserted.

A related criticism argues that the cues themselves arouse sexual stereotypes in the subjects. Unlike the pictures used in McClelland's TAT, which are ambiguous, Horner's cue is quite specific. Since medical school is (and certainly was in the 1960s when Horner's research was conducted) a male-dominated culture, Anne's success was achieved in a nontraditional and highly competitive domain. Further, she didn't just do well, she was at the top of her class, and she seemed surprised to "find" herself there, suggesting that she hadn't expended unusual effort or demonstrated unusual ability. Perhaps these role-deviant suggestions can explain the high incidence of FOS that Horner found (Shaver 1976). In studies where the cue is changed to place Anne and John in neutral settings, the results tend to show no significant differences between women and men. In these studies, both women and men who succeed in a typical masculine setting are seen as more masculine, but women who succeed in a neutral setting are seen as competent but not necessarily masculine (Juran 1979).

Another question raised about FOS is whether it really differs from Fear of Failure. As noted above, a field study of men and women found that both exhibited ambivalence about success, although for different reasons. Women worried about the social consequences and the role conflicts of success while men worried about the personal sacrifices and the effect on the competition (Wood and Greenfield 1976). When Patty (1976) measured the performance patterns of FOS-present versus FOS-absent women, she found them to be quite like those expected of high fear-of-failure men. That is, men high on achievement motivation did best on tasks of moderate difficulty, while men with high fear of failure did better on familiar, simple, or noncompetitive tasks. When the cue was varied so that Anne or John was lower than at the very top of the class, the outcome revealed more Fear of Failure—discouragement or anticipation of future failure—than Fear of Success. Negative imagery is elicited for both Anne and John when they are ranked near the bottom of the class and for John even when he was near the middle of the class, with John receiving more negative imagery than Anne (Fogel and Paludi 1984).

Despite the many criticisms of Horner's work, and the failure of succeeding researchers to validate her findings, the Fear of Success theory remains an important tool in understanding women's achievement motivation. The efforts to replicate her work have led to elaboration of her theory, greater complexity, and to improved instruments—including questionnaire measures. Tresemer (1976), one of the first to raise concerns over the overapplication of the theory, has also warned about the overinterpretation of his criticism. He cautions that to negate the theory altogether because of its flaws is like "throwing out the baby with the bathwater." Researchers have continued, and will continue in the future, to struggle with the questions of sex differences in Fear of Success, the extent to which it differs from Fear of Failure, and, perhaps most importantly, the definition of success.

What we have learned from the research, briefly stated and oversimplified, is that there is some combination of sex-role socialization and situational constraints that leads some women and some men to inhibit their performance in some circumstances. The relationship is a great deal more complex than Horner's original work suggested. The motive, if indeed it can properly be called a motive, is a good deal less stable and certainly less pervasive than her work suggested. But all of that is the nature of theory building. It is from the continual process of theorizing and testing that understanding and knowledge arises.

POWER MOTIVATION

After years of study, McClelland has concluded that achievement motivation "leads people to behave in very special ways that do not necessarily lead to good management" (McClelland and Burnham 1976). Achievement-oriented people, who like to do things for themselves and who seek short-term feedback on their performance, are well suited to entrepreneurial endeavors. Management, however, requires the ability to delegate tasks and to accomplish organizational goals by influencing the behavior of others.

Effective managers must have a greater need for power than need to achieve; they must also be disciplined and controlled so that their exercise of power "is directed toward the benefit of the organization and not toward the manager's personal aggrandizement. Moreover, the manager's need for power ought to be greater than his need for being liked."

Good managers, McClelland and Burnham argue, are high on Power Motivation, low on Affiliation Motivation, and high on inhibition and control. Managers high on Affiliation Motivation have a need to be liked and want to stay on good terms with everybody; they may behave in ways that enhance their popularity but that are detrimental to the overall goals of the organization. They often make decisions based upon what's best for the individual and ignore orderly procedures and long-range goals.

However, this is not to argue that the best manager is insensitive or self-serving; a distinction must be made between "personal power" and "socialized power." The individual who abuses power or seeks personal aggrandizement is using personal power; managers who combine power motivation with "controlled action or inhibition" are using socialized power. Those high on personal power often exercise their power impulsively; they are rude, drink too much, try to exploit others sexually, and collect such status symbols as fancy cars and big offices. Those high on socialized power, found to be the most successful managers, are more "institution minded," drink less, and want to serve others.

Because people experience power in different ways, McClelland (1975) has developed a typology of power that fits into a developmental model, as shown in Figure 8.1. Using the two dimensions of "source of power" and "object of power," either of which is either internal (self) or external (others), he identifies four stages of power development:

Stage 1: The source of power is others, and the object of power is self. The person derives his strength from others. In infancy, the child derives strength from a caretaker who nurtures and protects and in so doing makes the child feel strong. In adulthood, the person continues to draw strength from external sources—from friends, spouse, or others he or she admires. They want to be around such people to draw strength from them. People in this stage are often described as being very dependent, but they are only dependent in the sense that it makes them feel strong to be near a source of strength.

FIGURE 8.1
McClelland's Stages of Power Development

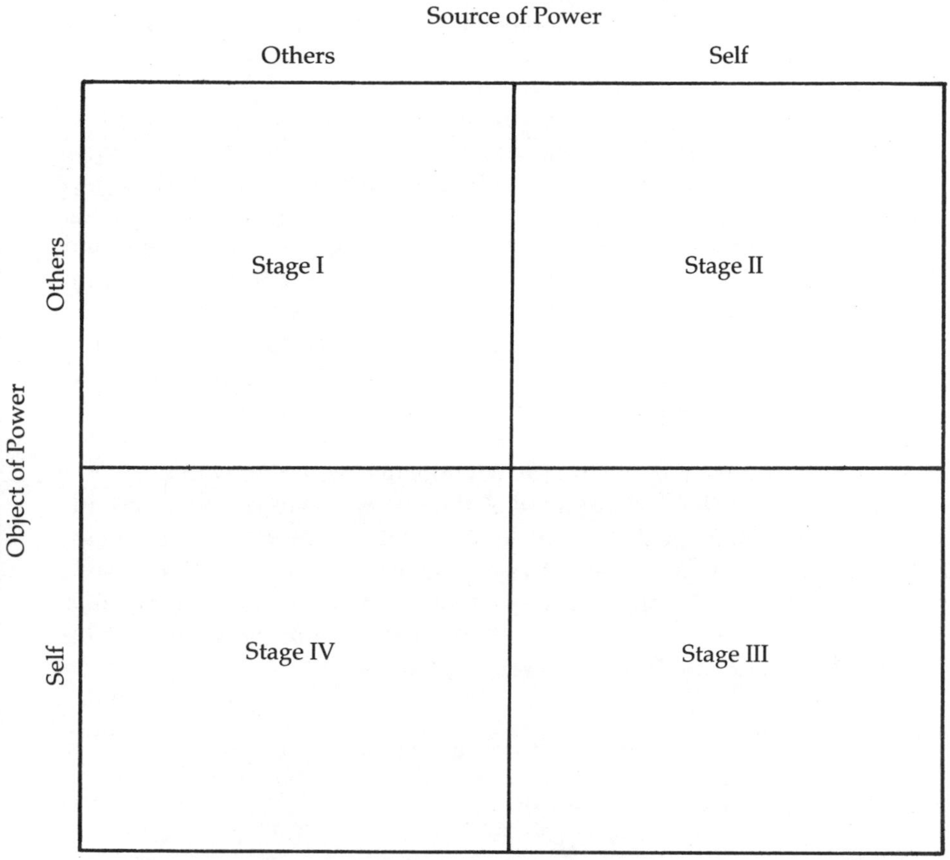

Source of Power

	Others	Self
Others	Stage I	Stage II
Self	Stage IV	Stage III

Object of Power

Stage 2: Both the source and the object of power is self. The person becomes internally strong. As children develop, they learn that they can gain control over their own bodies and minds and can decrease the control by and dependency on their mothers. In adulthood, the person in this mode feels powerful by accumulating possessions that are a part of the self—status symbols such as an expensive car or home—and by controlling the body through dieting, exercise, or yoga. The goal here is to feel strong and in control, but not necessarily to influence others.

Stage 3: The source of power is the self and the object is others. Soon after children learn that they can control themselves, they learn that they can control, or at least maneuver, others. As they grow older, they learn more subtle methods of control—bargaining, persuading, manipulating. Adults in this stage are often competitive and exploitive. However, somewhat surprisingly, some kinds of helping behavior also fall into this quadrant. Giving and receiving help can be looked at as a two-way interaction not unlike winning and losing. People who receive help from others tacitly acknowledge that they are weaker than the givers, at least at that point. The person who gives help without a reciprocal receiving of help achieves a kind of dominance over the receiver.

Stage 4: Both the source and the object of power is external. In this most advanced stage the person sees him- or herself as an instrument of higher authority (God, law, the larger group), which moves him or her to try to influence or serve others. The religious or political leader at this stage, and many business managers as well, willingly subvert their own self-interest for the greater good of the collectivity. People in this stage are more responsible in organizations, less ego-involved, more willing to seek expert help when appropriate, and more open to intimates. However, the person who has reached this state of maturity has the ability and the opportunity to use power behaviors in any of the three stages.

It would appear at first glance that effective managers would fall into Stage 4, but McClelland argues that they more likely represent an advanced phase of Stage 3. The Leadership Motive Pattern—the set of motives most associated with effective management at high levels of organizations—includes being at least moderately high in power motivation lower in affiliation motivation, and high in self-control or activity inhibition. McClelland and Boyatzis (1982) explain:

> High n-Power is important because it means the person is interested in playing the "influence game," in having an impact on others; lower in n-Affiliation is important because it enables the manager to make difficult decisions without worrying unduly about being disliked; and high on self-control is important because it means the person is likely to be concerned with maintaining organizational systems and following orderly procedures.

Are there sex differences in n-Pow? The small amount of research available suggests that women and men do not differ in the extent to which they are motivated by the opoportunity to use power (Van Wagner and Swanson 1979), but McClelland's research suggests men and women do differ in the way they express power; he found differences at every stage. In a general and oversimplified sense, he found that men high in power motivation tend to be "assertive in one way or another and emotional." They get into arguments, share information (boast) about their sex lives with family and friends, and have difficulty sleeping. Women, on the other hand, show a quite different pattern, which he again attributes to the possibility that the questionnaire may be inappropriate for women.

Women, he found, tend to focus more on themselves and to be concerned about their bodies, in the sense both of disciplining the body through diet and exercise and of being concerned with clothing. "Women are more concerned about having and sharing; men more about pushing ahead." McClelland concludes that women and men in a sense revert to sex roles in a reciprocal expression of power motivation. Men with high power motivation have an emotionally assertive approach to life and find strength in action; women with high power motivation focus on building up the self and on being internally strong.

McClelland and others have demonstrated that his Leadership Motive Pattern is correlated with successful management careers for men in nontechnical management positions, but not for men in engineering-dominated positions. To date no research has asked whether this Leadership Motive Pattern is present in successful female managers, although we shall see in Chapter 9 that on other leadership traits very few differences exist between women and men.

If McClelland is correct that power motivation, plus high socialized power orientation and low affiliation motivation, are the characteristics of successful male managers, and that women tend to differ from men in the way that they express their power motivation, then these findings have considerable implications for women in or aspiring to management positions. Chapter 9 gives a detailed look at the differential ways in which women and men perceive power, attain power, and use power.

But before we take up that issue, we turn to a cognitive theory of motivation. McClelland has asserted that achievement-motivated people prefer to attribute their success or failure to their own efforts or ability, rather than to chance or luck. Critics of Expectancy Value theories like McClelland's and Horner's have increasingly looked to cognitive theories to explain the apparent differential motivation of women and men.

ATTRIBUTION/ASPIRATION THEORY

A model of Attribution/Aspiration Theory categorizes the way women's successes or failures are perceived, to what causes they are attributed, and the effect of those attributions on future performance (Frieze 1975). It is based on research that is focused on three areas, showing that

1. Men and boys consistently hold higher expectations for personal success than do women and girls,
2. Women and men consistently attribute their own successes and failures to different causes, and
3. Other people also attribute success or failure to different causes of failure depending on the sex of the performer.

Differential Expectations

Both sexes tend to err when it comes to predicting success or failure. Men tend to have higher levels of expectations than women, especially when the task could be perceived as a masculine one. When objective measures of ability are available, it can be shown that men tend to over-state their expectation of success relative to their ability, whereas women tend to understate theirs. On the whole, however, even though women tend to be less optimistic, they tend to be more accurate (Frieze 1975). This higher level of self-esteem is apparent even among children. For instance, when children were required to state their expectations before the first trial in an experimental situation, the boys showed considerably more persistence in trying to reach their stated goals. Under similar cir-cumstances the girls showed more persistence when they were not re-quired to state their expectations or when they stated them only before the last trial (Dweck and Gilliard 1975). These differences in expectation are more pronounced when the task is labeled masculine or is new and unfamiliar. Predictions are more accurate when we have experience at the task or when it is seen as sex-appropriate (Frieze et al. 1982).

Self-Attributions

Are differences in expectations related to differences in the perceived causes of success or failure? Four attributional causes are possible: ability, effort, luck, and task ease or difficulty. A person may be seen as having achieved success because of unusual ability or unusual effort, or simply because of good luck or because the task was relatively undemanding. Failure may be laid to incompetence or lack of effort, or to bad luck or diffi-culty (Miner 1980). Attributions differ along two dimensions; whether they are stable or unstable, and whether they are internal or external. The stable, internal, causes are ability and effort; they lie within the indi-vidual. Success or failure attributed to stable factors might be expected to be repeated. The unstable, external, dimensions are luck and task diffi-culty; they lie within the environment. It is difficult to predict whether success or failure will reoccur when they are attributed to unstable causes (Frieze 1975).

Are there sex differences in attribution? In a very general sense, it can be said that men tend to attribute their successes to internal and stable causes (ability and task difficulty) while women tend to attribute their successes to external and unstable causes (good luck and exceptional ef-fort). On the other hand, men tend to attribute their failures to external and unstable causes (bad luck and lack of effort) while women attribute their failures to internal and stable causes (lack of ability and task diffi-culty). This generalized statement would support an argument that women, failing to attribute their success to their own ability, would be less likely to seek to repeat their successes or to set higher expectations for themselves. The research results show that while to some extent these generalizations are valid, a number of situational variables reduce the sex differences in attributions. These variables include job level, Achievement Motivation, Fear of Success, sex-role orientation, and the sex labeling of the task.

Job-Level: When job level was held constant (in a study of male and female first-level managers), no sex differences were found in attribution to luck, effort, or task. But some sex differences occurred. The men rated their own performance more favorably, saw themselves as having higher intelligence and greater ability, and attributed their success more to ability than the women did (Deaux 1979).

Achievement Motivation: Achievement motivation appears to be a more important predictor of attributions than sex. College students with high motivation made relatively higher ratings for ability and lower ratings for task difficulty when attributing the cause of their success or failure. Some sex differences did occur, however. Females tended to employ higher ratings for luck, and females with high achievement motivation made maximal use of effort as a causal factor (Bar-Tal and Frieze 1977). In a similar test under very competitive conditions, level of achievement motivation, not sex, again proved to be the critical factor. Males attributed their outcomes to ability more than did females; females attributed their outcomes more to effort than did males. Winners attributed outcome more to effort than did losers; and females attributed more to luck than did males. But again, all sex differences in attribution to ability, effort, and luck were explained by differences in achievement motivation (Levin, Gillman, and Reis 1982).

Fear of Success: Feather and Simon (1973) found a tendency for both male and female students with high Fear of Success to attribute success less externally and failure more externally than subjects who did not express Fear of Success. There was no relationship between Fear of Success and performance.

Sex Role Orientation: Orlofsky (1981) found that women who scored low on masculinity (feminine or undifferentiated scores on the Bem Sex Role Inventory) attributed their success to luck more than masculine or androgynous women. Women with high masculinity scores attributed their success to skill more than did the feminine of the undifferentiated group.

Sex Labeling of the Task: Expectations for success are related to the sex typing of the task. When a task is labeled as masculine, males tend to expect success and females failure. When these expected outcomes are achieved (success for males and failure for females) they are likely to be attributed to stable causes, while unexpected outcomes (failure for males and success for females) are more likely attributed to unstable causes (Weiner et al. 1971). These results hold true for children as well as adults (Etaugh and Brown 1975). McHugh, Frieze, and Hanusa (1982) found that, contrary to predictions, males rated themselves as luckier than females in competitive situations but, consistent with predictions, they made fewer attributions to ability on a female task.

Attributions of Others

The third element of the Attribution/Aspiration Theory speaks to the aspirations of others, and again the evidence is mixed. It's been frequently demonstrated that when objectively equal performance is being evaluated by third-party observers, men are consistently rated higher than women by both male and female raters (see Chapter 10 for a fuller discussion). The question here is not whether there are actual differences in performance but whether outcomes are attributed to different causes. Once again, an overview of the literature shows that the same bias that exists with self-attribution persists with the attributions of others; success of males is attributed to internal causes and of females to external causes, while the opposite holds true for failure (Galper and Luck 1980). But once again, there are situational variables that tend to ameliorate the effect of stereotypes:

Sex Labeling of the Task: On two tasks, one labeled masculine, one feminine, both male and female subjects attributed success to different causes depending on the sex label. A male's successful performance on a masculine task was attributed to skill, while the same performance by a female was attributed to luck. But the reverse conditions did not hold true. On the feminine task, ratings for men and women were almost identical. Further, performance on the masculine task was seen as better by the subjects, even though there were no differences in task difficulty. Women were rated as luckier than men; their outcomes were attributed about half to luck and half to skill (Deaux and Emswiller 1974). The sex labeling of a task or behavior affected not only its causal attribution but also judgments about whether the behavior is "good" or "bad." Attributions and judgments supported the notion of a double standard; identical behavior by males and females were attributed to different causes and judged by different standards. Behavior by males that was seen as incongruent with the masculine role was attributable to personal (internal) causes, while behaviors that were judged "bad" (socially unacceptable) were attributed to external causes. However, the reverse was true for women. Role-deviant behaviors were attributed to external causes and "bad" behaviors to internal causes. These data seem to support the general notion that "male is normal" and suggest there is a tendency to attach greater social blame to women than to men for identical undesirable behaviors (Galper and Luck 1980).

Expectations of Success: Feather and Simon (1971), using only the dimensions of ability and luck, found that unexpected outcomes were attributed to luck more often then expected outcomes. If a person did well on the first trial of a test, he or she would be expected to do well the second time, and in that case success would be attributed to ability. On the other hand, if the subject was unsuccessful in the first trial, the expectation would be that failure would be repeated on the second trial, and success would be attributed to ability. These results have not been confirmed in further studies, however. Two studies by Feldman-Summers and Kiesler (1974) found that both males and females expected males to do better on a masculine task, but these expectations did not affect the kinds of attributions that were made. Regardless of expectations or outcome, more effort was attributed to women than to men. When the experiment involved judgments between medical specialties perceived as masculine or feminine (surgery or pediatrics), all subjects thought that women would be more successful in the feminine field than in the masculine one and that the women would be less successful than men regardless of specialty. More motivation was attributed to females than males.

Attitudes toward Women as Managers: Males who hold an essentially negative attitude toward women as managers, as measured on the Women As Manager's Scale, were inclined to attribute the success of a woman manager to the external factors of luck or an easy job, while men with a positive attitude toward women managers were more likely to ascribe their success to internal factors of ability and effort. However, when the women managers were unsuccessful, no clear pattern of attribution was found. Success or failure of the women managers did not change the attitudes of the subjects toward women managers in general (Garland and Price 1977). Attitudes toward women as managers appears, however, to be a better predictor of male attributions than of females (Stevens and DeNisi 1980).

Aspirations

The implications of these differential attributions are fairly clear. If success is the result of ability and effort, one can take pride in the achievement and assume that it will be repeated. If success is attributed to a lucky break or if the task is seen as being relatively easy, there is little pride in the achievement and little expectation of future success. If failure is seen as the result of too little effort or of bad luck, then one can hope to achieve better results with increased effort and a change in fortune. But if the failure was caused by incompetence, then little change could be expected on future tries. Hence pride of accomplishment is more closely related to the internal and stable factors of ability and task difficulty, and success under these conditions would lead the performer to expect that future effort would lead to future success. Failure attributed to external and unstable causes could also lead the performer to expect that future tries, especially if they included increased effort, would result in success. Either of these cases should induce the individual to attempt future success, since he or she could reasonably expect to succeed. The opposite set of conditions, however—success attributed to external and unstable causes and failure attributed to internal and stable causes—would lead not only to a loss of self-esteem but also to an expectation of future failure, or at best of a lack of control over future outcomes.

If it were true, then, that there are sex differences in attributions, it could be argued that women are less motivated than men. But the evidence clearly shows that what sex differences do appear in self-attribution or the attributions of others are very slight (Frieze et al. 1982) and are largely explained by situational and "dispositional" variables. Situational variables include both the task itself (whether it is perceived as masculine or feminine, socially acceptable or unacceptable, easy or difficult, novel or familiar) and the context (the amount of competition inherent in the situation, the sex balance of actors in the situation, group versus individual efforts). Dispositional variables deal with the problem of treating men or women as a homogeneous group. They include motivational variables (achievement motivation, Fear of Success, self-esteem) and gender-role variables (androgyny, Attitudes toward Women) that cut across gender distinctions. As with the confusion surrounding Fear of Success, these results indicate that early studies may have overgeneralized their findings. They point the direction for new and more sophisticated research, but rather than negate the theory, they simply call for its elaboration (McHugh, Fisher, and Frieze 1982).

The research results have not obliterated the basic connection, that is, that expectations of success or failure are related to effort and outcome, and that expectations are a function of the attributions of self and others of causes of past outcomes. To the extent that, and under the conditions that, women and men make different attributions in like circumstances, their aspirations and their outcomes will also be different. And that is a difference that has profound implications for both individuals and management.

CONCLUSION

In this chapter we have reviewed both content and process theories of motivation with the hope of identifying sex differences. We have found repeatedly that neither men nor women can be treated as a homogenous group. Men and women do differ in terms of the value they attach to various organizational rewards, their commitment to work, the satisfactions they receive from work and the sources of that satisfaction, the extent to which they are motivated by achievement, affiliation or power needs, and the sources to which they and others attribute their successes or failures. However, all of these differences are eliminated or greatly mitigated by a number of variables.

Occupation and organizational level are major factors in explaining motivation differences. Individuals in low-status jobs, with little power and little opportunity for promotion, tend to value extrinsic rewards and the social aspects of the job regardless of gender. Managers and professional workers tend to differ very little from each other but a good deal from other occupational groups in their preference for rewards, their job commitment, their job satisfaction, and their achievement and power motivation.

Other personal variables include age, education, income, sex-role orientation, tenure on the job, attitudes and feelings associated with success or failure, marital status (including whether the spouse works), the presence or absence of children in the home, and occupational choice. Other situational variables that affect motivation include the sex labeling of the job and the causal attributions of self and others.

The dilemma is compounded by the fact that none of these variables works in isolation; there is clearly an interactive effect between them that has not been, and probably never will be, fully explored. To do so would be enormously time consuming and no doubt unproductive. Would we be better off it we understood the differences in motivation between a married, college-educated woman with teen-age children working as a bank officer and a divorced man with preschool-aged children with a high school education working on an assembly line? Probably not. Would we be better off to acknowledge that any perceived sex differences are much more likely to be a function of individual differences or of some combination of the above variables? Probably so.

9
Leadership and Power

The study of management has alternately concentrated on the study of leaders and the study of power. The study of leaders and leadership began with the study of traits, on the assumption that leadership was an inherent characteristic. Not surprisingly, trait theory was known synonymously as the "great man" theory of leadership. It was thought that if social science could identify the traits common to successful leaders, it could then measure these traits in incipient managers and predict which ones would be successful. When trait approaches proved disappointing, the study of leadership moved on to theories of leadership style, which generally looked at the two dimensions of "consideration" and "initiating structure," and subsequently to theories that added situational factors to these two.

Only very recently has the study of power been a serious concern of organizational research. Even though Max Weber's (1947) seminal work looked at the importance of legitimate power and the acceptance of authority, the issue of power has been mostly ignored until very recently. However, partly because of McClelland's findings that power motivation is more significantly related to managerial success than achievement motivation, and partly because of the rising concern of the women's movement for the powerlessness of women, there has of late been increasingly serious study of power and power styles in organizations.

It shouldn't surprise us to learn that the study of leadership or of power rarely includes sex or sex role as organizationally significant variables; the unchallenged assumption is that "male is normal" and all leaders are not only male but quite masculine. Very little research asks the relationship between masculinity or femininity and managerial effectiveness. Recent studies have, however, addressed the issue of female leadership and female power usage. These studies frequently explore the extent

to which female leaders display masculine characteristics and their success in doing so. Another popular topic asks how subordinates respond
to having a female supervisor or manager. No research, apparently, has
ever asked the parallel question of how workers feel about having a male
boss.

This chapter will review the findings of the literature on masculine
and feminine leadership and power behaviors. It will start with the trait
literature and proceed chronologically to the study of leadership studies
and then to the studies of situational variables. In the final section we will
look at the literature of power as it applies to masculinity and femininity.
The study of power, as we shall see, is approached in two different ways.
The more traditional approach looks at power from the individual or situational viewpoint; the other approach looks at power as a function of the
organizational structure.

TRAIT THEORIES

Literally hundreds of studies of the traits or characteristics of "natural
leaders" have been conducted over time. They became particularly popular between about 1920 and 1950 when the rapid development of
psychological testing instruments made personality assessment more a-
vailable. The kind of traits most frequently studied included physical
characteristics, personality, and ability (Yukl 1981). Certain traits were
found to be common among leaders: for instance, they tend to be tall; of
high socioeconomic status; intelligent, exhibiting superior judgment, decisiveness, knowledge, and verbal ability; have good interpersonal skills;
and have high achievement needs (Aldag and Brief 1981). These traits are
more related to the probability of being selected as a leader than to success
as a leader. They may, however, tell us something about why women are
less likely to be chosen as leaders, since on the average women are shorter
than men, and are seen stereotypically as being less intelligent, decisive,
and motivated. Women are, of course, perceived as having good interpersonal skills, but they are not seen as being powerful or influential.

Trait theory starts with the belief that leaders differ in some fundamental way from nonleaders. The early research was conducted in order
to determine empirically just what those trait differences were. However,
after many years and many hundreds of studies, efforts to distill the information proved disappointing. One review found that only 5 percent of all
traits thought to be related to leadership or success showed up in four or
more studies (Bird 1940). Another showed that while certain traits differentiated leaders from nonleaders, the relative importance of the dif-
ferentiating traits changed from one situation to another and could also be
related to the traits of followers (Stogdill 1948). So persuasive were these

writers that trait theory was virtually abandoned as organizational researchers sought for significant situational and style variables and the interactions between them. However, when Stogdill again reviewed the literature on trait studies in 1974, he concluded that researchers had overreacted to his criticisms. He argued that while there are no traits that will guarantee managerial success or are essential to it, the very personal nature of leadership should not be ignored.

Recent work with trait theories has concentrated on managerial assessment and selection. Assessment-center approaches, which use a variety of projective tests in simulated situations, plus some longitudinal studies, have provided important knowledge about managerial effectiveness and the importance of managerial motivations, interests, values, and technical, interpersonal, and conceptual skills (Yukl 1981). These studies have led to sex role being considered as an occupationally relevant variable and have produced insights not found elsewhere on the differential effects of sex role on leader behavior.

Before looking at what actual differences have been found between women and men, we should make explicit the existence of perceived differences. A survey of personnel directors showed that, despite contrary evidence, the majority of the subjects did not have high expectations for the effectiveness of women managers.

> Virtually every perceived difference between male and female employees was unfavorable to women aspiring to higher level occupations. Women were seen as less favorable in terms of knowledge, aptitudes, skills, motivation, interests, temperament, and work habits demanded in most managerial roles (Rosen and Jerdee 1978).

Women were also seen to "cry easily," perhaps with good reason. The study tells us nothing about the traits of women managers; it tells us a good deal about the perceptions of personnel managers.

Schein (1973, 1975) conducted two studies of perceived sex differences. Using a list of 92 adjectives, she asked 300 middle-line male managers to choose the items that they thought described either a successful manager, a man, or a woman. The results showed great similarity between masculine stereotypes and managerial stereotypes. Managers were seen to be more similar to men than to women on such characteristics as Emotionally Stable, Aggressive, Leadership Ability, Self-Reliant, (not) Uncertain, Vigorous, Desires Responsibility, (not) Frivolous, Objective, Well-Informed, and Direct. Disappointingly, when Schein replicated her study two years later on a population of women managers, she found that they were only slightly less likely than men managers to subscribe to these managerial stereotypes. The women managers, however, were more likely to describe a similarity between women and managers and between women and men. One surprise, however, came when the responses of male managers were broken down by age. The conventional wisdom holds that younger men, raised in an era of women's liberation, will hold less-stereotyped views of women as managers. But Schein found the opposite to be true. Older men managers, who are more likely to have actually worked with women in managerial positions, were less traditional in their perceptions of women. A more recent replication of this study, using the same list of adjectives and testing male and female managers simultaneously, found very little change over time (Massengill and DiMarco 1979).

The concept of psychological androgyny seemed to offer a fresh perspective to the study of managerial traits. If, as Bem and others have demonstrated, the androgynous individual is a more mentally healthy and more effective individual in nonorganizational settings, it seemed reasonable to speculate that the good manager would be perceived as androgynous. However, the hypothesis was soundly rejected by both males and females, who concurred with the other research that good managers are masculine (Powell and Butterfield 1979). However, by contrast, bad managers are not perceived as feminine, as might have been expected, but as undifferentiated, that is, as low on both masculine and feminine qualities (Powell and Butterfield 1984).

These studies show us that managers themselves, both men and women, tend to subscribe to the "great man" theory of leadership. We need to know further whether, in fact, sex or sex role does affect managerial success. It will also be useful to know whether there are in fact trait differences between male and female managers or between women managers and nonmanagers. One study explicitly included sex role as a variable and found it to be of no importance to success. Ghiselli (1971) used a "self-description inventory" to measure leader traits, then correlated these traits with success on the job to determine their differential importance. The trait most highly correlated with managerial success was "supervisory ability." At the very bottom of the list, showing no part in managerial effectiveness, was masculinity-femininity. However, since these were self-descriptions, and since the managerial stereotype so closely parallels the masculine stereotypes, one has to ask if successful managers would be likely to describe themselves as having feminine traits.

What evidence exists suggests that there are few, if any, trait differences between women and men managers. Significant differences were found on only two fairly insignificant variables in an extensive study using both trait and style approaches and relying heavily on Maslow's need concepts. Women scored higher on "social and work incentive" dimensions; men scored higher than females on interpersonal competence between managers and their peers (Donnell and Hall 1980; Hall and Donnell 1979). Similarly, a study of male and female MBA (Master's degree in Business Administration) candidates found no significant differences in male and female personality traits (Pfeifer and Shapiro 1978). A three-year longitudinal study of career advancement found strong similarities between women and men managers. One surprising outcome of this study, however, was the realization that men had considerably more career problems than expected. Neither women nor men seemed to have focused career plans or to have evaluated their strengths and weaknesses. It appears that past studies may have compared women's experiences to a successful male myth rather than to actual experiences, resulting in misleading conclusions about the nature of barriers to women (Harlan and Weiss 1981).

Perhaps the best-known and most frequently cited study comparing women managers and nonmanagers is Hennig and Jardim's *The Managerial Woman* (1977). This work demonstrates, perhaps better than any other, the strengths and the fallacies of the trait approach. The book was based on research that studied the life experiences of 25 highly successful women managers. All 25 held top-level line management positions in large or medium-sized firms. The women had achieved their positions through progressive career advancement, and their current positions were ones not generally designated as feminine. Data were obtained through interviews, autobiographical accounts, and a questionnaire. The same questionnaire was administered to three other groups of women to provide comparisons, and the 25 subjects were matched as closely as possible with a group of 25 women similar in background, education, and early career experience who had given up their careers at middle management. The data were arranged in five periods: childhood, adolescence, college, the first career decade, and career maturity. The comparison was intentionally between these 25 successful women and other women, not men. The question was how these women managed to depart from traditional female roles to achieve success in what the authors describe as "a man's world."

This, then, is traditional trait theory. Its purpose was to find out what made these high-achieving women different from their more traditional sisters, and the assumption was that "their accounts of their own experience would be the best source of explanation for the question raised." The approach was frankly psychoanalytic and the conclusions were inevitably deterministic. Remarkable similarities were found. All 25 were first-born children. Each was either an only child or the eldest in an all-girl family of no more than three children. All were born into very traditional upwardly mobile middle-class families, and all had happy childhoods with warm and loving families. Each identified more with her father than her mother and received support and encouragement from her father to succeed.

The career development of the group was also remarkably homogeneous. All went to college; most majored in career fields, rejecting the traditional feminine choices. Almost all started work in a secretarial position; in the Depression era, most of them were able to find jobs through the assistance or intervention of their fathers or family friends. Several changed jobs during the first two years, but after that all of them had stayed with the same firm for 30 years. None reported making a career decision until she was in her early 30s, and none married before age 35. The first ten years of their careers consisted of starting off as a secretary or administrative assistant to a rising executive and moving up in the company as he moved up. By the end of that first decade each had reached a responsible position, at least in middle management, and was well launched on a satisfying and rewarding career.

By their middle to late 30s, each of these women reached a "job plateau" and experienced what male executives would call a "mid-life crisis." Many began to cut back on their career involvement and to concentrate on their personal lives. Many began to reassess their attitudes toward femininity and traditional feminine values. Half of them eventually married, all to divorced men or widowers at least ten years older. Each of the husbands had children from previous marriages; none of the women bore children of her own.

The similarities among this group of women are certainly surprising. But what does all this tell us? First of all, these women were all born before 1915, the period in which the first women's movement was at its height. They went to college during the 1930s, and the financial hardships that kept many Depression-era young people out of college seems not to have affected their lives at all. Much of their early career progress took place during World War II, when a shortage of men workers created unusual career opportunities for women and when fewer young men were available for dating and marriage (Epstein 1971). Each of them had a male executive who served as an important mentor in her career progress.

To what extent can we generalize from these findings? Considering the results from other studies that suggest the first born or last born may be a "special child" who receives certain advantages (West 1976), can we say that women who are first born or only children are more likely than others to have successful careers? These 25 women all had high-achieving fathers and, with one exception, full-time homemaker mothers with very traditional values. Yet other studies show that high-achieving women are more likely to have nontraditional mothers or that the daughter's role may be related to both the mother's role and the mother's satisfaction with her role (Epstein 1971). Do we have to conclude that women who want to become successful managers must delay marriage and forego motherhood altogether? Obviously not. It's true that other studies confirm that women in the top ranks are much more likely than other women or than men in comparable positions to be unmarried (Epstein 1971). However, the last decade has seen an enormous increase in the number of married women in the work force at all levels and an increasing awareness of the possibilities of combining family and career. In fact, *The Managerial Woman* suffers from many of the weaknesses of trait theory. It tells us the traits that characterized these women managers, but not the relative strengths of the traits, the impact of the environment on their success, or the relationship between relevant traits and situational variables.

Nevertheless, there do appear to be more differences between women managers and nonmanagers than there are between women and men managers. A comparison of women in nontraditional occupations (20 percent or fewer female occupants) and women in nursing found that the nontraditional women were more achieving, emphasized production more, saw themselves as having characteristics more like managers and men, and saw no self-characteristics that conflicted with those ascribed to male managers. Although they had not foregone marriage, the businesswomen considered the domestic role less important, had fewer children, and had fewer children living at home than did the nurses. The groups did not vary in their attitudes toward the importance of their careers, their perceptions of their husband's attitudes, nor in the education level of their spouses and parents (Moore and Rickel 1980).

To sum up, we can say that trait theory has been generally discredited, although perhaps more so than it deserves. Early trait research, based on the "great man" theory of leadership, sought to identify the characteristics that separated leaders from nonleaders with respect to physical characteristics, personality, and ability. These studies were generally unsuccessful. Later studies have attempted to identify the traits that distinguish effective leaders from less-effective ones and have looked at a wider range of traits and characteristics, including motivation to manage, interests, values, and specific managerial skills such as technical, interpersonal, and conceptual ability. These studies have helped managers to assess and select successful leaders.

Much of the research that has been conducted on women managers has been trait research. The studies tell us something about the differences or lack of differences that exist between effective and ineffective women and men managers and between women managers and nonmanagers. They suggest that effective women managers differ very little from effective men managers in terms of their attitudes, motivation, and behavior, except that they are less likely than their male peers to be married and have children and that their career progress is slower. They further suggest that women managers differ considerably from women nonmanagers in their motivation, attitudes, and behaviors. Finally, and perhaps most importantly, they tell us the traits that are perceived by most managers as being related to managerial success, and reveal that women are not perceived stereotypically as possessing many of these traits.

STYLE THEORIES

Almost every approach to the study of leadership style identifies two dimensions of leadership behaviors that are seen as instrumental to effective management. Studies conducted at the Ohio State University beginning in the 1940s called these Consideration and Initiating Structure, and these terms have been used fairly consistently ever since. Consideration includes such specific behaviors as leader supportiveness, friendliness, consideration, consultation with subordinates, representation of subordinate interests, openness of communication with subordinates, and recognition of subordinate contributions. These relationship-oriented behaviors are all instrumental for establishing and maintaining good relationships with subordinates. Initiating Structure includes behavior items concerned with directing subordinates, clarifying subordinate roles, planning, coordinating, problem solving, criticizing poor work, and pressuring subordinates to perform better. These task-oriented behaviors are instrumental for efficient utilization of human and material resources in the attainment of group goals (Yukl 1981).

Over time it became apparent that leadership style alone was insufficient to explain leader effectiveness and that elements of the context in which the leader behaved were perhaps equally predictive. One of the first to introduce situational variables into leadership style theory was Fiedler (1965). He agreed with the basic premise of the Ohio State studies that style could be divided into two categories. However, he argued that the effectiveness of a given style was contingent upon certain situational variables that were not easily manipulated. The variables he found to be significant were:

- Leader-Member Relations: the degree to which group members like and trust their leader and are willing to follow his or her guidance;
- Task Structure: the degree to which the task is either highly specific or vague and ambiguous; and
- Position Power: the amount of legitimate and sustained power that the leader possesses.

Combinations of these three variables create eight separate types of organizational climate, each of which is favorable to one or the other leadership style. The leader's style is determined by the Least Preferred

Co-worker Scale (LPC), a controversial but widely used instrument. Leaders are trained to identify the situations in which their style will be most effective, rather than to try to adopt new styles. Fiedler argues that it is nearly impossible to "turn a cold and hard manager into a warm and fuzzy manager" through training, but if you can train people to recognize and avoid the situations in which they are likely to fail, then they cannot help but succeed. As we will see shortly, despite the criticisms of the theory, the LPC score has been shown to be a better predictor of leadership success than sex.

Other situational approaches have added new variables or have refined these existing ones. The research that we are concerned with here attempts to look at the sex or the sex role of the leader and the followers, at the perceived masculinity or femininity of the task or of the environment, and at the attitudes of the followers.

However, before we proceed, a cautionary statement is in order. Much of the style research involves questionnaires administered to a leader's subordinates to measure the leader's effectiveness and the subordinates' satisfaction. The results are assumed to be related to the manager's style. However, other interpretations are possible. The independent variable could be the subordinates' job satisfaction itself, or perhaps the subordinates are highly productive and their performance is the cause of the managerial style. Perhaps the managerial style, organizational effectiveness, and job satisfaction are all caused by some other variable not included in the research designs.

In addition, much of the research is done in experimental settings using students. While one can manipulate leader behavior to determine causality, the laboratory conditions lack the highly complex set of interactions that typify real-world conditions. On the other hand, field experiments often lack the control of variables that laboratory studies permit (Yukl 1981). Recognizing, then, the limitations as well as the strengths of existing literature, we can review some of the studies that compare male and female managerial style.

The work of Rosen and Jerdee, Stein, and Massengill and DiMarco on sex role and managerial stereotypes, reviewed above, leads to a hypothesis that feminine leaders will be more likely to adopt a leadership style high on Consideration, that masculine leaders will adopt styles high on Initiating Structure, and that subordinates will see the masculine style as more effective. A small but growing body of research is investigating that assumption as well as attempting to find out to what extent, if any, stereotypical managerial style is effective, how it is perceived by subordinates, and what contingencies may affect either actual or perceived style and effectiveness.

Do women and men adopt different managerial styles? Apparently not. There is scant evidence to support the stereotype that women managers are higher on Consideration and men higher on Initiating Structure. Male high school department chairs were seen by their subordinates as more aloof and more production oriented than female chairs, who were seen as higher on Consideration (Rousell 1974). In the self-descriptions of a matched sample of managerial employees, male managers at every level described themselves as more task-oriented than female managers, while female managers described themselves as more relationship-oriented than male equivalents (Brenner and Vinacke 1979). Since these were self-reports, the results may be more a reflection of the respondents' stereotypical self-perceptions than of actual behavior. Still others have found a relationship between masculinity and structuring behavior but not between femininity and consideration. In fact, subjects (both students and practicing managers) generally agreed that all managers should be high in both structure and consideration and have a masculine sex-role identity (Inderlied and Powell 1979). One of the few studies that actually measured behaviors and not perceptions of behavior found that women and men managers used a very similar communication style in their staff meetings, and that, in fact, they indicated a similar "masculine" perception of themselves as managers (Birdsall 1980).

Most research has found no sex differences in leader style. Male and female civilian supervisors in the U.S. Air Force were found by their subordinates to be very similar in terms of leader behavior and also in terms of effectiveness—a promising outcome given the masculine environment (Day and Stogdill 1972). In female-dominated organizations (two mental health clinics) researchers again found no sex differences in leadership style and also found no differences in subordinate satisfaction (Osborn and Vicars 1976). In some cases the stereotype has not only been disconfirmed, but contrary results have been found: Women leaders were perceived as higher on Initiating Structure than men leaders (Bartol and Wortman 1975). In one field study, no sex differences were found, but as the number of male subordinates rose, the female leaders' style became increasingly task-oriented (Chapman 1975). It seems likely that whatever differences exist are a function of other variables, not of sex.

Is there a connection between sex of leader, leadership style, and job satisfaction? Apparently not. We might predict that leadership styles high on Consideration would lead to greater job satisfaction, while styles high on Initiating Structure would lead to greater effectiveness, and such a relationship was found among employees in a social service agency. Employees reported greater job satisfaction when supervisors conformed according to stereotypical expectations. Consideration behaviors performed by females and Initiating Structure performed by men were both related to the job satisfaction of their subordinates (Petty and Miles 1976). And Consideration has been associated with job satisfaction for male leaders as well as female leaders (Petty and Bruning 1980). On the other hand, high school teachers expressed greater intimacy and group cohesiveness in male-led departments, even though women chairs were rated higher on Consideration. Since there were no women above the department chair, it seems at least possible that the blocked mobility of the women leaders may have influenced their style or the job satisfaction of their followers (Rousell 1974). Others have found no differences in job satisfaction based on the leaders' sex or leadership behavior (Osborn and Vicars 1976; Bartol and Wortman 1975).

Is there a connection between sex of leader, leadership style, and effectiveness? Apparently not. As noted above, no differences in effectiveness were found between women and men civilian managers in the Air Force. The only differences found were in career advancement. For males, effectiveness tended to result in rapid advancement, but for females, rate of advancement was unrelated to effectiveness (Day and Stogdill 1972). For managers in two service agencies, Initiating Structure was effective for both male and female managers (Petty and Bruning 1980). A laboratory study at West Point did find that groups headed by women performed slightly less well on an experimental task than did male-led groups. However, the outcomes, and the perception of those outcomes by participants, were affected by two variables. One was the extent to which the task was structured; the other was the followers' attitudes toward women (Rice, Bender, and Vitters 1980).

Is leadership style evaluated differently depending on gender? Perhaps. College students rated women and men differently when they performed in identical ways. Females were evaluated more favorably than males on Consideration behavior and males were evaluated more favorably than females on Structuring behavior (Bartol and Butterfield 1976). But the sex of the subordinate also makes a difference in how behavior is evaluated. Women have been shown to be judged more harshly when they exerted authority over a male subordinate and when they were lenient with a female subordinate (Jacobson et al. 1977).

Do men always emerge as leaders in groups where no leader is designated? Probably not, although it is often asserted that they do. The cause is laid to sex-role enculturalization and to the higher status attached to male behavior (Lockheed and Hall 1976). An oft-quoted study (Megargee 1969) found that in single-sex groups, individuals who were rated as high on "dominance" in a personality test consistently emerged as leaders, regardless of who made the decision about who should lead. When high-dominance women were paired with low-dominance men, however, the women typically made the final decision about who should assume the leader role, and 91 percent of the time they appointed their low-dominance male partner as leader. The results were interpreted as demonstrating female deference to sex-role expectations. However, a recent replication of the study sheds some new light on the outcomes. The assigned task in the original study was a clearly masculine one—assembling a machine part. When the original study was repeated, the results were very similar, but when a feminine task (sewing on a button) was assigned, the high-dominance women assigned themselves as leader more frequently. It may be that the leadership role lies in who makes the decision, not in who is annointed leader, and that the high-dominance women made the decision based upon their perceived competence in a masculine or feminine task (Carbonell 1984).

Emergent leadership may also be a function of the situation. Students who were assigned to task groups that met regularly over a 16-week semester were asked to name their group's leader at the end of the semester. The situation was one that, using Fiedler's theory, would call for a style high on Initiating Structure. Indeed, the results showed that style was a more important predictor of emergent leadership than sex. Of 42 emergent leaders, 26 were male and 16 female. The leaders' LPC scores showed them to be significantly higher on Initiating Structure than the remaining members of their groups. In 75 percent of the groups, the emergent leader had the highest score on Initiating Structure of any member of the group (Schneier 1978).

What does all of this prove? There are apparently no gender differences between women and men in terms of leadership style. Women do not adopt a more Considerate style; men do not exhibit higher Initiating Structure. What differences appear to exist seem to disappear when other variables are taken into account. Further, there is little relationship between sex, leadership style, and either effectiveness or the job satisfaction of subordinates. Men appear to assume the leadership role more frequently in unstructured groups, but in fact women may be exercising influence in other ways. Any understanding of the dynamics of leadership must include consideration of such variables as the situation, including Fiedler's variables, but also adding the sex composition of the organization, the opportunity structure of the organization, the perceived sex-role constraint of the tasks being performed, and probably others.

One cannot, however, ignore the implications of the research on managerial stereotypes. Even though the preponderance of the evidence shows scant differences at most, stereotypes continue to favor the "male is normal" model of leadership. There is clearly a conflict between behaviors that are sex-role appropriate and those that are situationally appropriate for both women and men. Those who behave in situationally appropriate ways run the danger of being perceived as sex-role deviants and the parallel danger of suffering from role conflict and role strain. The most encouraging implication from the research is that stereotypes tend to become less important as experience increases. Field studies repeatedly find less impact of stereotypes than laboratory studies, suggesting that in the real world men and women, leaders and followers, adapt their behaviors and their attitudes to the situation.

POWER THEORIES

Interest in the whole area of power has greatly increased in recent years. Once treated almost as a taboo, recent evidence has begun to demonstrate that power may be a great deal more important than previously thought in understanding organizational behavior. We saw earlier that the motivation to acquire and use power has been found by McClelland to be more closely associated with managerial success than Achievement motivation.

Studies of leadership traits and style, of the kind that we have been reviewing, may be far too limited to really explain what it is that managers do and what it is that differentiates the successful from the unsuccessful manager. Mintzberg (1975) has made extensive studies of what, exactly, managers do. He concludes that the classic stereotype of a manager is based largely on four myths: that the manager is a reflective, systematic planner; that the manager has no regular routine duties to perform; that the manager relies on a formal, integrated system for acquiring information; and that management is, or is becoming, a science or a profession. In short, Mintzberg is challenging that stereotype of the manager so firmly held by both women and men in the business world. In reality, he argues, the manager's job imbues him or her with a certain status, to which are attached certain ascribed roles. The formal authority of the manager's status gives rise to certain *interpersonal* roles, which in turn give rise to *informational* roles, which in turn enable the manager to play certain *decisional* roles.

The ten roles that every manager plays, to a greater or lesser extent, represent the use of the power that is associated with the role of manager:

Interpersonal Roles:
1. The Figurehead Role—the ceremonial duties that go with the position.
2. The Leader Role—the performance of duties necessary to accomplish the task of the unit. This role includes both Initiating Structure and Consideration, although Mintzberg does not use these terms.
3. The Liaison Role—the contacts the manager makes with peers or others outside of the regular chain of command.

Information Roles:
4. The Monitor Role—scanning the environment for relevant information.

5. The Disseminator Role—sharing and disseminating the information she or he has gathered.
6. The Spokesman Role—representing the organization to the larger society.

Decisional Roles:

7. The Entrepreneurial Role—seeking to maintain and improve the organization, initiating and monitoring developmental projects that enhance the organization.
8. The Disturbance Handler Role—commonly known as "putting out fires," responding to the unexpected disruption of the organization.
9. The Resource Allocator Role—allocating the scarce resources of the organization, including his or her own time. In designing the structure of the organization, the manager allocates power and access to power.
10. The Negotiator Role—engaging in negotiations (with workers, suppliers, or any other entity) that commit the organization's resources.

This model of managerial behavior is important for two reasons. First, it greatly expands our conception of what a manager does. In this view, the trait, style, and contingency theories all represent a fairly small share of the total picture. Further, it puts the emphasis on the manager's ability to acquire and use power. The important question for our purposes is the extent to which women and men differ in these dimensions. There are two distinct but not mutually exclusive approaches to the issue. One looks at the notion of "interpersonal power"—the extent to which sex-role expectations affect the use, perception, and effectiveness of given power styles. The other looks at "structural power"—the extent to which organizational structure and processes differentially affect men and women in their search for power.

Interpersonal Power

Interpersonal power can be defined as the ability to get another person or persons to act, think, or feel in a way that they would otherwise not have done (Frieze et al. 1978). Despite the negative connotations of the word, power (or influence) is something that everyone exerts a good deal of the time. The father who insists that his daughter finish her homework before she may watch television is exerting power. The manager who congratulates her administrative assistant when he has done a particularly good job is also exerting power. It is the coercive or abusive use of power, not power itself, that we find offensive. We use terms like "Machiavellian" or more recently "Nixonian" to suggest abuses of power.

We often recall Lord Acton's axiom that "Power corrupts, and absolute power corrupts absolutely." We accuse aggressive leaders of being "on a power trip." It is perhaps not surprising, given these negative attitudes, that we have shunned the study of power. And yet, in another sense, the failure of organizational scholars to more seriously consider the dynamics of power is surprising indeed.

A seminal analysis of interpersonal power was explicated by French and Raven (1959). They developed a typology of six power bases, sources of power that exist in a particular relationship between influencer and influence.

1. *Coercive Power* refers to the ability of one person to threaten another with punishment. The punishment might be physical or verbal. It can take tangible forms such as levying fines, firing, or withholding some valued outcome like a promotion or a raise.

2. *Reward Power* is the ability to administer a reward that the influencee values. Again, the reward might be tangible, such as a raise or bonus, or it might be intangible, such as praise or gratitude.

3. *Referent Power* is based on similarity and liking. If one admires another person and wishes to model him- or herself after that person, then the person has referent power. She or he is a point of reference to the admirer.

4. *Expert Power* is based on having superior skills or knowledge in a particular area or on a particular topic. If one is perceived as an expert, others will defer to him or her. Expert power tends to be particularized to the influencer's unique area of expertise.

5. *Legitimate Power* is based on one's position in the organization. Power is legitimate when it is based on the legally constituted authority of the office. It is concerned with "rank." Legitimate power depends for its effectiveness on subordinates' perceiving the legitimacy of the influencer's authority.

6. *Information Power* is based on influencing others by having specific information or data relevant to a particular issue. If one knows what time the plane leaves, one can influence one's fellow travelers to leave for the airport in time.

These power bases are available to a greater or lesser degree to individuals, depending on a number of factors. When faced with a situation requiring the use of power, one must choose from among the bases available at the moment. How does one choose which to use? First there is a cost/benefit analysis, which may be done consciously or unconsciously. How effective will this strategy be? What will it cost in terms of time, effort, money, or bargaining chips? Second, there is an evaluation of the reactions of others to a particular strategy. This step involves not so much questioning the effectiveness as questioning the subjective reactions. What will others think of me? Finally, one's own attitudes, values and beliefs, and personality affect the choice. How will I feel? What will I think of myself (Raven and Kruglanski 1970)?

Not everyone has access to power in the same way, however. There are four factors that influence how much power a person can have and use: status, concrete, resources, expertise, and self-confidence (Tedeschi 1972, in Frieze et al. 1978).

Status is socially determined. Every social system has a consensual set of values assigned to certain traits, positions, or achievements. We have seen over and over that in our society, male traits and male accomplishments are more highly valued than female ones. Those with high status have access to a wide range of power bases. Further, they are able to accumulate "idiosyncrasy credits," that is, they are able to behave in ways that would be unacceptable for a low-status person.

Concrete Resources include time, money, material possessions, physical strength, and other personal resources, such as sexual favors and warmth and affection.

Expertise is a special form of resources, including knowledge, information, or skills.

Self-confidence is related to possession of status, concrete resources, and expertise. People with self-confidence attempt to influence others more; people with low self-confidence expect less success, attempt less influence, and use less-risky power bases.

Clearly on all these grounds—power bases, power determinants, and power opportunities—men and women have different experiences. Power behaviors that are seen as appropriate for men will not, as we shall see, be seen as appropriate for women. The cost and outcomes for women and men of a given power base will often be different, and women and men will feel differently about using them. The opportunities for power use that are routinely available to men are often lacking for women.

Differences exist between women and men in both the opportunity and use of interpersonal power. Basing her work on the theoretical constructs described above, Johnson (1976) posited three dimensions of power styles: indirect versus direct power; personal versus concrete/power, and helplessness versus competence.

Indirect Power is often called manipulation. It occurs when the influencer acts, or attempts to act, without the receiver being aware of the action. Dropping hints, starting rumors, feigning illness, are all examples of indirect power. It is a form of behavior associated with women, who are proscribed from using more direct, unfeminine forms, and it is often effective for women. Men may use indirect power but may also use direct power without negative sanctions. Indirect power may be effective for women in the short run, but it has negative consequences. If it is effective, the influencer may obtain the objective but will get no recognition and will not be perceived as being powerful. If it is not effective, the influencer may be seen as being manipulative or exploitative. Further, the influencer is not likely to see him- or herself as strong and will not build a sense of self-confidence.

Personal versus Concrete Power refers to the types of resources one controls, those that depend on a personal relationship such as liking or respect and those that are concrete, such as money, knowledge, and physical strength. Again sex differences are apparent. Women tend to possess stereotypically feminine personal resources—liking, affection, love, or approval. Men tend to possess and control the concrete resources. Even when women do control concrete resources, they are discouraged from using them directly. Again, the resources available to women tend to be successful only in the short run. In order for personal resources to be effective, the influencer must have a personal relationship with the influencee. This makes him or her highly dependent on others.

Helplessness versus Competence rests largely on one's own sense of competency. Women often do not feel competent and they are not perceived by others as being competent, except perhaps in traditional female tasks. Displays of competence in traditional masculine tasks may be perceived as unfeminine behavior. Helplessness can be effective in the short run; even men can use it, as for instance the man who influences a woman to sew a button on his shirt by being unable to thread the needle. Although helplessness can be quite effective in the short run, the person who trades on weakness may bargain away the right to trade on strength at some later point, and once again it may have an important depressing influence on self-image.

Women, if they act in the socially acceptable feminine manner, will rely on indirect, personal, and helpless forms of power. Analysis of the interplay of these sex role expectations and opportunities for power reveals the actual differences in male and female power styles (Johnson 1976).

Reward and coercion are more commonly used by men than women, and the use of these styles is considered masculine. Physical coercion is seen as used by males with males but not with females, although the battered-wife syndrome suggests that, within the family at least, men do use physical coercion against women. Reward and coercion power can be used directly or indirectly. Indirect reward is essentially the process of operant conditioning or behavior modification. The influencer shapes the behavior of another by subtly reinforcing desired responses. Direct reward or coercion can also be based on personal resources, as when the influencer uses the giving or withholding of affection. Both the indirect use of reward and the direct use of reward with personal resources are seen as stereotypically feminine and are more frequently used by women than men. Although personal coercion is seen as feminine, men may also use it effectively; the risks are much less than for a woman using direct coercion. As a result, women are limited in their use of this power base to those situations and relationships where their personal resources are of value, while men have the opportunity for a much wider sphere of influence.

Referent power is based on the psychological process of identification and is open to women, possibly more so than to men. It is not seen as stereotypical to either males or females. However, because it relies on perceived similarities, it is often used by women with other women and men with other men.

Informational power differs from expert power in that the influencer does not just say she or he knows best but uses information to explain why. It relies upon having access to information, rather than to concrete or personal resources. Since women do not have access to information and are not seen as being as logical or competent as men, information power is seen as masculine and more often used by males. If a woman does have information and uses it directly, she may be seen as acting out of role and may arouse hostility. She may be more effective if she presents her information in a stereotypically feminine way, using a soft voice or hesitating manner. Men, on the other hand, are seen as effective when presenting information in a direct way.

Expert power is seen as highly masculine and is used more often by men than women. Men are more likely to be in expert positions; when women use expert power it is seen as aggressive and out of role. An exception occurs, however, in areas that are seen as legitimate domains of female expertise such as childrearing or cooking.

Legitimate power is the most complex form because it is based on prior learning of influence norms, of the rules of who has the legitimate right to influence whom. Women have less access to legitimate power than men and use it very little; when they do use it, they may be seen as highly aggressive. An exception is legitimate helplessness, which appeals to the norm of social responsibility; social norms mandate that a woman in a helpless position be rescued. Legitimate helplessness is more effective for women to use than legitimacy of position but, as with a missing shirt button, it is acceptable for men to use in some cases (Frieze et al. 1978).

For women in managerial positions, the incongruency between femininity and these power bases, determinants, and opportunities represents a serious dilemma. Women who use power styles that are considered masculine are perceived as being less effective and suffer interpersonal costs. For instance, a group of experienced male managers consistently assumed other male managers to be higher up in the organization than female managers, regardless of the power strategy used. But strategy did make a difference. Males were rated more positively when they used expert power, a masculine strategy and one that is considered very reliable. Females were rated more positively when they used reward power, a feminine but generally unreliable strategy. Further, those who supervised men were regarded more highly than those who supervised women (Wiley and Eskilson 1982).

Since women often find themselves in the position of supervising women, it seems that, regardless of the power style that a woman manager employs, she will be viewed as less powerful and less effective than her counterparts who supervise male employees. Further, she is in a double bind. If she uses expert power, a more effective style for a man, she will be viewed as acting in a deviant manner and will be seen as less effective than a man using the same strategy; if she uses reward power she will be seen as acting in a stereotypically female manner but will still be seen as less powerful and less effective than the man.

Role theory suggests that individuals who deviate from expected role norms will experience negative consequences, but power or powerlessness may be more of a predictor of role stress than deviance. First, people who occupy powerful roles have been found to have fewer symptoms of distress than those who are powerless. Second, a deviation from sex-role expectations produces distress only when the deviant occupies a powerless role. "People in powerful roles have little distress, regardless of whether they conform to or deviate from sex-role expectations" (Horwitz 1982).

Other evidence, however, confirms that there are interpersonal costs to using the power bases associated with the opposite sex. In a laboratory experiment, speakers using opposite-sex power bases (expertise for women, helplessness for men) were rated as less likable, less competent, and less qualified than speakers using bases appropriate to their sex. Speakers delivering messages consistent with their sex (gun control for men, child care for women) were also rated as more persuasive and more believable than the reverse (Falbo, Hazen, and Linimon 1982).

To recap what has been said so far, there are six bases of power: reward power, coercive power, expert power, legitimate power, referrent power, and information power. There are at least four factors that determine opportunities to use power; status, control of concrete resources, expertise, and self-confidence. In addition there are several factors that determine what power base we will use in a given situation, including the perceived costs and outcomes of a particular strategy, the effect it will have on others, and our own internal reactions. Finally, power strategies operate across a number of dimensions; direct versus indirect power, concrete versus personal resources, and helplessness versus competence.

The evidence all points to the same conclusions. Successful managers are those who are able to acquire and use power strategies effectively. Those power styles and strategies that are most associated with being perceived as powerful and competent, with being effective or persuasive, are also associated with being masculine. These are also the strategies that are associated with direct and concrete use of power. Further, people who are successful at getting and using power tend to acquire self-confidence and to exhibit fewer symptoms of psychological distress. On the other hand, those strategies that are perceived as being least effective and are least associated with being powerful are those indirect and personal styles commonly associated with femininity. Finally, the evidence suggests that both masculine and feminine styles may be effective if used by men, but masculine styles are not effective when used by women. The ineluctable conclusion is that women have the choice of using power in an indirect (manipulative) way and risking either being ineffective or unrecognized, or using direct styles and risking being both ineffective and disliked.

This view of power, as noted above, looks at the relationship between sex role stereotypes and perceptions of power styles to explain women's relative powerlessness in organization. Another approach looks, instead, at the structure of organizations themselves for an explanation.

Structural Power

A look at Mintzberg's ten roles of the contemporary manager reveals that a great deal of what the manager does requires a combination of direct and indirect power styles. The successful performance of the managerial role requires not only the downward use of authority but also the upward and outward use of influence. It requires that managers not only have the legitimate authority of their positions but also that they are seen as having power and influence in the larger organization. It requires, in short, that they be successful at organizational politics. The word *politics,* like the word *power,* has negative connotations, but it is used here in a nonpejorative sense to mean the use of aggregate, rather than personal, influence or power. It means the forming of alliances or coalitions with other powerful people in the organization in order to accomplish mutual goals. It implies a synergistic accumulation of individual power, that is, the power of a coalition is greater than the sum of the powers of the individuals (Pfeffer 1981).

Organization members tend to look on power as a finite quantity and hence at the distribution of power as a zero-sum game in which what one person gains another must have lost. Organizational politics create power within the organization, because a powerful person can, by association, empower a less-powerful ally without reducing his or her own power. On the contrary, the ability to empower another may in fact increase an individual's perceived power. This kind of structural power is essential to the accomplishment of the organization's goals; it may also be necessary to the accomplishment of individual ambitions. It is also consensual. You can poll any sample of organizational members as to who are the most influential actors and achieve a very high degree of agreement (Salancik and Pfeffer 1983).

Kanter (1979) argues that productive power is a function of one's connections with other parts of the system, rather than of one's sexual orientation. Organizational power evolves from two kinds of capacities: access to the resources, information, and support necessary to do the job; and the ability to get cooperation in doing what is necessary. A manager is seen as being powerful in the organization when he or she can accomplish such goals as interceding on behalf of someone in trouble with the organization or getting a desirable promotion for a talented subordinate, getting regular or fast access to top decisionmakers, or gaining access to early information about important events.

> Thus, people who look like they can command more of the organization's resources, who look like they can bring something that is valued from outside into the group, who seem to have access to the inner circles that make the decisions affecting the fate of individuals in organizations, may also be more effective as leaders . . . and be more liked in the process (Kanter 1977).

Two vital elements of this kind of structural power are credibility and dependency. When Kanter surveyed a sample of executives and asked them to define the characteristics of effective leaders, their conclusion was that *credibility* was more important than anything else. Credibility meant *competence* plus *power*. People with credibility were able to command the resources of supplies, information, and support necessary to get the job done. Those who had credibility upward in the organization also had it downward. Credibility downward was based on the subordinates' perceptions of their manager's importance in the organization and was in turn related to their effectiveness. Consideration, or "people sensitivity," was a good thing to have but was of very little value in terms of eliciting subordinate support without the respect that comes with credibility (Kanter 1977).

The degree to which credibility is related to power is a function of the amount of dependency in the situation. If power is related to the ability to acquire and control resources, then it follows that the scarcer and more critical the resource the greater the amount of power that attaches to it. Leaders who are able to define what resources are critical to the organization and who can control the distribution of those resources are able to make others dependent upon them. Their departments or units become critical to the survival and success of the larger organization (Hickson et al. 1971; Kotter 1977; Salancik and Pfeffer 1983).

Dependency occurs in organizations because of the complexity of the division of labor and because of the uncertainties created by the environment. Virtually no group can accomplish its task without dependence on others, for materials, for personnel, for consumption of output. Virtually no group can control completely all of the uncertainty that arises from the environment, from market or technological shifts, from economic conditions, from competition. The extent to which one group is dependent upon the other for either internal or external control of uncertainty is a measure of the power relationship between those groups and hence between their leaders. It is the reciprocity of these dependencies that makes the exercise of power possible (Kanter 1977).

Hence organizations have "power structures," which are not solely a function of job title or of position on the organizational chart. Kanter asserts that it is one's position in the power structure that determines one's leadership style, not one's personality traits or motivation. Power positions are achieved in one of two ways: through activities or through association. Activities, in order to increase power, must meet three criteria: they must be *extraordinary*—being first in a new position, taking major risks and succeeding, making organizational changes; they must be *visible*; and they must be *relevant*—being identified with the solution to critical organizational problems. However, in addition to activities, power almost always comes from social connections outside the immediate work group: through having or being a sponsor, through peer acceptance, and through powerful subordinates (for example, having a subordinate who is recognized as a "comer" or a "water walker" in the organization). To the extent that women in organizations are "tokens," that is, that there are very few of them and they are fairly isolated, it becomes very difficult for them to gain control of the critical activities or establish the essential alliances. Fear of sexual entanglement is substantially increased when women are tokens, increasing their isolation.

Certain positions within the hierarchy are associated with powerlessness, according to Kanter. The first two, not surprisingly, are first-line supervisors and staff (as opposed to line) managers, positions frequently held by women. The third is surprising, since it is the chief executive officer, a position rarely held by a woman. First-line supervisors are people in the middle, caught between higher management and their subordinates. They have little chance to gain power through activities and few chances to make power-enhancing alliances. They have little credibility, since they have little chance for upward mobility. They have moved from the ranks of the workers, but the next ranks, the entry levels of middle management, are generally filled with entry-level college graduates or MBAs. They have little or no impact on the making of policies or rules that affect their workers, they have few rewards to administer, and they may suffer resentment from their former co-workers. First-line supervisors tend to act out their powerlessness by oversupervising, by overcontrolling, and by overreliance on rules. Powerless themselves, they deny to their subordinates any opportunity for individual autonomy or freedom.

Staff professionals are the people who supply the support services to line departments. They have no direct authority in the larger organization and must use persuasion and bargaining techniques to get line managers to carry out their recommendations. They are perceived as useful (although sometimes as an unnecessary hindrance) but not as critical to the organization's survival. They are often hired because they have expertise in a particular area; they have little opportunity for upward mobility outside of their speciality, so have little opportunity to reach the ranks of upper management. Their work can be, and frequently is, assigned to outside consultants. They have little credibility and less dependency in the larger organization and little opportunity to form reciprocal alliances. Staff managers tend to respond to their powerlessness by becoming turf-minded, creating islands in the organization. They create a false sense of their own expertness and often engage in jurisdictional disputes with other staff departments.

Top managers, Kanter argues, can become powerless for similar reasons—lack of supplies, information, and support. Mintzberg found that, contrary to myth, managers do a good deal of routine work. And routine work drives out nonroutine work. The chief executive who allows himself to become immersed in the daily routine of the organization, in putting out fires, fails to exercise the power inherent in his or her office. Credibility comes from doing the nonroutine things, the planning, creative, innovative things. Leaders at the top are faced with a dilemma. In order to accomplish these nonroutine duties, they must isolate themselves from the daily affairs of the organization, but they must do so without cutting themselves off from essential sources of information or from sufficient exposure to the larger organization to maintain their credibility (Kanter 1979).

Powerless people respond to their powerlessness in a number of ways: by controlling behavior and close supervision, by being rules minded, and by exerting territorial and domain control. These behaviors are unlikely to produce effective results, and subordinates often respond by slack performance, leading in a vicious downward spiral to more control, more frequent application of rules, more territoriality. These are behaviors typical of all managers in powerless positions, regardless of sex. But since women managers are most frequently found in powerless positions, these behaviors have often been associated with female managers and have contributed to the stereotype of the mean, bitchy, woman boss.

There is a common and well-founded presumption that most workers, male or female, prefer a male boss to a female (Forgionne and Nwacukwu 1977). However, as we saw in the leadership studies, resistance to women as managers is greatly reduced when respondents have actually worked for a woman. Kanter (1977) argues that this discrepancy can be explained by the power structure of the organization. The preference for male bosses is really a preference for power, and in most organizations women do not hold positions in the power structure. But "power wipes out sex," and women who acquire power use leadership styles and behavior very similar to those used by men and no longer arouse anxiety about the quality of their leadership.

SUMMARY AND CONCLUSION

This chapter has looked in detail at the research on leadership. It began with a review of trait theories, moved on to the leadership style and contingencies studies, and finally considered the power issue, from the standpoint of both interpersonal and structural power. The major area of interest is the extent to which differences exist between women and men managers.

The trait literature suggests that successful women managers tend to be more like successful men managers and less like nonmanagerial women. They also suggest some important differences between male and female managers based on sex role expectations, both in the way women exercise leadership and in the way their leadership behavior is viewed and accepted. While these studies give us some interesting insights into the backgrounds, personalities, and experiences of successful women managers, they tell us little about the situational factors that affected their career development.

An extensive review of style and contingency studies turns out after all to be confusing. The evidence is at best inconclusive, at worst contradictory. The general perception that styles high on Consideration are more effective for women, are used more frequently by women, and are considered more appropriate by subordinates is not supported. The perception that men or women subordinates would respond differently to Consideration style on the part of women supervisors is not supported. The most positive conclusion that one can come to is that, in any given situation, it is the appropriateness of the leadership style, rather than the gender of either the leader or the subordinate, that is important.

Finally, the literature on power has been reviewed. Here some rather significant differences were noted. The study of interpersonal power suggests that there are strongly sex-linked power styles, power dimensions, power opportunities, and power determinants. Those styles that are closely related to managerial success are direct styles associated with status, competence, concrete resources, and self-confidence, and are based on expertise and legitimacy. They are the style most closely linked to masculinity. Power styles considered feminine are indirect styles associated with helplessness and personal resources and based on referent or legitimate power. These styles are manipulative, they are less effective, and even when successful, they fail to establish the credibility of the influencer. Women, however, who adopt direct styles may find their behavior regarded as inappropriate and deviant, and the styles may be ineffective for them. Men may find indirect styles less effective but not inappropriate, but women may find direct styles both inappropriate and ineffective.

The final section has looked at power as a structural phenomenon. Organizational politics award power to individuals who can exert influence upward and outward in the organization. This power is based on achieving credibility and creating dependency through the control of resources of supply, information, and knowledge. The more critical one's activities are to the organization's success and survival, the more dependent other elements of the organization become, and the more power is generated. One achieves power through activities, which must be extraordinary, visible, and relevant, and more importantly, through alliances with other powerful people, either of which may be more difficult for women, especially if they are relative isolates. Hence organizations create informal power structures that are independent of formal organizational charts. Certain positions in these power structures are particularly powerless, including first-line supervisors and staff managers, the kind of management positions most frequently held by women. The leadership style of incumbents in these positions is often characterized by close supervision, strict adherence to rules, and zealous protection of territory and domain. These characteristics are often attributed to the fact that the managers are women and contribute to the stereotype of the mean, bitchy, woman boss. They are, however, characteristic of powerless people regardless of gender.

Kanter's solution to the problem of powerlessness is the restructuring of organizations. She urges decentralization and the flattening of hierarchical structures as a means of distributing power, along with job redesign strategies that create more discretion and autonomy, especially for women in clerical positions. However, as we saw in Chapter 6, hierarchical management is probably inevitable in large and complex organizations, and the holders of power have much to lose and very little to gain by distributing it. Feminist rhetoric has attacked the whole concept of hierarchy as antithetical to the goals of the women's movement and has promulgated the idealistic notion of collectivity or structurelessness.

However, these structures, or the absence of structure, have proved ineffective even in women's groups (Freeman 1972) and are unlikely to find their way into utilitarian organizations.

Others put the burden on women themselves. One model suggests that women can undertake two activities in seeking more power. When considering a job, transfer, or promotion, they can assess the potential power of positions according to structural conditions, or they can seek to incorporate into their present jobs the structural functions (for example, resource and uncertainty control) that will increase their power (Smith and Grenier 1982). It is no doubt true that women, if they better understand the dimensions of power, can adopt these suggestions, but once again it's important to remember, as Shirley Chisholm once said, women will have to take power, because "no one is giving it away." And taking power may mean overcoming a great deal of social baggage.

10
Performance and
Perceptions of Performance

In Chapter 8, an extensive review of the literature of motivation found virtually no sex differences that did not disappear when situational variables were considered. Men and women similar in age, experience, educational level, and occupation, with equivalent opportunity and power in the organization, varied not at all in terms of their desired outcomes from work and their job satisfaction and very little in terms of their commitment to work. When situational factors were taken into account they also varied little on their motivation to achieve, their fears of failure or success, and their attributions for their successes and failures.

In Chapter 9 we found a similar lack of significant sex differences. Although it's clear that managers are stereotypically perceived to have masculine traits and to behave in masculine ways, in fact very little difference actually exists in either traits or styles between women and men managers. However, women and men do differ in their ability to get and to use power. Women have difficulty in exercising the power styles and behaviors that are successful and appropriate for men, they have difficulty in forming power alliances in the organization, and they have difficulty finding their way into the powerful positions in the organizational hierarchy.

Why?

In Chapter 9 we said, citing Kanter (1977), that power positions are achieved in one of two ways: through activities or through association. Activities, in order to increase power, must meet three criteria: they must be extraordinary, they must be visible, and they must be relevant.

Mere competence is not enough; it is expected. In order to have credibility, employees must be seen as people who make organizational changes, task risks, and offer solutions to pressing organizational problems. And they must have social connections outside the immediate work group with sponsors, peers, and subordinates. The process works in a circular way. In order to form powerful associates, one needs the visibility that comes from extraordinary activities, but in order to get the visibility one may need the help of powerful associates, especially sponsors. If there are sex differences in the performance of activities, or in the ways in which performance is perceived, that might account in part for differential access to power positions.

In this chapter we will look at the individual and organizational constraints on women's achievement. In the first section we will discuss male and female differences in performance, specifically in mixed-sex groups, to try to identify what sex differences, if any, occur and where the root of those differences lie. The second section will examine real and perceived differences in performance. The third will look at real and perceived differences in organizational decisionmaking. The final section will look at women's career aspirations in light of these differences in performance and the perception of performance.

CONFORMITY/COMPETENCE/CONFIDENCE

There are some differences in male and female behavior in mixed-sex organizational settings. A review of the literature suggests that these differences occur in three ways: (1) Men are more active than women, that is, the average man initiates more "verbal acts" than the average woman; (2) Men are more influential than women; and (3) Men initiate a higher proportion of their acts than women in task-oriented categories of behavior, while women initiate a higher proportion of their acts in social-emotional categories (Lockheed and Hall 1976).

Either men have more ability than women, or something operates in these settings to restrict the performance of women. Clearly there are no sex differences in intelligence or other forms of ability that would explain the persistence of these findings. One explanation is that, since the goals of femininity and of competence are not the same, women are not socialized to be competent. Further, little is known about how to go about raising females to be competent (Sherman 1976). As the Fear of Success literature demonstrates, women sometimes inhibit their own performance in the presence of men. In one study, highly competent women achieved at a higher level when working with an incompetent female than with an incompetent male. Worse yet, less-competent males and females achieved a lower level of performance when working with a competent female than with a competent male (Swanson and Tjosvold 1979). If you extend that logic it appears that, given a choice, a group would be better off with an incompetent male than with a competent female.

It is often argued that differences in behavior have to do with women's minority status in the group. But token males in female-majority groups have been found to behave quite differently from token females in male-majority groups (Webber 1976a). In an experiment in which managers were to prepare a final draft of a written report, four-person groups contained either three women and one man or the reverse. In male-majority groups, far more men than women claimed to be the de facto leader of the group or to have been the major contributor to the group. Only 10 percent of the women saw themselves as nonconforming to group norms. The men did the substantive work of the group and the women were relegated to typing; the women's suggestions were rejected or ignored. The women seemed to accept their role, to adhere to group norms, and to be helpful.

The men in a minority status behaved very differently. Every single man in a female-majority group claimed that he was the group leader. More women than in the male-majority groups claimed to be the leader or to be the major contributor, but these came nowhere near matching the male claims. A third of the men in the female-majority groups claimed to be nonconformers to group norms; none of the women did. In both types of groups, far more men than women were seen by others as the group leader.

There was no difference in performance between the groups, and women were more active in seeking leadership in the female-majority groups, but these groups had more conflict and both male and female members were less satisfied than in the male-majority groups. In fact, the most satisfied of all were women in male-majority groups. Tokenism that keeps women in minority status in organizations may keep women from full participation in the extraordinary activities of the group, but it doesn't explain why these women were apparently satisfied with their role.

Women are alleged to be, by nature or through sex role socialization, more conforming, more persuasable, and less independent than men (Sashkin and Maier 1971; Adams and Landers 1978). In a 1969 review of the literature, Nord (in Maccoby and Jacklin, 1974) concluded that "it has . . . been well established, at least in our culture, that females supply greater amounts of conformity under almost all conditions than males." But Maccoby and Jacklin (1974) found little support for this conclusion, and even found some studies in which males were more conforming than females. Recent research tends to bear them out by demonstrating that differences in conformity and persuasability are a function of situational variables rather than sex.

The sex typing and the difficulty of the task are significant. Males tend to conform more when the task is considered feminine; females conform more when the task is considered masculine; and both conform more as the task becomes more difficult (Sistrunk and McDavid 1971; Sistrunk 1972).

Feedback may have differential effects in inducing conforming behavior. In a situation where contribution was anonymous, success was measured by group achievement only, and there was no individual feedback, there were no sex differences in willingness to accept influence from an advisor. But when the advisor was aware of whether the subject had accepted the advice and whether the answer was right or wrong, males and females again showed themselves equally susceptible to influence. But surprisingly, their responses were in opposite directions. The women tended to become more conforming, but the males, perhaps concerned with appearing to others as independent, actually became merely "anticonforming" (Newton and Schulman 1977).

Men and women also tend to differ on whom they turn to for influence. For example, in one study, as task difficulty increased on a difficult masculine task, women tended to turn not to male but to female sources for advice (Sistrunk and McDavid 1971). A similar phenomenon was found in an experiment involving a difficult and important decisionmaking situation. Neither males nor females were more conforming, but the males were least influenced by their peers and became more susceptible to influence as the source became more expert. The females, on the other hand, were most influenced by their peers, even though they were the least expert source (Hansson, Allen, and Jones 1980). The tendency is to conclude from this kind of research that women are more concerned with social relationships while men are more concerned with task. But anticonformity among males was attributed to their desire to appear independent. Perhaps women turn to female sources, even less expert ones, to avoid appearing incompetent.

So while men and women on the average do not differ in their conformity or their independence, they do appear to differ in the circumstances under which they are subject to persuasion. The vast majority of people working in managerial positions or seeking managerial positions are working in male-majority situations and participating in tasks that may be perceived as masculine. Under these circumstances we would expect the men to be more independent and the women more conforming. As the task difficulty increases, the men may become more persuasible, but they would be more likely to turn to a male than a female for advice, unless the female were perceived as particularly expert in the field. Absent such expertise her suggestions are apt to be rejected or ignored and her efforts resented. Thus it's not surprising to find that women are often seen as more conforming; perhaps their survival depends on it.

Another explanation for women's lack of achievement is that they lack self-confidence and therefore inhibit their own performance. And in fact Maccoby and Jacklin's (1974) review of the literature did conclude that "self-confidence, defined in terms of both performance expectancies and self-evaluations of abilities and completed performances, is lower among women than men." However, once again subsequent research has shown that women do not display lower self-confidence in all achievement situations but rather in response to specific situations. There are at least three kinds of situational variables that influence women's self-confidence relative to men's (Lenney 1977).

First, whether women are lower in self-confidence than men depends upon the nature of the specific task. Women tend to have higher expectancy for success on tasks they perceive as feminine; men on tasks they perceive as masculine. But women and men in supervisory positions showed no differences in their work-related sense of competence (Snyder and Bruning 1979). Specifically, women's self-confidence has been found to be lower than men's in tasks involving spatial-mechanical ability and creativity (even though their performance was no different). In tasks requiring verbal ability and interpersonal perceptiveness, no differences were found (Lenney 1981).

Second, women often have lower self-confidence than men when they are given minimal or ambiguous feedback on their abilities or performances. In achievement situations in which subjects are provided with clear information on their task-specific abilities, the sexes respond similarly to this information and report equal levels of confidence. Also, in achievement situations in which unambiguous performance feedback is not available, women report lower levels of self-confidence than men.

Third, women's estimates of their own abilities appear to be lower than men's when the situation emphasizes the social environment, particularly when their work is compared with others' or evaluated by others. For women, but not for men, confidence varies remarkably depending upon both the sex and the perceived ability of the person to whom one is being compared (Lenney 1981).

The higher one goes in a career or profession, the more difficult it becomes to receive clear and unambiguous feedback and the closer the comparison and evaluation of one's work by others. Epstein's (1970) brilliant analysis of limits to women in the professions points out that clear and specific criteria for judging performance rarely exist. Instead "the professions depend on intense socialization of their members, much of it by immersion in the norms of professional culture before entry." Those employees who are excluded from the collegial network are "excluded from the situations in which they can learn and are also excluded from the social control system which lets them know how well they perform."

So while it may be true that women's lower self-confidence occurs only in very specific situations, it's clear that those situations are ones that often occur in organizational life.

Another way of explaining these differences in male and female behavior relies in a Theory of Diffuse Status Characteristics and Expectations States, which argues that under four specific conditions group members will expect high-status individuals to be more competent. These conditions are (1) when a group is working on a valued task, (2) when there is some competence that is instrumental to the successful completion of the task, (3) when the individuals in the group are task-focused and collectively oriented, and (4) when the individuals involved differ on one and only one diffuse status characteristic. Sex qualifies as a "diffuse status characteristic" because "male" and "female" are evaluated differently; there are specific expectations associated with being male or female, and males are generally expected to be better than females (Lockheed and Hall 1976). Since men have higher status than women, men are expected to be more competent than women, and competitive or dominating behavior is seen as legitimate for men but not for women (Meeker and Weitzel-O'Neill 1977).

The theory describes the process in this way: Groups expect some members to perform better than others. Group members who are expected to perform better will receive and take more opportunities to make task contributions, will have more influence and prestige, and will get more agreement and approval than those for whom expectations are lower. In the absence of information to the contrary, group members will assign performance expectations to themselves and others based upon external status characteristics, such as sex, and males have higher status. In the absence of information to the contrary, a task contribution that is accepted by other members of the group will be assumed by self and others to raise the relative status of the contributor. But raising one's own status in the group is legitimate only for those with high external status, so will be legitimate for men but not for women.

The "information to the contrary" might be information that the person is motivated to help others in the group rather than to raise her self-status, or legitimately assigned higher status, such as being appointed group leader by an outside authority. Acts that will result in raising one's own status relative to others will be expected from those from whom it is legitimate but will not be expected or accepted from those for whom it is not legitimate. Thus women must satisfy both themselves and others that they are competent and also that their motives are not self-serving before their contributions will be perceived as legitimate and their suggestions accepted.

Status rather than task/social differentiation is the crucial concept, as status affects performance expectations and expectations for legitimacy of competitive or dominating behavior. Information, accepted by self and others, that the females present are at least as competent as the males establishes one kind of situation in which sex differences in task behavior are minimized. Information, accepted by self and others, that task behavior by the women is not motivated by competitive status enhancement or that competitive status enhancement is legitimate in this particular case establishes another situation. (Meeker and Weitzel-O'Neill 1977).

The above helps to explain the differences in behavior in male majority and female majority groups but doesn't offer a sufficient explanation for differences in same-sexed groups. While actual performance differs relatively little, all male groups are often seen as being primarily task-oriented, all female groups as more socially oriented. All male groups may suffer because everyone wants to be the leader; all female groups may suffer because no one does. But the Theory of Diffuse Status Characteristics and Expectations States can be taken one step further to explain this apparent difference by consideration of the formal organizational setting in which work groups operate, and specifically of the structural concepts of division of labor and legitimacy (Fennel et al. 1978).

Division of labor occurs in all task-oriented groups, starting with the simple distinction between leader and nonleader. Each group faces two classes of problems: task content and task procedure. How the group solves these problems depends on legitimacy; competency is related to legitimacy for task content but not for task procedure. In mixed-gender groups Expectations States Theory predicts that white males will have legitimacy in the procedural area because of their higher external status. In single-sex groups no such prediction can be made, so legitimacy is decided by what is "empirically usual." In all-male groups, all white males are perceived as equally legitimate incumbents of the leadership role, and a division of labor is likely to develop. A male in a leadership role and his attempts to exercise authority will be viewed as legitimate unless there is evidence to the contrary. In an all-female group, all of the females are equally questionable incumbents of an authority role, and it is unlikely that a highly differentiated division of labor in the procedural area will develop. Thus, lack of legitimacy of the female leadership role contributes to difference in differentiation between all-male and all-female groups, not sex role socialization or biological predisposition.

In this section we have looked at the differences in performance between women and men. It seems to be generally true that in some circumstances women do tend to take a less-active role, to be more conforming and persuasable, and to exhibit less confidence than men do. We have emphasized the situational nature of these differences, recognizing at the same time that these situations—female minority status, masculine sex typing of tasks, lack of clear and unambiguous feedback on performance, and comparison with others—all contribute to greater conformity and lower self-confidence among women. We have also rejected the explanation that women are biologically less competent than men, or even that these differences are the result of sex role socialization. Instead we have advanced the Theory of Diffuse Status Characteristics and Expectation States to reason that the cause lies in the differential status of women and men, and specifically in the higher external status accorded men.

We turn now to another complex and disturbing problem, the differential evaluations of women's and men's performance. In order for women to gain credibility, their performances must not only be extraordinary and relevant, they must be recognized as such by managers, peers, and subordinates. If women's work is devalued relative to men's, they will never get the opportunities to acquire and use power.

PERFORMANCE EVALUATION

Management theorists have struggled for a very long time to devise objective measurements of employee productivity and performance. A variety of methods, some quite simplistic, some very sophisticated, have been developed. But regardless of how carefully constructed the measurement instrument, evaluations are and will always be inherently subjective. Some imperfect human must ultimately decide what tasks or responsibilities adhere to a particular job, what skills, knowledge, and ability are essential to it, what outcomes are desired, and what standard represents acceptable performance. And further, once these determinations have been made, some equally imperfect human being must measure or observe outcomes to determine to what extent the individual incumbent meets the expectations. One of the great fallacies of organizational life is that these evaluations are implicitly valid and reliable measures of individual and relative performance.

Considerable evidence shows that there tends to be an overall male bias in evaluation, and that this bias interacts with other variables such as the sex typing of the task, the sex of the rater, similarities between rater and ratee, and physical attractiveness. For example, when college and university department chairs in psychology were asked to judge the qualifications of young Ph.D.s, women were rated as less-desirable candidates than men with identical qualifications. The men were more likely to be offered positions at the associate professor level, the women at the lower assistant professor level (Fidell 1970). Identical work—essays, paintings—is rated higher when it is attributed to a male than to a female (Mischel 1974; Pheterson, Kiesler, and Goldberg 1971).

However, others have found an opposite effect that is equally discriminatory, the "you're pretty smart for a girl" syndrome. It seems to occur in situations where women perform in circumstances where they are not expected to. For example, women attorneys were rated as more vocationally competent than identically qualified males (Abramson et al. 1977); women responding to an emergency situation were rated as more deserving of a reward than men who performed identically (Taynor and Deaux 1973).

In a comprehensive review of the literature, Nieva and Gutek (1980) have identified three factors affecting these findings: (1) the level of inference required in the evaluation situation, (2) the effects of sex role incongruence, and (3) the effect of level of qualifications and performance involved.

Level of inference refers to the amount of speculation involved. At one extreme is the evaluation of past performance. It requires only the scrutiny of behavior or outcome that is exhibited. At the other extreme is the judgment of an individual's qualifications for a job, since this situation requires speculation about the future, about which little is known. The rater is asked to make inferences—based on such information as education, experience, or past performance—on how the person will behave in the future. Also, situations that require judgments about the causes or the value of performance call for high levels of inference.

Level of inference explains some of the disparity between the studies. In simple terms, the more ambiguity built into a situation, either in terms of the performance criteria or the actual performance, the higher the level of inference required and the more likely that stereotypes will affect the rating. Hence the more information available about the task or about the individual performer, the less likely that sex bias will affect the evaluation. The less-specific and -concrete information available about the individual, the more likely that judges will make inferences based upon what is generally known about the group to which the person belongs.

In a field study of 200 male and female candidates for work in a bank, a male-dominated environment, records of the actual selection interviews showed that on the three most important scales there were no sex differences. The scales in question—impact on workmates, impact on customers, and overall rating—all required a fairly high level of inference. If we can assume that the interviewers had concrete and specific information both about the job requirements and the candidates, that would tend to support the assertion that information reduces bias (Elliot 1981).

On the other hand, evaluation can be affected by very "subtle, nonfocal cues of affect and innuendo" (Brown and Geis 1984). Consensus about a leader's competence can be achieved in two ways: legitimation by an authority figure or expert, and peer-group approval. Identical leader performance was evaluated differently when an authority figure expressed or withheld confidence in a leader's ability, even though he never directly praised or denigrated. Also, the leader was evaluated less positively when group members revealed occasional subtle, nonverbal cues of either approval or disapproval. The evaluators in this experiment really believed that "the reality determining their evaluations [was] the performance itself." The study showed that "the reality of others' affective reactions to a performance significantly altered its perceived quality."

Sex role incongruence, or, more precisely, the absence of sex role congruence, seems to be a factor in many cases where a pro-male bias has appeared. Both males and females suffer to some extent when applying for sex-atypical jobs, but women also suffer in other, more fundamental ways. Often norms regarding work-related behaviors are incompatible with norms regarding behaviors appropriate to the female sex role. For example, the behavior of women managers was found to be in greater agreement than men's with a "normative model" of decisionmaking, and males and females who were perceived to be participative (an acceptable female behavior) were judged equally favorably. But in using the autocratic style, even when the situation called for it, females were rated negatively while males were rated somewhat positively (Jago and Vroom 1982).

A woman who performs well on work-related behaviors—a woman who is competent, assertive, or competitive—may be perceived as lacking in femininity, but worse, her performance may be attributed to chance or some other external cause, rather than to ability. For example, women who were appointed to leadership positions *because they were women* were rated less positively than those who became leaders through more equitable methods (chance, ability), regardless of whether their groups succeeded or failed (Jacobson and Koch 1977). However, as noted above, women may also be subject to overevaluation. Either way, women are being judged by different criteria, and the emphasis is on their sex, rather than their performance.

The level of performance or of qualifications may also affect the way in which bias operates. The more demanding the job, the more likely that males will be preferred. When women and men are equally competent, men tend to be rated higher, but when they are equally incompetent, women are rated higher. Competent men are liked better than competent women (Spence and Helmreich 1972); people would rather work with a competent man than a competent woman. In fact they would prefer an incompetent woman to a competent one (Hagen and Kahn 1975).

> Bias, then, tends to work in both directions. Competent males are rated more positively than equally competent females, while incompetent males are rated lower than equally incompetent females (Nieva and Gutek 1980).

"Beauty Is Its Own Reward"

Women have always been valued for and judged by their appearance. Looking attractive, looking sexy, and especially looking young are the criteria by which women are evaluated as women. Men as they grow older are thought to become distinguished; women as they grow older are thought to become ugly. Yet stereotypes apply here as well—women are said to be "beautiful but dumb"; to be "blond" is synonymous with being a "dumb blond." Surely everyone has heard the story of the man who spends a whole day interviewing candidates for a secretarial job. He questions each one about her education and experience, her clerical skills and her administrative skills. He evaluates each one on her judgment, intelligence, and maturity. At the end of the day he announces "I'll take the blond with the great legs."

Is there any truth to that? Unfortunately there is. But there is a peculiar kind of paradox in reactions to physical appearance. Physically attractive people, both male and female, are assumed to possess more socially desirable personality traits than unattractive ones. They are also expected to achieve more prestigious occupations, to be more competent and successful spouses, to have happier and more successful professional lives, and overall to be happier than less-attractive people (Dion, Berscheid, and Walster 1972). What's more, physical attractiveness appears to be a more potent factor in the evaluation of females than of males. Males tend to be evaluated on more objective grounds, for instance, the amount of money they earn, while females are evaluated on more subjective grounds, including their perceived ability to attract a successful husband, which in turn is perceived as related to their physical attractiveness (Bar-Tal and Saxe 1976).

These judgments are based on an overall evaluation of the individual's worth. But the evaluation of performance on a specific task is affected by the relative attractiveness of the individual, and once again men and women are treated differently. Male judges rated an attractive female author as more talented than an unattractive one, and they rated her essay as better, although both were being rated on the basis of the same essay. The attractive female was also rated higher than one whose appearance was unknown to the raters, and the impact of attractiveness was greatest when the essay was of poor quality (Landy and Sigall 1974). However, one exception was found: males with liberal attitudes toward women rated an unattractive incompetent female higher than her attractive counterpart (Holahan and Stephan 1981). Female judges were less influenced by a female author's attractiveness, and neither male nor female judges were affected by physical attractiveness when evaluating essays attributed to a male author (Kaplan 1978).

These findings should bode well at least for the attractive female. If males evaluate her work more positively than that of unattractive females, especially when the quality of the work is poor, then the effects of other forms of discrimination should be ameliorated. But, alas, it's not that simple. Competent women have been found to be just as attractive as competent men, but incompetent women are seen as more attractive than incompetent men (Rhue, Lynn, and Garske 1984). Further, attractiveness tends to enhance perceptions of masculinity and femininity and of social desirability (Gillen 1981). Thus, attractiveness may enhance evaluations on sex role congruent tasks, but it may work against women when the task is perceived as masculine (Cash and Trimer 1984).

For example, women who were judged both by themselves and others as physically attractive described themselves as likely to be successful in social situations, but they showed little confidence in their expected success on masculine tasks that required manipulative, skilled, or intellectual abilities (Abbott and Sebastian 1981). Attractive men applying for any white-collar organizational position and attractive women applying for nonmanagerial positions were rated higher than their less-attractive counterparts. But for managerial positions attractiveness worked against women, exaggerating the disparity between their perceived femininity and the typical masculine traits considered relevant to work performance (Heilman and Saruwatari 1979). These findings are consistent with Kanter's (1977) observation that at Indsco "personal appearance—attractiveness and social skills—was a factor in the career prospects of secretaries, with task-related skills . . . playing a smaller role as secretaries moved up the ranks." Appearance was so important that secretaries would be sent to secretarial school as much to learn dress and grooming as skills. But moving up the ranks meant moving up the secretarial ranks; the chances of moving into management were almost nonexistent.

Simply put, what this means is that being attractive makes women appear more feminine and more appreciated as women. It causes them to be more highly evaluated when they are involved in role-consistent behaviors. But it enhances the incongruities between their sex role and roles that are perceived as traditionally masculine. The blond with the great legs may have a better chance of getting the secretarial job but a lesser chance of getting a managerial one.

"In the Eye of the Beholder"

Another aspect of performance evaluation that deserves some attention is what is sometimes called the "similar to me" phenomenon. Managers have been found to give their highest ratings to those employees they perceive as holding values similar to their own (Senger 1971) or as being "similar kinds of people" (Pulakos and Wexley 1983). Candidates were assigned higher ratings of job suitability, intelligence, personal attributes, and attraction when they presented biographical information similar to that of their white middle-class interviewers (Rand and Wexley 1975).

One might predict that women would be rated higher by women and lower by men, and the reverse, but of course no such simple conclusion is possible. In fact, it is sometimes argued that women are more harsh in their judgments of women than of men. Philip Goldberg (1968) found that women value the professional work of men more highly than the identical work of women. However, other studies have had other outcomes. In one, females actually rated an essay allegedly written by a female as better than the same essay as written by a male (Levenson et al. 1975). But, perhaps reflecting again women's greater tendency to conformity, women rated a painting by a woman artist higher when its superiority had already been demonstrated by the awarding of a prize (Pheterson, Kiesler, and Goldberg 1971) and an essay by a woman writer higher when it was attributed to a person with high professional status (Peck 1978).

So we do know that both the sex and the personality of the rater affect perceptions of performance (Lord, Phillips, and Rush 1980). We also know that women tend to be more consistent in their perceptions of female performance than of male performance, a difference not found among male raters (Wexley and Pulakos 1982). But the strength or direction of these differences remains to be determined. We know that past experience makes a difference. Both men and women who have been supervised by a woman are more positive about women's motivation to manage, but not necessarily about their managerial ability, than those who have not (Ezell, Odewahn, and Sherman 1981). We know that androgyny level seems not to make a difference; androgynous individuals were no less affected by stereotypes in their evaluations than nonandrogynous ones; both showed subtle levels of discrimination against women (Gutek and Stevens 1979).

All of these studies tend to treat women and men as homogeneous groups, which may account for some of the anomalies. It's not at all clear to what extent men and women see ratees as "similar to me" on the basis of gender alone. More research is needed to determine to what extent sex, biographical similarity, or other characteristics—age, race, religion, or nationality—might affect the perceptions of similarity and how those perceptions might affect evaluations. In the meantime we are left with the reality that men do seem to rate more favorably the work of subordinates that they perceive as like themselves in terms of values and personalities. Men are also more likely to let their judgments of a woman and her work be affected by her physical attractiveness. The potential for discrimination against women is enormous, since men are far more likely to be in the position of making judgments. However, even if women do achieve the power, it may not always work to the advantage of other women. Women evaluators are relatively unaffected by attractiveness, but they are affected by status. Women seem to undervalue the work of other women unless it has already been demonstrated that the work itself or the person performing the work has achieved recognition.

To recap: Performance evaluation is not and can never be value free. A review of the literature shows that sex of the ratee, and to a lesser extent the sex of the rater, has a distinct impact on judgments of both the performer and the work. Most often this impact takes the form of a pro-male bias, although in some cases the result is an overevaluation of female work. Three factors that affect the level of bias are (1) the level of inference required—the less concrete and specific the situation, the more likely that males will be preferred; (2) sex role congruence—males tend to be favored over females in tasks that are perceived as masculine, but the reverse effect is less strong; (3) level of qualifications and performance—the greater the demands, the more likely that males will be preferred. Being physically attractive helps for males in most situations but for females only in situations that are not perceived as incongruent with the female sex role. Having shared values or personality traits with the rater tends to enhance the evaluation, but gender may or may not contribute to feelings of similarity. The pro-male bias is demonstrated by both sexes, except that women rate other women higher when their accomplishments have already received recognition. And perhaps most discouraging of all, it can be evoked by very subtle, nonverbal cues of approval or disapproval from either authority figures or subordinates.

So, while we have found so far no significant differences in female competence, we have found differences in the way female performance is perceived and evaluated. The next, and perhaps the most critical, decision is how these differential evaluations enter into organizational decisionmaking.

DISCRIMINATION

Under Title VII of the Civil Rights Act of 1964, and under statute in most states, it is unlawful to discriminate in employment decisions on the basis of race, religion, national origin, or sex. Most people, including many women, believe that those laws have at least eliminated most overt sex discrimination, giving women equal access to job opportunities. Yet despite the law, women continue to be absent altogether or to be found in very small numbers in male-dominated occupations. A number of factors may contribute to that situation, including women's occupational choices. But it is impossible to ignore the evidence that shows that women still receive differential and discriminatory treatment in organizational decisionmaking.

This discrimination takes two forms, *access* discrimination and *treatment* discrimination. Access discrimination refers to the problems women face in terms of the availability to them of particular jobs. Treatment discrimination is the situations they confront once they have obtained jobs (Levitan, Quinn, and Staines 1971).

Access Discrimination

Public policy and contemporary values require that when a man and woman are equally qualified they should be given equal treatment in applying for work. Most personnel decisionmakers undoubtedly believe that they comply with that standard. But a good deal of evidence shows that in reality they show a preference for male applicants, although a number of factors in addition to sex enter into the equation.

One study concentrated on only one occupation, Accounting, still a male-dominated field despite a substantial increase in the number of female accountants. Letters of application were sent in answer to newspaper advertisements for accounting jobs at several levels of skill. Efforts were counted as "successful" if the employer sent back an application form to be completed or scheduled an interview. Male applicants had considerably more success than identically qualified females. Yet when, several months later, the same employers were asked to respond to a survey on their hiring practices, 85 percent said they treat males and females equally when it comes to job decisions. A majority of the respondents said they thought there was no discrimination in the accounting field (Firth 1982).

In another study, male and female students made duplicate telephone inquiries in response to 256 different classified job advertisements. Clear-cut discrimination was found in over one-third of the cases ("This job isn't suitable for a man/woman," or "I don't think a man/woman would like this job"). In another third the answers were ambiguous ("Well, I guess you could come in and apply" or "Are you sure you're really qualified for this job?"). In only one-third of the cases was there no discrimination. One outcome of legal attempts to eliminate discrimination was apparent, however. Employers were more likely to discriminate against a male than a female seeking a sex-inappropriate job, apparently in recognition of the legal perils involved in discrimination against women (R. Levinson 1975).

These advertised jobs were mostly fairly low-level, low-skilled jobs, while the accounting jobs obviously required higher levels of education and training. Job recruiters at two university placement offices, presumably well versed in the relative competencies of male and female applicants for professional jobs, were asked to evaluate a hypothetical applicant— either male or female—for a male-oriented or female-oriented position. And once again discrimination was present: Significantly more females were recommended for the female-oriented position and males for the male-oriented one (Cohen and Bunker 1975). Similar results were apparent when professional personnel consultants rated the suitability of applicants for sex-typed jobs (Cash, Gillen, and Burns 1977).

Thus it's clear that men and women do receive differential treatment, but it is simplistic to say that men are preferred over women for all jobs or even that women and men are preferred for sex-specific jobs. Other variables enter in, including the sex-role orientation of the interviewer, the difficulty of the job, the scholastic performance and educational background of the applicants, the gender of the manager's subordinates, the level of inference required in the decision, the age and competence of the applicants, their attractiveness, even their choice of perfume (R. Baron 1983).

The sex-role orientation of the applicant may be more important than biological sex in determining perceived suitability for a sex-typed job. Jackson (1983a) found that androgynous as well as masculine people were considered suitable for masculine jobs, while both androgynous and feminine people were considered suitable for a feminine one. Surprisingly, feminine and androgynous persons were preferred for sex-neutral occupations.

The sex role orientation of the interviewer also affects the way she or he perceives an applicant's suitability for a sex-typed job. Those who hold conventional sex role stereotypes are more likely to discriminate in evaluating job applicants than those who do not endorse such beliefs and are more likely to discriminate against a woman applicant for a male-oriented job than the reverse (Sharp and Post 1980).

A disturbing corollary is found in the fact that women have been shown to behave in a more stereotypically feminine way when they have information that suggests that the interviewer holds conventional stereotypes. In both verbal and nonverbal ways, and even in their dress, they present themselves to traditional males in a more typically feminine manner (von Baeyer, Sherk, and Zanna 1981). Obviously, if they are applying for female-oriented positions, the behavior might enhance their job prospects, but for a male-dominated occupation it would probably decrease their chances. These data might be less alarming if it could be demonstrated that there is a decrease in sex role stereotyping among decisionmakers, but even among undergraduate business majors, substantial numbers of males, and more males than females, have been found to hold conventional stereotypes (Tomkiewicz and Brenner 1982).

The composition of the applicant pool is significant, especially for masculine positions. When women are tokens—less than 25 percent of the applicants—their qualifications are rated lower and they are less likely to be recommended for hiring. As the number of women candidates rises, so too does their perceived suitability for the job (Heilman 1980).

When a managerial job is highly demanding, male applicants are seen as more suitable than equally qualified females. They are also seen as higher on potential for long service with the organization and on potential for fitting in well (Rosen and Jerdee 1974c). Females in this study were seen as more suitable for a routine managerial job than for a demanding one. The lowest acceptance rates and the poorest overall evaluations were given to women applying for the demanding and challenging positions.

Men were also preferred when the job called for supervising men, and women were seen as more suitable for jobs requiring the supervision of women (Rose and Andiappan 1978).

A fascinating inversion of this phenomenon shows that when women and men are applying for the same position, the job itself may be perceived differently depending on the sex of the applicant. Job descriptions for a job described only as "white collar" were written so that either a male or a female might perform it. When the applicant was female, the evaluators perceived the job as primarily a clerical one, and characteristics they considered to be relevant were "Personality/Appearance" and "Skills/Education." When the applicant for the job was male, the job was perceived as more of an administrative management position, and the relevant characteristics were "Motivation/Ability" and "Interpersonal Relations" (Cecil, Paul, and Olins 1973).

Although this job description was perhaps artificially vague, managerial positions, as we noted above, are characterized by a good deal of ambiguity, requiring a fairly high level of inference, and therefore of risk, on the part of the decisionmaker. It has been argued that employment interviews are in reality "a search for negative information" (Webster, in Shaw 1972). Since interviewers are rarely rewarded for hiring good people and often criticized for hiring misfits, they tend to become cautious and to develop a sensitivity for negative evidence. This sensitivity is especially acute when the evaluation is based on ambiguous information. Decisions on managerial occupations, which are based on the interviewer's implicit personality theory and require a high level of inference, are therefore riskier than those on occupational categories that require specialized, advanced training, such as engineer or scientist. It follows that "negative traits" such as female gender or physical disability have a differential impact and are more central to some occupations than to others. Thus, when the job description is specific and the tasks are challenging and demanding, or when the job requires supervising other men, men are more likely to be seen as suitable for the job. When the job description is vague or ambiguous, the perceived difficulty, and therefore the perceived qualifications, vary depending on who is applying.

Obviously factors other than gender are involved. Grade point average (GPA), educational background, and competence are in some ways more important predictors of access than gender, but the gender factor always mediates their effect. Professional interviewers ranking bogus resumes rated scholastic standing as the most important criteria, but they showed a strong bias in favor of males over females having equal scholastic standing (Dipboye, Fromkin, and Wiback 1975). Corporate personnel directors responded more favorably to applicants with high grades than to those with average ones. But applicants who were identified only by first initial (hence whose gender was unspecified) fared better than those identified as female, regardless of GPA. The highest response was to an applicant with high grades whose gender was unspecified. The smallest response (0 out of 15) came to the female applicant with only average grades (Zikmund, Hitt, and Pickens 1978). Employers in another study clearly preferred competent to barely competent employees. They made little distinction between barely competent males and barely competent females, but for individuals with high competence, males were preferred over females (Haefner 1977). What all of this seems to suggest is that the highly qualified female will have a difficult time competing with men of equal ability, and the average female will have little chance at all against the average male.

On the other hand, the applicant's undergraduate or graduate degree proved to be important factors in selecting managerial candidates, overriding the effects of sex or marital status. Candidates with undergraduate degrees in business administration were regarded as most suitable for a managerial position, followed in order by industrial sociology, industrial engineering, history, and English literature. Applicants with an MBA were perceived as more suitable than those with an MS in administration, particularly for a job requiring interaction with others in the company. The authors conclude: "The job applicant's particular field of specialization and graduate degree play a more influential role in selection decisions than do personal characteristics such as sex or marital status" (Renwick and Tosi 1978).

Attractiveness, as we saw above, affects performance evaluation, although not in a straightforward way. It also affects job access. Males are preferred for masculine jobs, females for feminine jobs, but within those roles, attractive applicants are preferred over less-attractive ones. For non-sex-typed jobs, attractive applicants are preferred (Cash, Gillen, and Burns 1977) and higher salaries are recommended (Jackson 1983a). Scholastic standing takes precedence over attractiveness, but among equally qualified applicants, interviewers will prefer males over females and attractive applicants over unattractive ones (Dipboye, Fromkin, and Wiback 1975). These results hold regardless of the sex or attractiveness of the interviewer (Dipboye, Arvey, and Terpstra 1977). The bias against women and against unattractive candidates is most pronounced when deciding who should be ranked first or which one candidate should be hired. Since in many cases there is, in fact, only one opening or one position, the impact of this bias is larger than at first appears.

Access discrimination, then, is still very much a part of the organizational world. Employers clearly believe that they evaluate candidates equally and equitably, considering only valid criteria such as scholastic standing, undergraduate or graduate education, or other specialized qualifications. Equally clearly, such invalid factors as the sex and the sex role orientation of the applicant, the sex typing of the job, the sex and sex role orientation of the decisionmaker, plus the attractiveness of the applicant, all contribute to the decision process. The greatest problem seems to exist in access to occupations that are perceived as masculine, to jobs that are seen as difficult and challenging, and to positions where the job description is ambiguous or unclear and the requirements are subjective. In these cases the decisionmaker must rely on less-specific information, make greater inferences, and take greater risks in choosing one applicant over others. Under those conditions, the decisionmaker is most likely to choose a well-qualified male over an equally qualified female, particularly if the male is physically attractive. Often the preference will be for an average male over a well-qualified female. Rarely will the preference go to the average female, even to an attractive one.

Treatment Discrimination

Once the selection decision has been made and the individual enters the organization, a new set of potentially discriminatory decision situations arises. These include the tasks or responsibilities to which newcomers are assigned, the career support they are given, and the rewards they receive. There are two perceptions of treatment discrimination. One is that it is less problematic than access discrimination, since the experience of working with competent women tends to reduce the influence of stereotypes. Indeed, there is support for the argument that stereotypes are most influential in the absence of specific information about the individual (Bartol and Butterfield 1976). The other is that observations of one competent female do not generalize to all females. Each new woman in the organization is faced with overcoming for herself the effect of feminine stereotypes. The weight of the evidence seems to support the notion that treatment discrimination is subtle, covert, pervasive, and real.

When individuals are hired by large organizations, they are typically not hired for a specific position. Rather they are placed according to the organization's needs at the time they enter, then rotated through a series of positions to develop their managerial skills and organizational expertise. The initial placement decision is important, since it is the newcomer's chance to demonstrate competence, to attract a mentor, and to prepare for further career development. It is also the place where the newcomer assesses his or her own competence and relative strengths in the organization and begins to set performance and career goals. If women do not have the same access as men to challenging, demanding tasks, then they would be disadvantaged from the start, both in terms of their credibility in the organization and their own aspirations.

In one study, both males and females, when asked to make initial placement decisions, were more likely to see females as more suitably placed in unchallenging rather than challenging positions. However, experience in observing a competent female did seem to reduce the extent to which females in general were seen as less suitable for high-challenge positions, that is, experience did tend to change the stereotype (Taylor and Ilgen 1981).

Somewhat different results were found in another study of placement decisions, in this case the choice of assignment to either a dull or a challenging task. Men again demonstrated a preference for men for the challenging task, but women tended to choose other women.

> Men and women chose same-sex others for the challenging job because they expected a more rewarding relationship with these individuals. Thus, the participants felt that there would be less conflict during the work with individuals of their own sex. In addition, men seemed to justify their prejudices on the basis of role stereotyping, i.e., Paul is more competent for the challenging task, and Jane is more competent for the dull task and she would be more interested in getting the job done (Mai-Dalton and Sullivan 1981).

The preference for same-sex others has also been shown in situations that involve sharing decisionmaking authority and encouraging others to assume leadership positions. According to the Vertical Dyad Linkage Model of leadership, a group may be conceived of as a series of dyads, each involving the leader and one group member. An exchange process occurring within the dyad depends on which of two types of role relationship is set up. If the leader and member are mutually "ingroup," they make decisions together; the member is thereby able to assume status as a de facto leader. Those with whom the leader becomes close are also those most likely to receive support from the leader in return. If the relationship is "outgroup," the leader merely tells the group member how to behave. Outgroup members are not privy to the decisionmaking process and are therefore less likely to be designated heirs-apparent to the leader. People tend to groom for leadership those with whom they enjoy an ingroup relationship; men tend to choose other men, women other women (Larwood and Blackmore 1978).

We could conclude that to the extent that women are in positions to support and encourage the career development of other women, treatment discrimination will be reduced. But, unfortunately, men still hold control over the majority of decisions, and they still do prefer to invest organizational resources in men, rather than women. For example, in an in-basket exercise often used in research projects and management training seminars, one incident asks participants to recommend an employee to attend a highly regarded supervisory training conference. Background information is provided for a candidate who is a business school graduate and who is described as "having demonstrated good potential for higher level supervisory positions." When this candidate is described as a male, about 60 percent of workshop participants recommend sending him for training, but when the candidate is a female, only 35 percent recommend the training (Rosen and Jerdee 1977). Very similar results have been found in a survey of 1,500 readers of *The Harvard Business Review* in which 95 percent of the respondents were male (Rosen and Jerdee 1974a), in a study of 95 male bank supervisors (Rosen and Jerdee 1974b), and in a group of college seniors, of whom half were male and half female (Kovach 1981).

Other forms of treatment discrimination have been revealed by Rosen and Jerdee's research, some of it against men. For example, managers clearly expect male exployees to give top priority to their jobs when career and family obligations conflict and expect women to sacrifice their careers for their families. A request for a month's leave of absence to resolve a child care problem was far more frequently judged as inappropriate for a male accountant than for a female accountant and was much more likely to be denied to the male. If it were granted, the woman was more likely than the man to be paid.

In most instances, however, respondents have continually shown greater concern for the success of their male employees than their female ones. Wives of young male executives were overwhelmingly expected to support their husbands' careers by participating in job-related social events, but young husbands were not expected to give reciprocal support to their wives' careers. Respondents indicated a good deal more willingness to try to retain a valued male employee who was considering following his wife to a new location than they would for a similarly situated female employee; and they indicated a good deal less willingness to promote a woman than a man who showed a strong commitment to family responsibilities. In disciplinary situations, when a company policy had been violated (tardiness) more severe sanctions were recommended for a female than for a male offender; but in a more ambiguous situation where the employee's private, off-the-job behavior threatened to interfere with work, the executives showed more willingness to intercede with the male than with the female employee.

Treatment discrimination is apparently the result of stereotypes held by the decisionmakers. Some recent research has focused on the sex typing of the job and the sex role orientation, rather than the sex, of the employee. When personnel consultants were given information about an employee's gender traits, they tended to use that information, rather than sex, in making their decisions. Thus, in a masculine occupation, masculine and androgynous individuals were more highly recommended for promotion than feminine ones. In a feminine occupation, feminine and androgynous employees received stronger promotion recommendations than masculine employees. In sex-neutral occupations, feminine and androgynous persons were more likely to be promoted than masculine ones. But regardless of the sex typing of the job, masculine employees were still preferred over feminine ones for the challenging job assignment while feminine employees were most likely to be assigned to the routine task. Also, regardless of the sex typing of the job, androgynous persons were more likely than masculine or feminine persons to receive recommendations for a special training program (Jackson 1983b).

In one area, however, sex and not sex role is the determining factor. Males still suffer discrimination when it comes to job/family conflicts. Regardless of sex role, males in this research, as in so many other studies, were more likely to be refused a leave of absence to attend to child care than females in identical circumstances (Jackson 1983b).

These results can be viewed positively or negatively. They suggest that knowledge of the gender traits of individuals overrides stereotypes in matching up actual traits with the situational requirements of the job. However, personnel decisionmakers must be able to distinguish individuals from categories. If they assume that traits are inextricably tied to sex they will continue to make discriminatory decisions. As we have noted above, personnel consultants, executives, even students who are managers of the future tend to hold very traditional stereotypes, and women tend to behave in more stereotypically feminine ways in the presence of someone they know to hold conventional sex-role attitudes. So we may have a dilemma of women actually reinforcing stereotypes among the people whose beliefs they most need to change.

A final form of treatment discrimination comes in the form of rewards. The whole issue of pay inequities is covered in detail in Chapter 3. It should suffice here to be reminded that just as women's contributions are evaluated differently, so also are they rewarded differently from men's work. This differential treatment can cut both ways. When women succeed at tasks that are perceived as masculine, their work is sometimes overevaluated. Sex role plays a part here also. When a woman performs a masculine task in a masculine mode of behavior, she tends to be more highly rewarded than an equally performing male, but the reverse is not true for the male. Further, when she performs a feminine task in a feminine way, her performance is rated more highly than when she uses a masculine mode of behavior, but her reward isn't increased (Taynor and Deaux 1975). The important point here is not who gets paid more or less, or for what performance, but the fact that rewards are allocated differently depending on sex and sex role.

In summary, we can say that there is some evidence to support the contention that treatment discrimination will decrease as more women enter traditionally masculine occupations. Males who have the experience of working with competent females may learn to reduce their reliance on stereotypes. On the other hand, there is substantial evidence that significant subtle, mostly unconscious discrimination continues to exist, particularly in areas of ambiguity and uncertainty. Employers continue to expect men to sacrifice their families for their careers and women to sacrifice their careers for their families. They continue to offer more personal and career support and encouragement to males, to assign males to more challenging tasks or positions, to promote them to more responsible positions, and to reward them generously for their efforts. There is encouragement in the fact that women in recent years are more likely to support and encourage other women, and also in the fact that knowledge of an individual's gender traits can override stereotypes, but these encouraging results cannot hide the fact that women have a long way to go to receive equal treatment in contemporary organizations.

SUMMARY

In this chapter we considered the actual and perceived differences in women's performance. We found that women are no less competent than men, although they do tend to be more conforming and persuasable, hence less amenable to risk taking. We found some differences in confidence, particularly in situations where women are in a minority, tasks are sex-typed as masculine, and ambiguity is high and feedback low. We offered as an explanation of these differences not biology but a theory of status characteristics and expectation states.

When it comes to performance evaluation, however, significant sex differences appear, mostly in the form of a pro-male bias. The factors that contribute to this bias were explored along with some of the situational variables. We found that the pro-male bias is exhibited by women as well as men, although to a somewhat lesser degree. And we learned that perceptions of competence can be manipulated by extremely subtle nonverbal behavior.

In the final section we addressed the question of the extent to which these differences in performance and performance evaluation have resulted in discriminatory actions. We found that, despite Civil Rights laws that prohibit it, women continue to suffer access discrimination. While qualifications such as grades, scholastic standing, or competence clearly override sex, they are also mitigated by sex. Given two equally highly qualified candidates, employers prefer a male over a female, an attractive candidate over an unattractive one. Employers clearly prefer a less-qualified male to an equally less-qualified female. The most discouraging finding is that some employers seem to prefer a less-qualified male to a more-qualified female.

Although some have argued that treatment discrimination is less of a problem than access discrimination, the evidence suggests that women still receive less challenging assignments and less career support than males, while males receive less support than females in family/career conflicts.

Nevertheless, it would be a mistake to end this chapter on such a discouraging note. While it is undeniable that a pro-male bias exists in organizations and results in discriminatory treatment for both women and men, it's also true that great strides have been made in recent years. Women still face access discrimination, but they have at least gained access to occupations and organizations that until recently were closed to them altogether. Women still face treatment discrimination, but they have gained the insight and the knowledge and the power to demand equal treatment. True equality may be a long way away, but as they say in the ad, "You've come a long way, baby."

11

Careers, Career Decisions, and Career Development

The previous chapters have shown that women's organizational experiences are very different from men's. At every organizational level and in every occupational group, we see women's achievements and accomplishments being devalued, we see women receiving lower pay and slower promotions, and we see women excluded from positions of power and influence.

But are women the passive victims of a sexist society and sexist organizations? Or do they deliberately choose to pursue professions, positions, and career paths that will result in differential treatment? Many will argue that the problem lies with women themselves. They assert that the majority of women simply are not willing to make the personal sacrifices necessary to achieve the same successes as their male counterparts. They believe that women do not invest in their "human capital" to the extent that men do, that women experience role conflict between career roles and other life roles that take higher priority, and that women, lacking role models in nontraditional occupations, perceive them as unfeminine and opt for the traditional female work roles.

Others, however, reject these explanations and argue that they are another example of "victim analysis." They assert that women, given equal access to opportunities for education, job training, and development, along with equal assessment, will be able to reach equal status.

In this chapter we compare the differences in career choice, career development, and career training between women and men.

CAREER DECISIONS

Women and men have different decisions to make. Men must decide between a job and career. But women start with a more fundamental choice. They must first decide between work and nonwork, that is, between market work and full-time homemaking. If they opt for market work, they again have two choices. They must decide between a career— a sequential and occupationally related set of increasingly responsible or technical positions—and a job. If they decide on a career, they again have two choices. They must decide between a career in a traditionally female-dominated occupation or one in a traditionally male-dominated occupation. And if they choose a career, they face another choice; whether to try to combine their career with marriage and children. What they choose at each decision point is at least partially a function of how they perceive their feminine role and how they value familial roles.

Career, Work, or Nonwork

Children begin to internalize sex stereotypes from a very early age. They understand that boys grow up to be men and that grown men work. Rarely do children see a man over school age and under retirement age who isn't working at a job or seeking work. By kindergarten age they have a fairly clear view of what kinds of work men do. They also understand that girls grow up to be women, but the roles of grown women may be less clear. Women do nurturing things in the home; they cook, clean, wash and iron clothes, and take care of children and other adults; they may also work for pay outside the home. Kindergarten-aged children already know what kinds of paid work women do and don't do. Rather surprisingly they are more likely to exclude women from men's sex-typed jobs than men from women's sex-typed jobs. It's apparently not so much that they feel that "women's place is in the home" as that women's place is in female-dominated occupations (Schlossberg and Goodman 1972).

Between kindergarten and sixth grade, little change occurs in the degree to which children stereotype occupations, and by the end of high school the majority of students have defined some clear occupational choice. In one study of high-school-age students, about 60 percent of males and 60 percent of females reported that they aspired to professional or technical careers, far more than could possibly be employed in these fields. (Fottler and Bain 1980).

For some women, the career choice may be homemaking. A controversial "Theory of Marriage" by political economist Gary Becker (1974) argues that a traditional division of labor within the marriage may be the most rational. In choosing a marriage partner, the optimal choice for most traits—ability, education, race, income, and height—is "a mating of likes." But for such traits as wage rates the mating of unlikes is preferable. Becker posits that among the motivations for marriage is the efficiency associated with specialization of male and female time within marriage. If the woman's potential earnings are lower than the man's but she is at least as productive as he within the household, then the marriage is most efficient if she uses her less-expensive time in doing homemaking tasks while he uses his more-expensive time earning the family's living.

Critics of the theory reply that it is at best a description of the status quo and at worst a justification for the further exploitation of women. It also may raise a moot point, since women as a group are increasing their earnings ability both through education and labor market participation.

Among high-school-aged women, only a small proportion expect to be full-time homemakers at age 30. These women are likely to come from very traditional, white, rural, working-class families, and to have low scholastic achievement. Consistent with Becker's theory, they would presumably have low earnings potential in the marketplace and might realistically expect to contribute their time to the homemaking role while their husbands apply their more expensive time to the breadwinner role (Falkowski and Falk 1983).

Among college-age women the number who choose homemaking as a career has declined steadily over the last 20 years (Betz 1984). Women currently in college report that they plan to combine career and family, although they expect to put the family first throughout their careers. They expect to interrupt their careers either altogether or on a part-time basis while their children are preschool age (Greenglass and Devins 1982). However, the number who expect to work all their lives appears to be on the increase (Betz 1984).

These expectations appear to be consistent with those of the men in their age cohort. Komarovsky (1973) found that while college males were quick to espouse feminist ideology, with further probing they often revealed a "modified traditionalist" position. Like the women students, they favored a sequential pattern of work for married women: work, withdrawal from work for childbearing, and eventual return to work. They varied as to the help they were prepared to give their wives with domestic and childrearing functions; even the most traditional men held homemaking in very low esteem, yet they expected their wives to do it. Only a handful (7 percent) were willing to modify their own roles to facilitate their future wives' careers.

More discouraging still is a study of dual-career couples in which 66 percent of the men and 75 percent of the women described themselves as feminists and espoused a belief in egalitarian marriage. Even among this group, when a decision had to be made that would adversely affect the career of one partner, that is, there was no option that provided for compromise, feminism gave way to traditional values and the wife's career was sacrificed to the husband's (Foster, Wallston, and Berger 1980).

Clearly at this stage there is a good deal of agreement about appropriate occupational choice. Even at the graduate school level these differences do not disappear. In a study of first-year students in a professional program, female students anticipated less career advancement than the males. More importantly, the women put less value than the men on higher level professional roles, which they perceived as being more demanding than lower level ones (Peterson-Hardt and Burlin 1979). When women and men in graduate schools in male-intensive fields (business, law, and medicine) were asked, "What do you expect to be doing in 2 years, 5 years, 10 years, and 20 years?" there were few differences, with one exception. The women expected to make greater accommodation to marriage and the family, especially at the five-year interval (Shann 1983).

Follow-up studies of college women show that those who expect to have careers and to combine career and family are probably fairly realistic. The number of women doing so has increased dramatically in recent years. Those who expect to be full-time homemakers may be less realistic; only a tiny fraction of college women has remained continuously out of the labor force. Those who expect extended interruptions for childrearing may also be unrealistic; a large and increasing number of women workers are continuously employed throughout their work lives (Betz 1984).

Thus we see that throughout the years in which career decisions are being formed, males and females are subject to different influences and different constraints. Social change has had its impact. We now see the great majority of girls from high school age on planning for some sort of occupational role. But rather than abandoning the more traditional role of homemaker, they expect to integrate that role with their occupational role and give it priority, an expectation that is consistent with those of their male cohorts.

However well these expectations are met, the chances are that individuals will experience some stress and role conflict. Noncareer employed women, that is, women who describe themselves as having a job, not a career, report more role conflict than career women, especially in the absence of role support from the husband (Holahan and Gilbert 1979a). Yet in dual-career families, women with high career aspirations experience more role conflict than those with lower ambition, while the opposite is true for men (Holahan and Gilbert 1979b). One might expect these situations to be reversed; the explanation probably lies in the fact that in the dual-career couple each individual is acting in a manner contrary to societal expectations, while the woman with a noncareer job is conforming to those expectations.

For some women, one choice is volunteer work as a primary career (Jenner 1981), a choice that allows participation in meaningful and satisfying work without defying social convention and without threatening the familial role. However, it is a choice that is not open to the majority of families that require two incomes and one that is not viable to many women who see it as exploitation of women and further reinforcement of sexual stereotypes.

Among those women who choose homemaking as their primary career, many will find themselves in the labor market, supporting themselves and their families. Among the majority of young people who choose ambitious plans for professional and technical careers, many will find these ambitions unrealized. Among those who reject the choice of a managerial career, many will become managers. Among the women and men who expect that women will interrupt their careers for childrearing, many will find this choice unrealistic and unaffordable. Among those women who combine a job (not a career) and homemaking, many will suffer role conflict. Among men in dual-career families who lower their own career aspirations to share familial roles, many will also experience role conflict.

Traditional Versus Nontraditional Careers

As increasing numbers of women enter career fields dominated by males (Betz 1984), much interest has focused on the influences that affect such a choice. Less has been written about men who enter female-intensive occupations. The issue is a highly complex one without definitive answers, but a cursory review of the literature will show that the myths of sex differences in influences, decisionmaking processes, or investment in human capital do not hold up to close scrutiny.

There are internal differences between those women who choose traditional and those who choose nontraditional roles in their perception of the feminine sex role. Most of these differences center around sex-role ideology. Women with traditional views of the feminine role are less likely to set high educational goals (Lipman-Blumen 1972), are more likely to choose traditional female professions, and are more conservative with respect to marital relationships (Crawford 1978). Women with high career aspirations have been shown to be nontraditional in their values and behaviors, and also to be satisfied with their lives and confident of their career plans. They are willing to postpone marriage (Parsons, Frieze, and Ruble 1978) but have as many romantic and friendship relationships with men as do their more traditional sisters, and often look to a boy friend for role support (Tangri 1972). Women with a traditional view tend to prefer a vicarious mode of achievement, while contemporary women are a good deal more likely to prefer to accomplish their goals through their own efforts (Lipman-Blumen 1972).

External influences may affect career choice directly and they may also affect ideology, which in turn affects career choice. But the impact of these influences is far from clear. Lipman-Blumen (1972) found that the only really significant determinant was a family in which parents had a fairly egalitarian marriage. She found no significance to such obvious socioeconomic factors as religion, rural versus urban or suburban background, family disruption through divorce or death, the presence or absence of siblings of either gender, birth order, or whether or not the mother worked for wages outside the home.

Mothers probably serve as role models for their daughters, but the nature of their influence is complex. It is too simplistic to say that mothers who work outside the home produce nontraditional daughters, as is sometimes asserted. Perhaps a more important predictor is the mother's overall satisfaction with life. Mothers who are dissatisfied with homemaking are more likely to be dissatisfied with life and to have nontraditional daughters (Lipman-Blumen 1972). And women with working mothers who were dissatisfied with life are also more likely to have high career aspirations (Parsons, Frieze, and Ruble 1978). However, women now employed in or pursuing graduate degrees in male-intensive occupations report that nontraditional careers are fostered by identification with and the emotional support of both parents—rather than just one (Lunneborg 1982).

Schools have come in for a great deal of criticism for the way in which they shape women's occupational roles. And indeed there is considerable evidence of sexism in the schools (Stacey, Bereaud, and Daniels 1974). Reading texts in the primary grades tend to show very traditional roles— men as both fathers and jobholders and women only as mothers. If women work it is only out of dire necessity and the work is in traditional female occupations. By junior high school boys are counseled into math and science courses, girls into language and literature. Counselors, both male and female, seem to respond more favorably to female students who hold traditional career goals and to take males' career plans more seriously. Male counselors have little knowledge of the extent of women's labor force participation (Wirtenberg and Nakamura 1976).

It should come as little surprise, then, that talented female high school seniors express a lack of information about steps in preparing for a technical career and feel they receive inadequate encouragement from teachers and counselors (McLure and Piel 1978). On the other hand, adult women who have entered nontraditional fields report that in addition to their parents they received strong support from teachers and other adults, as well as siblings and peers (Lunneborg 1982).

The vocational tests often given to high school students also come in for criticism. Much research confirms that there is considerable sex typing in these vocational interest inventories. However, what limited evidence exists suggests that these tests have relatively little impact on career choice (Wirtenberg and Nakamura 1976).

Occupational prestige affects decisions, but again the relationship is unclear. Traditional male occupations have always carried more status and prestige than traditional female ones. As occupations move from male to female dominance, their occupational prestige tends to decrease, a relationship that is usually assumed to be cause and effect. Laboratory studies have seemed to confirm this notion; as students were convinced that certain prestigious male-dominated occupations would, in the next five years, admit increased numbers of women, they found them increasingly less prestigious and desirable (Touhey 1974a). Increased male participation in female-dominated professions increased the prestige and desirability of the occupation (Touhey 1974b). However, for a sample of business undergraduates, the prospect of increasing numbers of women entering either business or the professions did not result in a decline in either the prestige or desirability of those professions (Crino, White, and DeSanctis 1983).

The influence of occupational prestige on career decisionmaking is complicated further by the fact that prestige is influenced not only by the sex type of the occupation but also by the sex of the incumbent. Women in nonprofessional, nontraditional jobs (carpenter, auto mechanic) receive less prestige than men in those jobs. Traditionally female occupations, both professional and nonprofessional, receive less prestige than corresponding male occupations, but male jobholders receive even lower ratings than women (Beyard-Tyler and Haring 1984).

What can be said, then, about the influences that affect the decision to enter a nontraditional career? Women who make these decisions do seem to have a different sex role orientation from their more traditional sisters; to have stronger ambitions both for education and career, to have a stronger sense of their own competence, to be more confident of their decisions and satisfied with their lives, and to prefer a direct mode of achievement. They have less conservative views about marriage and are willing to delay marriage for the sake of their careers. Yet they have as many and as important relationships with males. They are influenced a good deal by their families. They come from families where both parents were supportive and where the parents had a fairly egalitarian marriage. Yet they often have mothers who are dissatisfied with their own lives— either as homemakers or as job holders. They are influenced by education—by textbooks, teachers and counselors, and to a much lesser extent by sex-biased vocational tests—but these influences tend to push them toward traditional, rather than nontraditional, choices. They are influenced by occupational prestige, which varies across occupational categories according to the sex composition of the occupation as well as within occupations according to the gender of the jobholder. If there is a trend or a pattern here it is hard to detect.

Decision Processes

It is sometimes argued that women and men differ in the way in which they make decisions. But again the evidence only partially supports such a belief and fails to explain those differences that do appear.

Women, unlike men, are likely to seriously consider only a relatively small subset of potential jobs when making career decisions. Their perceptions about probable entry into or success in jobs differ from the perceptions of men and may not be particularly accurate. They are likely to expect different outcomes from men (surely an accurate expectation), and they attach different values to these outcomes (Brief, Van Sell, and Aldag 1979). Not unlike most males, they tend to use an "intuitive" as opposed to a "planning" decisionmaking style (Lunneborg 1978). They do not differ from males in the age at which they make career decisions (Neice and Bradley 1979), and progress in the decision process is affected by sex role self-concept for both women and men (Moreland et al. 1979).

As in other forms of organizational behavior, sex doesn't seem to make much difference, but sex role may.

Investment in Human Capital

The theory of human capital as an explanation for occupational segregation was discussed in Chapter 3. It refers to the "investment" that people and their employers make in education and training. This education and training brings increased productivity, which in turn is rewarded by higher income or status. Time spent in the labor force represents a gain in one's human capital—and for men age and time in the labor force are roughly equivalent. Decisions to invest in human capital, by both employer and employee, are influenced by age and time in the labor force on a cost-benefit basis. The older one is, or the less time one will remain in the labor force, the less time there is to recover the costs of investment and reap benefits.

The human capital approach argues that the interruptions in women's employment histories will result in early decisions to invest less in human capital, in less time to accumulate human capital while in the labor market, and in depreciation of previously acquired human capital during breaks in employment. In general women would be expected to have less effective human capital than men (Rosenfeld 1979). Differences between women's and men's labor force experiences are often explained by human capital theory. It is used to argue that women fail to enter male-dominated occupations because, anticipating that their careers will be discontinuous, they decline to invest in the required schooling or experience, and there is some evidence to support this argument (McLure and Piel 1978). It is used to explain why women do enter female-dominated professions such as nurse, teacher, or social worker, where presumably the depreciation of human capital over breaks in employment is less (Polachek 1981). It has been used to explain the differences in male and female wages (Mincer and Polachek 1978). And it is used to justify employers' reluctance to hire women in occupations that require extended training and development time.

Human capital theory has an intuitive appeal, and in fact can be used to explain part of the difference between male and female labor market experience. But it is at best only a partial explanation (Rosenfeld 1979). Women do, in fact, invest in their human capital very much to the same extent that men do, although their investment strategies tend to vary. Men more frequently than women will use job training or job changes to increase their human capital while women are more likely to invest in additional schooling (Gurin 1981). However, a survey of MBA students found that women and men did not differ in their willingness to accept various investment strategies, such as changing employers, changing functional area, or relocating to a new geographical location. Both men and women were most favorable toward changing functional areas and least favorable toward changing employers (Rynes and Rosen 1983).

It's possible that differences in choice of strategies may be a function of differential access, specifically of women's opportunities to participate in career development and training programs. In other words it may be the employer, rather than the employee, side of the equation that is deficient. It may be that many women willing and anxious to invest in their own human capital are denied equal access to the training and development opportunities that their employers offer to equally qualified males. We turn now to a discussion of access to two resources in the development spectrum: training and mentoring.

TRAINING

Training can take many forms in an organization, and the most effective training no doubt includes elements of a variety of forms. The least formal training method is on-the-job, which can be nothing more than casual observation or can include an intense and protracted mentoring relationship. The most formal is highly structured classroom lectures, seminars, or workshops, either on site or off site. Other types of available training include self-paced individual courses of study, tuition reimbursements for college and university credits, and attendance at conferences. In a perfect world employers would offer the combination of training programs that would have optimal utility for the firm and the individual and offer them without prejudice to all employees. This is not a perfect world.

For example, a recent survey of middle management training and development programs, a follow-up of a study done in 1963, showed little if any significant trends or new developments over the 20-year period. There are more firms engaged in the training business, that is, professional training firms, and more university and education and training, but expenditures remained constant when corrected for inflation. The most frequently covered subjects in both surveys were communications, principles of management, and interpersonal skills (Middlebrook and Rachel 1983).

The state of the training art in the public sector seems no more encouraging. Most agencies make formal training available to staff, either on site or off site. The most frequently covered topics are very similar to those in the private sector—managerial techniques, human relations, and communications. Only three out of five employers have procedures for identifying dead-end career ladders in organizations. Only half evaluate all jobs before designing training programs to ensure that the training is job related. Fewer than one in five conduct skills surveys to find employees who, given special training, might be eligible for higher level jobs. About half have "explored ways of bridging employees from dead-end jobs into professional or para-professional jobs with more room for advancement," and only 43 percent have actually restructured existing jobs or created new ones (*IPMA News* 1981).

Women-Only Training

In this context, it shouldn't come as a surprise that there is substantial disagreement among trainers and also advocates for women as to the most desirable approach for training women for managerial careers. The questions involve whether women should be given segregated instruction, and, if so, which women should receive it and what the course content should be.

The arguments for women-only training speak to two issues: the problems of overcoming the socialization of women into feminine roles and behaviors, and the organizational skills that women lack. For example it is argued that because of their feminine socialization:

- When men are present women tend to revert to the comfortable, established pattern of deferring to men for advice and leadership (Larwood, Wood, and Inderlied 1978).
- Management courses dominated by men replicate the "outsider" situation women already have to deal with at work, a setting that breeds sex-role stereotyping.
- When men are present women may be assigned stereotypically feminine roles in group activities and simulations (for example, personnel or consumer functions) and not get the opportunity to practice and develop skills in the stereotypically male functions of finance or production (Hartnett and Novarra 1980).
- An otherwise outspoken woman may be easily intimidated into silence by a class of assertive men.
- Women may be unable to speak as honestly as they would like in front of men (Larwood, Wood, and Inderlied 1978). (This argu-

ment could presumably be used in favor of excluding women from all-male classes.)

- In some areas women, who are likely to be older, more mature, and to have better formal qualifications and more varied work experience, may be held back by the men.
- In women-only courses, women experience the feeling of shared competence, enjoy the association of other competent women, and have the opportunity to establish a network of female peers.
- In women-only classes women have the experience of women role models as teachers and can participate in stereotype-free career planning (Hartnett and Novarra 1980).

As a further argument in favor of women-only training it is often pointed out that graduates of women's colleges tend to have a much higher record of career achievement than women graduates of coeducational institutions. The problem with that approach is that it ignores the fact that women's colleges tend to be private, expensive, and elite. The same argument can be made for male-only training, that is, that a disproportionate percentage of successful males are graduates of all-male, or virtually all-male, colleges, most of which are highly exclusive.

In addition to the arguments based on roles and stereotypes, there are also arguments that speak to the special training needs of women, for example:

- Women need to raise their self-esteem, to learn new behaviors for managing interpersonal conflict, and to develop leadership and team-building skills (Heinen et al. 1975).
- Women need help with career planning (Heinen et al. 1975).
- Women need to learn the perceptions, strategies, and behavioral skills needed in the corporate arena (White, Crino, and DeSanctis 1981).
- Women need to become more politically sophisticated. The tendency, strongest among women in middle management, is to overemphasize the importance of education and hard work and to underestimate the importance of political awareness in moving up in the organization (Radin 1980).
- Few women have the technical background or training necessary to fill management positions and their opportunity for exposure to relevant experience has been severely restricted in the past (Gomez-Mejia and Balkin 1980).

All of these arguments speak to the need for special training programs for women. Few, however, would argue that women should be restricted to sexually segregated training. Most urge special training in addition to or as a preliminary to sex-integrated training programs.

Even so, there is strong opposition to any segregated instruction for women. Among the arguments against it are:

- These programs assume that women have unique problems that can't be resolved through traditional development programs (White, Crino, and DeSanctis 1981),
- They assume that women, but not men, need training to overcome the effects of role socialization, to be assertive, to plan careers, to make a commitment to work, to learn to manage their time.
- If women have difficulty asserting themselves with men, they are not going to get over it in a segregated classroom. Sooner or later they are going to have to learn to deal with men (Larwood, Wood, and Inderlied 1978).
- The presence of such programs creates the appearance that the environment either should not or cannot be changed and the onus is on women to adapt to the organizational climate as it exists (White, Crino, and DeSanctis 1981).
- These programs are ineffective because it is the structure of the organization, not the behavior of individuals, that needs to be changed (Kanter 1977).
- These programs perpetuate stereotypes about occupational and personality differences (Bolton and Humphreys 1977; Shockley and Staley 1980).
- The "separate but equal" doctrine doesn't work here any better than it did in public education. Regardless of the quality of the program, men will be perceived as having had training and women will be perceived as having had *remedial* training.
- Most training is designed for a relatively homogeneous work force with similar skills, and women are not a particularly homogeneous class of workers. They tend to be at different stages in their training needs (Albrecht 1978).
- Many of the requisite managerial skills are now taught in schools of business and public administration, both graduate and undergraduate, which are now well attended by women. Those who need training are the women 10 or 20 years out of school (Hammer 1983).
- There are more similarities than differences between women and men, and women managers are more like men than they are like women nonmanagers (Bolton and Humphreys 1977).

Despite these criticisms a good many organizations are offering special training for women or sending women managers and potential women managers to off-site seminars. Some of these programs are very expensive and of questionable value. Typically they cover a range of topics that include intrapersonal, interpersonal, and technical areas. The content of the courses varies widely, but there are a number of common themes that reflect the assumptions mentioned above. Most programs include a segment on communication, which often includes some emphasis on assertiveness training (Paul 1979; Ames 1977); goal setting (Marcum 1976), consciousness raising and confidence building (Buzenberg 1975), or other approaches to overcome feminine passivity and dependence. Many also include substantive topics such as human resource management, financial management, problem analysis, planning and decision-making, leadership skills, and team dynamics (Gomez-Mejia and Balkin 1980).

Perhaps the disagreements about segregated training and the wide range of topic areas result from both the lack of perspective on what type of training is needed and the absence of rigorous evaluation of training programs. An exploratory study aimed at trying to identify the training needs of women in state and local government found that, in the public sector at least, there is no clear model of a successful career pattern (Radin 1980). In the absence of such a pattern it is difficult, indeed, to design training and development programs that will help to move women up.

At the same time the evaluation of most training programs consists of a survey of the attitudes of the participants at the close of the program. What they measure is not learning but the sense of euphoria that can be created by an adept trainer. Even programs that make an effort to measure change more often than not measure attitude rather than behavioral change (Shockley and Staley 1980; Middlebrook and Rachel 1983; *IPMA News* 1981). Unfortunately, neither public nor private sector organizations are willing to undertake pretraining and posttraining studies, production records analysis, or other special longitudinal studies to validate the cost-effectiveness of their programs. In the absence of such studies it is impossible to tell whether women are in any way benefited or harmed by women-only training.

Even those who argue in favor of women-only training suggest it as a supplement to and not an alternative to mixed-sex training. The question then becomes which women should receive this training. Some organizations have required some special training for all women, for example, a course in assertiveness training. Such requirements are insulting to some women and probably a misuse of training resources. While some women clearly benefit from assertiveness training, others have no need of it. While some men have no need of assertiveness training, others would clearly benefit from it. And the same can probably be said for most training programs.

If we assume for the moment that at least some women will benefit from special, remedial training, then the question becomes: Who should get it. Some employers adopt a low-risk policy. One author, for instance, suggests that training efforts should be directed at those women who are perceived by others as having the characteristics that are considered most important for managers [and] have expertise in their field which is clearly superior to the great majority of those to be supervised (Brenner 1972).

Brenner also recommends that the initial placement of women managers should be in positions where the majority of the subordinates are experienced, the superior is exceptionally supportive, and where expertise is a large and important component of authority, as in staff positions.

A woman staff manager with a high level of expertise, surrounded by experienced subordinates, and supervised by an exceptionally supportive manager wouldn't appear at first glance to be in dire need of special training. However, she may be the very woman who is most "trainable." An evaluation of an extensive, well-funded, and carefully designed training program for women managers in city government showed that significant gains were made in both Assertiveness and Attitudes Toward Women (the two dimensions measured). But when the trainees were divided by occupational class it became apparent that the greatest gains were made by women already in the professional and managerial classifications. In the fourth group, made up of secretarial supervisors, scores actually declined. This group was also older, less educated, lower in self-concepts, and significantly more traditional in their attitudes toward the female role than those in the other groups (Rader 1979). In other words, the training was successful for those women who needed it least and actually counterproductive for those who needed it the most.

We come back then, to the questions that we raised at the beginning of this section. Should organizations sponsor or encourage special training programs for women only? If so, what should that training consist of? And who should be trained? The first answer has to be that the whole process of training needs to be studied. There is little agreement about what constitutes appropriate training for entry-level and middle managers, male or female, and what form it should take. Until we understand better what the requirements are for management jobs, until we can set some clear and measurable objectives for training, until we agree to conscientiously assess the outcomes of training and development programs, then each class or seminar constitutes little more than a shot in the dark.

It's also clear that in the absence of good information it is impossible to prescribe course work exclusively for women. It's no doubt true that women find it personally rewarding to work and study with a group of women peers and role models, away from competition with men. It's probably equally true that men enjoy the experience of training sessions away from the distractions of women. But it is exactly this situation that women have objected to for so long, for obvious reasons. The danger exists that when women have completed their women-only training, they may have completed all their training. Even though few people argue that women-only training is a substitute for mixed-sex training, there is a real and present danger that it will, in fact, become so. In all organizations at all times, resources are scarce. When women's training resources have been spent on women-only training there may be nothing left over for further offerings.

It's surely clear that not all women need remedial training, or that all men do not. Any sensible approach to training must start with a skills assessment and a carefully drawn, individual career plan. Training should be matched to the developmental needs of the individual and coordinated with the staffing needs of the organization. Training resources should be allotted to those who need them, not on the basis of sex.

So far in this discussion we have talked about a limited concept of training, the self-contained course or seminar. A broader and more informal approach is on-the-job training, often supervised and monitored by a mentor. We turn now to this form of career development.

Mentors and Mentoring

The issue of mentoring has created enormous interest and discussion in recent years. Epstein's (1971) study of women in the professions identified the exclusion of women from the protégé-sponsor system as a major deterrent to the career development of women. Kanter's (1977) study of a large manufacturing corporation showed that successful male managers often enjoyed what she called "sponsored mobility"; their careers were enhanced by the support and encouragement of mentors, referred to in the firm as "rabbis" or "godfathers." But perhaps the greatest impetus to the study of mentoring came from a study by a group of Yale University researchers of the stages of adult development in the lives of a group of males (D. Levinson et al. 1978). Levinson's study confirmed what women had been saying for a long time: that mentoring was a crucial element in career development and that it is often unavailable to women. However, as we shall see, it is also unavailable to the majority of men, and there may be alternatives that can accomplish the same objectives.

First, let's look at some aspects of the mentor/protégé relationship.

The Prevalence of Mentoring

Do all successful executives have mentors? There is some evidence that the phenomenon is widespread if not universal. An extensive survey of practicing managers found that these relationships are fairly extensive among the elite of the business world and have tended to become more common in the last 20 years. Roughly two-thirds of the respondents had had a mentor, and about one-third had had two or more; nearly all of the mentors were male. Fewer than 1 percent of the respondents to the study were women, and all of them had had mentors, again nearly all of them male. The women tended to have had more mentors, an average of three to the men's two (Roche 1979). Among the 25 top women executives interviewed by Hennig and Jardim (*The Managerial Woman* 1977) all had had a mentor, but other studies show the percentages are fairly consistent with those of men managers. Phillips (1978) found that about two-thirds of the 300+ top women executives in the United States had had at least one mentor, and the majority of them had had two or more. Missarian (1982) winnowed the list of top female executives to 90 and found that the vast majority had had mentors, usually two or three of them, and that most of the mentors were men.

The Role of the Mentor

What do these mentors do for their protégés? Their functions seem to be a combination of utilitarian career-related roles and personal affective roles.

Career roles include

- teacher: enhancing the young person's skills and intellectual development,
- sponsor: using his or her influence to facilitate the young person's entry and advancement,
- host and guide: welcoming the initiate into a new occupational and social world and acquainting him or her with its values, customs, resources, and cast of characteres (Levinson et al. 1978.)

Activities included among these utilitarian functions are

- fighting for the protégé: standing up for him or her in meetings if controversy arises, promoting his or her candidacy for promising opportunities and challenging assignments, publicizing accomplishments (Kanter 1977; Kram 1983; Missarian 1982),
- giving feedback on performance (Lunding et al. 1978).
- teaching "tricks of the trade" (Missarian 1982).
- giving maximum responsibility and exposure to new functional areas (Missarian 1982).
- bypassing the hierarchy: getting inside information, short-cutting cumbersome procedures or red tape (Kanter 1977),
- providing reflected power: putting the resources of the sponsor behind the protégé (Kanter 1977), to provide exposure and visibility, but also protection (Kram 1983).

Affective roles include

- role model: through his or her own virtues, achievements, and way of living, being an exemplar that the protégé can admire and seek to emulate (D. Levinson et al. 1978; Phillips 1977).
- counselor: providing advice and moral support, providing help in problem solving and in defining and redefining goals (Phillips 1977; D. Levinson et al. 1978).

The activities that mentors engage in in enacting these roles include

- active listening: reflecting thoughts back, helping to identify options, and providing suggestions and advice (Phillips 1977).
- encouraging: showing unfailing confidence, (Phillips 1977), and "bestowing one's blessing" (D. Levinson et al. 1978).

This bestowing of blessing is the crucial element for male mentor/protégé relationships, according to Levinson. Young men, he found, have "a Dream"—a vision or dream of their own future. The crucial function of the mentor is the "realization of the Dream."

> He fosters the young adult's development by believing in him, sharing the youthful Dream and giving it his blessing, helping to define the newly emerging self in its newly discovered world, and creating a space in which the young man can work on a reasonably satisfactory life structure that contains the Dream.

The functions and activities that mentors perform for women differ very little from those performed for men, but the emphasis tends to be different. At lower organizational levels women typically need more of the affective roles—providing encouragement, support, and advice. At this level the mentor can use his or her status to give the protégé legitimacy and also ensure that she receives credit for her work so she can build her own reputation. At higher levels the mentors spend more time on the utilitarian functions, "selling" their protégés (Fitt and Newton 1981).

Stages in the Mentor/Protégé Relationship

Mentor/protégé relationships go through a series of stages that seem to be quite predictable. They are labeled in various ways by various researchers; for our purposes here we will use a four-stage model (Kram 1983).

Initiation: This stage starts with a fantasy—the young manager admires and respects the senior person for his or her competence and capacity to provide advice and guidance. The senior person sees the junior as someone with potential, "coachable," and enjoyable to work with. The senior sees the possibility of contributing to the junior's growth and success. During the first year fantasy becomes transformed into concrete positive expectations.

Cultivation: This stage typically lasts two to five years (although duration can range up to 10 or 12 years (D. Levinson et al. 1978). The career functions emerge first; in time as the interpersonal bond grows the affective functions emerge.

Separation: This usually occurs "from six months to two years after a significant change in the structural role relationship and/or in the emotional experience of the relationship" (Hunt and Michael 1983). For example, the protégé is promoted to a new job or transferred to another location. Or it may end gradually—part of the growing up process. Levinson et al. (1978) says "men do not have mentors after 40." Separation is always a period of adjustment for both mentor and protégé and is often accompanied by anxiety, resentment, turmoil, and feelings of loss, especially if it occurs prematurely. Levinson et al. (1978) explain that

> mentoring is best understood as a form of love relationship. It is difficult to terminate in a reasonable, civil manner. In this respect, as in others, it is like the intense relationship between parents and grown offspring, or between sexual lovers or spouses.

Redefinition: This stage sometimes leads to an uneasy truce, to peer status characterized by ambivalence and discomfort, hostility and resentment, and bitterness. But after a cooling-off period it often resolves into a lasting friendship. Levinson et al. (1978) found that after the separation the personality of the mentee is enriched further as he makes the valued qualities of the mentor more fully a part of himself. In some respects, the main value of the relationship is created after it ends, but only if there was something worthwhile there while it was happening.

Mentoring and Power

Mentors are typically 8 to 15 years older than their protégés and two or more organizational levels senior in rank. They have, almost without exception, been protégés themselves. This means that they are old enough to be a big brother but too young to be a father. It also means that they are powerful enough to be able to provide concrete assistance. The issue of power is critical to the issue of mentoring and, not unexpectedly, the stages of development of the mentor/protégé relationship can be equated to McClelland's (1975) stages of power development discussed in Chapter 6.

In stage 1 of power development, the individual's source of strength and power is others. In the initiation stage of the mentor/protégé relationship the young person seeks out a more powerful senior person as mentor, or in the absence of such a person seeks to build a peer network.

In stage 2 of power development, the individual learns self-control and begins to experience his or her own strength. In the cultivation stage of the mentor/protégé relationship the young person begins to take on added responsibility, to become more independent and autonomous.

In stage 3 of power development, the individual learns to control others, either by being exploitative and competitive or by being helpful. Following the separation and redefinition stages of the mentor relationship, the former protégé often experiences power by mentoring others (Hunt and Michael 1983).

The power implications of the mentor relationship cannot be underestimated. The person who can successfully identify and sponsor the future managers of an organization has both exercised and demonstrated power. The affective roles of a mentor can be, and often are, performed by powerless people, but the utilitarian roles can be performed successfully only by people who have both influence and control of concrete resources in the organization. One result of this reflected power is that the protégé who is able to move upward through what Kanter calls "sponsored mobility"—with the help of a mentor—receives substantially more support and encouragement from others than the person who moves up through "contest," or open, mobility. The former often finds the upward path smooth and easy, the latter finds it steep and rough. The former will most likely use his or her own power, when it is acquired, to sponsor others; the latter will insist that others climb the rocky path. If the latter is female, she will be called a "queen bee."

This power dimension helps to explain both why managers choose to be mentors and why some relationships end in bitterness. The mentor's reward is the success of the protégé. The mentor may get genuine pleasure from the ward's successes but is not unaware of the impact on his or her own power sources. If the protégé fails to meet expectations, the mentor's judgment may be questioned and valuable resources will have been squandered. On the other hand, if the mentor lacks the political power to intercede for the protégé, or declines to do so, the protégé may have decreased his or her credibility by being aligned with a loser. If the relationship is successful, both careers have been enhanced; if it is unsuccessful, both careers may be damaged.

Mentoring and the Organization

Organizations gain a good deal from mentoring activities. Employees who have been protégés are better educated, better paid, less mobile, and more satisfied with their work and career progress than those who have not (Hunt and Michael 1983). They also earn more money at a younger age, are more likely to follow a career plan, and sponsor more protégés (Roche 1979). For the organization, mentoring not only aids in the development of young talent but also provides an opportunity for greater utilization of older managerial talent. The mentor often experiences a sense of rejuvenation and achievement not offered by his or her formal organizational duties. A few organizations consider mentoring so important that they have institutionalized formal mentoring programs for all employees (Lunding et al 1978) or for women and minority employees (Cook 1979).

Not all organizations lend themselves to mentoring, however. Mentors are most important in large organizations, in organizations with only a small number of women managers, and in hierarchical organizations characterized by multiple management levels and intense competition for an ever-narrowing pyramid of positions. They can be more influential if promotion and assignment decisions are made by committee. They flourish in "an organization with enhanced opportunity, with enthusiasm for innovation versus conservative resistance, and with structural supports for more equal treatment of women and minorities" (Hunt and Michael 1983). Access to mentor relationships is probably easier if the organization uses such devices as management by objectives (MBO), formalized career planning, special assignments spanning several management levels, job rotation, fast-track career development plans, and Affirmative Action plans that encourage relationships by increasing exposure. Paradoxically, mentor/protégé relationships are probably least vital in the organizations in which they are easiest to establish (Fitt and Newton 1981).

Mentors and Women

As we saw earlier, most successful managers of either sex have had mentors. For the most part the mentors have been men, partly because there have been no powerful women to act as mentors. We need now to ask three questions: Can women mentor other women? Will men mentor women? Do women, or men, really need mentors?

Can women mentor other women? In the strictest sense of the word the answer is probably still "no." Mentoring is a power behavior, and while the number of women managers has risen in recent years, the number of women in positions of real power still remains small. Many women with management titles are in staff positions where their organizational power is limited. Women who do possess sufficient influence can, and obviously do, act as mentors to both men and women juniors. These women must husband their power carefully, though, particularly if they are in relatively isolated positions. The risks that all managers take in assuming a protégé are magnified for a woman, so women may be reluctant to act as mentors to women and may demand greater performance from a female protégé than from a male.

Will men mentor women? Of course, and many have done so and will continue to do so. Kanter (1977) argues that they do so for different reasons. Rather than assisting a younger version of themselves in "the realization of the Dream," they take on female protégés to demonstrate the organization's commitment to promoting women or their ability to solve the organization's problem. But other motives operate as well, particularly the desire to develop talent (Fitt and Newton 1981).

Mentoring women presents risks for men as well as for women. As with the woman mentor, the greater visibility of the relationship heightens the risk that the mentee's failure will cause peers to question his judgment. An even greater risk, though, is the perception of others that a close association will evolve into sexual entanglement—a perception often reinforced by spouses, especially when the work involves travel (Fitt and Newton 1981). And unquestionably such a relationship is often marked with a degree of sexual tension. Missarian (1982) attributes this problem to our failure to distinguish between the Greek concept of *agape* (platonic love between equals and thought to be possible only between men), *philia* (family love), and *eros* (romantic love or sexual love). In our society love and sex are inexorably linked. Sex without love is accepted for men and to some extent is becoming so for women, but love without sex is considered suspect, particularly between a man and a woman.

These perceptions contribute to the fear that is associated with male/female mentor/protégé relationships. Individuals seem to cope with it by adopting family roles such as father/daughter or brother/sister so that incest taboos reduce the sexual tensions. Others throw themselves into a flurry of work and maintain a professional behavior at all times. In either case the strategy is to put physical and psychological distance between themselves and the other and to learn to cope with the rumors that inevitably arise.

There are, of course, other drawbacks to male/female mentoring. Women sometimes complain that no matter how supportive their male mentors are, they can never fully understand or empathize with the situations and constraints facing a woman in a male-dominated environment. Nor can a man, however willing, serve as a fully adequate role model for a woman mentee. Worse, a male mentor may encourage such stereotypical behaviors as feelings of dependency and incompetence (Kram 1983). Levinson et al. (1978) summed up the problem this way:

> This cross sex gendering can be of great value, but its value is often limited by the tendency to make her less than she is: to regard her as attractive but not gifted, as a gifted woman whose sexual attractiveness interferes with work and friendship, as an intelligent but impersonal pseudo-male or as a charming little girl who cannot be taken seriously.

Do women need mentors? The literature seems to support the common belief that a mentor is a vital ingredient to success and that mentors are less available to women than to men. But there are some contrary arguments and some alternative approaches.

Mentors may not be as important or as prevalent as appears at first glance. The research suggests repeatedly that those managers who have had a mentor are younger, better educated, make more money, are more satisfied, and are less mobile. But there is no evidence that this is a cause-and-effect relationship. How can we be sure that these people would have been less successful without the attentions of a mentor? Presumably they were what Kanter calls "comers" or "water walkers," bright and able young people who were selected as protégés because of their obvious ability and promise. It's interesting to note that executives who have had mentors do not credit their mentors with their success. Rather, they ascribe their success to their own personal characteristics: ability to make decisions, motivation, ability to motivate others, ability to lead, energy level, ability to complete assignments, and willingness to work long hours. They even rank luck as more important than having a mentor for their own success (Roche 1979).

It's possible that the mentor/protégé is simply an artifact of the patriarchal system that has characterized many large, hierarchical organizations. To be sure, this system has benefited the elite among young males and excluded all others. It has also clearly benefited those organizations that reaped the benefits of an informal and essentially cost-free management development program. However, it suffers from the same problems as formal training and development programs in that its objectives have never been clearly defined, its processes and mechanisms have never been fully understood, and its results have never been measured.

It's also possible that when it is neither possible nor necessary to find one person to play all of the roles of a mentor it is quite possible, and perhaps preferable, to have a number of people, each of whom plays one or two of the roles. The kind of mentoring relationship we have been describing here is both comprehensive and mutual (Clawson 1980). It is also "intense, exclusionary, and elitist" (Shapiro, Haseltine, and Rowe 1978). Mentorship is not democratic, and the reality is that many women and men will not find mentors. Some may even choose not to have a single mentor, because of the political and sexual hazards involved (Cook 1979), and because so many sources of knowledge and information are available that it may be unwise to rely on only one (Clawson 1980). The alternatives range along a continuum from the very paternalistic relationship of a mentor/protégé, to "sponsors," "guides," and finally, at the other end, "peer pals" (Shapiro, Haseltine, and Rowe 1978).

Sponsors serve as strong patrons but are less powerful than mentors in promoting and shaping the careers of the protégés. These may be direct supervisors, too close in age and experience to act as mentors but senior enough to provide significant assistance.

Guides are individuals who are less able than mentors or sponsors to fulfill the roles of benefactor, protector, or champion, but are invaluable in explaining the system. Secretaries and administrative assistants often enact these roles.

Peer Pals are people helping each other to succeed and progress by reciprocally sharing information and strategies and providing sounding boards and advice for one another.

In summary we can say that mentors and mentoring relationships seem to be an important part of the career development of successful men and women and that they seem to contribute something important to the organization's career development goals. Mentor/protégé relationships can be enormously gratifying for both individuals. Successful mentoring involves an overt use of power, and there are risks on both sides of the relationship. These risks are even greater in cross-sexed relationships. Since there are few women managers with the power to serve as successful mentors, and since mentoring women increases the risks for women and men, women have tended to have less access to mentoring than perhaps equally qualified men. One solution has been to try to institutionalize or formalize mentoring within the organization, although it seems unlikely that a true mentor relationship could be mandated.

Another approach is for the individual to develop a range of less-intense relationships—sponsors, guides, or peer pals—to serve in partial roles to fulfill the essential functions. We turn now to a broader discussion of these peer relationships.

Networks and Networking

Women have long faced with anger and frustration their exclusion from the "old boys' network." These illusive, informal relationships seem to control the power and the resources of the organization, sharing vital information and reaching prior consensus on important decisions, all the while excluding all of the women and most of the men from full participation in organizational activities. The outcome of this resentment has been the formation of women's organizations, sometimes referred to as "new girls' networks." These take various forms: occupational groups, organizational groups, and regional groups. Their stated purposes have usually been to replicate the advantages that men enjoy from their wide range of contacts. What little evaluation has been done on these groups suggests that they may not be very successful in achievement of that purpose, but they may be useful in teaching women the importance of building contacts and the fine art of doing so.

There is little question that successful managers do develop and use networks. Kaplan (1984) calls these "trade routes" and defines them as "a reciprocal set of relationships that stabilizes the manager's world and gives it predictability." These networks includes people both higher and lower in the organizational hierarchy as well as people at the same level in other units or functions. They also include people outside of the organization. The lateral relationships are important, and they must be reciprocal—hence the name "trade routes."

> Managers enter these trade relationships with lateral network members for one compelling reason; they depend on these people and literally can't get their jobs done without them (Kaplan 1984).

However, instead of trading goods, they trade services: accurate information, technical expertise, advise, political backing, moral support. They obtain these services by setting up reciprocal relationships. Reciprocation does not always occur instantly; a balance is struck over time. Network members are allowed to open charge accounts so long as the debt is later repaid in needed services. They exchange help for a promise of future help.

This kind of network cannot be mandated by management. Managers must cultivate their own networks. Most managers do it deliberately but it is also something that occurs naturally. It takes time and is a continuous process. Every promotion or change in position requires rebuilding the network, but even as a manager remains in the same job, the environment is dynamic. The network must be constantly tended.

Women's networks differ from these "trade routes" in that they are formally organized for the purpose of career enhancement. But they may be premature, since the number of women needing support is far greater than the number available to give it. A case study of a network in a large Midwestern city found that the majority of the participants were at the supervisory or middle management level; very few had executive-level positions. While middle- and upper-level managers could increase their contacts at their own level, there were few opportunities to find career links and role models among executive-level women (DeWine and Casbolt 1983).

The shortage of upper-level women was also revealed in a survey of women managers across the country. Over half perceived themselves as receiving minimal to no support from women above them in their organizations, often because there were none. On the other hand, most respondents perceived themselves as giving support to those below them. In other words, women perceive themselves to be giving more support to those below them than those women perceive themselves as receiving (Warihay 1980). Because of this paucity of executive-level women, formally organized women's networks that limit sources of support to women only may narrow, rather than widen, the opportunities for developmental activities.

But formal networks may serve another useful purpose. Women need to develop skill in building their trade routes, including their network of peer pals, from a wide range of sources, both male and female. Some women seem to need help either in understanding the importance of network building or in making maximum use of the opportunities available. About one-third of the women in the network studied by De-Wine and Casbolt reported that they never attended meetings and never met with women outside their own organizations for the purpose of networking. For those who did make contacts, they were most frequently with friends or internal business associates, seldom with new acquaintances from the formal network. Masculine and androgynous women reported that they met with women outside their organizations for the purpose of networking, and androgynous women had the most frequent contacts. Overall, the women who were most active networkers were less likely to affiliate with formal networks. Participants were for the most part not making much use of their network contacts outside of the organized meetings; they were using friends and business acquaintances as their primary contacts rather than initiating contacts with less-familiar individuals.

So the formal network may not be the place to build trade routes. But it can be a place where women begin to develop the skills of initiating contacts, of seeking and giving information, and of building alliances. Some women, particularly those with a highly feminine role orientation, may find these skills difficult to learn. Sooner or later they are going to have to develop reciprocal network relationships with men as well as with women, and a formal network will probably never be able to replace an informal, carefully developed one. But it can provide a relatively safe place to practice.

SUMMARY

Men must choose an occupation or a career. Women, unlike men, must choose between work and nonwork, work and career, and traditional and nontraditional careers. Fewer and fewer women opt for full-time homemaking, and more and more aspire to careers in traditionally male-dominated professions. The vast majority of young people have unrealistically high career ambitions and very few aspire to management careers. However, the decisionmaking process that young people undergo in choosing these life roles shows no significant sex differences.

There are no differences in the investment that women and men make in their human capital, but they tend to invest in different strategies. Women invest more in education and training, men more in job changes. Women in the past have tended to choose careers in which interruptions in service would not decrease their capital investment, but as more and more women plan for uninterrupted careers, those differences seem to diminish.

What is available in formal training classes and seminars is a hodgepodge of skill training and attitude adjustment. There are a number of persuasive arguments in favor of women-only training, as an adjunct of mixed training, but while such training may provide a satisfying experience for women, its disadvantages outweigh its advantages. Training opportunities should be allocated on the basis of individual and organizational need, not of sex. Women and men must have the same developmental experiences; men and women ultimately have to learn to work together.

Overall, it appears that the whole state of the training art has advanced little in the last two decades; there is little understanding of the essentials of career development, little knowledge of what kinds of training are needed, and little evaluation of the effectiveness of the training that is being given.

Mentoring and networking provide training opportunities that are perceived as being essential to managerial careers and largely unavailable to potential women managers. While these relationships are usually of value to all concerned, they also involve significant risks. They are almost by definition elitist and exclusionary, and they certainly are not available to the majority of potential managers, male or female. They also appear to be more important in some organizational structures and more possible in others. However, the advantages of a mentor can be approximated by building a number of relationships with others in the organization: sponsors, guides, and peer pals.

Successful managers build networks—trade routes—both horizontally and vertically, both in and out of their organizations. These networks are informal and spontaneous, but they must be carefully nurtured. Attempts to replicate these informal trade networks with formally organized women's networks have not, apparently, been successful in building trade routes. These networks do provide an opportunity for women to enhance and practice their skills in making and maintaining contacts. But ultimately women and men must learn to work together and to include each other in their networks.

12

A Look at the Future

The young people in the 1960s who set out to change the social and political world taught us: "If you're not part of the solution you're part of the problem."

Over and over again throughout this book we have confronted the reality of sex and gender differences—in the family, in the labor force, in the organization, and even within occupations. While to a very great extent women fare much worse than men in terms of opportunities and rewards, men suffer from sex-role expectations that lock them into a narrow and restrictive repertoire of behaviors and lifestyles. Both women and men could be justified for feeling angry or frustrated at the state of the world they live in.

But those who accentuate the negative are part of the problem. To be part of the solution one needs to begin to think creatively and optimistically about the shape of the future. Evidence has been presented throughout the book to try to paint as clear as picture as possible of "what is." At the same time, we have tried to gain a better understanding of "what was" by tracing the history and the evolution of the family and the division of labor within the family, the social change brought about by manufacturing technology, and the persistence of moral and religious views about sex roles and sexuality.

We turn now to a forecast of the future. In Chapter 2 we suggested one rather depressing scenario—of increasing sex differentiation and decreasing opportunity. We now present an alternative, and very positive, scenario, along with some guideposts about how to get there.

First, however, we return to our point of departure from Chapter 1 to review to what extent we were successful in challenging the assumptions of extant organizational theory.

POINT OF DEPARTURE REVISITED

Chapter 1 promised that this book would differ from others by challenging three sets of assumptions: the male model of work, the breadwinner model, and the industrial model.

The Male Model of Work

The male model of work assumes that work is central to the lives of men but not women. Indeed, Protestant Work Ethic values, promulgated by the church during the Industrial Revolution, persuaded men that they were serving God by enduring long hours and abysmal working conditions. "Women's work" was housewifery; women entered the paid labor force only for brief periods before marriage. After marriage they worked only in the event of dire financial necessity or during wartime labor shortages.

But over time, hours have shortened, working conditions have improved, income, benefits and pensions have increased, and the average life span has lengthened; the proportion of their lives that men devote to employment is greatly decreased. Religion plays a less salient role than it did a century ago, and other values have become more important. Work continues to be a major role for men, but not necessarily the primary or central one. Participation in family life, church, community, sports, and other leisure activities also helps to define the individual to himself and to others.

At the same time, women's relationship to work has undergone substantial change. While the majority of women still attach greater significance to family roles than to work roles, they now spend the majority of their lives in the paid labor force. High school and college-age women expect to work most of their lives, interrupting their careers only briefly for childbearing and childrearing. Increasing numbers expect to work without interruption throughout their lives. In terms of their job attitudes, expectations, commitment to work, motivation, and performance, women workers differ very little from their male counterparts. The greatest difference is in their salary expectations: They expect to earn substantially less than men—a not unrealistic expectation.

The male model of work, by assuming that typically male behavior in the organization is the norm, manages to ignore the whole issue of human sexuality. But both women and men bring their sexuality and their sex role orientation with them to the workplace. Sexuality affects a great deal of the communication, conflict, and cooperation that takes place on the job, both in same-sex and mixed-sex relationships. Women workers are often seen as putting more emphasis on their friendships with women co-workers than on their jobs themselves, but in reality those relationships are often a substitute for other rewards that are lacking from female-intensive jobs. Women in professional and managerial ranks often find themselves in competition with other women at their own level and cut off from other women both above and below them on the hierarchy.

Men often see the workplace as an arena for validating their masculinity. Fear of revealing themselves or of appearing less than fully masculine may prevent them from confiding in, cooperating with, or seeking help from others. Competitiveness may lead them to exchange "war stories"—exploits about sports, business, or sexual conquests. The male model of work assumes that men workers are rational, logical, instrumental, and unemotional; it fails to consider the extent to which behavior is affected by the need to maintain the masculine sex role, even to the detriment of the organization.

Fear of sexual involvement, or of the perception of involvement, may prevent men from forming close working relationships with women colleagues or from acting as mentors to women protégés. Since men and women in our society have little experience with any kind of relationship other than a romantic or sexual one, women and men co-workers often have difficulty in establishing satisfactory nonsexual working relationships. When romantic relationships disrupt the workplace, they present a problem to managers, but when women and men avoid interaction for fear of "entangling alliances," that too presents a problem to management.

The assumptions of the male model of work, rooted in the Industrial Revolution and dependent on rigid division of labor within the family and occupational segregation within the organization, mask the implications of sex and gender in the organization. If we truly want to understand organizational behavior we have to understand the impact of sex and sex role on both women and men in the workplace.

The Breadwinner Model

The breadwinner model assumes that workers live in traditional nuclear families in which the male head of household is the primary earner and the wife, if she works at all, is a secondary earner only casually attached to the labor market.

In reality the traditional family with a breadwinner husband, a full-time homemaker wife, and two or three dependent children now represents only a small fraction of all households. While most people still live in families, the number of two-earner families has increased enormously, the number of children per family has decreased substantially, the number of single-parented families has increased somewhat, and the number of single-person households has multiplied. The traditional nuclear family has now been replaced with an enormous variety of family forms.

Men's labor force participation has decreased steadily in recent years, while women's participation has increased rapidly. Women now make up almost half of the labor force and their numbers are growing. For most families, the wife's earnings are not "secondary," a supplementary income to enhance the breadwinner's earnings. For the majority of families, two incomes are essential. Often it is the second income that lifts the family out of poverty. The growing army of single women, including those with children, are themselves the breadwinners.

The breadwinner model assumes investments in human capital for male workers, as in experience and training, are likely to have a payoff in future productivity. Transfers, training, promotions, travel—all are seen as safe investments for breadwinners. Many corporations, in fact, expect executive wives to invest their own human capital in their husband's careers, on the assumption that they will reap the benefits of his career advances. On the other hand, the model regards investment in the human capital of women workers as carrying considerably higher risk.

Men and women vary little in their willingness to invest in their own human capital; women are somewhat more likely to invest in education and men in job-specific experience. But organizations are still more willing to choose men over women for positions that require considerable expenditure of training and development resources.

The Industrial Model

Among the major outcomes of the Industrial Revolution were the growth of the large corporation, increased standardization (including standardization of pay and hours), and specialization.

Standard hours were necessary because of the enormous demand for unskilled and semiskilled labor to keep factories operating. Shift work was necessary to keep the machinery in use around the clock. Productivity was a function of the number of hours expended, and workers' hours were determined by the productive process. As the labor unions bargained for shorter hours and the Congress adopted legislation regulating hours, the workday gradually became shorter and shorter, but no less rigid. The typical full-time worker now works five eight-hour shifts a week, regardless of the type of work she or he does or of any other factors.

Mass-production processes required large aggregations of men, materials, and machines. As the administrative component of industry grew in size, white-collar work also became centralized in large offices. While the telephone and the telegraph greatly enhanced communication, information and technology continued to be concentrated in central locations.

Workers went to the factory or to the office to do their work because that was the only place where the necessary resources were available.

Labor and government also succeeded in improving the pay and benefits of workers, again in standardized forms. The government specifies minimum wages for workers of various classes—age, industry, occupation. Union contracts and company job evaluation schemes set wages for the job, rather than for the worker. While some pay scales do make allowances for productivity or some other measure of merit, they continue to consider primarily the input, that is, the number of hours worked. Hourly wages are set at least partially on the basis of the perceived needs of the worker and his or her family. Higher wages for male-intensive occupations are justified on the assumption that men have families to support, and presumably women don't. Fringe benefits, once only a small fraction of the workers' compensation, now often add as much as 40 percent to the employer's payroll costs. These benefits also tend to be highly standardized and to be designed for the breadwinner family; for example, they may provide full health and dental insurance coverage for the worker and his or her spouse and dependent children.

Factory work and mass production contributed to the division of labor in several ways. Mechanization brought about widespread "deskilling" of jobs; in the name of efficiency, tasks were broken down into ever smaller and more repetitive segments. Because of the long hours and the necessity of women's household production, men took over most factory work. Because they were breadwinners, and because they were essential to production, men were able to bargain for increasingly higher wages. Office work became women's work when repetitive clerical tasks were separated from administrative duties; copy work was done by women in the home and paid by the word. When the typewriter replaced the quill pen, clerical work was brought back into the office, but it remained women's work. Both factory women and clerical women typically left the labor force when they married; neither successfully bargained for higher wages. Protective legislation reduced the hazards they faced on the job but also reduced their job opportunities and probably their pay.

Information processing has replaced manufacturing as the primary sector of the economy, and computer technology greatly reduces the necessity for standardized hours and central work stations. The majority of workers are what Peter Drucker (1966) calls "knowledge workers," people whose occupations require mental rather than physical effort; their productivity is governed by a number of factors—their ability, their energy level or attention span, the number of interruptions, the difficulty of the task, the quality of the work, cycles and fluctuations in the work flow—but not by the pace of an assembly line. Any of these factors makes a more rational method for designing work schedules than an arbitrary basis of eight hours a day for five days a week. Technology makes it possible to design job schedules around the task rather than the reverse. For many contemporary workers, it is no longer necessary or even sensible to require a rigid and fixed schedule.

Nor is it necessary for people to "go to work" in the conventional sense. Through the use of microcomputers and telecommunications, the information necessary to do one's job is available from central data banks wherever the worker happens to be, anywhere in the world. Completed work can be transmitted to wherever it is needed, stored for access from any location, or kept secret and hidden if necessary. The central aggregation of all the means of production is no longer either efficient or practical.

Standardized pay and fringe benefit packages may also be unnecessary and inefficient. Pay based on input (on hours) is rational for the industrial worker when physical effort is the only factor affecting productivity. But for the information worker, input is less important than output; the number of hours expended may have little to do with either the quality or the quantity of work produced. Hours are certainly easier to determine than other measures of productivity, but the computer makes possible not only enormous increases in productivity but also innovative ways of measuring it.

Fringe benefits can also be made more flexible. Because most benefit programs are based on the assumption of a typical nuclear family with a breadwinner husband, employers are paying a great deal for compensation components that may benefit only a fraction of their employees. A two-earner family may have duplicate health insurance packages, far in excess of its needs. Working parents may have redundant health and dental insurance, from which they derive no payoff, when what they need most is child care—still offered by very few employers. Standardized benefits were rational when they were designed; but because of the myriad family forms that now characterize the society, they are now about as useful as a horse and buggy for many workers.

The size of corporations takes on a new meaning. Mass production brought about the creation of huge corporations. Size has traditionally been measured by the number of employees, a measure that becomes meaningless with the computer's potential for productivity. Highly automated firms can produce enormous amounts of work with a relatively small number of employees. While economies of scale will continue to make very large organizations more efficient in some industries, in others we will see an increasing number of firms providing highly specialized products with relatively few workers. These organizations with smaller staffs will be less bureaucratic and less hierarchical. The administrative component will be smaller, and the job of "manager" will be redefined. The whole concept of career development will undergo change.

The factors that contributed to the division of labor within the family and occupational segregation in the workplace no longer exist. Men no longer work long hours in unsafe and unhealthy factory conditions; housework no longer requires a full day's work; women now share the breadwinner role if they don't hold it exclusively; to a somewhat lesser extent men share the homemaker role. Women no longer leave the labor force when they marry; most don't leave it even after they have children. Clerical jobs have undergone a "deskilling" process similar to that experienced by factory jobs earlier, but women workers are increasingly turning to the labor unions to raise pay and benefits.

The postindustrial model makes it possible to go beyond the notion of flextime or compressed work weeks, which are already fairly widely practiced. It now becomes possible to redefine the word "job." A job has typically been defined as 40 hours of work a week, performing a particular task or set of tasks, for a particular sum of money and benefits. Instead, a job could be defined as a particular set of outcomes, almost like a contract. Employer and employee could agree on what tasks were to be performed, what quality and quantity of work would be expected, and when the work was to be completed. They would agree on what combination of money or benefits would be paid (Harriman 1982).

This plan has benefits for both employee and employer. The employee can decide how much of his or her time to devote to market work and how much to devote to family or leisure activities. She or he can decide where—office, home, a neighborhood computer center—and when— days, nights, weekends—to do the work. The employer can smooth cycles in the flow of work; it is no longer necessary to keep all workers steadily engaged at all times. Job content can be varied with need and the availability of workers; it's not necessary to pay someone for a "full-time" job when the job takes less than 40 hours a week to complete. The supervisor's concern becomes not whether the employee comes to work on time, makes personal phone calls, or works as fast or slow as others; rather the supervisor would be concerned only with whether the work was timely and accurate.

Of course there are many objections to such a plan, and of course it can't work in every organization and every occupation. Some public contact jobs are regulated by the flow of customers and the necessity to keep business hours. Technology that involves sequential dependency requires careful scheduling to avoid slack time. Technology that requires frequent interactions or communications must be at least coordinated, if not standardized. Nevertheless, a great deal more flexibility is possible than is currently found. The administrative complexities could create chaos, but managing complex information is one of the things that computer technology handles best. The greatest impediment to a highly flexible, dynamic workplace is tradition—the tradition of the industrial model.

The male model of work, the breadwinner model, and the industrial model, are all outmoded by electronic technology, yet all continue to influence and shape our perceptions of organizations. The first two are, to a very significant degree, artifacts of the third. The industrial era brought about enormous social change, most of it for the better, but it did increase the divisions between the sexes. The postindustrial era will surely bring about enormous social change as well. We turn now to a hopeful prediction about what these changes might bring.

PREDICTING THE FUTURE

While a good deal of attention is being paid in the media to the wonders of electronic technology, less attention of a serious nature is paid to the social implications of that technology. As at the start of the Industrial Revolution, some workers, or more particularly some unions, are predicting dire consequences, social upheaval resulting from mass unemployment, and the deskilling of jobs. Others are predicting a Utopian world of personal robots, bionic bodies, and intergalactic travel. No one, of course, can really predict the future, and those who try are often embarrassed by the degree to which events prove them wrong. Nevertheless, armed with the knowledge that what follows is pure speculation, let us indulge in some fantasies about the world we would like to see develop.

For the sake of our fantasy, we will assume that the world will be free of nuclear disaster, global war, or other man-made or natural disasters. We will assume that humankind will make rational choices to protect the natural environment and to conserve natural resources. We are primarily concerned with the social changes that might stem from technological change, holding the physical world constant.

The End of Civilization As We Know It

In 1952 Kurt Vonnegut's futuristic novel, *Player Piano,* predicted a world in which man was freed from all necessity, indeed from almost all opportunity, for paid employment. The ordinary events of life were so automated that the only people with jobs were Ph.D.-bearing scientists, engineers, and managers. Virtually all decisionmaking was done by computer, including decisions about education and occupation, and of course the computers were programmed by the professional elites. Those people not selected for advanced education, and therefore for technical jobs, were assigned either to the Army or to the Reconstruction and Reclamation Corps—the "reeks and the wrecks." The only employed women were secretaries—with Ph.D. degrees.

Despite the lack of meaningful work, there was no poverty. Industry was managed, controlled, and coordinated by a committee of business leaders to prevent wasteful competition. Government taxed the part of industry's income that once went into labor, and this money was redistributed to the "average man." Every household was provided with the latest labor-saving devices; the standard of living was higher than before the onset of automation.

Nevertheless, there was widespread dissatisfaction with the system. Jobs in the Army or the Reeks and Wrecks were demeaning and repetitious. Individuals with ability and ingenuity mourned the lack of opportunity to develop their skills, to work with their hands, to use their intelligence; they whiled away their time drinking, playing mindless games, and marching in parades. But when a revolution, led by dissident elites, failed, they immediately began to rebuild the broken machines that had been the source of their discontent.

Chapter 2 suggested a scenario for the future not unlike that sketched by Vonnegut: an increasing income gap between small, elite, upper-middle-class families and larger, less-privileged lower-class families; enormous increases in productivity leading to technological unemployment; machines increasingly replacing man's mental as well as physical effort; many occupations eliminated, others deskilled, with traditionally female-intensive occupations disproportionately affected. Some of these changes are already in process; others seem to be just on the horizon. What might occur to change the course of the future?

The Dawn of a New Age of Enlightenment

Those who protested that the industrial age would lead to widespread unemployment were wrong; many more jobs were created than were eliminated. Those like the Luddites who predicted that the need for many skills would be eliminated were right. Working conditions got better, hours got shorter, and wages increased; the standard of living for the average worker improved. But for many workers, the work itself became less skilled, less demanding.

The Reeks and Wrecks in Vonnegut's story were like the Luddites. They were not without income, indeed they enjoyed a high standard of living. They were not without jobs, although the jobs were essentially meaningless; the tasks could surely have been done more efficiently by machines. They were without dignity; only those elites who worked in highly technical positions enjoyed status and power. Vonnegut makes much of the fact that these people lack freedom. They are like pampered prisoners, well cared for but lacking the ability to exercise choice or will.

In our scenario for the future we could incorporate or adapt much from Vonnegut that is positive:

- As technology becomes more and more productive, eliminating more and more jobs, taxes can be levied on the owners of the means of production and redistributed through transfer payments to those without jobs.
- For those with skills and abilities, public sector employment, funded by taxes on the enhanced productivity of the private sector, can be used to perform labor-intensive services in a wide range of social areas that are now neglected: child care for the young, health and recreation for the elderly and the handicapped, subsidies for the arts, education for people of all ages, clean-up of the environment.
- Technology itself can be used to improve the quality of our lives, by eliminating tasks that are dirty, dangerous, or otherwise distasteful, by improving our health and the quality of medical care, by enhancing our communications ability, by providing information and entertainment.

We would want to improve on Vonnegut in some ways, however, especially in reducing the disparity in sex roles.

- Technological change, up to now, has created new jobs that required high levels of technical skill and knowledge. But computer software and applications are becoming more and more sophisticated and at the same time less and less technically demanding. Jobs that are neither physically nor technically demanding are less likely to be sex segregated. If men and women are not occupationally segregated, and work is paid on the basis of output, the pay disparity should decrease.
- Computer technology makes possible, even desirable, a redefinition of what constitutes a job: shorter, more flexible working hours, schedules designed around tasks and work flow, rather than around hours, and more flexible working conditions, salaries, and benefits. Conflict between work and family will be reduced. Marriages will become more egalitarian, since earnings will be relatively equal and each partner will have equal time to contribute to family roles. Men will become more involved in nurturing, and as they do they will unlearn some of the inhibitions and restrictions of the inexpressive masculine role.
- Changes in the division of labor within the family will lead to greater equality within the workplace. Status and power will be more equally distributed; language, both verbal and nonverbal, will come to reflect that equality, just as it now reflects inequality. As women become more integrated into the power and opportunity structure of the organization, there will be fewer "token" women;

in turn, women's contributions will be evaluated more equitably as emphasis shifts from their feminine role to their organizational role. Interpersonal communication will be enhanced as roles become more equal. The decline of tokenism will also reduce the fear of sexual attraction and involvement; it may even mean a decline in homophobia—allowing men to be more expressive not only with women but with other men as well. Androgyny will be seen as the appropriate sex role for managers, whether male or female.

None of these changes, however, will come about if, as Vonnegut predicted, people are held captives in a world controlled by the values of scientists, engineers, and managers. But those values are simply a modern adaptation of the Protestant Work Ethic. In the industrial age, the church preached a doctrine that work, however menial, was a way of serving God. Workers endured the present on the promise of a better life in the hereafter. In contemporary management literature we call it Achievement Motivation. The Reeks and Wrecks had internalized the values of achievement and then were denied the opportunity to experience it. Their problem was not that machinery had denied them the right to achievement, but that the society had taught them that the appropriate arena for achievement was in their jobs.

In our scenario, then, we will predict another value change, equivalent to the rise of Protestantism. Workers will *not* unlearn the need for achievement; they will *not* unlearn the desire for activities that are rewarding and fulfilling. They *will* unlearn the notion that those needs must be satisfied on the job. We will return, pehaps, to an earlier age, when leisure, not work, was valued. Men, but not women, were defined by their participation in the church or the community, by their accomplishments in arts and letters, by their contributions to the health and well-being of others. In our scenario, those values will reemerge and be extended to women as well.

Our scenario presents the best of all possible worlds. Technology frees mankind from the necessity to toil at unpleasant and unrewarding tasks. It provides the means to increase productivity to the point where the term itself is meaningless. Government frees us from poverty and deprivation; it redistributes the wealth generated by enhanced productivity while supporting much-needed social services and esthetic opportunities. And social values free us from the need to define ourselves through our jobs; they make it possible to redefine in infinitely more satisfactory ways both sex roles and the sexual division of labor.

Skeptics will argue that anything is possible in a fantasy, and so it is. This fantasy calls for a major redefinition of social values, a not inconsiderable barrier. However, they should recall that in the history of the world, our present value system is very young. We talk about social revolution when we should in fact speak of evolution. Values and beliefs do change over time, and they tend to change in response to technological change. A grim scenario of increasing unemployment, decreasing opportunity, and greater inequality is possible. But so also is one of hope for a better future for both women and men. We have the power to shape the kind of social world we want. It's not too soon to begin. If you're not part of the solution, you're part of the problem.

References

Abbott, Aaron, and Richard Sebastian. 1981. "Physical Attractiveness and Expectations of Success." *Personality and Social Psychology Bulletin* 7:481–486.

Abramson, Joan. 1979. *Old Boys New Women: The Politics of Sex Discrimination.* New York: Praeger.

Abramson, Paul, Philip Goldberg, Judith Greenberg, and Linda Abramson. 1977. "The Talking Platypus Phenomenon: Competency Ratings as a Function of Sex and Professional Status." *Psychology of Women Quarterly* 2:114–124.

Acker, Joan. 1978. "Issues in the Sociological Study of Women's Work." In *Women Working,* edited by Ann H. Stromberg and Shirley Harkess, pp. 134–162. Palo Alto, Calif.: Mayfield.

Acker, Joan, and Donald R. Van Houten. 1974. "Differential Recruitment and Control: The Sex Structuring of Organization." *Administrative Science Quarterly* 19 (June):152–163.

Adams, J. Stacey. 1963. "Wage Inequities, Productivity, and Work Quality." *Industrial Relations* 3:9–16.

Adams, Kathrynn, and Audrey Landers. 1978. "Sex Differences in Dominance Behavior." *Sex Roles* 4:215–223.

Albrecht, Maryann. 1978. "Women, Resistance to Promotion and Self-Directed Growth." *Human Resource Management* 17:12–17.

Aldag, Ramon, and Arthur Brief. 1981. *Managing Organizational Behavior.* St. Paul: West Publishing.

_____. 1979. "Some Correlates of Women's Self-Image and Stereotypes of Femininity." *Sex Roles* 5:319–327.

Allen, Robert, and Lyman Porter (Eds.). 1983. *Organizational Influence Processes.* Glenview, Ill.: Scott, Foresman.

Alpander, Guvenc, and Jean Gutmann. 1976. "Contents and Techniques of Management Development Programs for Women." *Personnel Journal* 55:76–79.

American Bar Association Journal. 1983. "Women in the Law." 69:1383–1393.

Ames, Michael. 1977. "Non-assertion Training Has Value Too." *Personnel Journal* 56:348–350, 366.

Ames, Michael, and Dorothy Heide. 1982. "Training and Developing Women Managers: Are They Really a Special Case?" *Personnel Administrator* 27(11):19–26.

Amsden, Alice (Ed.) 1980. *The Economics of Women and Work.* New York: St. Martins Press.

Anderson, Rosemarie. 1978. "Motive To Avoid Success: A Profile." *Sex Roles* 4:239–248.

Andrisani, Paul, and Mitchell Shapiro. 1978. "Women's Attitudes Toward Their Jobs: Some Longitudinal Data on a National Sample." *Personnel Psychology* 31:15–34.

Archer, Frank. 1984. "Charting a Career Course." *Personnel Journal* 63(4):60–64.

Argyle, Michael, Veronica Salter, Hilary Nicholson, Marylin Williams, and Philip Burgess. 1970. "The Communication of Inferior and Superior Attitudes by Verbal and Non-verbal Signals." *British Journal of Clinical Psychology* 9:222–231.

Argyris, Chris. 1957. *Personality and Organization.* New York: Harper.

Arkin, William. 1978. "Military Socialization and Masculinity." *Journal of Social Issues* 34:151–168.

Arnett, Matthew, Richard Higgins, and Andre Priem. 1980. "Sex and Least Preferred Co-Worker Score: Effects in Leadership Behavior." *Sex Roles* 6:139–152.

Aronson, Elliot. 1966. "The Effect of a Pratfall on Increasing Interpersonal Attractiveness." *Psychonomic Science* 4:227–228.

Arrow, Kenneth. 1976. "Economic Dimensions of Occupational Segregation: Comment I." *Signs* 1:233–249.

Atkinson, John, and Joel Raynor. 1974. *Motivation and Achievement.* Washington, D.C.: Winston.

Baer, Judith. 1978. *The Chains of Protection: The Judicial Response to Women's Labor Legislation.* Westport, Conn.: The Greenwood Press.

Backhouse, Constance, and Leah Cohen. 1981. *Sexual Harassment on the Job.* Englewood Cliffs, N.J.: Prentice Hall.

Balswick, Jack, and Charles Peek. 1971. "The Inexpressive Male: A Tragedy of American Society," *The Family Coordinator* 20:363–368.

Bane, Mary Jo. 1976. *Here To Stay: American Families in the Twentieth Century.* New York: Basic Books.

Bane, Mary Jo, and George Masnick. 1980. *The Nation's Families: 1960–1980.* Boston: Auburn House.

Baron, Alma. 1977. "Selection, Development and Socialization of Women into Management." *Business Quarterly* 42(4):61–67.

Baron, Alma, and Ken Abrahamsen. 1981. "Will He—or Won't He—Work with a Female Manager." *Management Review* 70(11):48–53.

Baron, Robert. 1983. "'Sweet Smell of Success?' The Impact of Pleasant Artificial Scents on Evaluation of Job Applicants." *Journal of Applied Psychology* 68:709–713.

Bar-Tal, Daniel, and Leonard Saxe. 1976. "Physical Attractiveness and Its Relationship to Sex-Role Stereotyping." *Sex Roles* 2:123–132.

Bar-Tal, Daniel, and Irene Frieze. 1977. "Achievement Motivation for Males and Females as a Determinant of Attributions for Success and Failure." *Sex Roles* 3:301–312.

Bartol, Kathryn. 1978. "The Sex Structuring of Organizations: A Search for Possible Causes." *Academy of Management Review* 3:805–815.

_____. 1976. "Expectancy Theory as a Predictor of Female Occupational Choice and Attitude Toward Business." *Academy of Management Journal* 19:669–675.

Bartol, Kathryn, and D. Anthony Butterfield. 1976. "Sex Effects in Evaluating Leaders." *Journal of Applied Psychology* 61:446–454.

Bartol, Kathryn, and Max Wortman. 1979. "Sex of Leader and Subordinate Role Stress: A Field Study." *Sex Roles* 5:513–517.

_____. 1975. "Male Versus Female Leaders: Effects on Perceived Leader Behavior and Satisfaction in a Hospital." *Personnel Psychology* 28:533–547.

Baruch, Grace. 1972. "Maternal Influences Upon College Women's Attitudes Toward Women and Work." *Developmental Psychology* 6:32–37.

Baxandall, Rosalyn, Elizabeth Ewen, and Linda Gordon. 1976. "The Working Class Has Two Sexes." *Monthly Review* 3 (July/August):1–9.

Baxandall, Rosalyn, Linda Gordon, and Susan Reverby. 1976. *America's Working Women*. New York: Vintage Books.

Becker, Gary. 1974. "A Theory of Marriage: Part II." *Journal of Political Economy* 82(2):S11–S33.

_____. 1971. *The Economics of Discrimination* (2nd edition). Chicago: The University of Chicago Press.

_____. 1965. "A Theory of the Allocation of Time." *The Economic Journal* 80:493–517.

Bellak, Alvin, Marsh Bates, and Daniel Glasner. 1983. "Job Evaluation: Its Role in the Comparable Worth Debate." *Public Personnel Management* 12:418–424.

Beller, Andrea. 1982. "Occupational Segregation by Sex: Determinants and Changes." *The Journal of Human Resources* 17:371–392.

_____. 1981. "The Effect of Economic Conditions on the Success of Equal Employment Opportunity Laws: An Application to the Sex Differential in Earnings." *Review of Economics and Statistics* 62:379–387.

Belohlav, James, and Eugene Ayton. 1982. "Equal Opportunity Laws: Some Common Problems." *Personnel Journal* 61:282–285.

Bem, Sandra. 1975. "Sex Role Adaptability: One Consequence of Psychological Androgyny." *Journal of Personality and Social Psychology* 31:634–643.

_____. 1974. "The Measurement of Psychological Androgyny." *Journal of Consulting and Clinical Psychology* 42:155–162.

Bem, Sandra, and Ellen Lenney. 1976. "Sex Typing and the Avoidance of Cross-sex Behavior." *Journal of Personality and Social Psychology* 33:48–54.

Bem, Sandra, Wendy Martyna, and Carol Watson. 1976. "Sex Typing and Androgyny: Further Explorations of the Expressive Domain." *Journal of Personality and Social Psychology* 34:1016–1023.

Bender, Marilyn. 1979. "The Changing Rules of Office Romances." *Esquire,* April 24: 46–56.

Berch, Bettina. 1982. *The Endless Day: The Political Economy of Woman and Work.* New York: Harcourt, Brace, Jovanovich.

Berg, J. 1976. *Managing Compensation.* New York: Amacon.

Bergmann, Barbara. 1974. "Occupational Segregation, Wages and Profits When Employers Discriminate by Race and Sex." *Eastern Economic Journal* 1:103–110.

Betz, Ellen. 1984. "A Study of Career Patterns of Women College Graduates." *Journal of Vocational Behavior* 24:249–263.

Beutell, Nicholas. 1983. "Integration of Home and Nonhome Roles: Women's Conflict and Coping Behavior." *Journal of Applied Psychology* 68:43–48.

Beyard-Tyler, Karen, and Marilyn Haring. 1984. "Gender-related Aspects of Occupational Prestige." *Journal of Vocational Behavior* 24:194–203.

Bird, C. 1940. *Social Psychology.* New York: Appleton-Century.

Birdsall, Paige, 1980. "A Comparative Analysis of Male and Female Managerial Communication Style in Two Organizations." *Journal of Vocational Behavior* 16:183–196.

Blau, Francine. 1978. "The Data on Women Workers, Past, Present, and Future." In *Women Working,* edited by Ann H. Stromberg and Shirley Harkess, pp. 29–63. Palo Alto, Calif.: Mayfield.

_____. 1977. *Equal Pay in the Office.* Lexington, Ky.: Lexington Books.

Blau, Francine, and Wallace Hendricks. 1979. "Occupational Segregation by Sex: Trends and Prospects." *The Journal of Human Resources* 14:198–210.

Blau, Francine, and Carol Jusenius. 1976. "Economists' Approaches to Sex Segregation in the Labor Market: An Appraisal." *Signs* 1(3-part 2):181–199.

Blau, Peter, Cecilia Falbe, William McKinley, and Phelps Tracy. 1976. "Technology and Organization in Manufacturing." *Administrative Science Quarterly* 21 (3):21 40.

Bloch, Tova. 1980. "Sex Differences in Interest Measurement." *Journal of Occupational Psychology* 53:181–186.

Block, W.E. and M.A. Walker (Eds.). 1982. *Discrimination, Affirmative Action, and Equal Opportunity.* Vancouver, B.C.: The Fraser Institute.

Bolton, Elizabeth, and Luther Humphreys. 1977. "A Training Model for Women—An Androgynous Approach." *Personnel Journal* 56:230–244.

Bradford, David, Alice Sargent, and Melinda Sprague. 1975. "The Executive Man and Woman: The Issue of Sexuality." In *Bringing Women Into Management,* edited by Francine Gordon and Myra Strober, pp. 39–58. New York: McGraw-Hill.

Bremer, Teresa, and Michele Wittig. 1980. "Fear of Success: A Personality Trait or a Response to Occupational Deviance and Role Overload." *Sex Roles* 6:27–44.

Brenner, Marshall. 1972. "Management Development for Women." *Personnel Journal* 51:165–169.

Brenner, O.C., and Joseph Tomkiewicz. 1979. "Job Orientation of Males and Females: Are Sex Differences Declining?" *Personnel Psychology* 4:741–751.

Brenner, Otto, and W. Edgar Vinacke. 1979. "Accommodative and Exploitative Behavior of Males versus Females and Managers versus Nonmanagers as Measured by the Test of Strategy." *Social Psychology Quarterly* 42:289–293.

Brief, Arthur, and Richard Oliver. 1976. "Male-Female Differences in Work Attitudes Among Retail Sales Managers." *Journal of Applied Psychology* 61:526–528.

Brief, Arthur, Gerald Rose, and Ramon Aldag. 1977. "Sex Differences in Preferences for Job Attributes Revisited." *Journal of Applied Psychology* 62:645–646.

Brief, Arthur, Mary Van Sell, and Ramon Aldag. 1979. "Vocational Decision Making Among Women: Implications for Organizational Behavior." *Academy of Management Review* 4:521–530.

Brief, Arthur, and Marc Wallace. 1976. "The Impact of Employee Sex and Performance on the Allocation of Organizational Rewards." *The Journal of Psychology* 92:25–34.

Broverman, I.K., D.M. Broverman, F.E. Clarkson, P.S. Rosenkrantz, and S.R. Vogel. 1970. "Sex Role Stereotypes and Clinical Judgements of Mental Health." Journal of Consulting and Clinical Psychology 34:1–7.

Broverman, I.K., S.R. Vogel, D.M. Broverman, F.E. Clarkson, and P.S. Rosenkrantz. 1972. "Sex-role Stereotypes: A Current Appraisal." *Journal of Social Issues* 28(2):59–78.

Brown, Randall, Marilyn Moon, and Barbara Zoloth. 1980. "Occupational Attainment and Segregation by Sex." *Industrial and Labor Relations Review* 23:506–517.

Brown, Stephen. 1979. "Male Versus Female Leaders: A Comparison of Empirical Studies." *Sex Roles* 5:595–611.

Brown, Virginia, and Florence Geis. 1984. "Turning Lead into Gold: Evaluations of Women and Men Leaders and the Alchemy of Social Consensus." *Journal of Personality and Social Psychology* 46: 811–824.

Bruning, Nealia, and Robert Snyder. 1983. "Sex and Position as Predictors of Organizational Commitment." *Academy of Management Journal* 26:485–491.

Bullard, Peter, and Paul Cook. 1975. "Sex and Workstyle of Leaders and Followers: Determinants of Productivity." *Psychological Reports* 36:545–546.

Bureau of National Affairs. 1963. *Equal Pay for Equal Work: Summary, Analysis, Legislative History and Text of the Federal Equal Pay Act of 1963; with Summaries of Applicable State Laws.* Washington, D.C.: Bureau of National Affairs.

Buzenberg, Mildred. 1975. "Training and Development of Women Executives: A Model." *Collegiate News and Views* Fall: 19–22.

Caldwell, Mayta, and Letitia Peplau. 1982. "Sex Differences in Same-Sex Friendships." *Sex Roles* 8:721–732.

Cano, Liane, Sheldon Solomon, and David Holmes. 1984. "Fear of Success: The Influence of Sex, Sex-Role Identity, and Components of Masculinity." *Sex Roles* 10:341–347.

Caplan, Paula. 1981. *Barriers Between Women.* New York: SP Medical and Scientific Books.

Carbonell, Joyce. 1984. "Sex Roles and Leadership Revisited." *Journal of Applied Psychology* 69:44–49.

Cary, Mark, and Dave Rubick-Davis. 1979. "Judging the Sex of an Unseen Person from Nonverbal Cues. *Sex Roles* 5:355–361.

Cash, Thomas, and Claire Trimer. 1984. "Sexism and Beautyism in Women's Evaluations of Peer Performance." *Sex Roles* 10:87–97.

Cash, Thomas, Barry Gillen, and D. Steven Burns. 1977. "Sexism and "Beautyism" in Personnel Consultant Decision Making." *Journal of Applied Psychology* 62:301–310.

Cecil, Earl, Robert Paul, and Robert Olins. 1973. "Perceived Importance of Selected Variables Used to Evaluate Male and Female Job Applicants." *Personnel Psychology.* 26:397–404.

Chacko, Thomas. 1982. "Women and Equal Employment Opportunity: Some Unintended Consequences." *Journal of Applied Psychology* 67:119–123.

Chapman, J. Brad. 1975. "Comparison of Male and Female Leadership Styles." *Academy of Management Journal* 18:645–650.

Clawson, James. 1980. "Mentoring in Managerial Careers." In *Work, Family, and the Career: New Frontiers in Theory and Research,* edited by C. Brooklyn Derr. New York: Praeger, pp. 144–156.

Clifton, A. Kay, Diane McGrath, and Bonnie Wick. 1976. "Stereotypes of Women: A Single Category?" *Sex Roles* 2:135–149.

Cohen, Stephen, and Kerry Bunker. 1975. "Subtle Effects of Sex Role Stereotypes on Recruiters Hiring Decisions." *Journal of Applied Psychology* 60:566–572.

Coleman, James. 1976. "Athletics in High School." In *The Forty-Nine Percent Majority: The Male Sex Role,* edited by Debra David and Robert Brannon, pp. 264–269. Reading, Mass.: Addison-Wesley.

Collins, Eliza. 1983. "Managers and Lovers." *Harvard Business Review* 61(5).

Collins, Eliza, and Timothy Blodgett. 1981. "Sexual Harassment: Some See It . . . Some Won't." *Harvard Business Review* 59(3):76–95.

Condry, John, and Sharon Dyer. 1976. "Fear of Success: Attribution of Cause to the Victim." *Journal of Social Issues* 32(3):63–82.

Cook, Mary. 1979. "Is the Mentor Relationship Primarily a Male Experience?" *Personnel Administrator* 24(11):82–86.

Costain, Anne. 1981. "Representing Women: The Transition from Social Movement to Interest Group." *Western Political Quarterly* 24:100–113.

Cox, D. 1982. "Inequality in the Lifetime Earnings of Women." *Review of Economics and Statistics* 64:501–504.

Crawford, Jim. 1978. "Career Development and Career Choice in Pioneer and Traditional Women." *Journal of Vocational Behavior* 12:129–139.

Crino, Michael, Michael White, and Gerry DeSanctis. 1983. "Female Participation Rates and Occupational Prestige: Are They Inversely Related?" *Journal of Vocational Behavior* 22:243–255.

Dalton, Gene, Paul Thompson, and Raymond Price. 1977. "The Four Stages of Professional Careers—A New Look at Performance by Professionals." *Organizational Dynamics* 6:19–42.

David, Debra and Robert Brannon (Eds.). 1976. *The Forty-Nine Percent Majority: The Male Sex Role.* Reading, Mass.: Addison-Wesley.

Davidson, Lynne. 1981. "Pressures and Pretense: Living with Gender Stereotypes." *Sex Roles* 7:331–347.

Dawson, Christopher. 1983. "Will Career Plateauing Become a Bigger Problem? *Personnel Journal* 62(1):78–81.

Day, David, and Ralph Stogdill. 1972. "Leader Behavior of Male and Female Supervisors: A Comparative Study." *Personnel Psychology* 23:353–360.

Deaux, Kay. 1979. "Self-Evaluations of Male and Female Managers." *Sex Roles* 5:571–580.

Deaux, Kay, and Tim Emswiller. 1974. "Evaluations of Successful Performance on Sex Linked Tasks: What Is Skill for the Male Is Luck for the Female." *Journal of Personality and Social Psychology* 29:80–85.

Deaux, Kay, and Janet Taynor. 1973. "Evaluations of Male and Female Ability: Bias Works Both Ways." *Psychological Reports* 32:262–272.

Depner, Charlene, and Virginia O'Leary. 1976. "Understanding Female Careerism: Fear of Success and New Directions." *Sex Roles* 2:259–268.

Derr, C. Brooklyn (Ed.). 1980. *Work, Family, and the Career: New Frontiers in Theory and Research.* New York: Praeger.

DeWine, Sue, and Diane Casbolt. 1983. "Networking: External Communication Systems for Female Organizational Members." *Journal of Business Communication* 20(2):57–67.

Dion, Karen, Ellen Berscheid, and Elaine Walster. 1972. "What Is Beautiful Is Good." *Journal of Personality and Social Psychology* 24:285–290.

Dipboye, Robert, Richard Arvey, and David Terpstra. 1977. "Sex and Physical Attractiveness of Raters and Applicants as Determinants of Resume Evaluations." *Journal of Applied Psychology.* 62:288–294.

Dipboye, Robert, Howard Fromkin, and Kent Wiback. 1975. "Relative Importance of Applicant, Sex, Attractiveness, and Scholastic Standing in Evaluation of Job Applicant Resumes," *Journal of Applied Psychology* 60:39–43.

Dipboye, Robert, Walter Zultowski, Dudley Dewhirt, and Richard Arvey. 1979. "Self Esteem as a Moderator of Performance-Satisfaction Relationships." *Journal of Vocational Behavior* 15:193–206.

Dixon, Ruth. 1976. "Measuring Equality Between the Sexes." *Journal of Social Issues* 32:19–31.

Doeringer, Peter. 1967. "Determinants of the Structure of Industrial Type Labor." In *The Economics of Women and Work,* edited by Alice Amsden, pp. 211–232. New York: St. Martin's Press.

Doherty, Mary Helen, and Ann Harriman. 1981. "Comparable Worth: The Equal Employment Issue of the 1980's." *Review of Public Personnel Administration* 1(3):11–32.

Donaghy, William. 1980. *Our Silent Language: An Introduction to Nonverbal Communication.* Dubuque: Gorsuch Scarisbrick.

Donnell, Susan, and Jay Hall. 1980. "Men and Women as Managers: A Significant Case of No Significant Differences." *Organizational Dynamics* 8(Spring):60–77.

Driscoll, Jeanne. 1981. "Sexual Attraction and Harassment: Management's New Problems." *Personnel Journal* 60:33–36.

Driscoll, Jeanne, and Rosemary Bova. 1980. "The Sexual Side of Enterprise" *Management Review* 69:51–54.

Drucker, Peter. 1966. *The Effective Executive.* New York: Harper and Row.

Dubbert, Joe. 1979. *A Man's Place.* Englewood Cliffs, N.J.: Prentice Hall.

Duberman, Lucile. 1975. *Gender and Sex in Society.* New York: Praeger.

Dubin, Robert, and Daniel Goldman. 1972. "Central Life Interests of American Middle Managers and Specialists." *Journal of Vocational Behavior* 2:133–141.

Dundes, Alan. 1978. "Into the Endzone for a Touchdown: A Psychoanalytic Consideration of American Football." *Western Folklore* 37:75–88.

Dweck, Carol. 1975. "The Role of Expectations and Attributions in the Alleviation of Learned Helplessness." *Journal of Personality and Social Psychology* 31:674–685.

Dweck, Carol, and Diane Gilliard. 1975. "Expectancy Statements as Determinants of Reactions to Failure: Sex Differences in Persistence and Expectancy Change." *Journal of Personality and Social Psychology* 32:1077–1084.

Eakins, Barbara, and R. Gene Eakins. 1978. *Sex Differences in Human Communication.* Boston: Houghton Mifflin.

EEOC. 1964. *Legislative History of Titles VII and IX of Civil Rights Act of 1964.* Washington, D.C.: U.S. Equal Employment Opportunity Commission.

Ehrenreich, Barbara, and Deidre English. 1980. "Reflections on the 'Woman Question.'" In *Family in Transition,* edited by Arlene Skolnick and Jerome Skolnick. pp. 217–230, Boston: Little, Brown.

Elliot, A.G.P. 1981. "Sex and Decision Making in the Selection Interview: A Real-life Study." *Journal of Occupational Psychology* 54:265–273.

Ellis, Rebecca, and Susan Taylor. 1983. "Role of Self-Esteem Within the Job Search Process." *Journal of Applied Psychology* 68:632–640.

Ellis, Robert, and Margaret Herrman. 1983. "Understanding Career Goals of College Women: Intradimensional Variation in Sex-typed Occupational Choice." *Sociology and Social Research* 68:40–55.

Ellul, Jacques. 1964. *The Technological Society.* New York: Vintage Books.

Epstein, Cynthia. 1971. *Woman's Place.* Berkeley: University of California Press.

_____. 1970. "Encountering the Male Establishment: Sex-Status Limits on Women's Careers in the Professions." *American Journal of Sociology* 75:965–983.

Ernst, Martin. 1982. "The Mechanization of Commerce." *Scientific American* 247(3):132–147.

Etaugh, Claire, and Barry Brown. 1975. "Perceiving the Causes of Success and Failure in Male and Female Performers." *Developmental Psychology* 11:103.

Evans, Christopher. 1979. *The Micro Millenium.* New York: Viking Press.

Ezell, Hazel, Charles Odewahn, and J. Daniel Sherman. 1981. "The Effects of Having Been Supervised by a Woman on Perceptions of Female Managerial Competence." *Personnel Psychology* 34:291–299.

Falbo, Toni, Michael Hazen, and Diane Linimon. 1982. "The Costs of Selecting Power Bases or Messages Associated with the Opposite Sex." *Sex Roles* 8:147–157.

Falkowski, Carolyn, and William Falk. 1983. "Homemaking as an Occupational Plan: Evidence from a National Longitudinal Study." *Journal of Vocational Behavior* 22:227–242.

Fairhurst, Gail, and Kay Snaveley. 1983a. "A Test of the Social Isolation of Male Tokens." *Academy of Management Journal* 26:353–361.

_____. 1983b. "Majority and Token Minority Group Relationships: Power Acquisition and Communication." *Academy of Management Review* 8:292–300.

Farrell, Michael, and Stanley Rosenberg. 1981. *Men at Midlife.* Boston: Auburn House.

Farrell, Warren. 1974. *The Liberated Man.* New York: Random House.

Fasteau, Marc. 1974. *The Male Machine.* New York: McGraw-Hill.

Feagin, Joe, and Clairece Feagin. 1978. *Discrimination American Style: Institutional Racism and Sexism.* Englewood Cliffs, N.J.: Prentice Hall.

Feather, N.T. and J.G. Simon. 1973. "Fear of Success and Causal Attribution for Outcome." *Journal of Personality* 41:525–542.

_____. 1971. "Causal Attributions for Success and Failure in Relation to Expectations of Success Based upon Selective or Manipulative Control." *Journal of Personality* 39:527–541.

Federal Register. 1980. "Equal Employment Opportunity Commission: Discrimination Because of Sex Under Title VII of the Civil Rights Act of 1964, as Amended: Adoption of Final Interpretive Guidelines." Rules and Regulations 45(219):74676–74677.

Federico, Suzanne, Pat-Anthony Federico, and Gerald Lundquist. 1976. "Predicting Women's Turnover as a Function of Extent of Met Salary Expectations and Biodemographic Data." *Personnel Psychology* 29:559–566.

Feirstein, Bruce, 1982. *Real Men Don't Eat Quiche.* New York: Pocket Books.

Feldberg, Roslyn, and Evelyn Glenn. 1983. "Technology and Work Degradation: Effects of Office Automation on Women Clerical Workers." In *Machina ex Dea,* edited by Joan Rothschild. pp. 59–78. New York: Pergamon Press.

Feldberg, Roslyn, and Evelyn Nakano Glenn. 1979. "Male and Female: Job Versus Gender Models in the Sociology of Work" *Social Problems* 26:524–538.

Feldman-Summers, Shirley, and Sara Kiesler. 1974. "Those Who Are Number Two Try Harder: The Effect of Sex on Attribution of Causality." *Journal of Personality and Social Psychology* 30:846–855.

Fennell, Mary, Patricia Barchas, Elizabeth Cohen, Anne McMahon, and Polly Hildebrand. 1978. "An Alternative Perspective on Sex Differences in Organizational Settings: The Process of Legitimation." *Sex Roles* 4:589–604.

Ferber, Marianne, and Bonnie Birnbaum. 1981. "Labor Force Participation Patterns and Earnings of Women Clerical Workers." *The Journal of Human Resources* 16:416–426.

Ferree, Myra. 1976a. "Working-class Jobs: Housework and Paid Work as Sources of Satisfaction." *Social Problems* 23:431–441.

_____. 1976b. "The Confused American Housewife." *Psychology Today* 10(4):76–80.

Festinger, Leon. 1957. *A Theory of Cognitive Dissonance.* Evanston, Ill.: Row, Peterson.

Fidell, L.S. 1970. "Empirical Verification of Sex Discrimination in Hiring Practices in Psychology." *Journal of Psychology* 25:1094–1098.

Fidell, Linda, and Jane Prather. 1976. "Women: Work Isn't Always the Answer." *Psychology Today* 10(4):78.

Fiedler, Fred. 1965. "Engineering the Job to Fit the Manager." *Harvard Business Review* 43(5):115–122.

Firestone, Shulamith. 1970. *The Dialectic of Sex.* New York: William Morrow.

Firth, Michael. 1982. "Sex Discrimination in Job Opportunities for Women." *Sex Roles* 8:891–901.

Fitt, Lawton, and Derek Newton. 1981. "When the Mentor is a Man and the Protege is a Woman." *Harvard Business Review* 59(2):56–60.

Flick, Rachel. 1983. "The New Feminism and the World of Work." *Public Interest* 71:33–44.

Fogel, Ric, and Michele Paludi. 1984. "Fear of Success and Failure, or Norms for Achievement." *Sex Roles* 10:431–434.

Forgionne, Giusseppi, and Celestine Nwacukwu. 1977. "Acceptance of Authority in Female Managed Organizational Positions." *University of Michigan Business Review* 29(May):23–28.

Forgionne, Giusseppi, and Vivian Peeters. 1983. "Race and Sex Related Differences in Job Satisfaction and Motivation Among Managers." *Personnel Administrator* 29(2): 66–72.

Foster, Lawrence, and Tom Kolinko. 1979. "Choosing to be a Managerial Woman: An Examination of Individual Variables and Career Choice." *Sex Roles* 5:627–633.

Foster, Martha, Barbara Wallston, Michael Berger. 1980. "Feminist Orientation and Job-Seeking Behavior Among Dual-Career Couples." *Sex Roles* 6(1):59–65.

Fottler, Myron, and Trevor Bain. 1980. "Sex Differences in Occupational Aspirations." *Academy of Management Journal* 23:144–149.

Frances, Susan. 1979. "Sex Differences in Nonverbal Behavior." *Sex Roles* 5:519–535.

Freedman, Sara. 1978. "Some Determinants of Compensation Decisions." *Academy of Management Journal* 21:397–409.

_____. 1979. "The Effects of Subordinate Sex, Pay Equity, and Strength of Demand on Compensation Decisions." *Sex Roles* 5:649–660.

Freeman, Jo. 1972. "The Tyranny of Structurelessness." *Berkeley Journal of Sociology* 27:151–164.

French, J.R.P., and Bertram Raven. 1959. "The Bases of Social Power." In *Studies in Social Power,* edited by D. Cartwright, pp. 150–167. Ann Arbor: University of Michigan Press.

Friedman, Howard. 1980. "The Scientific Error of Sexist Research." *Sex Roles* 6:747–873.

Friedrich, Lynette. 1976. "Achievement Motivation in College Women Revisited: Implications for Women, Men, and the Gathering of Coconuts." *Sex Roles* 2:1976.

Frieze, Irene. 1975. "Women's Expectations for and Causal Attributions of Success and Failure." In *Women and Achievement,* edited by Martha Mednick, Sandra Tangri, and Lois Hoffman. Washington, D.C.: Hemisphere.

Frieze, Irene, Jacqueline Parsons, Paula Johnson, Diane Ruble, and Gail Zellman. 1978. *Women and Sex Roles.* New York: W.W. Norton.

Frieze, Irene, and Sheila Ramsey. 1976. "Nonverbal Maintenance of Traditional Sex Roles." *Journal of Social Issues* 32:133–141.

Frieze, Irene, Bernard Whitley, Barbara Hanusa, and Maureen McHugh. 1982. "Assessing the Theoretical Models for Sex Differences in Causal Attributions for Success and Failure." *Sex Roles* 8:333–342.

Friss, Lois. 1982. "Equal Pay for Comparable Work: Stimulus for Future Civil Service Reform." *Review of Public Personnel Administration* 2(3):37–48.

Fulghum, Judy. 1984. "The Newest Balancing Act: A Comparable Worth Study." *Personnel Journal* 63:32–38.

_____. 1983. "The Employer's Liabilities Under Comparable Worth." *Personnel Journal* 62:400–412.

Fullerton, Howard, and John Tschetter. 1983. "The 1995 Labor Force: A Second Look." *Monthly Labor Review* 106(11):3–10.

Gagnon, John. 1976. "Physical Strength, Once of Significance." In *The Forty-Nine Percent Majority: The Male Sex Role,* edited by Debra David and Robert Brannon. pp. 169–178. Reading, Mass.: Addison-Wesley.

Galper, Ruth Ellen, and Dana Luck. 1980. "Gender, Evaluation, and Causal Attribution: The Double Standard is Alive and Well." *Sex Roles* 6:273–282.

Garland, Howard, and Kenneth Price. 1977. "Attitudes Toward Women in Management and Attributions for Their Success and Failure in a Managerial Position." *Journal of Applied Psychology* 62:29–33.

Ghiselli, Edwin. 1971. *Explorations in Managerial Talent.* Santa Monica, Calif.: Goodyear.

Gilbreath, Jerri. 1977. "Sex Discrimination and Title VII of the Civil Rights Act." *Personnel Journal* 56:23–26.

Giles, William, and Hubert Field. 1982. "Accuracy of Interviewers' Perception of the Importance of Intrinsic and Extrinsic Job Characteristics to Male and Female Applicants." *Academy of Management Journal* 25:148–157.

Gillen, Barry. 1981. "Physical Attractiveness: A Determinant of Two Types of Goodness." *Personality and Social Psychology Bulletin* 7:277–281.

Ginzberg, Eli. 1982. "The Mechanization of Work." *Scientific American* 247(3):66–75.

Giuliano, Vincent. 1982. "The Mechanization of Office Work." *Scientific American* 247(3):148–165.

Glazer, Nathan. 1975. *Affirmative Discrimination: Ethnic Inequality and Public Policy*. New York: Basic Books.

Goldberg, Andrea, and Samuel Shiflett. 1981. "Goals of Male and Female College Students: Do Traditional Sex Differences Still Exist?" *Sex Roles* 7:1213–1223.

Goldberg, Herb. 1976. *The Hazards of Being Male*. New York: Nash.

Goldberg, Philip. 1968. "Are Women Prejudiced Against Women?" *Transaction* 5:28–30.

Goldberg, Steven. 1973. *The Inevitability of Patriarchy*. New York: Morrow.

Golden, Gail, and Frances Cherry. 1982. "Test Performance and Social Comparison Choices of High School Men and Women." *Sex Roles* 8:761–772.

Golembiewski, Robert. 1977a. "Testing Some Stereotypes About the Sexes in Organizations: Differential Satisfaction with Work?" *Human Resource Management* 16(2):30–32.

_____. 1977b. "Testing Some Stereotypes About the Sexes in Organizations: Differential Centrality of Work?" *Human Resource Management* 16(4):21–24.

Gomez-Mejia, Luis. 1983. "Sex Differences During Occupational Socialization." *Academy of Management Journal* 26:492–499.

Gomez-Mejia, Luis, and David Balkin. 1980. "Can Internal Management Training Programs Narrow the Male-Female Gap in Managerial Skills?" *Personnel Administrator* 25(5):77–83.

Goode, William J. 1971. "World Revolution and Family Patterns." *The Journal of Marriage and the Family* 33:624–635.

Goodstadt, Barry, and Larry Hjelle. 1973. "Power to the Powerless: Locus of Control and the Use of Power." *Journal of Personality and Social Psychology* 27:190–196.

Gordon, Francine, and Myra Strober. 1975. *Bringing Women Into Management*. New York: McGraw-Hill.

Gould, Robert. 1976. "Measuring Masculinity by the Size of the Paycheck." In *The Forty-Nine Percent Majority: The Male Sex Role*, edited by Debra David and Robert Brannon, pp. 113–117. Reading, Mass.: Addison-Wesley.

Gould, Sam. 1978. "Career Planning in the Organization." *Human Resource Management* 17:8–11.

Gould, Sam, and James Werbel. 1983. "Work Involvement: A Comparison of Dual Wage Earner and Single Wage Earner Families." *Journal of Applied Psychology* 68:313–319.

Gray, Mary, and Elizabeth Scott. 1980. "A 'Statistical' Remedy for Statistically Identified Discrimination." *Academe* May:174–181.

Green, Thayer. 1967. *Modern Man in Search of Manhood.* New York: Association Press.

Greenfield, Sue, Larry Greiner, and Marion Wood. 1980. "The 'Feminine Mystique' in Male-Dominated Jobs: A Comparison of Attitudes and Background Factors of Women in Male-Dominated Jobs." *Journal of Vocational Behavior* 17:291–309.

Greenglass, Esther, and Reva Devins. 1982. "Factors Related to Marriage and Career Plans in Unmarried Women." *Sex Roles* 8(1): 57–71.

Greenlaw, Paul, and Diana Foderaro. 1979. "Some Practical Implications of the Pregnancy Discrimination Act." *Personnel Journal* 58:677–681, 708.

Greenlaw, Paul, and John Kohl. 1982. "The EEOC's New Equal Pay Act Guidelines." *Personnel Journal* 61:517–521.

Grimm, James, and Robert Stern. 1974. "Sex Roles and Internal Labor Market Structures: The 'Female' Semi-Professions." *Social Problems* 21:690–705.

Gross, Alan. 1978. "The Male Role and Heterosexual Behavior." *Journal of Social Issues* 34:87–107.

Gross, Barry. 1978. *Discrimination in Reverse: Is Turnabout Fair Play?* New York: New York University Press.

Gruder, Charles, and Thomas Cook. 1971. "Sex Dependency and Helping." *Journal of Personality and Social Psychology* 19:290–294.

Grune, Joy, and Nancy Reder. 1983. "Pay Equity: An Innovative Public Policy Approach to Eliminating Sex-based Wage Discrimination." *Public Personnel Management* 12:395–403.

Gunn, Thomas. 1982. "The Mechanization of Design and Manufacturing." *Scientific American* 247(3):114–131.

Gurin, Patricia. 1981. "Labor Market Experiences and Expectancies." *Sex Roles* 7:1079–1092.

Gutek, Barbara, and Bruce Morasch. 1982. "Sex-Relations, Sex-Role Spillover, and Sexual Harassment of Women at Work." *Journal of Social Issues* 38:55–74.

Gutek, Barbara, Bruce Morasch, and Aaron Cohen. 1981. "Interpreting Social-Sexual Behavior in a Work Setting." *Journal of Vocational Behavior* 22:30–48.

Gutek, Barbara, and Denise Stevens. 1979. "Effects of Sex of Subjects, Sex of Stimulus Cue, and Androgyny Level on Evaluations in Work Situations which Evoke Sex Role Stereotypes." *Journal of Vocational Behavior* 14:23–32.

Hacker, Helen. 1975. "Class and Race Differences in Gender Roles." In *Gender and Sex in Society,* by Lucille Duberman, pp. 134–184. New York: Praeger.

Hacker, Sally. 1983. "The Mathematization of Engineering: Limits on Women and the Field." In *Machina ex Dea,* edited by Joan Rothschild, pp. 38–58, New York: Pergamon Press.

_____. 1979. "Sex Stratification, Technology and Organizational Change: A Longitudinal Case Study of A.T.&T." *Social Problems* 26:539–557.

Haefner, James. 1977. "Race, Age, Sex, and Competence as Factors in Employer Selection of the Disadvantaged." *Journal of Applied Psychology* 62:199–202.

Hagen, Randi, and Arnold Kahn. 1975. "Discrimination Against Competent Women." *Journal of Applied Social Psychology* 5:362–376.

Hall, Douglas, and Francine Gordon. 1973. "Career Choices of Married Women: Effects on Conflict, Role Behavior, and Satisfaction." *Journal of Applied Psychology* 58:42–48.

Hall, Douglas, and Francine Hall. 1976. "Effects of Job Incumbents' Race and Sex on Evaluations of Managerial Performance." *Academy of Management Journal* 19:476–481.

Hall, Jay, and Susan Donnell. 1979. "Managerial Achievement: The Personal Side of Behavioral Theory." *Human Relations* 32:77–101.

Hallblade, Shirley, and Walter Mathews. 1980. "Computers and Society: Today and Tomorrow." In *Monster or Messiah? The Computer's Impact on Society,* edited by Walter Mathews, pp. 25–36. Jackson: University Press of Mississippi.

Hammer, Nancy. 1983. "Companies Must Communicate Their Commitment to Promoting Women." *Personnel Administrator* 28(6):95–98.

Hamner, Clay, Jay Kim, Lloyd Baird, and William Bigoness. 1974. "Race and Sex as Determinants of Ratings by Potential Employers in a Simulated Work-Sampling Task." *Journal of Applied Psychology* 59:705–711.

Hansson, Robert, Madalyne Allen, and Warren Jones. 1980. "Sex Differences in Conformity: Instrumental or Communal Response." *Sex Roles* 6:207–212.

Hantover, Jeffrey. 1978. "The Boy Scouts and the Validation of Masculinity." *Journal of Social Issues* 34:184–195.

Harlan, Anne, and Carol Weiss. 1981. *Moving Up: Women in Managerial Careers* (Final Report). Working Paper No.86, Wellesley College Center for Research on Women.

Harragan, Betty. 1978. *Games Mother Never Taught You: Corporate Gamesmanship for Women.* New York: Warner Books.

Harren, Vincent, Richard Kass, Howard Tinsley, and John Moreland. 1978. "Influence of Sex Role Attitudes and Cognitive Styles on Career Decision Making." *Journal of Counseling Psychology* 25:390–398.

Harriman, Ann. 1983. "The Summer of '81: Comparable Worth in San Jose." Paper presented to the American Society for Public Administration, Annual Conference, New York City.

_____. 1982. *The Work/Leisure Trade-off: Reduced Work Time for Managers and Professionals*. New York: Praeger.

Harriman, Ann, and June Horrigan. 1984. "Rip Van Winkle Was a Woman: The Awakening of the Comparable Worth Issue." Paper presented to the Western Political Science Association Annual Meeting, Sacramento.

Hartmann, Heidi. 1976. "Capitalism, Patriarchy, and Job Segregation." *Signs* 1(3-part 2): 137–169.

Hartmann, Heidi, and Donald Treiman. 1983. "Notes on the NAS Study of Equal Pay for Jobs of Equal Value." *Public Personnel Management* 12:404–417.

Hartnett, Oonagh, and Virginia Novarra. 1980. "Single Sex Management Training and a Woman's Touch." *Personnel Management* 12(3):33–35.

Hayge, Howard. 1982. "Marital and Family Patterns of Workers: An Update." *Monthly Labor Review* 105(5):53–56.

_____. 1981. "Husbands and Wives as Earners: An Analysis of Family Data." *Monthly Labor Review* 104(2):46–53.

Heilbrun, Alfred, Jr., and Harvey Schwartz. 1982. "Sex-gender Differences in Level of Androgyny." *Sex Roles* 8:201–214.

Heilman, Madeline. 1980. "The Impact of Situational Factors on Personnel Decisions Concerning Women: Varying the Sex Composition of the Applicant Pool." *Organizational Behavior and Human Performance* 26:386–395.

Heilman, Madeline, and Kathy Kram. 1978. "Self-Derogating Behavior in Women—Fixed or Flexible: The Effects of Co-Worker's Sex." *Organizational Behavior and Human Performance* 22:497–507.

Heilman, Madeline, and Lois Saruwatari. 1979. "When Beauty is Beastly: The Effects of Appearance and Sex on Evaluations of Job Applicants for Managerial and Nonmanagerial Jobs." *Organizational Behavior and Human Performance* 23:360–372.

Heinen, Stephen, Dorothy McGlauchin, Constance Legeros, and Jean Freeman. 1975. "Developing the Woman Manager." *Personnel Journal* 54:282–287.

Heller, Trudy. 1982. *Women and Men as Leaders*. New York: Praeger.

Helmreich, Robert, Elliot Aronson, and James LeFan. 1970. "To Err Is Humanizing—Sometimes: Effects of Self-esteem, Competence and a Pratfall on Interpersonal Attraction." *Journal of Personality and Social Psychology* 16:259–264.

Hemmer, Joan, and Douglas Kleiber. 1981. "Tomboys and Sissies: Androgynous Children?" *Sex Roles* 7:1205–1211.

Henderson, R.I. 1976. *Compensation Management.* Reston, Va.: Reston Publishing.

Henle, Peter, and Paul Ryscavage. 1980. "The Distribution of Earned Income Among Men and Women, 1958–1977." *Monthly Labor Review* 103:3–10.

Henley, Nancy. 1977. *Body Politics: Power, Sex and Nonverbal Communication.* Englewood Cliffs, N.J.: Prentice Hall.

_____. 1976. "Nonverbal Communication and the Social Control of Women." *Science for the People* 8(4):16–19.

_____. 1973–74. "Power, Sex and Nonverbal Communication." *Berkeley Journal of Sociology* 18:1–26.

Hennig, Margaret, and Anne Jardim. 1977. *The Managerial Women.* New York: Anchor Books/Doubleday.

Herzberg, Frederick. 1966. *Work and the Nature of Man.* New York: World.

Hickson, D.J., C.R. Hinings, C.A. Lee, R.E. Schneck, and J.M. Pennings. 1971. "A Strategic Contingencies' Theory of Intraorganizational Power." *Administrative Science Quarterly* 16:216–229.

Hively, Janet, and William Howell. 1980. "The Male-Female Management Team: A Dance of Death?" *Management Review* 69:44–50.

Hoffman, Carl, and John Reed. 1981. "The Strange Case of the XYZ Corporation." *Across the Board* 18(4):27–38.

Hoffman, Donnie, and Linda Fidell. 1979. "Characteristics of Androgynous, Undifferentiated, Masculine, and Feminine Middle-Class Women." *Sex Roles* 5:765–781.

Hoffman, Lois. 1972. "Early Childhood Experiences and Women's Achievement Motives." *Journal of Social Issues* 28:129–155.

Holahan, Carole, and Cookie Stephan. 1981. "When Beauty Isn't Talent: The Influence of Physical Attractiveness, Attitudes Toward Women, and Competence on Impression Formation." *Sex Roles* 7:867–876.

Holahan, Carole, and Lucia Gilbert. 1979a. "Interrole Conflict for Working Women: Careers Versus Jobs." *Journal of Applied Psychology* 64:86–90.

_____. 1979b. "Conflict Between Major Life Roles: Women and Men in Dual Career Couples." *Human Relations* 32:451–467.

Horner, Matina. 1972. "Toward an Understanding of Achievement-Related Conflicts in Women." *Journal of Social Issues* 28:157–175.

Horwitz, Allan. 1982. "Sex Role Expectations, Power, and Psychological Distress." *Sex Roles* 8:607–623.

Hoult, P.P., and M.C. Smith. 1978. "Age and Sex Differences in the Number and Variety of Vocational Choices, Preferences and Aspirations." *Journal of Occupational Psychology* 51:119–125.

Houseknect, Sharon, Suzanne Vaughan, and Anne Macke. 1984. "Marital Disruption Among Professional Women: The Timing of Career and Family Events." *Social Problems* 31:273–284.

Hoyenga, K.B., and K.T. Hoyenga. 1979. *The Question of Sex Differences.* Boston: Little, Brown.

Hoyman, Michele, and Ronda Robinson. 1980. "Interpreting the New Sexual Harassment Guidelines." *Personnel Journal* 59:996–1000.

Huckle, Patricia. 1981. "The Womb Factor: Pregnancy Policies and Employment of Women." *Western Political Quarterly* 34:114–126.

Hunt, David, and Carol Michael. 1983. "Mentorship: A Career Training and Development Tool." *Academy of Management Review* 8:474–485.

Hunt, John, and Peter Saul. 1975. "The Relationship of Age, Tenure and Job Satisfaction in Males and Females." *Academy of Management Journal* 18:690–702.

Hunter, Jean E. 1976. "Images of Women." *Journal of Social Issues* 32:7–15.

Inderlied, Sheila, and Gary Powell. 1979. "Sex-Role Identity and Leadership Style: Different Labels for the Same Concept?" *Sex Roles* 5:613–625.

IPMA News. 1981. "Training and EEO Survey Results." December.

Ireson, Carol. 1978. "Girls' Socialization for Work." In *Women Working,* edited by Ann Stromberg and Shirley Harkess, pp. 176–200. Palo Alto, Calif.: Mayfield.

Jackson, Linda. 1983a. "The Influence of Sex, Physical Attractiveness, Sex Role, and Occupational Sex-linkage on Perceptions of Occupational Suitability." *Journal of Applied Social Psychology* 13:31–44.

_____. 1983b. "Gender, Physical Attractiveness, and Sex Role in Occupational Treatment Discrimination: The Influence of Trait and Role Assumptions." *Journal of Applied Social Psychology* 13:443–458.

Jacobson, Marsha, Judith Antonelli, Patricia Winning, and Dennis Opeil. 1977. "Women as Authority Figures: The Use and Nonuse of Authority." *Sex Roles* 3:365–375.

Jacobson, Marsha, and Walter Koch. 1977. "Women as Leaders: Performance Evaluation as a Function of Method of Leader Selection." *Organizational Behavior and Human Performance* 20:149–157.

Jago, Arthur, and Victor Vroom. 1982. "Sex Differences in the Incidence and Evaluation of Participative Leader Behavior." *Journal of Applied Psychology* 67:776–783.

Jamison, Kaleel. 1983. "Managing Sexual Attraction in the Work Place." *The Personnel Administrator* 28(8).

Jancic, Marion. 1981. "Diversifying Women's Employment: The Only Road to Genuine Equality of Opportunity." *International Labor Review* 120:149–163.

Jenkins, Clive, and Barrie Sherman. 1979. *The Collapse of Work.* London: Eyre Methuen.

Jenner, Jessica. 1981. "Volunteerism as an Aspect of Women's Work Lives" *Journal of Vocational Behavior* 19:302–314.

Johnson, Beverly, and Elizabeth Waldman. 1983. "Most Women Who Maintain Families Receive Poor Labor Market Returns." *Monthly Labor Review* 106(12):30–34.

Johnson, Paula. 1976. "Women and Power: Toward a Theory of Effectiveness." *Journal of Social Issues* 32:99–109.

Johnson, Ronald, and Joan MacDonnell. 1974. "The Relationship Between Conformity and Male and Female Attitudes Toward Women." *The Journal of Social Psychology* 94:155–156.

Jones, Ethel, and James Long. 1981. "Part-Week Work and Women's Unemployment." *Review of Economics and Statistics* 52:70–76.

Josefowitz, Natasha. 1982. "Sexual Relationships at Work: Attraction, Transference, Coercion or Strategy." *The Personnel Administrator* 27(3):91–96.

_____. 1980. "Management Men and Women: Closed Vs. Open Doors." *Harvard Business Review* 58(5):56, 58, 62.

Jourard, Sidney. 1974. "Some Lethal Aspects of the Male Role," In *Men and Masculinity,* edited by Joseph Pleck and Jack Sawyer, pp. 21–29. Englewood Cliffs, N.J.: Prentice Hall.

Juran, Shelley. 1979. "A Measure of Stereotyping in Fear-of-Success Cues." *Sex Roles* 5:287–297.

Jurgensen, Clifford. 1978. "Job Preferences (What Makes a Job Good or Bad)?" *Journal of Applied Psychology* 63:267–276.

Kanter, Rosabeth Moss. 1979. "Power Failure in Management Circuits." *Harvard Business Review* 57(4):65–75.

_____. 1977. *Men and Women of the Corporation.* New York: Basic Books.

_____. 1976. "The Impact of Hierarchical Structures of the Work Behavior of Women and Men." *Social Problems* 23:415–430.

Kaplan, Joel, and Richard Lieberman. 1980. "Comparable Pay: A Management Perspective." *EEO Today* 17:145–158.

Kaplan, Robert. 1984. "Trade Routes: The Manager's Network of Relationships." *Organizational Dynamics* 12(4):37–52.

_____. 1978. "Is Beauty Talent? Sex Interaction in the Attractiveness Halo Effect." *Sex Roles* 4:195–203.

Kaufman, Debra, and Michael Fetters. 1980. "Work Motivation and Job Values Among Professional Men and Women: A New Accounting." *Journal of Vocational Behavior* 17:251–262.

Kavanagh, Michael, and Michael Halpern. 1977. "The Impact of Job Level and Sex Differences on the Relationship between Life and Job Satisfaction." *Academy of Management Journal* 20:66–73.

Kaye, Harvey. 1974. *Male Survival.* New York: Grosset and Dunlap.

Kemper, Susan. 1984. "When to Speak Like a Lady." *Sex Roles* 10:435–443.

Key, Mary Ritchie. 1975. *Male/Female Language.* Metuchen, N.J.: Scarecrow Press.

Klein, Deborah. 1983. "Trends in Employment and Unemployment in Families." *Monthly Labor Review* 106(12):21–25.

Klopfer, Frederick and Thomas Moran. 1978. "Influences of Sex Composition, Decision Rule, and Decision Consequences in Small Group Policy Making. *Sex Roles* 4:907–915.

Komarovsky, Mirra. 1976. *Dilemmas of Masculinity: A Study of College Youth.* New York: W.W. Norton.

_____. 1973. "Cultural Contradictions and Sex Roles: The Masculine Case." *American Journal of Sociology* 78:873–885.

Korman, Abraham. 1976. "Hypothesis of Work Behavior Revisited and an Extension." *Academy of Management Review* 1(1):50–62.

Kotler, Philip. 1980. *Marketing Management.* Englewood Cliffs, N.J.: Prentice Hall.

Kotter, John. 1977. "Power, Dependence, and Effective Management." *Harvard Business Review* 55(4):125–136.

Kovach, Kenneth. 1981. "Implicit Stereotyping in Personnel Decisions." *Personnel Journal* 60:716–722.

_____. 1980. "Women in the Labor Force: A Socio-economic Analysis." *Public Personnel Management Journal* 9:318–326.

Kram, Kathy. 1983. "Phases of the Mentor Relationship." *Academy of Management Journal* 26:608–625.

Kramer, Cheris. 1974. "Stereotypes of Women's Speech: The Word from Cartoons." *Journal of Popular Culture* 8:624–644.

Kronenberger, George, and David Bourke. 1981. "Effective Training and the Elimination of Sexual Harassment." *Personnel Journal* 60:879–883.

Lakoff, Robin. 1975. *Language and Woman's Place.* New York: Harper and Row.

Landy, David, and Harold Sigall. 1974. "Beauty is Talent: Task Evaluation as a Function of the Performer's Physical Attractiveness." *Journal of Personality and Social Psychology* 29:299–304.

Larwood, Laurie, and John Blackmore. 1978. "Sex Discrimination in Managerial Selection: Testing Predictions of the Vertical Dyad Linkage Model." *Sex Roles* 4:359–367.

Larwood, Laurie, Marion Wood, and Sheila Inderlied. 1978. "Training Women for Management: New Problems, New Solutions." *Academy of Management Review* 2:584–592.

Lasch, Christopher. 1980. "'Endangered Species' or 'Here to Stay': The Current Debate About the Family." In *Family in Transition,* edited by Arlene Skolnick and Jerome Skolnick (3rd edition), pp. 80–91. Boston: Little, Brown.

Laws, Judith. 1976. "Work Aspirations of Women: False Leads and New Starts." *Signs* 1(3-part 2):33–49.

Ledgerwood, Donna, and Sue Johnson-Deitz. 1981. "Sexual Harassment: Implications for Employer Liability." *Monthly Labor Review* 104(4):45–47.

Lehne, Gregory. 1976. "Homophobia Among Men." In *The Forty-Nine Percent Majority: The Male Sex Role,* edited by Debra David and Robert Brannon. pp. 66–88. Reading, Mass.: Addison-Wesley.

Lemkau, Jeanne. 1984. "Men in Female-Dominated Professions: Distinguishing Personality and Background Features." *Journal of Vocational Behavior* 24:110–122.

_____. 1983. "Women in Male-Dominated Professions: Distinguishing Personality and Background Characteristics." *Psychology of Women Quarterly* 8:144–165.

_____. 1979. "Personality and Background Characteristics of Women in Male-Dominated Occupations: A Review." *Psychology of Women Quarterly* 4:221–240.

Lenney, Ellen. 1981. "What's Fine for the Gander Isn't Always Good for the Goose: Sex Differences in Self-Confidence as a Function of Ability Area and Comparison with Others." *Sex Roles* 7:905–924.

_____. 1979a. "Androgyny: Some Audacious Assertions Toward Its Coming of Age." *Sex Roles* 5:703–719.

_____. 1979b. "Concluding Comments on Androgyny: Some Intimations of Its Mature Development." *Sex Roles* 5:829–840.

_____. 1977. "Women's Self Confidence in Achievement Settings." *Psychological Bulletin* 84:1–13.

Leontief, Vassily. 1982. "The Distribution of Work and Income." *Scientific American* 247(3):188–204.

Levenson, Hanna, Brent Burford, Bobbie Bonno, and Loren Davis. 1975. "Are Women Still Prejudiced Against Women? A Replication and Extension of Goldberg's Study." *The Journal of Psychology* 80:67–71.

Levine, Robert, Michael-Judith Gillman, and Harry Reis. 1982. "Individual Differences or Sex Differences in Achievement Attributions?" *Sex Roles* 455–464.

Levine, Robert, Harry Reis, Eleanor Sue Turner, and Gary Turner. 1976. "Fear of Failure in Males: A More Salient Factor than Fear of Success in Females?" *Sex Roles* 2:389–398.

Levinson, Daniel, Charlotte Darrow, Edward Klein, Maria Levinson, and Braxton McKee. 1976. "Periods in the Adult Development of Men: Ages 18 to 45." *The Counseling Psychologist* 6:21–25.

_____. 1978. *Seasons of a Man's Life.* New York: Knopf.

Levinson, Richard. 1975. "Sex Discrimination and Employment Practices: An Experiment with Unconventional Job Inquiries." *Social Problems* 22:533–547.

Levitan, Sar, and John Belous. 1981. *What's Happening to the American Family.* Baltimore: Johns Hopkins University Press.

Levitin, Teresa, Robert Quinn, and Graham Staines. 1971. "Sex Discrimination Against American Working Women." *American Behavioral Science* 15:237–254.

Lewin, Ellen, and Virginia Olesen. 1980. "Lateralness in Women's Work: New Views of Success." *Sex Roles* 6:619–629.

Lewis, Robert. 1978. "Emotional Intimacy Among Men." *Journal of Social Issues* 34:108–121.

Lewis, Sinclair. 1922. *Babbitt.* New York: Harcourt Brace.

Linenberger, Patricia, and Timothy Keaveny. 1981. "Sexual Harassment in Employment." *Human Resource Management* 20(1):11–17.

Lipman-Blumen, Jean. 1975. "Toward a Homosocial Theory of Sex Roles: An Explanation of the Sex Segregation of Social Institutions." *Signs* 2:15–31.

_____. 1972. "How Ideology Shapes Women's Lives." *Scientific American* 226(1):34–42.

Livingston, Joy. 1982. "Responses to Sexual Harassment on the Job: Legal, Organizational, and Individual Action." *Journal of Social Issues* 38(4):5–22.

Lockheed, Marlaine, and Katherine Hall. 1976. "Conceptualizing Sex as a Status Characteristic: Applications to Leadership Training Strategies." *Journal of Social Issues* 32:111–123.

Lord, Robert, James Phillips, and Michael Rush. 1980. "Effects of Sex and Personality on Perceptions of Emergent Leadership, Influence and Social Power." *Journal of Applied Psychology* 65:176–182.

Lunding, F.L., G.L. Clements, and D.S. Perkins. 1978. "Everyone Who Makes it Has a Mentor." *Harvard Business Review* 56(4):89–101.

Lunneborg, Patricia. 1982. "Role Model Influencers on Nontraditional Professional Women." *Journal of Vocational Behavior* 20:276–281.

_____. 1978. "Sex and Career Decision-making Styles." *Journal of Counseling Psychology* 25:299–305.

Lyles, Marjorie. 1983. "Strategies for Helping Women Managers—or Anyone." *Personnel* 60:67–77.

Maccoby, Eleanor, and Carol Jacklin. 1974. *The Psychology of Sex Differences.* Stanford, Calif.: Stanford University Press.

Maccoby, Michael. 1976. *The Gamesman.* New York: Bantam Books.

Macklin, Eleanor. 1980. "Nontraditional Family Forms: A Decade of Research." *The Journal of Marriage and the Family* 42:905–922.

Mahoney, Thomas. 1983. "Approaches to the Definition of Comparable Worth." *Academy of Management Review* 8:14–22.

Mai-Dalton, Renate and Jeremiah Sullivan. 1981. "The Effects of Manager's Sex on the Assignment to a Challenging or a Dull Task and Reasons for the Choice." *Academy of Management Journal* 24:603–612.

Major, Brenda. 1979. "Sex-Role Orientation and Fear of Success: Clarifying an Unclear Relationship." *Sex Roles* 5:63–70.

Major, Brenda, and Ellen Konar. 1984. "An Investigation of Sex Differences in Pay Expectations and their Possible Causes." *Academy of Management Journal* 27:777–793.

Marcum, Patricia. 1976. "Men and Women on the Management Team." *University of Michigan Business Review* 28(6):8–11.

Martin, Elmer, and Joanne Martin. 1980. "The Black Family: An Overview." In *Family in Transition,* edited by Arlene Skolnick and Jerome Skolnick (3rd edition), pp. 468–478, Boston: Little, Brown.

Maslow, Abraham. 1943. "A Theory of Human Motivation." *Psychological Review* 50:370–396.

Massengill, Douglas, and Nicholas DiMarco. 1979. "Sex-Role Stereotypes and Requisite Management Characteristics: A Current Replication." *Sex Roles* 5:561–570.

Mathews, Patricia. 1984. "The Changing Work Force: Dual-career Couples and Relocation." *Personnel Administrator* 29(4):55–62.

McClelland, David. 1975. *Power: The Inner Experience.* New York: Irvington.

_____. 1965. "Toward a Theory of Motive Acquisition." *American Psychologist* 20:321–333.

McClelland, David, and Richard Boyatzis. 1982. "Leadership Motive Patterns and Long Term Management Success." *Journal of Applied Psychology* 67:737–743.

McClelland, David, and David Burnham. 1976. "Power Is the Great Motivator." *Harvard Business Review* 54:100–110.

McGregor, Douglas. 1960. *The Human Side of Enterprises.* New York: McGraw-Hill.

McHugh, Maureen, Joan Fisher, and Irene Frieze. 1982. "Effect of Situational Factors on the Self-Attributions of Females and Males." *Sex Roles* 8:389–397.

McHugh, Maureen, Irene Frieze, and Barbara Hanusa. 1982. "Attributions and Sex Differences in Achievement: Problems and New Perspectives." *Sex Roles* 8:467–487.

McLennan, Barbara. 1982. "Sex Discrimination in Employment and Possible Liabilities of Labor Unions: Implications of County of Washington v. Gunther." *Labor Law Review* 33(1):26–35.

McLure, Gail, and Ellen Piel. 1978. "College-Bound Girls and Science Careers: Perceptions of Barriers and Facilitating Factors." *Journal of Vocational Behavior* 12:172–183.

McMillan, Julie, Clifton A. Kay, Diane McGrath, and Sanda Gale. 1977. "Women's Language: Uncertainty or Interpersonal Sensitivity and Emotionality." *Sex Roles* 3:545–559.

Mednick, Martha, Sandra Tangri, and Lois Hossman (Eds.). 1975. *Women and Achievement: Social and Motivational Analyses.* Washington, D.C.: Hemisphere Publishing.

Meeker, B.F. and P.A. Weitzel-O'Neill. 1977. "Sex Roles and Interpersonal Behavior in Task-Oriented Groups." *American Sociological Review* 42:91–105.

Megargee, Edwin. 1969. "Influence of Sex Roles on the Manifestations of Leadership." *Journal of Applied Psychology* 53:377–382.

Mellor, Earl. 1984. "Investigating the Differences in Weekly Earnings of Women and Men." *Monthly Labor Review* 107(6):17–28.

Middlebrook, Bill, and Frank Rachel. 1983. "A Survey of Middle Management Training and Development Programs." *Personnel Administrator* 28(11):27–31.

Miller, Casey, and Kate Swift. 1976. *Words and Women: New Language in New Times.* New York: Anchor Press/Doubleday.

Miller, Jon, Sanford Labovitz, and Lincoln Fry. 1975. "Inequities in the Organizational Experiences of Women and Men." *Social Forces* 54:365–381.

Mincer, Jacob, and Solomon Polachek. 1978. "Women's Earnings Reexamined." *The Journal of Human Resources* 13:118–134.

_____. 1974. "Family Investments in Human Capital: Earnings of Women." *Journal of Political Economy* 82:S76–S110.

Miner, John. 1980. *Theories of Organizational Behavior.* Hinsdale, Ill.: The Dryden Press.

Mintzberg, Henry. 1975. "The Manager's Job: Folklore and Fact." *Harvard Business Review* 55.

Mischel, Harriet. 1974. "Sex Bias in the Evaluation of Professional Achievements." *Journal of Educational Psychology* 66:157–166.

Missarian, Agnes. 1982. *The Corporate Connection: Why Executive Women Need Mentors to Reach the Top.* Englewood Cliffs, N.J.: Spectrum.

Mitchell, Terence. 1974. "Expectancy Models of Job Satisfaction, Occupational Preference and Effort: A Theoretical, Methodological and Empirical Appraisal." *Psychological Bulletin* 81:1053–1077.

Moore, Dorothy. 1984. "Evaluating In-Role and Out-of-Role Performers." *Academy of Management Journal* 27:603–618.

Moore, Loretta, and Annette Rickel. 1980. "Characteristics of Women in Traditional and Non-Traditional Managerial Roles." *Personnel Psychology* 33:317–333.

Moreland, John, Vincent Harren, Eileen Krimsky-Montague, and Howard Tinsley. 1979. "Sex Role Self-concept and Career Decision Making." *Journal of Counseling Psychology* 26:329–336.

Myers, Anita, and Hilary Lips. 1978. "Participation in Competitive Amateur Sports as a Function of Psychological Androgyny." *Sex Roles* 4:571–578.

Narus, Leonard, and Judith Fischer. 1982. "Strong but Not Silent: A Reexamination of the Expressivity in the Relationships of Men." *Sex Roles* 8:159–168.

Neice, David, and Richard Bradley. 1979. "Relationship of Age, Sex, and Educational Groups to Career Decisiveness." *Journal of Vocational Behavior* 14:271–278.

Neugarten, Dale, and Jay M. Shafritz (Eds.). 1980. *Sexuality in Organizations.* Oak Park, Ill.: Moore Publishing.

Newman, Winn. 1983. "Statement to the Equal Pay Joint Committee, Des Moines, Iowa." *Public Personnel Journal* 12:382–389.

_____. 1976. "The Policy Issues: Presentation III." *Signs* 1(3-part 2):265–272.

Newsweek. 1983. "A Portrait of America." January 17:20–36.

Newton, Rae, and Gary Schulman. 1977. "Sex and Conformity: A New View." *Sex Roles* 3:511–521.

Nielsen, Joyce. 1978. *Sex in Society.* Belmont, Calif.: Wadsworth.

Nieva, Veronica, and Barbara Gutek. 1980. "Sex Effects on Evaluation." *Academy of Management Review* 5:267–276.

Nilsen, Sigurd. 1984. "Recessionary Impacts on the Unemployment of Women and Men." *Monthly Labor Review* 107(5):21–25.

Norris, B.A. 1983. "Comparable Worth, Disparate Impact, and the Market Rate Salary Problem: A Legal Analysis and Statistical Application." *California Law Review* 71:730–775.

Norton, Steven, David Gustafson, and Charles Foster. 1977. "Assessment for Management Potential: Scale Design and Development, Training Effects, and Rater/Ratee Sex Effects." *Academy of Management Journal* 20:117–131.

O'Farrell, Brigid. 1982. "Craftworkers and Clerks: The Effect of Male Co-worker Hostility on Women's Satisfactions with Non-traditional Jobs." *Social Problems* 29:252–264.

O'Leary, Virginia. 1974. "Some Attitudinal Barriers to Occupation Aspirations in Women." *Psychological Bulletin* 81:809–826.

O'Leary, Virginia, and James Donoghue. 1978. "Latitudes of Masculinity: Reactions to Sex Role Deviance in Men." *Journal of Social Issues* 34:17–28.

Orlofsky, Jacob. 1981. "A Comparison of Projective and Objective Fear-of-Success and Sex-Role Orientation Measures as Predictors of Women's Performance on Masculine and Feminine Tasks." *Sex Roles* 7:999–1018.

Orth, Charles, and Frederic Jacobs. 1971. "Women in Management: Pattern for Change." *Harvard Business Review* 71(4):139–146.

Osborn, Richard, and William Vicars. 1976. "Sex Stereotypes: An Artifact in Leader Behavior and Subordinate Satisfaction Analysis?" *Academy of Management Journal* 19:439–449.

Osterman, Paul. 1979. "Sex Discrimination in Professional Employment: A Case Study." *Industrial and Labor Relations Review* 32:451–276.

Parsons, Jacquelynne, Irene Frieze, and Diane Ruble. 1978. "Intrapsychic Factors Influencing Career Aspirations in College Women." *Sex Roles* 4: 337–347.

Parsons, Jacquelynne, Judith Meece, Terry Adler, and Caroline Kaczala. 1982. "Sex Differences in Attributions and Learned Helplessness." *Sex Roles* 8:421–432.

Parsons, Jacquelynne, Diane Ruble, Karen Hodges, and Ava Small. 1976. "Cognitive-Developmental Factors in Emerging Sex Differences in Achievement-Related Expectancies." *Journal of Social Issues* 32:47–59.

Patty, Rosemarie Anderson. 1976. "Motive to Avoid Success and Instructional Set." *Sex Roles* 2:81–83.

Paul, Nancy. 1979. "Assertiveness Without Tears: A Training Program for Executive Equality." *Personnel Management* 11(4): 37–39.

Peck, Teresa. 1978. "When Women Evaluate Women, Nothing Succeeds Like Success: The Differential Effects of Status Upon Evaluations of Male and Female Professional Ability." *Sex Roles* 4:205–213.

Pemberton, John (Ed.). 1975. *Equal Employment Opportunity—Responsibilities, Rights, and Remedies.* New York: The Practicing Law Institute.

Persing, Bobbye. 1977. "Sticks and Stones and Words: Women in the Language." *Journal of Business Communication* 14:11–19.

Peterson-Hardt, Sandra, and Frances-Dee Burlin. 1979. "Sex Differences in Perceptions of Familial and Occupational Roles." *Journal of Vocational Behavior* 14:306–316.

Petty, M.M., and Nealia Bruning. 1980. "A Comparison of the Relationships Between Subordinates' Perceptions of Supervisory Behavior and Measures of Subordinates' Job Satisfaction for Male and Female Leaders." *Academy of Management Journal* 23:717–725.

Petty, M.M., Gail McGee, and Jerry Cavender. 1984. "A Meta-Analysis of the Relationships Between Individual Job Satisfaction and Individual Performance." *Academy of Management Review* 9:712–721.

Petty, M.M., and Robert Miles. 1976. "Leader Sex-role Stereotyping in a Female Dominated Work Culture." *Personnel Psychology* 29:393–404.

Pfeffer, Jeffrey. 1981. *Power In Organizations.* Mansfield, Mass.: Pitman Publishing.

Pfeifer, Pat, and Stanley Shapiro. 1978. "Male and Female MBA Candidates: Are There Personality Differences?" *Business Quarterly* 43(Spring):77–80.

Phelps, Edmund. 1980. "The Statistical Theory of Racism and Sexism." In *The Economics of Women and Work,* edited by Alice Amsden, pp. 206–210. New York: St. Martin's Press.

Pheterson, Gail, Sara Kiesler, and Philip Goldberg. 1971. "Evaluation of the Performance of Women as a Function of Their Sex, Achievement and Personal History." *Journal of Personality and Social Psychology* 19:114–118.

Phillips, Linda. 1977. "Mentors and Proteges: A Study of the Career Development of Women Managers and Executives in Business and Industry." Unpublished Doctoral Dissertation, University of California, Los Angeles.

Pines, Ayala, and Ditsa Kafry. 1981a. "The Experience of Tedium in Three Generations of Professional Women." *Sex Roles* 7:117–134.

_____. 1981b. "Tedium in the Life and Work of Professional Women as Compared with Men." *Sex Roles* 7:963–977.

Pleck, Joseph. 1977. "The Work-Family Role System." *Social Problems* 24:417–427.

_____. 1976. "The Male Sex Role: Definitions, Problems, and Sources of Change." *Journal of Social Issues* 32:155–164.

Pleck, Joseph, and Jack Sawyer. 1974. *Men and Masculinity.* Englewood Cliffs, N.J.: Prentice Hall.

Polachek, Solomon. 1981. "Occupational Self-selection: A Human Capital Approach to Sex Differences in Occupational Structure." *The Review of Economics and Statistics* 58:60–69.

Powell, Gary. 1983. "Sexual Harassment: Confronting the Issue of Definition." *Business Horizons* 26(4):24–28.

_____. 1980. "Career Development and the Woman Manager—A Social Power Perspective." *Personnel* 57(3):22–32.

Powell, Gary, and D. Anthony Butterfield. 1984. "If 'Good Managers' are Masculine, What are 'Bad Managers'?" *Sex Roles* 10:477–484.

_____. 1981. "A Note on Sex Role Identity Effects on Managerial Aspirations." *Journal of Occupational Psychology* 54:299–301.

_____. 1979. "The 'Good Managers': Masculine or Androgynous?" *Academy of Management Journal* 22:395–403.

Prather, Jane. 1971. "When the Girls Move In: A Sociological Analysis of the Feminization of the Bank Teller's Job." *Journal of Marriage and the Family* 33:777–782.

Public Administration Times. 1983. "Black Leaders Face the Fatherless Family." 6(10):2.

Pulakos, Elaine, and Kenneth Wexley. 1983. "The Relationship Among Perceptual Similarity, Sex, and Performance Ratings in Manager-Subordinate Dyads." *Academy of Management Journal* 26:129–139.

Quinn, Robert. 1977. "Coping With Cupid: The Formation, Impact, and Management of Romantic Relationships in Organizations." *Administrative Science Quarterly* 22(March):30–45.

Rader, Martha. 1979. "Evaluating a Management Development Program for Women." *Public Personnel Journal* 8:139–145.

Radin, Beryl. 1980. "Leadership Training for Women in State and Local Government." *Public Personnel Management* 9:52–61.

Rand, Thomas, and Kenneth Wexley. 1975. "Demonstration of the Effect, 'Similar to me,' in Simulated Employment Interview." *Psychological Reports* 36:535–544.

Ratner, Ronnie. 1980. "The Paradox of Protection: Maximum Hours Legislation in the United States." *International Labour Review* 119:185–197.

Raven, Bertram, and A. Kruglanski. 1970. "Conflict and Power." In *The Structure of Conflict,* edited by P. Swingle. New York: Academic Press.

Reha, Rose. 1979. "Preparing Women for Management Roles." *Business Horizons* 22:68–71.

Reif, William, John Newstrom, and Robert St. Louis. 1976. "Sex as a Discriminating Variable in Organizational Reward Decisions." *Academy of Management Journal* 19:469–476.

Remick, Helen. 1983. "An Update on Washington State." *Public Personnel Journal* 12:390–394.

Renick, James. 1980. "Sexual Harassment at Work: Why it Happens, What to do About it." *Personnel Journal* 59:658–662.

Renwick, Patricia, and Henry Tosi. 1978. "The Effects of Sex, Marital Status, and Educational Background on Selection Decisions." *Academy of Management Journal* 21:93–103.

Rhue, Judith, Steven Lynn, and John Garske. 1984. "The Effects of Competent Behavior on Interpersonal Attraction and Task Leadership." *Sex Roles* 10:925–937.

Rice, Robert, Lisa Bender, and Alan Vitters. 1980. "Leader Sex, Follower Attitudes Toward Women, and Leadership Effectiveness: A Laboratory Experiment." *Organizational Behavior and Human Performance* 25:46–78.

Rice, Robert, Jan Yoder, Jerome Adams, Robert Priest, and Howard Prince II. 1984. "Leadership Ratings for Male and Female Military Cadets." *Sex Roles* 10:885–901.

Riche, Richard. 1982. "Impact of Electronic Technology." *Monthly Labor Review* 105(3):37–39.

Riger, Stephanie, and Pat Galligan. 1980. "Women in Management: An Exploration of Competing Paradigms." *American Psychologist* 35:902–910.

Roche, Gerard. 1979. "Much Ado About Mentors." *Harvard Business Review* 57(1):14–16, 20, 24.

Rose, Gerald. 1978. "Sex Effects on Effort Attributions in Managerial Performance Evaluation." *Organizational Behavior and Human Performance* 21:367–378.

Rose, Gerald, and P. Andiappan. 1978. "Sex Effects on Managerial Hiring Decisions." *Academy of Management Journal* 21:104–112.

Rosen, Benson, and Thomas Jerdee. 1978. "Perceived Sex Differences in Managerially Relevant Characteristics." *Sex Roles* 4:837–843.

_____. 1977. "On-the-Job Sex Bias: Increasing Managerial Awareness." *The Personnel Administrator* 22(1):12–18.

_____. 1974a. "Sex Stereotyping in the Executive Suite." *Harvard Business Review* 52(2):45–58.

_____. 1974b. "Influence of Sex Role Stereotypes on Personnel Decisions." *Journal of Applied Psychology* 59:9–14.

_____. 1974c. Effects of Applicant's Sex and Difficulty of the Job on Evaluations of Candidates for Managerial Positions." *Journal of Applied Psychology* 59:511–512.

Rosen, Benson, Thomas Jerdee, and Thomas Prestwich. 1975. "Dual-Career Marital Adjustment: Potential Effects of Discriminatory Managerial Attitudes." *Journal of Marriage and the Family* 37:565–572.

Rosen, Benson, Sara Rynes, and Thomas Mahoney. 1983. "Compensation, Jobs and Gender." *Harvard Business Review* 61(4):170–190.

Rosen, Benson, Mary Ellen Templeton, and Karen Kichline. 1981. "The First Few Years on the Job: Women in Management." *Business Horizons* 24(6):26–29.

Rosenbach, William, Robert Dailey, and Cyril Morgan. 1979. "Perception of Job Characteristics and Affective Work Outcomes for Women and Men." *Sex Roles* 5:267–277.

Rosenfeld, Carl, and Scott Brown. 1979." The Labor Force Status of Older Workers." *Monthly Labor Review* 102(11):12–18.

Rosenfeld, Rachel. 1979. "Women's Occupational Careers: Individual and Structural Explanations." *Sociology of Work and Occupations* 6:283–311.

Rosenthal, Doreen, and Diane Chapman. 1982. "The Lady Spaceman: Children's Perceptions of Sex-Stereotyped Occupations." *Sex Roles* 8:959–965.

Rothschild, Joan (Ed.). 1983. *Machina ex Dea.* New York: Pergamon.

Rousell, Cecile. 1974. "Relationship of Sex of Department Head to Department Climate." *Administrative Science Quarterly* 19:211–220.

Rowe, Mary. 1981. "Dealing With Sexual Harassment." *Harvard Business Review* 59(3):42–46.

Rubery, Jill. 1980. "Structured Labor Markets, Worker Organization and Low Pay." In *The Economics of Women and Work,* edited by Alice Amsden, pp. 242–270. New York: St. Martin's Press.

Rubin, Lillian. 1976. *Worlds of Pain: Life in the Working-Class Family.* New York: Basic Books.

Rynes, Sara, and Benson Rosen. 1983. "A Comparison of Male and Female Reactions to Career Advancement Opportunities." *Journal of Vocational Behavior* 22:105–116.

Rytina, Nancy. 1982. "Tenure as a Factor in the Male-Female Earnings Gap." *Monthly Labor Review* 105(5):32–34.

Rytina, Nancy, and Suzanne Bianchi. 1984. "Occupational Reclassification and Changes in Distribution by Gender." *Monthly Labor Review* 107(3):11–17.

Safilios-Rothschild, Constantina. 1977. *Love, Sex and Sex Roles.* Englewood Cliffs, N.J.: Prentice Hall.

Safran, Claire. 1976. "What Men Do to Women on the Job." *Redbook* November:149–223.

Salancik, Gerald, and Jeffrey Pfeffer. 1983. "Who Gets Power—And How They Hold on to It: A Strategic-Contingency Model of Power." In *Organizational Influence Processes,* edited by Robert Allen and Lyman Porter, pp. 52–71. Glenview, Ill.: Scott, Foresman.

Sandell, Steven, and David Shapiro. 1978. "An Exchange: The Theory of Human Capital and the Earnings of Women. A Reexamination of the Evidence." *The Journal of Human Resources* 13:103–117.

Sashkin, Marshall, and Norman Maier. 1971. "Sex Effects in Delegation." *Personnel Psychology* 24:471–476.

Sattel, Jack. 1976. "The Inexpressive Male: Tragedy or Sexual Politics?" *Social Problems* 23:469–477.

Sawhill, Isabel. 1976. "Discrimination and Poverty Among Women who Head Families." *Signs* 1:201–211.

Sawyer, Sandra, and Arthur Whatley. 1980. "Sexual Harassment: A Form of Sex Discrimination." *The Personnel Administrator* 25(1):36–44.

Scanzoni, John. 1978. *Sex Roles, Women's Work, and Marital Conflict: A Study of Family Change.* Lexington, Mass.: Lexington Books.

Scanzoni, Letha, and John Scanzoni. 1981. *Men, Women and Change.* New York: McGraw-Hill.

Schein, Virginia. 1978. "Sex Role Stereotyping, Ability and Performance: Prior Research and New Direction." *Personnel Psychology* 31:259–268.

_____. 1975. "The Relationship Between Sex Role Stereotypes and Requisite Management Characteristics Among Female Managers." *Journal of Applied Psychology* 60:340–344.

_____. 1973. "The Relationship Between Sex Role Stereotypes and Requisite Management Characteristics." *Journal of Applied Psychology* 57:95–100.

Schlossberg, Nancy, and Jane Goodman. 1972. "A Woman's Place: Children's Sex Stereotyping of Occupations." *The Vocational Guidance Quarterly* 20:266–270.

Schnebly, John. 1982. "Comparable Worth: A Legal Overview." *Personnel Administrator* 27(4):43–48, 90.

Schneier, Craig. 1978. "The Contingency Model of Leadership: An Extension to Emergent Leadership and Leader's Sex." *Organizational Behavior and Human Performance* 21:220–239.

Schonberger, Richard, and Harry Hennessey. 1981. "Is Equal Pay for Comparable Work Fair?" *Personnel Journal* 60:964–968.

Scott, Joan. 1982. "The Mechanization of Women's Work." *Scientific American* 247(3):166–187.

Sekaran, Uma. 1983. "How Husbands and Wives in Dual-Career Families Perceive Their Family and Work Worlds." *Journal of Vocational Behavior* 22:288–302.

_____. 1982. "An Investigation of the Career Salience of Men and Women in Dual Career Families." *Journal of Vocational Behavior* 20:111–119.

Sekas, Maria. 1984. "Dual Career Couple—A Corporate Challenge." *Personnel Administrator* 29(4):37–45.

Senger, John. 1971. "Managers' Perceptions of Subordinates' Competence as a Function of Personal Value Orientation." *Academy of Management Journal* 14:415–423.

Seymour, William. 1979. "Sexual Harassment: Finding A Cause of Action Under Title VII." *Labor Law Journal* 30:139–156.

Shack-Marquiz, Janice. 1984. "Earnings Differences Between Men and Women: An Introductory Note." *Monthly Labor Review* 107(6):15–16.

Shann, Mary. 1983. "Career Plans of Men and Women in Gender Dominant Professions." *Journal of Vocational Behavior* 22:343–356.

Shapiro, Eileen, Florence Haseltine, and Mary Rowe. 1978. "Moving Up: Role Models, Mentors, and the 'Patron System.'" *Sloan Management Review* 19:51–58.

Sharp, Cheryl, and Robin Post. 1980. "Evaluation of Male and Female Applicants for Sex-Congruent and Sex-Incongruent Jobs." *Sex Roles* 6:391–401.

Shaver, Philip. 1976. "Questions Concerning Fear of Success and Its Conceptual Relatives." *Sex Roles* 2:305–320.

Shaw, Edward. 1972. "Differential Impact of Negative Stereotyping in Employee Selection." *Personnel Psychology* 25:333–338.

Sherman, Julia. 1976. "Social Values, Femininity, and the Development of Female Competence." *Journal of Social Issues* 32:181–195.

Shockley, Pamela, and Constance Staley. 1980. "Women in Management Training Programs: What They Think About Key Issues." *Public Personnel Management Journal* 9:214–224.

Sieling, Mark. 1984. "Staffing Patterns Prominent In Female-Male Earnings Gap." *Monthly Labor Review* 107(4):29–33.

Sigelman, Lee, H. Brinton Milward, and Jon Shepard. 1982. "The Salary Differential Between Male and Female Administrators: Equal Pay for Equal Work?" *Academy of Management Journal* 25:664–671.

Signs. 1976. "Occupational Segregation in International Women's Year." Volume I, Issues 3 and 4.

Siklula, Andrew, and John McKenna. 1983. "Individuals Must Take Charge of Career Development." *Personnel Administrator* 26(10):39–97.

Silvern, Louise, and Victor Ryan. 1979. "Self-Rated Adjustment and Sex-typing on the Bem Sex-Role Inventory: Is Masculinity the Primary Predictor of Adjustment?" *Sex Roles* 5:739–763.

Simpson, Peggy. 1983. "Washington: The Fight for Equity." *Working Woman* April:70–77.

Sistrunk, Frank. 1972. "Masculinity-Femininity and Conformity." *The Journal of Social Psychology* 87:161–162.

Sistrunk, Frank, and John McDavid. 1971. Sex Variable in Conforming Behavior." *Journal of Personality and Social Psychology* 17:200–207.

Smith, Catherine. 1979. "Influence of Internal Opportunity Structure and Sex of Worker on Turnover Patterns." *Administrative Science Quarterly* 24:362–381.

Smith, Diane, and Walter Plant. 1982. "Sex Differences in the Job Satisfaction of University Professors." *Journal of Applied Psychology* 67:249–251.

Smith, Howard, and Mary Grenier. 1982. "Sources of Organizational Power for Women: Overcoming Structural Obstacles." *Sex Roles* 8:733–747.

Smith, Shirley. 1982. "New Worklife Estimates Reflect Changing Profile of Labor Force." *Monthly Labor Review* 105:15–20.

Snyder, Robert and Nealia Bruning. 1979. "Sex Differences in Perceived Competence: An Across Organizations Study." *Administration in Social Work* 3:349–359.

Sorrentino, Constance. 1983. "International Comparisons of Labor Force Participation, 1960–1981." *Monthly Labor Review* 106(2):23–36.

Sowell, Thomas. 1982. "Weber and Bakke, and the Presuppositions of 'Affirmative Action.'" In W.E. Block and M.A. Walker (Eds.), *Discrimination, Affirmative Action, and Equal Opportunity*. Vancouver, B.C.: The Fraser Institute.

Spelfogel, Evan. 1981. "Equal Pay for Work of Comparable Value: A New Concept." *Labor Law Journal* 32:31–39.

Spence, Janet, and Robert Helmreich. 1979. "On Assessing 'Androgyny.'" *Sex Roles* 5:721–737.

_____. 1972. "Who Likes Competent Women: Competence, Sex-Role Congruence of Interests, and Subjects' Attitudes Toward Women as Determinants of Interpersonal Attraction." *Journal of Applied Social Psychology* 2:197–213.

Spence, Janet, Robert Helmreich, and J. Stapp. 1974. "The Personal Attributes Questionnaire: A Measure of Sex-role Stereotypes and Masculinity-femininity." *JSAS Catalog of Selected Documents in Psychology* 4:43 (Ms. No.617).

_____. 1975. "Ratings of Self and Peers on Sex Role Attributes and Their Relation to Self-esteem and Conceptions of Masculinity-Femininity." *Journal of Personality and Social Psychology* 32:29–39.

Sproat, Kezia. 1983. "How Do Families Fare When the Breadwinner Retires?" *Monthly Labor Review* 106(12):40–44.

Stacey, Judith, Susan Bereaud, and Joan Daniels (Eds.) 1974. *And Jill Came Tumbling After*. New York: Laurel.

Staines, Graham, Robert Quinn, and Linda Shepard. 1976. "Trends in Occupational Discrimination, 1969–1973." *Industrial Relations* 15:88–98.

Staines, Graham, Carol Tavris, and Toby Jayaratne. 1974. "The Queen Bee Syndrome." *Psychology Today* 7(January):55–60.

Stake, Jayne. 1976. "The Effect of Information Regarding Sex Group Performance Norms on Goal-Setting in Males and Females." *Sex Roles* 2:23–28.

_____. 1979. "Women's Self-estimates of Competence and the Resolution of the Career/Home Conflict." *Journal of Vocational Behavior* 14:33–42.

Stein, Aletha, and Margaret Bailey. 1975. "The Socialization of Achievement Motivation in Females." In *Women and Achievement: Social and Motivational Analyses,* edited by Martha Mednick, Sandra Tangri, and Lois Hoffman, pp. 151–157. Washington, D.C.: Hemisphere Publishing.

Stein, Peter, and Steven Hoffman. 1978. "Sports and Male Role Strain." *Journal of Social Issues* 34:136–150.

Stephan, Walter, and Dale Woolridge. 1977. "Sex Differences in Attributions for the Performance of Women on a Masculine Task." *Sex Roles* 3:321–328.

Stephensen, Harriet. 1975. "De-stereotyping Personnel Language." *Personnel Journal* 54:334–335.

Stern, Barbara. 1981. *Is Networking for You?: A Working Woman's Alternative to the Old Boy System.* Englewood Cliffs, N.J.: Spectrum.

Stevens, George, and Angelo DeNisi. 1980. "Women as Managers: Attitudes and Attributions for Performance by Men and Women." *Academy of Management Journal* 23:355–361.

Stillman, Nina. 1978. "Women in the Workplace: A Legal Perspective." *Journal of Occupational Medicine* 20:605–609.

Stogdill, R.M. 1974. *Handbook of Leadership: A Survey of Theory and Research.* New York: The Free Press.

_____. 1948. "Personal Factors Associated With Leadership: A Survey of the Literature." *Journal of Psychology* 25:35–71.

Stouffer, Samuel. 1976. "Masculinity and the Role of the Combat Soldier." In *The Forty-Nine Percent Majority: The Male Sex Role,* edited by Debra David and Robert Brannon, pp. 179–182, Reading, Mass.: Addison-Wesley.

Sturgess, Brian. 1984. "Telecommunications and Mass Media." In *People, Science and Technology,* edited by Charles Boyle, Peter Wheale, and Brian Sturgess. pp. 169–194. Totowa, N.J.: Barnes and Noble Books.

Summerhayes, Diana, and Robert Suchner. 1978. "Power Implications of Touch in Male-Female Relationships." *Sex Roles* 4:103–110.

Swanson, Marcia, and Dean Tjosvold. 1979. "The Effects of Unequal Competence and Sex on Achievement and Self-Presentation." *Sex Roles* 5:279–285.

Tangri, Sandra. 1972. "Determinants of Occupational Role Innovation Among College Women." *Journal of Social Issues* 28:177–199.

Tangri, Sandra, Martha Burt, and Leanor Johnson. 1982. "Sexual Harassment at Work: Three Explanatory Models." *Journal of Social Issues* 38(4):33–54.

Tannahill, Reay. 1980. *Sex in History.* New York: Stein and Day.

Tavris, Carol, and Carole Offir. 1977. *The Longest War: Sex Differences in Perspective.* New York: Harcourt, Brace, Jovanovich.

Taylor, Daniel, and Edward Sekscenski. 1982. "Workers on Long Schedules, Single and Multiple Jobholders." *Monthly Labor Review* 105(5):47–53.

Taylor, Frederick. 1947. *Scientific Management.* New York: Harper and Row.

Taylor, Susan, and Daniel Ilgen. 1981. "Sex Discrimination Against Women in Initial Placement Decisions: A Laboratory Investigation." *Academy of Management Journal* 24:859–865.

Taylor, Ronald, and Mark Thompson. 1976. "Work Value Systems of Young Workers." *Academy of Management Journal* 19:522–536.

Taynor, Janet, and Kay Deaux. 1973. "When Women are More Deserving than Men: Equity, Attributions, and Perceived Sex Differences." *Journal of Personality and Social Psychology* 28:360–367.

_____. 1975. "Equity and Perceived Sex Differences: Role Behavior as Defined by the Task, the Mode, and the Actor." *Journal of Personality and Social Psychology* 32:381–390.

Teich, Albert (Ed.). 1981. *Technology and Man's Future.* New York: St. Martin's Press.

Terry, Sylvia. 1982. "Unemployment and its Effect on Family Income in 1980." *Monthly Labor Review* 105(4):35–43.

Terborg, James. 1977. "Women in Management: A Research Review." *Journal of Applied Psychology* 62:647–664.

Terborg, James, Lawrence Peters, Daniel Ilgen, and Frank Smith. 1977. "Organizational and Personal Correlates of Attitudes Toward Women as Managers." *Academy of Management Journal* 20:89–100.

Tharenou, Phyllis. 1979. "Employee Self-Esteem: A Review of the Literature." *Journal of Vocational Behavior* 15:316–346.

Tiger, Lionel. 1969. *Men in Groups.* New York: Random House.

Tilly, Louise A., and Joan W. Scott. 1978. *Women, Work and Family.* New York: Holt Rinehart and Winston.

Time. 1980. "The Robot Revolution." December 8:72–83.

Toffler, Alvin. 1980. *The Third Wave.* New York: William Morrow.

Tolson, Andrew. 1977. *The Limits of Masculinity.* New York: Harper and Row.

Tomkiewicz, Joseph, and O.C. Brenner. 1982. "Organizational Dilemma: Sex Differences in Attitudes Toward Women Held by Future Managers." *The Personnel Administrator* 27(7):62–65.

Touhey, John. 1974a. "Effects of Additional Women Professionals on Ratings of Occupational Prestige and Desirability." *Journal of Personality and Social Psychology* 29:86–89.

_____. 1974b. "Effects of Additional Men on Prestige and Desirability of Occupations Typically Performed by Women." *Journal of Applied Social Psychology* 4:330–335.

Treiman, Donald, and Heidi Hartmann (Eds.). 1981. *Women, Work and Wages: Equal Pay for Jobs of Equal Value.* Washington, D.C.: National Academy Press.

Trescott, Martha. 1983. "Lillian Moller Gilbreth and the Founding of Modern Industrial Engineering." In *Machine ex Dea,* edited by Joan Rothschild. pp. 23–27. New York: Pergamon Press.

Tresemer, David. 1976. "Current Trends in Research on 'Fear of Success.'" *Sex Roles* 2:211–216.

Trotter, Richard, Susan Zacur, and Wallace Gatewood. 1982a. "The Pregnancy Disability Amendment: What the Law Provides: Part I." *The Personnel Administrator* 27(2):47–54.

_____. 1982b. "The Pregnancy Disability Amendment: What the Law Provides, Part II." *The Personnel Administrator* 27(3):55–58.

Tsui, Anne, and Barbara Gutek. 1984. "A Role Set Analysis of Gender Differences in Performance, Affective Relationships, and Career Success of Industrial Middle Managers." *Academy of Management Journal* 27:619–635.

Tziner, Aharon, and Shimon Dulan. 1982. "Validity of an Assessment Center for Identifying Future Female Officers in the Military." *Journal of Applied Psychology* 67:728–736.

Vanek, Joann. 1978. "Housewives as Workers." In *Women Working: Theories and Facts in Perspective,* edited by Ann Stromberg and Shirley Harkess, pp. 392–414. Palo Alto, Calif.: Mayfield.

Van Wagner, Karen, and Cheryl Swanson. 1979. "From Machiavelli to Ms: Differences in Male-Female Power Styles." *Public Administration Review* 39:66–72.

Varca, Philip, Garnett Shaffer, and Cynthia McCauley. 1983. "Sex Differences in Job Satisfaction Revisited." *Academy of Management Journal* 26:348–353.

Veevers, J.E. 1978. "Voluntarily Childless Wives: An Exploratory Study." In *Family in Transition,* edited by Arlene Skolnick and Jerome Skolnick (3rd ed.), pp. 546–554. Boston: Little, Brown.

Viscusi, Kip. 1980. "Sex Differences in Worker Quitting." *The Review of Economics and Statistics* 62:388–398.

von Baeyer, Carl, Debbie Sherk, and Mark Zanna. 1981. "Impression Management in the Interview: When the Female Applicant Meets the Male (Chauvinist) Interviewer." *Personality and Social Psychology Bulletin* 7:45–51.

Vonnegut, Kurt. 1952. *Player Piano*. New York: Delta.

Waldman, Elizabeth. 1983. "Labor Force Statistics From a Family Perspective." *Monthly Labor Review* 106(12):16–20.

Walker, James. 1978. "Does Career Planning Rock the Boat?" *Human Resource Management* 17(1)2–7.

Walker, Jon, Curt Tausky, and Donna Oliver. 1982. "Men and Women at Work; Similarities and Differences in Work Values Within Occupational Groupings." *Journal of Vocational Behavior* 21:17–36.

Warihay, Philomena. 1980. "The Climb to the Top: Is the Network the Route for Women?" *Personnel Administrator* 25:55–60.

Weaver, Charles. 1978. "Sex Differences in the Determinants of Job Satisfaction." *Academy of Management Journal* 21:265–274.

Webber, Ross. 1976a. "Perceptions and Behaviors in Mixed Sex Work Teams." *Industrial Relations* 15:121–129.

_____. 1976b. "Career Problems of Young Managers." *California Management Review* 18(4):19–33.

Weber, Max. 1930. *The Protestant Ethic and the Spirit of Capitalism*. London: George Allen and Unwin.

_____. 1947. *The Theory of Social and Economic Organization*. Translated and edited by A.M. Henderson and Talcott Parsons. New York: Oxford University Press.

Wehrenberg, Stephen. 1984. "Accommodating the Stages of Career Development." *Personnel Journal* 63(5):19–20.

Weiner, B., I. Frieze, A. Kukla, S. Best, and R. Rosenbaum. 1971. *Perceiving the Causes of Success and Failure*. New York: General Learning Press.

Weitz, Shirley. 1976. "Sex Differences in Nonverbal Communication." *Sex Roles* 2:175–184.

Wesman, Elizabeth. 1983. "Shortage of Research Abets Sexual Harassment Confusion." *The Personnel Administrator* 28(11):60–65.

West, Naida. 1976. *Leadership With a Feminine Cast*. San Francisco: R. and E. Research Associates.

Wexley, Kenneth, and Elaine Pulakos. 1982. "Sex Effects on Performance Ratings in Manager-Subordinate Dyads: A Field Study." *Journal of Applied Psychology* 67:433–439.

Whaley, George. 1982. "Controversy Swirls Over Comparable Worth Issue." *Personnel Administrator* 61(5):51–61,92.

Wheale, Peter. 1984. "Scientific Management and Work." In *People, Science, and Technology,* edited by Charles Boyle, Peter Wheale, and Brian Sturgess. pp. 195–211. Totowa, N.J.: Barnes and Noble Books.

Wheeler, Kenneth. 1981. "Sex Differences in Perceptions of Desired Rewards, Availability of Rewards, and Abilities in Relation to Occupational Selection." *Journal of Occupational Psychology* 54:141–148.

White, Michael, Michael Crino, and Gerry DeSanctis. 1981. "A Critical Review of Female Performance, Performance Training and Organizational Initiatives Designed to Aid Women in the Work Role Environment." *Personnel Psychology* 34:227–248.

Whyte, William. 1956. *The Organization Man.* New York: Simon and Schuster.

Wiley, Mary, and Arlene Eskilson. 1982. "The Interaction of Sex and Power Base on Perceptions of Managerial Effectiveness." *Academy of Management Journal* 25:671–677.

Williams, Gregory. 1976. "Trends in Occupational Segregation by Sex." *Sociology of Work and Occupations* 3:38–62.

Wirtenberg, T. Jeana, and Charles Nakamura. 1976. "Education: Barrier or Boon to Occupational Roles of Women?" *Journal of Social Issues* 32:165–179.

Wittig, Michele, and Paul Skolnick. 1978. "Status Versus Warmth as Determinants of Personal Space." *Sex Roles* 4:493–503.

Wood, Marion and Susan Greenfield. 1976. "Women Managers and Fear of Success: A Study in the Field." *Sex Roles* 2:375–387.

Woodward, Bob, and Carl Bernstein. 1976. *The Final Days.* New York: Simon and Schuster.

Work in America Institute. 1980. *The Future of Older Workers in America: New Options for Extended Working Life.* Scarsdale, N.Y.: Work in America Institute.

Wright, Paul. 1982. "Men's Friendships, Women's Friendships and the Alleged Inferiority of the Latter." *Sex Roles* 8:1–20.

Wymer, John III. 1983. "Compensatory and Punitive Damages for Sexual Harassment." *Personnel Journal* 62:181–184.

Yankelovich, Daniel. 1981. *The New Rules.* New York: Random House.

Yorburg, Betty. 1974. *Sexual Identity: Sex Roles and Social Change.* New York: John Wiley.

Young, Anne. 1982. "Educational Achievement of Workers, March 1981." *Monthly Labor Review* 105(4):52–55.

Young, Michael, and Peter Willmott. 1973. *The Symmetrical Family.* New York: Pantheon.

Yukl, Gary. 1981. *Leadership in Organizations.* Englewood Cliffs, N.J.: Prentice Hall.

Zellman, Gail. 1976. "The Role of Structural Factors in Limiting Women's Labor Force Participation." *Journal of Social Issues* 32:33–45.

Zikmund, William, Michael Hitt, and Beverly Pickens. 1978. "Influence of Sex and Scholastic Performance on Reactions to Job Applicant Resumes." *Journal of Applied Psychology* 63:252–254.

Author Index

Subject Index

About the Author

ANN HARRIMAN is Professor of Human Resource Management at California State University, Sacramento.

Professor Harriman has written extensively in the area of organizational behavior, in particular on topics concerning the effects of social change on organizations. Her book, the *Work/Leisure Trade-off: Reduced Work Time for Managers and Professionals,* was published by Praeger in 1982. Her articles have appeared in *Review of Public Personnel Administration* and the *National Forum.*

Professor Harriman holds a B.S. degree from the University of California at Berkeley, an M.B.A. from California State University, Sacramento, and M.P.A. and D.P.A. degrees from the University of Southern California.